THE OUTDOOR TRAVELER'S GUIDE
CARIBBEAN

THE OUTDOOR TRAVELER'S GUIDE
CARIBBEAN

TEXT BY
KAY
SHOWKER

PRINCIPAL PHOTOGRAPHY BY
GERRY ELLIS

STEWART, TABORI & CHANG
NEW YORK

Frontispiece: The northeast coast of St. Kitts.

Published in 1989 and distributed in the U.S. by Stewart, Tabori & Chang, Inc., 575 Broadway, New York, New York 10012

Distributed in the English language elsewhere in the world (except Canada and Central and South America) by Melia Publishing Services, P.O. Box 1639, Maidenhead, Berks. SL6 6YZ England. Canadian and Central and South American Accounts should contact Sales Manager, Stewart, Tabori & Chang.

Library of Congress Cataloguing-in-Publication data

Showker, Kay.
  Caribbean/text by Kay Showker; principal photography by Gerry Ellis.
  Includes Index.
  ISBN 1-55670-012-1
  1. West Indies—Description and travel—1981- —Guide-books.
  2. Caribbean Area—Description and travel—1981- —Guide-books.
  3. Outdoor recreation—West Indies—Guide-books. 4. Outdoor recreation—Caribbean Area—Guide-books. 5. National parks and reserves—West Indies—Guide-books. 6. National parks and reserves—Caribbean Area—Guide-books. I. Ellis, Gerry. II. Title. III. Series.
  F1609.S48 1989   89-11341
  917.2904'52—dc20   CIP

Additional photographs copyright © 1989 photographers listed below. © Tony Arruza: 102, 123, 173, 230–1, 412. © Frederick D. Atwood: 82–3. © Tom Bean: cover, 94–5. © Susan Blanchet/M.L. Dembinsky, Jr., Photography Associates: 55. © Nicholas Devore III/Photographers/Aspen: 382–3. © Derek Fell: 188. © French West Indies Tourist Board: 294. © Michael Graybill: 22, 27, 47 center. © Al Grotell: 484 right. © Steven Holt/VIREO: 450 top, 450 center left. © Chris Huss: 177 top, 177 center top, 177 center bottom, 198 bottom, 484 left. © Everett C. Johnson/Folio Inc.: 184–5, 206–7. © Burt & Maurine Jones/Ellis Wildlife Collection: 65 center right, 176. © Alex Kerstitch: 65 bottom left. © Gea Koenig: 72, 202, 235. © Sid Lipschutz/VIREO: 427 bottom right. © Felix Lopez: 135, both. © Edward Monnelly: 54, 62. © Willy Nicolas: 76, 77, 80. © Kathi Porter: 430. © Porterfield-Chickering: 467, 485. © Robert Rattner: 30, 47 bottom, 51, 63 right, 262, 326, 327 left, 327 right, 366. © R. Ridgely/VIREO: 427 top left. © Carl Roessler: 65 top left and right, left top center, right bottom; 439. © Jeff Rotman: 63 left, 65 left bottom center, 177 bottom. © Nancy Sefton: 198 top. © Kay Showker: 34–5. © Joe Smoljan: 58. © Tim Thompson: 172.

MAPS: Guenter Vollath
NATURAL-HISTORY CONSULTANT: John Farrand, Jr.
DESIGN: Jeff Batzli
PHOTO RESEARCH: Sarah Longacre
CAPTIONS: Joan Scobey
INDEX: Pat Woodruff

Printed in Japan
10 9 8 7 6 5 4 3 2

CONTENTS

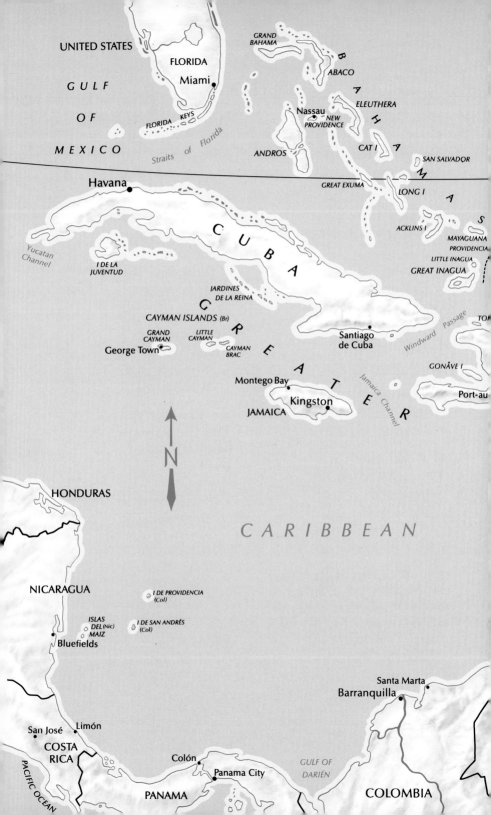

THE CARIBBEAN

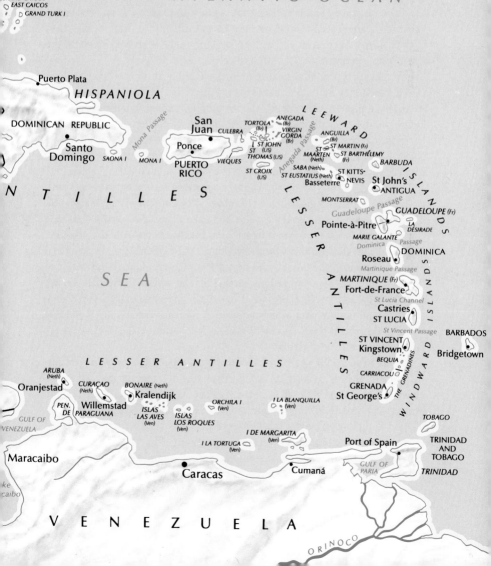

TROPIC OF CANCER

ATLANTIC OCEAN

RKS AND CAICOS ISLANDS (Br)
RTH CAICOS
GRAND CAICOS
EAST CAICOS
GRAND TURK I

Puerto Plata

HISPANIOLA

DOMINICAN REPUBLIC

Santo
Domingo

SAONA I

MONA I

Mona Passage

San
Juan

CULEBRA

Ponce

VIEQUES

PUERTO
RICO

ST CROIX
(US)

TORTOLA
(Br)

ANEGADA
(Br)

VIRGIN
GORDA
(Br)

ST JOHN
(US)

ST
THOMAS (US)

SABA (Neth)

ST EUSTATIUS (Neth)

ANGUILLA
(Br)

ST MARTIN (Fr)

ST
MAARTEN
(Neth)

ST BARTHÉLEMY
(Fr)

ST KITTS-
NEVIS

Basseterre

LEEWARD

BARBUDA

St John's
ANTIGUA

ISLANDS

ANTILLES

MONTSERRAT

Guadeloupe Passage

GUADELOUPE (Fr)

Pointe-à-Pitre

LA
DÉSIRADE

MARIE GALANTE

Dominica Passage

Roseau

DOMINICA

Martinique Passage

SEA

MARTINIQUE (Fr)

Fort-de-France

St Lucia Channel

Castries

ST LUCIA

St Vincent Passage

BARBADOS

ST VINCENT

Kingstown

BEQUIA

CARRIACOU

GRENADA

St George's

LESSER   ANTILLES

ARUBA
(Neth)

Oranjestad

CURAÇAO
(Neth)

BONAIRE (Neth)

Kralendijk

PEN.
DE
PARAGUANA

Willemstad

ISLAS
LAS AVES
(Ven)

ISLAS
LOS ROQUES
(Ven)

ORCHILA I
(Ven)

I LA BLANQUILLA
(Ven)

THE GRENADINES

Bridgetown

WINDWARD ISLANDS

A N T I L L E S

LESSER

TOBAGO

I DE MARGARITA
(Ven)

Port of Spain

TRINIDAD
AND
TOBAGO

TRINIDAD

GULF OF
VENEZUELA

Maracaibo

ke
caibo

I LA TORTUGA
(Ven)

Caracas

Cumaná

GULF OF
PARIA

V E N E Z U E L A

ORINOCO

INTRODUCTION

TO MY KNOWLEDGE, *The Outdoor Traveler's Guide to the Caribbean* is the first book of its kind for the region. It is intended to provide information on an aspect of the Caribbean that has largely been overlooked by writers, tourist officials, and, indeed, by most vacationers.

Although writers since Columbus have been seduced by the Caribbean's natural beauty and have lured readers there with descriptions of its magnificent, exotic landscapes, most travelers see only the fringes of these beautiful islands. Their image of the Caribbean is one of a place to laze away the days on pearly sands rather than a place to explore. If an "outdoors" vacation is suggested, travelers may be more likely to think of Colorado than the Caribbean. And yet, for the growing ranks of active travelers, the Caribbean is a natural.

Few places in the world can match the Caribbean in the diversity and range of outdoor activities it offers together with ease, convenience, and weather to match. Year-round, the swimming, sailing, windsurfing, snorkeling, and scuba diving are superb. There is hiking, biking, birding, horseback riding, deep-sea fishing, river rafting, surfing, and even whitewater canoeing and whale-watching. Throughout the Caribbean there are bird sanctuaries, botanic gardens, nature reserves, and marine parks.

The islands of the Caribbean, where nature has been so extravagant with its beauty, have the geographic characteristics and variety of continents. There are islands with soaring volcanic peaks from which waters cascade through rain-forested slopes into streams that meander over the countryside until they disappear into wide swamps. Other islands are low-lying and offer the drama of the desert with cactus as tall as trees, ever-shifting sand dunes, and eerie rock formations carved by the wind. No two islands are alike. Large and small, each island has distinctive and special features—and the land is only part of nature's show. Beneath the sea are wondrous worlds of exotic fish and spectacular reefs that await exploration by novice snorkelers and expert divers.

As you prepare for your outdoor Caribbean adventure, there are practical considerations to keep in mind. Year-round temperatures along the coast hover around 80°F/26°C but can go to 70°F/21°C from December to March, and to 90°F/32°C between July and September. Trade winds cool the air and keep days pleasant but the tropical sun is very strong. You should always use screening lotions for skin protection.

Walking—whether in old colonial towns or along mountain trails—is more rigorous in the tropics than in temperate climates. The heat and humidity or aridity can make one mile feel like ten. If you walk a mile in twenty minutes in temperate climates, allow thirty minutes or more in the tropics. Always carry water and drink plenty of it, especially in arid regions where it is easy to become dehydrated quickly. Be sure you are in good health before attempting any activities that are more strenuous than those to which you are accustomed.

Distances are deceptive, too. An island road of 20 mi/32 km can take two hours to drive. What might appear to be a few miles on a map could turn out to be a torturous four-hour trek. Sudden downpours are common and come without warning, disappearing as quickly as they arrive and refreshing the air but leaving trails muddy and slippery. Roads that might have been paved often are washed out by heavy rains or blocked by mud slides. Footpaths deteriorate quickly or disappear under fast-growing vegetation unless they are constantly maintained.

Generally, the rainy season, characterized by short tropical downpours, lasts from May to October but, in fact, rain falls throughout the year. Clouds shift quickly; there can be rain in one part of an island and none only a few miles away. In rain forests and at high altitudes rain falls almost daily. Mountain regions can be chilly, particularly in winter, and cloud-shrouded volcanic peaks are pelted by winds and rains most of the year.

Never underestimate weather conditions. Carry a jacket when hiking in the mountains and take a sweater and windbreaker when you are going to high peaks. For normal hiking, loose-fitting cotton attire is recommended. You should wear long-sleeved shirts and trousers for protection against thorny bushes, poisonous plants, and the sun. Sneakers or running shoes are more suitable than boots, except on sharp limestone and rocky mountain terrain when sturdy-soled shoes or light tropical boots are better. Be careful around cacti and bushes; they can scrape the skin and puncture shoes. Take insect repellent on hikes in the forest and for birding in the wetlands.

Never succumb to a sense of security—it will probably be a false one. Whether in a rain forest, on desert tracks, or at the beach, the danger of injury is ever present and aid and rescue are seldom near at hand. Particularly on the more developed islands, the presence of tourists in large numbers helps to feed drug and crime problems. On most islands, service stations and phones are few and far between. Always seek advice locally about sea and trail conditions.

Never hike alone, particularly in a rain forest; it is too easy to become disoriented and lost. Do not wander off tracks without a local guide. Thick vegetation often hides cave openings and sinkholes and obscures faults that can plunge hundreds of feet. At the seashore, do not swim alone at isolated beaches. Coastlines, particularly on the Atlantic, have strong undertows.

Although in the past it may have been easier to discover the Caribbean's beaches than its mountains, this is changing. New interest and awareness about the environment and the islands' natural attractions are leading island governments to make their interiors more accessible.

As each island has obtained its independence in recent years, it has had to grapple with the problems of growth and development. Some, but not all, have recognized the dire results of denuding their mountains, overdeveloping their beaches, and destroying their wetlands. They understand that their natural endowment is their most precious resource and that the future of their islands rests on its protection. Conservation is under way. A cadre of young technicians is beginning to be heard. Environmental-impact studies are being demanded before new building is approved, and ecologists are working alongside developers. Many new land and marine parks have been created in the last few years; reforestation and projects to save endangered species are ongoing across the region.

After spending two years researching this book, I am heartened by the growing awareness and activity I found. The influence outdoor travelers can have by their presence in conveying the value of conservation should not be underestimated. Every visitor can help preserve the environment by following the adage, "Take only photographs; leave only footprints."

This book could easily have been twice its length, but even then it would have been impossible to include every trail, cove, and flower. The aim instead is to stimulate your interest and point you in the right direction. The book contains a great deal of the information that has never been published before, or has been published only in research reports and books for specialists. The material has come from my own personal experience and from the legion of naturalists, ecologists, foresters, botanists, marine biologists, and other specialists who were extraordinarily generous in sharing their knowledge and experience with me.

Information on flora and fauna is written in language everyone can understand. Scientific names are noted after common names in the index of this book to help readers identify species that often have several local names. Readers with more than a passing interest in trees and flowers might want to carry Penelope Honychurch's *Caribbean Wild Plants and Their Uses* (London: Macmillan Caribbean, 1986) and John Kingsbury's handy *200 Conspicuous, Unusual or Economically Important Tropical Plants of the Caribbean* (Bullbrier Press, Ten Snyder Heights, Ithaca, NY 14850). Serious bird-watchers should have James Bond's *Birds of the West Indies* (London: Collins, 1985). A standard reference on reefs is Eugene Kaplan's *Peterson Field Guide to Coral Reefs* (Boston: Houghton Mifflin, 1982). Other books are suggested in the "Exploring the Island" section of each chapter.

Some helpful books and pamphlets, often available in bookstores in the region, are: C. Dennis Adams, *Caribbean Flora* (Surrey, England: Nelson

Caribbean, 1976); Gildas Le Corre and Andre Exbryat, *Flowers of the Tropics* (Fort de France, Martinique: Edition Exbryat, 1985); G. W. Lennox and S. A. Seddon, *Flowers of the Caribbean* (London: Macmillan Caribbean, 1978); S. A. Seddon and G. W. Lennox, *Trees of the Caribbean* (London: Macmillan Caribbean, 1980); and Ian F. Took, *Fishes of the Caribbean Reefs*. London: Macmillan Caribbean, 1978.

Space has not permitted more than the briefest mention of history but I would urge you to read up on the islands you visit. It will greatly enhance your experience.

The Caribbean islands are spectacular in their natural splendor and diversity. They will delight your senses and refresh your spirits. I hope *The Outdoor Traveler's Guide to the Caribbean* will open the door to this new Caribbean for you.

KAY SHOWKER

AUTHOR'S ACKNOWLEDGEMENTS

THE AUTHOR RECOGNIZES with deep appreciation the enormous contribution made by experts, researchers, and other writers in the preparation of the text. In addition to the government tourist boards who helped to facilitate my work without any obligation on my part, many specialists and long-time associates in the Caribbean were tireless in their efforts to help me. I wish I could name them all but space allows me only these few.

ANGUILLA: Hon. Emile Gumbs, Chief Minister and Minister of Tourism; Don Mitchell, Solicitor of the Supreme Court; Dave Carty, Anguilla Archaeological and Historical Society. ANTIGUA: Desmond Nicholson,

Black sand beach, St. Eustatius.

Director, Museum of Antigua and Barbuda; Martha Watkins-Jilkes, writer; Douglas J. M. Howie, Antigua and Barbuda Department of Tourism. ARUBA: Julio Maduro, Aruba National Parks Foundation and Corvalu Tours; Watti Chai, Aruba Tourist Board. BARBADOS: Dr. W. W. Denham and Nancy J. Habley, School for Lifelong Learning/University of New Hampshire; Richard Goddard, Duke of Edinburgh Awards; Philippa Newton, Curator (Natural History), Barbados Museum. BRITISH VIRGIN ISLANDS: Ruthanne Devlin, writer; Bertram Letsom, Director, British Virgin Islands National Parks; Robert L. Norton, B.V.I. National Parks Trust. CAYMAN ISLANDS: John Andresen, Caymans National Trust; Patricia Bradley, author of Birds of the Cayman Islands. CURAÇAO: Jeffrey Sybesma, Netherlands Antilles National Parks Foundation and Curaçao Underwater Park. DOMINICA: Marie-Jose Edwards, Director of Tourism; Tom Economou, Nature Trails, Inc., Miami, Florida. DOMINICAN REPUBLIC: Dr. Tom A. Zanoni, Botanic Gardens, Santo Domingo; Mario Delgado, Dominican Foundation for the Research and Conservation of Marine Life. GRENADA: Richard M. Huber, Jr., ecologist, Organization of American States. FRENCH WEST INDIES: Cecille Graffin, French Government Tourist Office; Myron Clement, Clement-Petrocik, New York. HAITI: Dr. Tom A. Zanoni. JAMAICA: Hon. John Drinkall, former British High Commissioner to Jamaica; Dr. Thomas Farr, Institute of Jamaica. MONTSERRAT: Mr. and Mrs. Bert Wheeler, Montserrat National Trust; Barbara Currie, writer. PUERTO RICO: Kathryn Robinson, writer, author of The Other Puerto Rico. SABA: Dr. Tom van't Hof, Director, Saba Marine Park; Natalie and Paul Pfanstiehl, authors of Saba, The First Guidebook; Eric Horstman, ecologist; Anne Keene, horticulturist. ST. KITTS AND NEVIS: Greg Pereira, Greg's Rainforest Tours; Pam Barry, Golden Rock Estate; R. L. Norton, BVI National Parks Trust; Ralph Field, Tropical Research and Development Corporation. ST. LUCIA: Mark Eckstein, British Volunteers Service Overseas; Robert J. Devaux and Gregor Williams, St. Lucia National Trust; G. Karolin Kolcuoglu, Anse Chastanet. ST. MAARTEN: Gail Knopfler, Museum Classics. ST. VINCENT AND THE GRENADINES: Dr. I. Earl Kirby, St. Vincent Archaeological Museum; Calvin Nicholls, Chief Agriculture Officer, Ministry of Trade and Agriculture. Madge Morris, St. Vincent and the Grenadines Tourist Office. TRINIDAD AND TOBAGO: Hans Boos, Director, Emperor Valley Zoo; Keith Musgrave, Nature Trail Tours; Kevin Kenny, Crusoe Reef Society; Ian Lambie, Asa Wright Nature Center; Victoria Soo Poy, Mount St. Benedict Guest House; Manuel Arias, Wonder Bird Tours, New York; Peter Ramrattan, BWIA. U.S. VIRGIN ISLANDS: Benjamin Kesler, St. George Village Botanical Gardens, St. Croix; Fred Sladen, St. Croix Environmental Association; Jan Smith.

KAY SHOWKER

PHOTOGRAPHER'S ACKNOWLEDGMENTS

MY DEEPEST AND WARMEST THANKS thanks to so many throughout the West Indies and New York City who made a very difficult project a pleasure. I wish to express a special note of thanks to Robert J. Bauer, Linda Collins, George Brennan, Becky Pastorick, June Moysten, Joe Scott, and Bill Dowse of EASTERN AIRLINES who, despite numerous delays and complications remained loyal to the project and assisted to the end. A gigantic debt is owed to the staff of the Ellis Wildlife Collection, in particular Victoria Karr, whose endless editing and organizing lent some sanity to the images I poured upon her. To "Shaz," friend and partner, while you never focused a lens, pressed a shutter, or loaded a camera, these photos would not exist without you: I can never begin to thank you enough. To everyone at Professional Camera in New York, in particular Herb, thanks ever so much for keeping my battery of Nikons in working order despite my ceaseless abuse. To Peg who came through, yet again, and again, when all the doors seemed closed, a warm hug and special thanks. For making island hopping more happiness than horrendous, thanks to Looch. To Pat Walter, owner of Air There Helicopters in St. Thomas, USVI, thank you for making many of the aerials that appear in this guide possible. To all the tourism office and public relations firms handling the West Indies, thank you for your support, sometimes given on short notice, and your assistance in providing hotel accommodations and guides when possible.

And to the following, thank you for your assistance, kindness, and patience: Joan Applewhite, Ardastra Gardens & Zoo, the Baulu family, Alison Beck, Bindley Benjamin, Hans Boos, Ed Buckley, Myron Clement, Katy Crowing, Andrew Dalton, Megan Davis, Marie Jose Edwards, Dave Eliot, Elyse Elkin, Lisa Fitzgerald, Guy-Claude Germain, Alistair Green, Lauren Halfacre, Chuck Hesse, Glen Holms, Richard Huber, Rita Itow, David Jardin, Indira Jose, Lenore Joseph, Bob Kirkpatrick, Karolyn Kalcuoglu, Gary Larson, Leonie Lee, Susan Lomenzo, Suzanne McManus, John Miller, Robert & Ginny Milne, Margaret Moran, Nicole Mounouchy, Jim & Henry Nixon, Joe Petrocik, Martin Peynado, Peter Rothholz, Arlene Stevens, Kass Vaughn, Daphne Anne Warner, Bari Weissman, Ingrid Whitfield, Marcia Wilson, Suzanne Worden.

A closing note to the reader. The West Indies is a region of great opportunity—a chance to discover great natural beauty. Much of it is hidden and does not embrace the traveler when he or she first sets foot on each island. Even so, discoveries fresh and exciting, those that will linger long after the tan has faded, do exist and welcome the adventurous. In the images presented here I hope a part of the searched-for paradise is revealed.

GERRY ELLIS

JAMAICA

THE CAYMAN ISLANDS

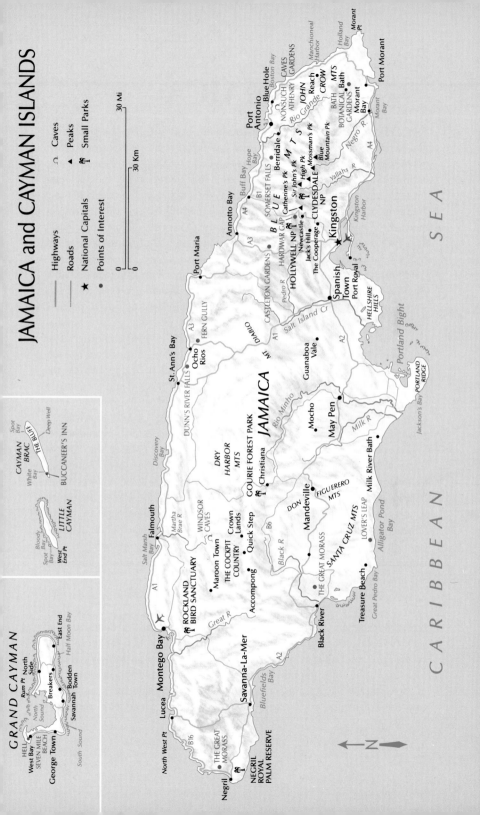

JAMAICA and CAYMAN ISLANDS

Highways

Roads

★ National Capitals

● Points of Interest

∩ Caves

▲ Peaks

🏛 Small Parks

30 Mi

30 Km

GRAND CAYMAN

HELL
West Bay
SEVEN MILE BEACH
George Town
Rum Pt North Side
North Sound
South Sound
Breakers
Bodden Town
Savannah Town
East End
Half Moon Bay

B16

N

CAYMAN BRAC
Spot Bay
Deep Well
The Bluff
White Bay
BUCCANEER'S INN

LITTLE CAYMAN
Spot Bay
Bloody Bay
West End Pt

Negril
NEGRIL ROYAL PALM RESERVE
THE GREAT MORASS
North West Pt

A2

Lucea
Montego Bay
ROCKLAND BIRD SANCTUARY
Savanna-La-Mer
Accompong
Maroon Town
THE COCKPIT COUNTRY
Quick Step
Crown Lands
WINDSOR CAVES
Martha Brae R
Salt Marsh Bay
Falmouth

A1

Great R

Black R
B6

Mandeville
DON
Black River
THE GREAT MORASS

SANTA CRUZ MTS
LOVER'S LEAP
Treasure Beach
Great Pedro Bay
Bluefields Bay

FIGUERERO MTS
Milk River Bath
Alligator Pond
Milk R

May Pen
Mocho

Christiana
GOURIE FOREST PARK
DRY HARBOR MTS

St. Ann's Bay
Ocho Rios
DUNN'S RIVER FALLS
FERN GULLY
A3
Discovery Bay

Port Maria
A4

MT DIABLO
A1
CASTLETON GARDENS
Salt Island Cr
Pedro R
Rio Minho
Guanaboa Vale

A2
Spanish Town
Port Royal
HELLSHIRE HILLS

Jackson's Bay
Portland Bight
PORTLAND RIDGE

JAMAICA

Annotto Bay
Buff Bay
Hope Bay
Port Antonio
Boston Bay
NONSUCH CAVES
Blue Hole
ATHENRY GARDENS
Rio Grande
JOHN CROW MTS
Reach
BATH BOTANICAL GARDENS
Morant
Morant R
Negro R.
A4
Port Morant
Morant Pt
Holland Bay
Manchioneal Harbor

Berridale
SOMERSET FALLS
Catherine's Pk
Sir John's Pk
HARDWAR GAP
HOLLYWELL NP
Newcastle
Jack's Hill
The Cooperage
CLYDESDALE NP
Mossman's Pk
High Pk
Blue Mountain Pk
Yallahs R
B L U E M T S

★ Kingston
Kingston Harbor

C A R I B B E A N

S E A

JAMAICA

Awesome green mountains of spectacular beauty drop to the palm-studded shoreline fringed with white sand beaches. Countless streams rushing down the thickly forested mountainsides carve their way through the luxuriant tropical growth, cascade over rocky precipices, and meander through marshland to the sea. Banana groves and sugarcane fields and orchards of mango and limes cover the foothills. From the northwest quarter, an eerie karst landscape of haystack hills cuts off the north coast from the south and helps create the impression that Jamaica is a big country rather than a small Caribbean island.

The original vegetation of Jamaica was virtually all forest and marshland. Little wonder the Arawaks called it *Xaymaca*, meaning land of wood and water. While much of the hillside terrain has long been cultivated, parts of Jamaica still have enough natural vegetation to give one an idea of what Columbus might have seen when he landed in 1492. Within a century after the Spaniards' arrival, the Arawaks on Jamaica had been wiped out by war, disease, and enslavement. The Spaniards were then thrown out by the English, who colonized the island and stayed 300 years. They encouraged settlers and missionaries, tolerated pirates, traded with Levantine merchants, and imported African slaves and indentured Asians to work the sugar plantations. From this hodgepodge grew Jamaica's distinctive culture.

In September 1988 Jamaica was hit by Hurricane Gilbert, the first in thirty-seven years and one of the worst storms of this century. Jamaicans moved quickly to repair the damage; however, it will be several years before accurate studies of the flora and fauna can be made to determine what species, if any, have been lost. Meanwhile, the Jamaicans are determinedly optimistic about the long-term outlook. While some parts of the country might not have recovered fully at the time of your visit, you will surely find more than enough of nature's handiwork to admire here than you can possibly fit into one, two, or even several visits.

KINGSTON

Overshadowed by the resorts of the north coast and burdened by bad publicity, Jamaica's capital is ignored by most tourists. Yet, for those eager to discover the country's natural attractions, Kingston is many things: gateway to the Blue Mountains; home of the Institute of Jamaica, guardian of the country's natural, historical, and cultural heritage; and a convenient base for exploring the little-known south, a treasure trove for naturalists.

Royal Botanic Gardens (Hope Gardens)

On the east side of the capital at the foot of the Blue Mountains are the Royal Botanic Gardens. Long recognized as one of the most important botanic gardens in the Caribbean, they have a park setting of spacious green lawns with stately royal palms and enormous flamboyant and other trees whose spreading arms offer respite from the strong Jamaican sun. There are hedges of pine and bougainvillea, periwinkle flower beds, and lily ponds. The gardens are known especially for their orchid collection.

The creator of the gardens was Sir Daniel Morris, a coffee scientist who had lived in Ceylon and who imported over 800 species from Asia and Africa to make the new setting a showplace. Kingston residents, able to obtain cuttings of the exotic new species from the gardens' nursery, were quick to imitate, and soon showy gardens and expansive lawns began to appear throughout the city and the island.

The legacy remains: Jamaica has more botanic gardens than any location in the Caribbean and perhaps more than any other island in the world (Britain excepted). The Botanic Gardens together with the many other gardens and parks around Kingston attract a great variety of birds; Jamaica has more than 256 bird species of which twenty-seven are endemic, and many more migratory birds visit in autumn and spring. Many species that live here as well as in neighboring islands have an added interest to birders because they have developed distinctive behavior and appearances that are peculiar to Jamaica. Among those seen frequently in Kingston gardens are Jamaica's two endemic species of hummingbirds—the Jamaican mango and the streamertail, or doctor bird. Occasionally, one might see the endemic Jamaican owl and common potoo; the bananaquit and Jamaican oriole are ubiquitous.

The Kingston foothills, particularly the woodlands around Hermitage Dam on the north and Mona Dam on the east, are birding locations for the endemic Jamaican lizard-cuckoo, Jamaican vireo, and yellow-billed parrot. Also present, in addition to grebes and a variety of ducks, are the stolid flycatcher, Greater Antillean pewee, gray catbird, olive-throated parakeet, and rufous-throated solitaire.

Morant Point

Along the coast between Kingston and Morant Point, the easternmost corner of Jamaica, the southern spurs of the Blue Mountains drop quickly to the sea. Here the vegetation has adapted to growth on dogtooth limestone and includes red birch, several species of cassia, and quinep; along the sea are seaside mahoe and seagrape. The road crosses the Yallahs River which, depending on the season, will be either a torrent or a small stream meandering through a wide, rocky gully. The east side of Morant Bay has several white sand beaches with public changing facilities.

The north side of Morant Point curves around Holland Bay, a public beach with a long ribbon of white sand and calm waters protected by the Point. The south side is marsh and mangrove swamp. This corner of Jamaica was one of the hardest hit by Hurricane Gilbert in September 1988.

BATH BOTANICAL GARDEN

Bath, north of Port Morant, has the second oldest botanic gardens in the Americas, established in 1779 after those in St. Vincent. The town of Bath was laid out in the seventeenth century after the discovery of the curative powers of the region's minerals waters, known as the Bath Fountain. Created for medicinal purposes, the gardens are adjacent to Bath hospital. They have not been well maintained in recent years and are hardly worth the trip unless one is touring the area. The mineral springs, located about a half-mile beyond the town in a lush tropical setting, are unusual in that the waters come from hot and cold springs. Bath is a starting place for hikes into the John Crow Mountains, the most difficult terrain in Jamaica. Also, one may see in these gardens the black-billed form of the streamertail, which is found only in eastern Jamaica.

THE BLUE MOUNTAINS

The lofty Blue Mountains that frame Kingston and dominate the eastern third of Jamaica make up the country's most scenic region and the most popular one for hiking. Some of the birds, butterflies, and vegetation here are found nowhere else in Jamaica. Born from violent uplift 5 million years ago, the ridge rises dramatically from the coast between Port Antonio on the north and Kingston on the south, and reaches its highest point in five peaks of the Grand Ridge: John Crow, 5,750 ft/1,753 m (and not to be confused with the John Crow Mountains); St. John's Peak, 6,332 ft/1,930 m; High Peak, 6,812 ft/2,076 m; Mossman's Peak, 6,703 ft/2,043 m; and Blue Mountain Peak, 7,402 ft/2,256 m above sea level. The ridge is drained by some of Jamaica's largest rivers—the Yallahs and Morant on the south; the Swift, Spanish, and Rio Grande on the north—and by many small ones. The northern slopes are still virtually unexplored.

The mountains are covered with forests and dotted with plantations of Caribbean pine and the famous Blue Mountain coffee, the most expensive in the world. Alas, its fame and price have reached such heights that

Five high peaks crown the ridge of the Blue Mountains in eastern Jamaica, and a network of roads, paths, and trails leads hikers through this beautiful and dramatic region.

precious soil-conserving woodlands are being cleared for coffee plantations at an alarming rate. Due to lumbering and coffee production, on the other hand, the mountains have a web of roads, tracks, trails, and footpaths, making almost any part accessible to determined hikers. Some mountain tracks can be negotiated by four-wheel-drive vehicles; others are passable only on foot or by mule. There are tiny farming communities throughout the Blue Mountains in astonishingly remote places.

The Blue Mountains are traversed by three north–south roads and can be approached from either coast. Hiking areas are on the south side of the mountains along the Kingston/Newcastle/Buff Bay road. This road provides access to Mount Horeb and Catherine's Peak on the southwest face of the Grand Ridge where there are extensive trails. At Irish Town, the Newcastle Road branches east to Gordon Town, Guava Ridge (Pine Grove), and Mavis Bank, all access points for roads and tracks into the high mountains. Some key locations, such as Jack's Hill and Mavis Bank, are served by public transportation from Kingston. At Mahogany Vale, beyond the plantation and coffee processing center of Mavis Bank, a country road leads upward to Whitfield Hall, the starting point for the trip to Blue Mountain Peak. Mahogany Vale is frequently impassable after a heavy rain. Distances between key locations are usually no more than 2 or 3 mi/3.2 or

4.8 km, and, generally, hiking along roads and tracks is not difficult. Hikers should not leave trails, however; if they do, they will quickly find the way impassable due to impenetrable vegetation, mud slides, boulders, or cliffs that drop several thousand feet. Topographical maps are available from the Land and Survey Department in Kingston and are essential for hikers who are not accompanied by local guides. *A Hiker's Guide to the Blue Mountains*, by former Peace Corps volunteer Bill Wilcox, is very useful.

JACK'S HILL

East of Kingston, across the hot Liguanea plain and past the Botanic Gardens, the Newcastle/Buff Bay road climbs quickly into the cool air of the mountains. Shortly after Papine, and before crossing a bridge that leads to Blue Mountain Inn, the Skyline Drive branches west (left) along the first ridge overlooking the city to the village of Jack's Hill at 2,059 ft/628 m. Here, too, is Maya, a rustic cottage and camping site operated by the Jamaican Alternative Tourism, Camping and Hiking Association, or JATCHA, a loosely knit group of privately owned cottage and camping operations around Jamaica. The 15-acre/6-hectare retreat is surrounded by a tropical landscape of montane forests, feathery ferns, bamboo, and fruit trees, with Mount Horeb (4,600 ft/1,402 m) and Catherine's Peak (5,060 ft/ 1,542 m) towering in the background. For those content with minimal accommodations, Maya makes a suitable base. (Iver, a restored nineteenth-century guesthouse in Jack's Hill, provides more deluxe accommodations.)

Maya's trained nature guides will take hikers on short mountain trails or on all-day treks up to and around the high peaks. Or hikers can set out on their own over developed trails from Jack's Hill to Peter's Rock (two hours), continuing on to Holywell National Park, situated on the western slope of Mount Horeb (two hours). The trail and dirt road pass through Caribbean pine plantation and elfin woodland and along boulder-strewn gullies watered by fast-flowing streams and falls.

If, instead of turning left to Skyline Drive and Jack's Hill, one continues straight across the bridge past the Blue Mountain Inn—one of Jamaica's best restaurants where night temperatures are often 30°F/15°C cooler than in Kingston—the road forks right to Gordon Town and left to Irish Town (and hence to Newcastle). Beyond Irish Town, a spur on the east leads to Strawberry Hill, a former guesthouse surrounded by pretty gardens with a large variety of plants. Note especially the tree ferns and thunbergia, whose lavender-blue flower resembles a cross between an orchid and a hibiscus, and Napoleon's hat, a tiny red or yellow flower with a crown resembling a Chinese parasol. The house is a good place to view the panorama of Kingston and to watch spectacular sunsets. Lunches and dinners are served only Thursday to Sunday; reservations are necessary.

CATHERINE'S PEAK

When the Newcastle Road, which borders the Hope River most of the way, climbs to 2,500 ft/762 m, the drop in temperature is noticeable immediately. From a distance, Newcastle, which comes into view several miles prior to reaching it, looks like a Swiss mountain village rather than the Jamaican army hill station that it is. Situated at about 3,500 ft/1,067 m above sea level on the southern flank of Catherine's Peak, Newcastle was founded in 1841 as an alternative training site for British troops who were being ravaged by yellow fever in the lowlands.

As part of their training, the army recruits race on the paved road to the peak and back to the base; some complete the course in under twenty-five minutes. Most people, however, take about forty-five minutes to reach the top and their reward is a magnificent view of the mountains, Kingston on the plain, and the Caribbean Sea. Newcastle is a starting point for hikes north to Woodcutter's Gap, Green Hills, and Silver Hill Gap, and south to Gordon Town—all developed trails that are fairly easy to find with a topographical map and local directions.

HOLYWELL NATIONAL RECREATION PARK

This park, managed by the Forestry Department, is 3 mi/4.8 km north of Newcastle at 4,000 ft/1,220 m altitude. The site, where nighttime winter temperatures can drop below freezing, offers panoramic views and the twinkling lights of Kingston in the evening. There are walking trails and sheltered picnic areas with tables and barbecue pits. A map near the park entrance provides information on specific trails. Three cabins, each with four beds and a fireplace, are available for rent; one must obtain a reservation in person in advance from the Forestry office in Kingston. Weekends and holidays must be booked weeks in advance; weekdays are more available. Users bring their own bed linen, food, kitchen utensils, and toiletries.

HARDWAR GAP

After the park, the road to Buff Bay passes through Hardwar Gap, a thickly wooded mountain pass at about 4,000 ft/1,220 m and one of the prettiest stretches on the drive. Here, clouds move through the forest daily, creating a cool and damp environment more closely resembling the tropical rain forests of the Lesser Antilles than other sections of the Blue Mountains. The woods, dense with tree ferns, blue mahoe, mahogany, and other native trees, are luxuriant with huge bromeliads and epiphytes, particularly marcgravia, whose scarlet flowers attract hummingbirds.

Blue mahoe is the national tree of Jamaica. Until one sees it in blossom, it is difficult to imagine that this enormous tree, which normally grows over

30 or 40 ft/9 or 12 m, belongs to the hibiscus family. Its blossoms change color from yellow to orange to red as they mature; it is not uncommon for one tree to display blossoms of three different colors at one time. The *blue* in its name comes from the bluish hue of the polished wood, which is easily recognizable in the furniture and crafts for which it is used. Blue mahoe is now found on many Caribbean islands and is planted frequently to aid in soil conservation and reforestation.

Beyond Hardwar Gap, the Kingston/Buff Bay Road continues to the north side of the ridge from where there is a splendid view down the valley to Buff Bay on the north shore. The winding road follows the Buff Bay River which flows through a wooded, steep-sided valley most of the way. In many places, the waters tumble over large boulders into pools where one might stop for a picnic and a dip. There is a beautiful triple cascade 2 mi/3.2 km after the Spring Hill Police Station. As is often the case in Jamaica, a river may be a swift-flowing torrent or a gentle stream, depending upon the rain and time of year.

CLYDESDALE NATIONAL PARK

At the northeast end of Hardwar Gap at a hamlet called Section, a road branching east leads to Silver Hill Gap where a dirt road turns south and then east to Clydesdale National Park and Cinchona. Once a coffee plantation and pine nursery at 3,700 ft/1,128 m, Clydesdale has been made into a park under the management of the Forestry Department. One of the structures there has been converted into a dormitory. At the approach to Clydesdale a stream running through thick vegetation cascades into a pool large enough for swimming—though the water is quite chilly. The area, shaded by a high canopy of mahogany, mahoe, and eucalyptus trees, invites picnicking and bird-watching. Among the Blue Mountains' endemics to be seen here are the crested quail-dove, chestnut-bellied cuckoo, Jamaican becard, Jamaican elaenia, white-eyed thrush, white-chinned thrush, Jamaican vireo, Blue Mountain vireo, and arrow-headed warbler.

CINCHONA GARDENS

Clydesdale is the starting point for the hike to Cinchona, a public garden at 5,000 ft/1,524 m, established in 1868. The name comes from the cinchona tree whose bark is a source of quinine, once a highly valued commodity for curing malaria and other tropical fevers. Cinchona was planted here as a commercial enterprise, but only a few of the trees remain. The dominant

Lichen, ferns, orchids, and bromeliads do not harm the trees they use for support; all are among the profuse vegetation of Jamaica's Blue Mountains.

tree now is the giant eucalyptus, of which there are twelve species. There are also Norfolk Island and massonia pines, podocarpus, and huge rhododendrons. The gardens, covering a sixth of their original size, are being renovated after years of neglect.

In this quiet, almost melancholy setting, footpaths wander through the gardens under an umbrella of lacy bamboo and explore hillsides planted with magnificent ferns, bushes of hydrangea and azalea, and beds of agapanthus lilies whose blue flowers carpet sections of the gardens in early spring. Beds with a large variety of show orchids cover one hillside. Streamertails often are seen darting about the flowering bushes. From Cinchona there is a breathtaking view down the valley and across to the Grand Ridge of the Blue Mountains.

There are several trails to Cinchona, but the road from Clydesdale is the most convenient. Through neglect, however, it has become a crude track that heavy rains and mud slides make impassable for vehicles. Only a strong, high-built vehicle can negotiate the deeply rutted road, even when it is dry. Consequently, one must be prepared to walk the 2.5 mi/4 km to the summit where the gardens are located, heart-pounding exercise for those who are not in good shape. At a comfortable pace, the hike up can take an hour and a half, forty-five minutes to return. Those with stamina can continue hiking down to Westphalia across the Green River to Penlyne Castle, and from there to Whitfield Hall, a hostel at 4,200 ft/1,280 m altitude at the end of the motor road, and the starting point for the hike to Blue Mountain Peak. With four-wheel-drive one can also motor from Clydesdale via Mahogany Vale and Mavis Bank to Whitfield Hall.

BLUE MOUNTAIN PEAK

Of all the hikes in the Blue Mountains, the most popular is the 3,000-ft/ 900-m ascent to Blue Mountain Peak, particularly at full moon, when hikers, departing from Whitfield Hall at 2 A.M., make the four- to five-hour trek 6.5 mi/10.4 km to the summit in time to watch the sun rise over the mountains. The peak trail starts a half-mile from the hostel on an undemanding path fresh with the scent of mountain heather. Soon, however, the rocky path begins to climb and wind up along terraced hillsides planted with coffee and vegetables and shaded by banana trees. It passes through tropical rain and montane forests entangled in vines and tight with ferns and bamboo that creaks in the wind. The final stretch passes through the moss-draped dwarf trees of elfin woodland.

Portland Gap, the halfway point, has a Forestry Department cabin and water. From here the climb gets steeper and narrower as it tracks through dense undergrowth of ferns under the canopied forest—all better enjoyed in the daylight of the return journey. The last mile passes through a dry, jagged riverbed called Jacob's Ladder, and is the steepest part, made only slightly easier for tired hikers by the light of dawn.

Out of the darkness, the island's peaks begin to emerge; below, one can see the mist rising like clouds of smoke from the valleys that stretch to the sea. Soon, if the morning is clear, the outline of the coast with Kingston on the south and the twin harbors of Port Antonio on the north comes into view. On the clearest days, one can see Cuba, 90 mi/144 km away. The trail at the summit levels onto a rough plateau covered with scrubby trees and bushes. The winds swirl the mist and clouds overhead, sometimes moving on, sometimes clinging to the sides obliterating all below. At the peak there are two huts—one with no roof, the other partly covered—belonging to the Forestry Department and intended for a caretaker who apparently is seldom there. Those who want to camp overnight can reserve a hut at the Forestry office in Kingston. Debris left by previous hikers does nothing to enhance the site.

On the return trip, provided the fog is not too thick, one can enjoy the dense vegetation and mountain panoramas that are missed in the darkness on the upward journey. At Portland Gap the view overlooks the green folds of Blue Mountain ridges all the way to the sea. In winter the mountainsides are brightened with the red blossoms of African tulip and orange immortelle. Hikers may chance upon some of the birds that live in the Blue Mountains, such as the endemic Jamaican tody, Jamaican woodpecker, rufous-tailed flycatcher, and crested quail-dove, known locally as the mountain witch. Others found in this region are the yellow-bellied sapsucker, Greater Antillean pewee, rufous-throated solitaire, and a dozen or more species of warblers.

The hike to the peak is not hazardous or particularly difficult for those with stamina. Those who do not want to walk the entire route can hire mules from Whitfield Hall to go to the peak. December to March, the dry season, is the preferred time for the hike, when one has a better chance of enjoying clear views and staying dry. But since the peaks get 150 in/381 cm or more of rain per year, "dry" is relative. Normally, hikers can expect the temperature to be in the 50s F/teens C at night, but they should never underestimate weather conditions, which can change quickly. Temperatures at the peak can drop from 50°F/10°C to freezing and seem even colder when there is rain and strong wind. The best preparation is to dress in layers—T-shirt, sweater, down vest or windbreaker, heavy socks, and cap. On clear days the sun warms the air quickly. Boots are not necessary; sturdy shoes or sneakers are adequate. A flashlight is essential on the trail for the nighttime climb.

Whitfield Hall, a hostel with an outdoor campsite, is set in a grove of giant eucalyptus trees. A four-wheel-drive vehicle is necessary to reach it from Mavis Bank, unless one prefers to make the four-hour hike. Arrangements for a vehicle and reservations for Whitfield Hall and a mule can be made through the Jamaica Tourist Board.

A practical alternative to Whitfield Hall for those who prefer greater comfort is Pine Grove (809-922-8705), a mountain lodge 2 mi/3.2 km north of Guava Ridge at Content. It has its own jeeps and arranges excursions to the peaks with guides and mules at very reasonable prices. (For an additional fee, one can be picked up from Kingston airport.) The lodge is a good base for nearby excursions and (if you are energetic) for hiking to Cinchona and Newcastle.

JOHN CROW MOUNTAINS

At the northeastern end of Jamaica are the John Crow Mountains, a limestone ridge younger than the Blue Mountains and an area for serious hikers and mountain climbers only. The limestone has eroded to form a rugged karst terrain, similar to the Cockpit Country but more irregular. The mountains lie directly in the path of the prevailing northeast tradewinds and receive almost daily rain. The lower reaches of the forest are typical lower-montane rain forest with a canopy of about 80 to 90 ft/24 to 27 m where the most abundant tree is the Santa Maria. Above 1,250 ft/380 m can be found one of the largest expanses of undisturbed native forest remaining in Jamaica; above 3,750 ft/1,143 m one enters the low tangle of trees and shrubs of elfin woodland, covered with mosses and epiphytes.

About their expedition in 1953, G. F. Asprey and R. G. Robbins wrote in their ecological monograph, *The Vegetation of Jamaica*: "Crevasses and small ravines lie at all angles and are from 6–20 ft./1.8–6 m in depth. The only possible progress is across the top of the tangled vegetation where every foothold must be tested before relinquishing the last. Large rock castles up to 20 ft./6 m in height are frequent and each must be circumnavigated. It is small wonder that such an area has been little explored." Indeed, an expedition that set out to explore it in the early 1980s needed two weeks to cover only 6 mi/10 km. Little wonder, too, that runaway slaves, known as Maroons, were able to hide out from the British here as they did in the Cockpit Country.

The lower reaches of the Rio Grande River, fed by streams from the John Crow Mountains, are popular for river rafting, an activity that takes one past rural villages far from the roadsides.

Nestled in the foothills of the John Crow Mountains lies Moore Town, which, along with Accompong on the edge of the Cockpit Country, is one of only two Maroon settlements that have their own chief, or "colonel." The Moore Town Maroons are descendants of those who once lived in Nanny Town on the western side of the Rio Grande River below Blue Mountain Peak. Nanny Town was destroyed by the British in the 1730s; the area is so remote that the town's location was lost to history for more than two centuries and only rediscovered about twenty years ago.

The Millbank area is of particular interest because it is the home of the spectacular Jamaican swallowtail, which lives in the eastern parts of the Blue Mountains and the Cockpit Country. This giant, bright yellow and black butterfly with a 6-in/15-cm wingspan is the largest in the Western Hemisphere. Coveted by collectors since its discovery in the eighteenth century, it is found near Millbank at the source of the Rio Grande. Although specimens have been collected at various times of the year, the summer months, especially May and June, are thought to be the best. The John Crow Mountains are also home to Jamaica's only endemic land mammal, the nocturnal coney, or Jamaican hutia, which has been described fancifully as a cross between a rabbit and guinea pig, and which has been hunted for its meat since Arawak times.

HELLSHIRE HILLS

Southwest of Kingston, by the sea, the limestone Hellshire Hills are a semidesert area covered with undisturbed dry scrub of cacti and cassia. The nice beaches along the coast are Kingstonians' favorite weekend playground, but they are less populated during the week. The road via the Caymanas Race Track leads as far as Port Henderson and Fort Clarence. Inland from the beaches there are no roads and no development. South of Port Henderson a hiking trail for the hardy leads up to Rodney's Lookout from where there is a superb view of Kingston and the coast.

On the south side of Fort Clarence and on the southwest coast of the hills, there are salt ponds and mangroves. The area has undeveloped caves, including some with petroglyphs; one must inquire locally for directions. In addition to the coney, which lives here, the hills are home to the endemic Jamaican boa, or yellow snake. Averaging 6 to 8 ft/1.8 to 2.4 m, it is one of the largest of the Caribbean's two dozen species, and one of Jamaica's five endemic snakes; none is poisonous. Ground iguanas, which have disappeared elsewhere, may possibly remain here because the hills are one of the few places in Jamaica where they could survive predation.

MILK RIVER BATH

From the four-lane highway that leads west of Kingston to Mandeville, several country roads turn off to the south coast. Only footpaths, however, extend as far as Portland Ridge, the southernmost point of Jamaica, an area unknown to tourists and, indeed, to most Jamaicans. The terrain south of the Brazilletto Mountains to Portland Ridge is made up of lowlands and marshes which together with the dozens of offshore islands of the bay, known as Portland Bight, have been proposed as a wildlife sanctuary in a project intended to be the basis of a national parks system.

Farther west at Milk River about a mile from the sea a spa has harnessed what are said to be the world's most radioactive waters, with an international reputation for curing nerve and liver disorders. The waters have been measured to be nine times more active than those of Bath in England and fifty times those of Vichy in France.

MANDEVILLE

Situated at 2,000 ft/600 m on a plateau of the Don Figuerero Mountains overlooking the south coast, Mandeville is the best location for touring the central area of the country. Grand old mahogany trees, flowering yellow poui and mango, and trees laden with ackee fruit, the national food passion, decorate the country lanes that wind through vales around the town. Mandeville is the center for several well-known Jamaican products—Pickapeppa sauce, coffee, chocolate—whose modest factories can be visited.

MARSHALL'S PEN

Marshall's Pen, 3 mi/4.8 km northwest of Mandeville, is a cattle farm and nature reserve surrounded by woodlands where 89 of Jamaica's bird species may be seen, including 23 endemics. A total of 51 bird species breed on the property. Among the common endemics that breed here are the chestnut-bellied cuckoo, Jamaican owl, Jamaican tody, Jamaican woodpecker, Jamaican elaenia, Jamaican becard, Jamaican vireo, Jamaican euphonia, and yellow-shouldered grassquit. The rare endemics are the yellow-billed and black-billed parrots.

Birders are welcome but by appointment only. Contact Ann or Robert Sutton, Marshall's Pen, Box 58, Mandeville, Jamaica (809-962-2260). The best times for viewing birds are 6 to 9 A.M. and 4 to 6 P.M. The property has many roads and paths that can be used for self-guided tours. There is a small charge. Tours with Jamaican ornithologists and naturalists can be arranged for groups.

GOURIE CAVE AND FOREST PARK

The countryside around Mandeville has been planted extensively with pines which help to prevent soil erosion while also providing timber. Christiana, a farming community north of Mandeville, has several pleasant hiking areas. In town, a country road on the east (starting in front of Kirby Hardware) leads about 2 mi/3.2 km to the Blue Hole River and waterfall where one can swim. About a mile north of the town, in a pine grove next to the main road, the Gourie Forest Park has two well-equipped cabins (keys available from the caretaker). From here, a 0.5-mi/0.8-km track leads down into a gully to a cave that has not been charted but which is said to be one of Jamaica's longest cave systems with water that runs underground to Oxford about 10 mi/16 km to the west. The path leading to the cave is surrounded by woods with trees including blue mahoe, broadleaf, Santa Maria, and candlewood, known locally as cantoo, among others.

THE COCKPIT COUNTRY

About 8 mi/13 km north of Christiana, the road becomes track leading to Troy and Crown Lands, settlements in the heart of the Cockpit Country. The Cockpit is a loosely defined region that encompasses parts of three parishes, or districts: southern Trelawny, the eastern edge of St. James, and the northern edge of St. Catherine.

A karst limestone region of caves, sinkholes, and haystack terrain, the Cockpit is basically a plateau of hard limestone built up layer by layer over millions of years. It rose above sea level by uplift that occurred about 20 million years ago. Over the eons the limestone has been eroded by rainfall whose carbonic acid content has gradually dissolved the limestone and seeped through to belowground, leaving behind a jumble of steep, rocky, conical hills of about the same height and separated by deep depressions, or "cockpits," each drained by a sinkhole at the bottom. Beneath the land are miles of uncharted caves and rivers.

The terrain, likened to an inverted egg carton, ranges from 1,000 to 2,500 ft/ 300 to 760 m and gets from 75 to 150 in/190 to 380 cm of annual rainfall. The tops and vertical hillsides have little or no soil to support vegetation, although some does grow out horizontally from the sides. But the cockpits where the minerals have been deposited as the water seeps through usually have very fertile soil, and when undisturbed they support thick vegetation and very large trees. Where roads provide access, the forest has been cut and small-scale banana and other crops are cultivated. The impenetrable

The endangered manatee, a massive mammal that can grow to 15 ft/4.6 m, lives on aquatic vegetation in shallow coastal waters and mangrove swamps.

subtropical-to-wet forest hosts a great variety of rare and endemic plants including a hundred or more species of ferns. The plants are often rare and endemic to very restricted locations.

The southeast corner of the Cockpit, north of Troy and Quick Step, is known as the District of Look Behind, and is often labeled on maps with "Me no sen, you no come." The phrase comes from the days when the region was the stronghold of the Maroons, who, after fighting the British to a truce in the eighteenth century, were able to gain autonomy, which continues in a diluted form to this day. "Maroon" comes from the Spanish word *cimarrón*, meaning wild or untamed.

The hillsides at the edge of the Cockpit can be covered by car on one's own, but there are no roads in the heart of the Cockpit. In addition to the road to Troy and Crown Lands, tracks from Balaclava and Windsor, northwest of Mandeville, lead to the villages of Aberdeen and Quick Step. From Appleton, the home of Jamaica's best-known rum, and Maggotty the road leads via Retirement to Accompong, the home of the chief of the Maroons, known as the Colonel. The road from Retirement to Elderslie, Mocho, and Maroon Town vaguely defines the western edge of the Cockpit. Windsor is the deepest penetration of the Cockpit on its north side and is accessible by road from Falmouth. Tours to Windsor Cave and villages at the western edge of the Cockpit depart from Montego Bay.

Hiking in the Cockpit is for serious hikers and cavers only; they must have a guide from the Cockpit accompanying them, not only because of the immense difficulty of the terrain, but also because of a certain danger an unaccompanied person could encounter. Ganja, the Jamaican marijuana, is grown here as well as in the less accessible areas of the John Crow and Blue mountains. Foreigners who are not accompanied by someone known to the people of the immediate area are likely to be suspected of being drug enforcement officers, who are not exactly welcomed visitors. Very few Jamaicans have ever ventured into the heart of the Cockpit.

LOVER'S LEAP AND TREASURE BEACH

Southwest of Mandeville the Santa Cruz Mountains form a backdrop to the south coast where miles of beaches are among the little-known gems of Jamaica awaiting discovery. Lover's Leap at the southeast end of the Treasure Beach area is a sheer cliff rising 1,000 ft/300 m above the sea. A rocky road leads to the clifftop and a lighthouse; a derelict building mars the site but not the spectacular view. A cliffside visit is not recommended for anyone troubled by heights.

Almost any place along secluded Treasure Beach is good for hiking; there

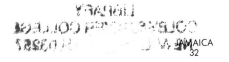

are no real trails, only footpaths or dirt tracks used by local fishermen and farmers. There are small villages slightly inland, but not directly by the sea. The area is a prime birding location.

BLACK RIVER AND GREAT MORASS

Black River is both the name of Jamaica's longest river and the little colonial town at its mouth where five rivers meet in the 80,000-acre/32,376-hectare Great Morass, which comprises marshland, swamps, and mangroves rich in vegetation and birdlife. At the mouth of the Black and Broad rivers where the fresh water meets the salt water from the sea, there are extensive mangroves dominated by red mangrove, whose aerial roots fall 30 to 40 ft/9 to 12 m into the swamp. Beyond it are white mangrove, ferns, and vines. Past the mangroves are large tracts of marsh or sedge savanna with a great variety of riverine vegetation, such as wild cane, bulrush, and wild ginger, known as ginger lily or butterfly ginger elsewhere in the Caribbean and as *mariposa* in Spanish. The savanna is dominated by sawgrass, and some bull thatch, the only palm natural to the open sedge marsh and the most important tree of the region economically, is found here. It is used for thatching houses and weaving baskets, particularly the pots used for shrimping, one of the main activities of the Morass. From the open marsh, the vegetation changes to jungle-thick marsh forest, the most distinctive feature of the Morass. Although the forest has been cut extensively, a tall royal palm endemic to Jamaica is abundant. Blue mahoe, boarwood, and several other species normally found only at high elevation thrive here apparently because of the high humidity.

The best examples of marsh forest are located near New Holland and Frenchman where giant trees form a high canopy over a dense undergrowth of ferns and vines; birdlife is abundant. About a half-mile upstream from the New Holland pumping station and stretching to Lacovia, the Black River is bordered by a remnant of logwood forest, completely different from the marsh forest downstream. A species introduced in 1715 for commercial reasons, logwood was prized by European textile makers for the dark blue and black dyes it produces.

The edges of the river are thick with water hyacinth, lilies, and a variety of rooted plants on whose floating leaves northern jacanas and purple gallinules scamper about in the late afternoon. Other birds of the Morass are herons and egrets, West Indian whistling-ducks, blue-winged teal, ring-necked ducks, and many shorebirds.

Pages 34 and 35: In the shallow waters of the Black River, red mangroves can grow to 40 ft/12 m by buttressing their trunks with prop roots sent down into the river bed.

In the great expanse of the Morass, there are several raised limestone islands—Cataboo, Slipe, Punch's, and Frenchman's—which have long been inhabited by people who depend almost entirely on the swamp for their livelihood, earned through shrimping, fishing, and basket-weaving. They move about in canoes whose design and construction have changed little from those of the Arawaks, while the pots they use for shrimping are woven like those found along the Niger River in West Africa where their ancestors came from more than 300 years ago.

From the town of Black River on the south coast, a boat excursion of an hour or so goes up the river to the mangroves and grassland. The river has snook, mullet, and carp and is one of the few places in Jamaica where there still are crocodiles, which, like the manatees, were once abundant. Known locally as alligators, the American crocodile can occasionally be seen sleeping in the sun along the mud banks. The rare manatee, believed to number less than a hundred in Jamaica, might be seen at the mouth of the river.

NEGRIL

One route from Black River to Montego Bay is along the southwest coast, a prime fishing area, to Negril. The road edges a series of beaches to Savanna-la-Mar, near the mouth of the Cabarita River, then cuts inland up the Negril River valley through pastureland and large sugarcane plantations. Once an obscure fishing village, Negril is the major resort of the west coast along 7 mi/11.2 km of idyllic palm-fringed, white sand beaches fronting an aqua sea protected by coral reefs. It was put on the map by the "flower children" of the 1960s and until recently had minimal development, enabling it to retain the laid-back lifestyle that made it famous. Although there are strict building codes—no building can be higher than the tallest tree—the pace of development has quickened and threatens to change Negril's character. Outdoor activity is oriented mainly to the sea, with facilities for boating, diving, snorkeling, windsurfing, and deep-sea fishing. North of Negril Beach, the coast rounds a series of rockbound coves to the picturesque eighteenth-century port of Lucea and Mosquito (Miskito) Cove, a popular destination for picnic and snorkeling excursions from Montego Bay.

MONTEGO BAY

Montego Bay, the country's major gateway, is most visitors' introduction to Jamaica. Begun in the eighteenth century as a sugar-loading station for the large number of plantations in the region, it is one of the main resorts of the north coast. It is a convenient base for exploring the western third of Jamaica and the Cockpit.

Rockland Bird Sanctuary

West of Montego Bay at Anchovy is the 3-acre/1.2-hectare Rockland Bird Sanctuary and Feeding Station, a reserve for Jamaica's three species of hummingbird: the vervain hummingbird, one of the two smallest birds in the world; the Jamaican mango; and the streamertail, or doctor bird. The latter two are endemic and protected by Jamaica's wildlife laws. The streamertail, the national bird, has brilliant plumage with a velvety crest, emerald breast, and long, scissors-like tail feathers. (A stylized version of the bird is used in the logo of Air Jamaica, the nation's airline.)

There are trails where as many as fifty-one species might be spotted on a three-hour walk. Among the endemics here are the Jamaican owl, Jamaican woodpecker, Jamaican becard, white-eyed thrush, and white-chinned thrush. Other species are common barn-owl, stolid flycatcher, gray catbird, scarlet tanager, summer tanager, saffron finch, indigo bunting, and ten species of warblers. The sanctuary closes about an hour before sunset.

The Great River

Beyond the turnoff to the Rockland Bird Sanctuary, the coastal highway crosses the Great River where bamboo rafts with an oarsman and seats for two people can be hired for an hour's leisurely cruise through the lush vegetation of the lower river valley. Three evenings a week an excursion called "A Jamaican Night on the Great River" takes guests up the torchlit river by boat to a landing where they enjoy a folklore show and reggae music and dine on local specialties. The Great River is one of several waterways becoming popular for white-water canoeing.

Montego River Valley

On a steep hillside east of Montego Bay is Sign Great House, an eighteenth-century plantation house once restored as an inn and bird sanctuary but no longer open. It is a starting place for hiking on short trails that lead to the Montego River where there are small rapids and places to swim in a quiet, green setting almost unknown to the tourists who crowd the beaches of Montego Bay. One should ask locally for directions. Here, as elsewhere in Jamaica, one will see the blue-flowered lignum vitae whose parts—wood, bark, leaves, blossoms, and fruit—have many practical and medicinal uses.

Cockpit and Train Excursions

From Montego Bay several excursions offer an easy and comfortable way to see some of the Cockpit Country and rural mountain life. *Cockpit Tours* takes passengers from Montego Bay via Maroon Town and Retirement to

Accompong where they meet the current Colonel of the Maroons and a bush doctor who explains the use of local herbs. *Governor's Coach*, a luxury diesel train once used by the governor of Jamaica for official travel, climbs the mountains stopping at several small villages along the edge of the Cockpit. At Ipswich passengers visit the caves, picnic by a mountain stream, and learn about the making of rum at the Appleton Rum Distillery. *Hilton High Day*, an excursion to Hilton Plantation, a working farm on 40 tropical acres/16 hectares in the hills, 20 mi/36 km from Montego Bay, is designed to show visitors the "real" Jamaica, with a Jamaican breakfast; a walking tour to explain the fruits, vegetables, and flowers growing on the farm; and a Jamaican lunch. Those who start at 6:30 A.M. can include a hot-air balloon ride over Jamaican mountainsides.

ROSE HALL GREAT HOUSE

East of Montego Bay en route to Falmouth, in a majestic garden setting on a hillside overlooking the sea, is Rose Hall Great House, the most beautiful plantation house on the north coast. Built around 1770, the mansion was a ruin before American millionaire John Rollins restored it as a museum in the early 1970s. The house is best known for its last occupant, Annie Palmer, a beautiful Englishwoman whose ghost haunts the house, according to local legend. Known as the White Witch of Rose Hall, she allegedly murdered three husbands and was herself murdered at age twenty-nine. Trails behind Rose Hall are popular for horseback riding, and there are several stables in the immediate vicinity.

FALMOUTH LAGOON AND MANGROVES

Immediately before Falmouth on the north side of the road is a phosphorescent lagoon and marsh; on the south is a mangrove swamp where crocodiles are the highlight of a modest tourist attraction, Jamaica Safari Village, created by the owners of a small hotel for naturalists in Montego Bay. There are boats for a trip into the mangroves, and the area is rich in bird-life, particularly herons, egrets, limpkins, clapper rails, and shorebirds. The Village has a small zoo of crocodiles, snakes, and other native animals.

MARTHA BRAE RIVER AND WINDSOR CAVE

At a landing site known as Rafter's Village, about 1 mi/1.6 km upstream from Falmouth on the Martha Brae River, rafts (for two) guided by experienced oarsmen are available for a gentle two-hour ride downriver through a serene, tropical country setting. Except during the rainy season, the Martha Brae is a calm waterway that flows from Windsor Cave, located farther up the mountains on a narrow country road via the Good Hope

Great House. The karstic caves, which run 2 mi/3.2 km into the Cockpit, are among the largest in Jamaica and have magnificent stalactite formations. Two chambers are accessible and are being developed by their new owner. To explore further, one needs lights and a guide; the caves have many levels.

DISCOVERY BAY AND ST. ANN'S BAY

About midway between Montego Bay and Ocho Rios, Discovery Bay is the traditional site where Christopher Columbus first sighted Jamaica in 1494. It is marked by a memorial park. Across the road from the Discovery Bay Marine Laboratory lies a small fragment of low scrub forest with figs, myrtles, and bromeliads, thought to be typical of the vegetation that covered the area when Columbus arrived. (One should wear sturdy shoes as protection against the forest's dogtooth limestone.) At Runaway Bay, the Green Grotto Caves are a tourist attraction with a guided tour along lighted paths and a boat ride on an underground lake. The area between Discovery Bay and Runaway Bay is slated for major development as a resort for diving and water sports.

In 1503, on Columbus's fourth voyage, two of his ships were damaged and had to be beached near St. Ann. Here, Columbus spent a year awaiting rescue, thus giving Jamaica the unique status as the only place in the New World where the great explorer lived.

Green-backed herons are equally at home near fresh and salt water and can be found in swamps, beside marshes, and among the prop roots of red mangroves.

OCHO RIOS

Known as the Garden of Jamaica, Ocho Rios is another of the large resort centers of the north coast. But hidden in the lush steep-sided mountains behind the town are botanic gardens, bird sanctuaries, beautiful waterfalls, and working plantations for sugar, bananas, mangoes, and other tropical produce. Any of these attractions makes an easy day's outing.

FERN GULLY

One of Jamaica's most distinctive plants is fern, of which 550 species are native, ranging from tiny lacy species to huge tree ferns that grow 30 ft/9 m or more in height. Ferns are found throughout the island but one of the most impressive, easily accessible collections can be seen at Fern Gully, a former riverbed that now comprises the first 3 mi/4.8 km of highway A1 from Ocho Rios to Kingston. The winding road is bordered by hundreds of fern species and a forest of bamboo and other giant trees that meet overhead to form a natural canopy over the road, cooling the air.

DUNN'S RIVER FALLS

Wherever one travels in Jamaica one is never far from a spring or water-fall—a particularly refreshing sight to hikers. Of all the cascades, the most famous, photographed, and accessible is the Dunn's River Falls on the north coast 7 mi/11.2 km west of Ocho Rios. It emerges abruptly from thickly wooded limestone cliffs 600 ft/180 m above the sea and tumbles down a wide stairway of huge rocks to the Caribbean. The tropical scenery is spectacular and changes at every level. The surefooted may climb the rocks (in a bathing suit and sneakers), fighting the rapids like salmon beating upstream. Since this is Jamaica's single most visited natural attraction, one usually climbs in a crowd. Guides are available and should be used, since the rocks are very slick in spots and the torrents are powerful enough to knock one off balance. Those who are not up to the adventure can view the setting from observation decks.

SHAW PARK BOTANICAL GARDENS

On a hillside directly above Ocho Rios is Shaw Park Botanical Gardens, a nature retreat with magnificent views of the town and coast. The grounds have formal gardens with cascading waters, beds of lilies, shrimp plants, and pretty lanes and walkways under bougainvillea trellises where one can wander through a variety of exotic flora. A gigantic seventy-year-old banyan tree is the showpiece of the gardens.

CARINOSA

The Gardens of Carinosa on a steep 20-acre/8-hectare hillside 1 mi/1.6 km from Ocho Rios were created around a natural gorge with a series of waterfalls where rain-forest vegetation of ferns and bromeliads has been interlaced with palms, heliconias, anthurium, and hibiscus. Walkways with bridges and viewing decks run up and down the hill along lily ponds and flower beds and there is a walk-through aviary containing a variety of endemics including doves, hummingbirds, the Jamaican tody, and the Jamaican woodpecker. The gardens have a theme-park look, complete with restaurant, gift shop, and safari-costumed guides wearing pith helmets. There is a high admission fee for non-Jamaicans.

PROSPECT PLANTATION AND OTHER EXCURSIONS

A convenient and pleasant way to become acquainted with Jamaica's many exotic fruits and vegetables is to tour a working plantation by jitney or on horseback. Several such excursions are available in the Ocho Rios area.

The most extensive, best organized, and best maintained is the 1,100-acre/445-hectare Prospect Plantation, about 4 mi/6.4 km east of Ocho Rios. It is probably the most satisfying of the plantation tours for visitors because the great many tree varieties are well labeled. The tour by jitney passes through woodlands that include samaan or guango, birch gum, breadnut, Jamaican cedar, flamboyant, cassava, logwood, tamarind, soursop, guava, cocoa, calabash, and ackee. The roadways are lined with plants and shrubs such as aloe vera, known locally as sinkle bible, and bulrush, a purple and green aloe-like plant, known as Moses-in-the-basket. Hiking trails lead to White River Gorge, 500 ft/150 m deep and almost obscured by thick woods. The estate can also be toured by horseback. Prospect Plantation produces mainly limes and allspice, which the Jamaicans call pimento.

The 600-acre/242-hectare Friendship Farms, high on a hill beyond Fern Gully, is a working cattle farm with a variety of indigenous fruit and flowering trees. There are groves of allspice, banana, black pepper, bayleaf, coconut, and coffee. The 200-year-old plantation house sits in a garden on a hill at 2,000 ft/600 m altitude and has a splendid view over the countryside. The farm has picnic sites and a fishing pond stocked with perch.

East of Ocho Rios overlooking Port Maria, the 175-year-old Brimmer Hall Estate has guided tours in a tractor-drawn jitney. En route one crosses the White River where an evening excursion, similar to the one at the Great River, is held several nights weekly departing from Ocho Rios.

Pages 42 and 43: Famous Dunn's River Falls, near Ocho Rios, cascades down a wooded gorge. One can climb the rocky falls or enjoy them from a side trail.

CASTLETON GARDENS

Annotto Bay is the turnoff for the middle of the three roads over the Blue Mountains to the south coast; it follows the Wag Water River most of the way. About 10 mi/16 km from the north coast the road passes through the center of the Castleton Gardens, begun in 1862 as a more convenient alternative to the gardens at Bath and Cinchona. Many of the exotic trees that now populate Jamaica, such as the flamboyant, were introduced here. Although the gardens have suffered from neglect and flooding from time to time, they still have an enormous variety of flora. On the west side of the road the gardens are tight with ferns and remnants of the 180 species of palms that were planted here originally. The delicate light green flowers of the jade vines are spectacular. The gardens east of the road have a more open park-like appearance where huge teak, mahogany, calabash, and other large trees provide shady picnic sites along the banks of the river.

PORT ANTONIO

Draped in heavy tropical vegetation with an irregular coastline of small coves backed by the towering ridges of the Blue Mountains, Port Antonio is for many people the most beautiful area of Jamaica. It offers a great diversity of outdoor activities, from an easy walk around the old port to trekking in the high mountains. Rewarding views can be gotten on a boat ride along the coast from Huntress Marina at the town dock.

ATHENRY GARDENS AND NONSUCH CAVES

In the hills directly behind Port Antonio is the 185-acre/75-hectare Seven Hills of Athenry Plantation encompassing show gardens and the Nonsuch Caves, which are lighted and have walkways for viewing. As the story goes, the estate was bought by its present American owner from an ad in the *Wall Street Journal*. The property is planted with acres of coconut, banana, and allspice trees whose wood is used for smoking jerk pork and chicken, a unique and very popular Jamaican specialty that originated in the Port Antonio area. From the Athenry Gardens there is a magnificent view of Port Antonio and the north coast and the Blue Mountains to the south.

RIO GRANDE

The Rio Grande, one of Jamaica's largest rivers, begins on the western slopes of the John Crow Mountains and is fed by dozens of rivers and streams that make their way through the rugged northern slopes of the Blue Mountains to flow through the Rio Grande Valley that lies between the two great mountain ranges. While the valley has long been cultivated even in many of its least accessible areas, the forests of the upper river basin have some of the least disturbed vegetation in Jamaica.

The lower reaches of the Rio Grande west of Port Antonio are the setting for the romantic, unique-to-Jamaica excursion of river rafting, begun as a pastime in 1911 when a United Fruit Company representative got the idea after watching bananas being towed on rafts downstream to the docks for loading onto ships. A half-century later movie star Errol Flynn popularized the idea by staging the first rafters' race. Today, it is Port Antonio's number-one tourist attraction. The excursion starts about 8 mi/12.8 km upstream from Port Antonio at Berrydale, where passengers board 30-ft/9-m bamboo rafts that seat two. With the Blue Mountains in the background, a skilled helmsman guides his raft at a leisurely pace for two to three hours down the Rio Grande while passengers enjoy the river's tropical setting. Along the way, one sees Jamaican rural life that cannot be glimpsed from the resorts and roadsides.

SOMERSET FALLS

At Hope Bay west of Port Antonio, immediately by the airstrip, a small road with a sign leads to a waterfall situated only about 30 yards/27 m off the road. Somerset Falls flows from the Daniels River and runs in dispersed fashion about 40 ft/12 m down the sides of a semicircular canyon into a large pool surrounded by the cool shade of a jungle-thick tropical canopy. One can take a raft or swim the short distance to the base of the falls where there are rocks on which to sit to enjoy the setting.

BLUE HOLE

The Blue Hole, 6 mi/10 km east of Port Antonio on the Caribbean coast, is often called the most beautiful spot in Jamaica. It gives the impression of being the submerged crater of a volcano; claims of its depth range from 185 to 282 ft/56 to 86 m. The lagoon is fed by freshwater springs, one of which has the power to increase virility, according to local lore. The site is under the care of the Jamaica National Trust, but one might wonder how much care the Trust gives since vendors are here in force. Beyond this annoyance, the Blue Hole is a lovely place to swim.

The Royal Botanic Gardens in Kingston, known as Hope Gardens until the name was changed to honor a visit by Queen Elizabeth II, are famous for their orchids.

OUTDOOR ACTIVITIES

HIKING: Jamaica does not have a fully developed national parks system, but efforts are being made to develop and improve trails and facilities. JATCHA (Jamaican Alternative Tourism, Camping and Hiking Association, P.O. Box 216, Kingston 7; 809-927-0357) has the best information on hiking, including hiking guide services and equipment for rent; it can also arrange longer excursions. Jamaica is a web of logging tracks and back-country roads, any of which can be used for hiking, but hikers should not stray off tracks and they must be prudent about wandering into remote areas without a local guide.

CAMPING: The Negril area in the west is a favorite camping place. However, for personal safety one should not camp in any area without first consulting the Jamaica Tourist Board or JATCHA. The latter has detailed information on safe sites and accommodations and can provide guides in areas where needed. Friendship Farms near Ocho Rios has a group of buses converted into two-room campers with bath in a secluded country setting.

CAVING: Jamaica is honeycombed with an estimated 900 caves, of which 400 have been registered by the Geological Survey Department. Caves are tied intimately to the history and folklore of Jamaica: Arawaks used them for ceremonial and burial purposes; pirates and smugglers hid in them; Maroons found them to be good places of refuge.

Many rivers and streams in the western half of the island disappear into caves and reappear elsewhere as springs, blue holes, and falls. The longest cave system is thought to be the one from which the Black River emerges. Others of interest to spelunkers are Windsor Cave, which runs almost 2 mi/3.2 km through the Cockpit Country, and Jackson's Bay Caves on the western side of the Portland Ridge. The latter have Arawak carvings; five entrances lead to chambers and enormous caverns with spectacular formations. The Jamaica Caving Club (c/o Dept. of Geology, University of the West Indies, Mona, Kingston; 809-927-6661) is a very active group; it collected most of the information contained in the book *Underground Jamaica* by Prof. Alan Fincham.

CANOEING AND RAFTING: As transportation, canoeing is as old as the Arawaks, but as a modern sport canoeing is new, made possible with the development of inflatable rafts that careen with ease over rocky rapids that would cause wooden canoes to break up. Only a fraction of Jamaica's 126 rivers have been scouted, but already white-water runs have been located on such waterways as the Great River near Montego Bay. Specialists say the river has more than a dozen consecutive white-water runs on the lower half of a 9-mi/14.4-km gorge near the village of Lethe. Canoeing and rafting conditions depend on the rainfall and time of year.

HORSEBACK RIDING: In the Ocho Rios area, Chukka Cove at St. Ann's Bay on the north coast is a full-scale equestrian center. It has eight pastures and stables for forty-one horses on 50 acres/20 hectares and offers beach rides, trail rides through working sugar and banana plantations, and mountain trekking. Polo matches are held here on

Green anole.

Jamaican oriole.

Thursdays and at Drax Hall Polo Field (5 mi/8 km west of Ocho Rios) on Saturdays. Prospect Plantation Stables offers one- and two-hour treks through its 1,100-acre/445-hectare woodland. The Montego Bay area has five stables. The 1,000-acre/404-hectare Good Hope Plantation at Falmouth claims to have 200 mi/320 km of trails; rides range from an hour of plantation, garden, and coastal views to longer treks to river gorges and wooded highlands.

SWIMMING: The north coast is the major resort area of Jamaica. Doctor's Cave Beach and Cornwall Beach in Montego Bay and Ocean Village in Ocho Rios

are body- and concession-filled beaches in the heart of town. While they have nothing to recommend them as natural settings, they are the most convenient places to enjoy water sports, if one's hotel does not have them. Elsewhere, the island offers quiet beaches of great variety.

The east coast from Port Antonio to Morant Bay has intimate coves hidden behind dense tropical foliage and miles of deserted beaches with the slopes of the John Crow Mountains behind them. However, there are places on this coast with dangerous undertow, especially around Long Bay; one should seek advice locally about safe places to swim. On the west coast, the 7-mi/11-km stretch of palm-fringed beaches at Negril is one of Jamaica's finest, as are the little-known sands of Treasure Beach on the south coast. And don't overlook the rivers, waterfalls, and blue holes that abound throughout the country.

Jamaican hutias.

SNORKELING AND DIVING: The shallow reefs and drop-offs of Jamaica's north coast offer good diving over unusual underwater sites whose highlights are tunnels, crevasses, mini-walls, and what Jacques Cousteau once called "some of the most dramatic sponge life in the Caribbean." In 1986 Jamaica enacted strict water-sports licensing laws that have made legitimate operators very safety-conscious; they require divers to have a certification card or take a scuba resort course (these are readily available) before they can don tanks. One should never dive with "freelance" guides who solicit business on the beach. Snorkeling off the beach is available at resorts along the north and west coasts. Negril is the best-known scuba and snorkeling location for tourists, but some of Jamaica's best snorkeling is found around the cays off Port Royal and the Hellshire Hills.

FISHING: Sport-fishing is one of Jamaica's main attractions and, in general, has the virtue of being less expensive here than in many other places of the Bahamas and Caribbean. Half-day and full-day boat charters, with bait and tackle provided, for blue marlin, tuna, dolphin, and wahoo are available from marinas near Montego Bay and Ocho Rios. They usually provide free pickup service from area hotels. The three-leg blue marlin tournament—an event that has elevated Jamaica to a premier marlin location—starts in early September with a five-day international meet sponsored by the Montego Bay Yacht Club. Two weeks later the competition moves on a second leg to Ocho Rios, and it concludes in Port Antonio in early October.

At Salt Marsh, a small village on the north coast near the Falmouth marshes, the local fishermen report fine catches of perch, marlin, and eel. The south coast from Morant Bay to Pedro is considered a major fishing area. Alligator Pond, one of the largest fishing beaches, has modern fiberglass motorboats available for hire. Stream fishing is strictly a local pastime due to the lack of facilities and information for tourists.

BOATING: Boat charters and large sailboats on day cruises that include snorkeling, picnic lunch, and drinks leave daily from marinas in Montego Bay, Ocho Rios, and Negril; any hotel can help you make arrangements.

SURFING: Boston Bay on the northeast coast has wave action large enough for surfing.

WINDSURFING: Most beachside resorts from Negril to Ocho Rios have boards for windsurfing. Sail conditions are ideal for beginners and recreational windsurfers, but probably are too tame for serious competitors.

EXPLORING THE ISLAND

Jamaica has one of the most extensive road systems of any island in the Caribbean, with roads ranging from good to terrible. A coastal highway circles the country, except for stretches of the south coast. Eight narrow, winding, but adequate north–south roads connect various points of the two coasts; inland, a maze of rural roads, country lanes, and logging tracks creates a web over the island. Except for the most rugged parts of the John Crow Mountains on the east and the interior of the Cockpit Country on the northwest, almost any part of the island is accessible. The best roads are the north-coast stretch between Montego Bay and Ocho Rios, the cross-island mountain highway between Ocho Rios and Kingston, and the expressway between Kingston and Mandeville. Road maps are available from the Tourist Board.

For travel in and around major towns and resorts, hiring a taxi for a half or a full day is a convenient, affordable way to travel if one can share the cost. Taxi fares may be shared among four passengers. Engage licensed taxis only. Although there are many freelance taxis available for lower prices (*if* one bargains well), stories are rampant about theft and other problems encountered by unsuspecting tourists who use them. JUTA (Jamaica Union of Travellers Association) is the government-licensed and -approved fleet of taxis. Government-approved fares between major locations are posted at hotels and other locations; nonetheless, one should always settle the fare *in advance*. Minibuses (actually large taxis) are available between major resorts at lower rates than a taxi.

Major U.S. car rental firms are present here, but rates are high to cover the extremely high Jamaican import duties on cars and parts; gas is expensive, too. During high season demand is often greater than supply. Four-wheel-drive vehicles, essential for travel in most parts of the Blue Mountains, are even fewer. Bikes, mopeds, and motorbikes can be rented in resort centers on the north coast, but it is imperative that one be experienced since driving on highways in Jamaica is very hazardous. Jamaicans drive fast with little regard for the rules of the road. Driving is on the LEFT. Inexpensive large and small intracity buses operate throughout the island. They are seldom used by tourists, because they do not run on set schedules and they stop frequently en route to pick up and discharge passengers. For those unconcerned about time, however, they are an inexpensive and convenient way to travel.

Even less expensive—and slower—is the cross-island train that goes between Montego 'Bay and Kingston, a trip of almost five hours. Visitors take this train for a sightseeing adventure as much as for transport. It stops at many small villages along the way, with passengers and vendors getting on and off at every stop and giving visitors a color-

ful glimpse of rural life, mountain scenery, and the Cockpit Country.

INFORMATION: In the U.S.: Jamaican Tourist Board, 801 Second Ave., 20th fl., New York, NY 10017; 212-856-9727. In Canada: 1 Eglinton Ave. East, Suite 616, Toronto M4P 3A1; 416-482-7850. In the U.K.: Jamaica House, 1-2 Prince Consort Road, London SW7 2BZ; 71-224-0505. In Jamaica: 2 St. Lucia Avenue, Kingston; 809-92-99200. At Montego Bay: Cornwall Beach, P.O. Box 67; 809-95-24425. At Ocho Rios: Ocean Village Shopping Center, P.O. Box 240; 809-97-42582. At Port Antonio: City Center Plaza, P.O. Box 151; 809-99-33051. The Board's uniformed "Courtesy Corps" are trained to help visitors and have the power of arrest, if that should be necessary. Meet-the-People is a Tourist Board–sponsored program that arranges for local hosts.

Forestry and Soil Conservation Department, Ministry of Agriculture, 173 Constant Spring Rd., Kingston.

The Institute of Jamaica, 12–16 East St., Kingston (92-77817) is an umbrella group comprising the Natural History Museum, which collects and studies the flora and fauna of Jamaica, the Jamaica National Trust, and the National Library; it also publishes *Jamaica Journal*, a quarterly on the natural environment and culture of Jamaica and the region. Gosse Bird Club (Box 1002, Kingston) is the major bird-watching club.

Books on Jamaica include: *A–Z of Jamaican Heritage* by Olive Senior (1984); *Tour Jamaica* by Margaret Morris (1985); *Adventure Guide to Jamaica* by Steve Cohen (1988); *Bird Watching in Jamaica* by May Jeffrey-Smith (1972); *Flowering Plants of Jamaica* by C. D. Adams (1972); *Wild Flowers of Jamaica* by A. D. Hawkes and B. Sutton (1974); D. A. Thompson, P. K. Bretting, and M. Humphreys, eds., *Forests of Jamaica*, papers from the 1983 Caribbean Regional Seminar on Forests of Jamaica symposium, published by the Jamaican Society of Scientists and Technologists, Kingston.

THE CAYMAN ISLANDS

LONG WHITE POWDERY BEACHES caressed by magnificently clear aquamarine waters, acres of mangroves and lagoons hosting a rich birdlife, and limestone bluffs honeycombed with caves—these are some highlights of the Cayman Islands on land. But these pale in comparison to the spectacular reefs, densely encrusted walls, and extraordinary marine life beneath the sea that have made the Caymans a mecca for divers from around the world.

The Cayman Islands are a British Crown Colony comprising three low-lying islands: Grand Cayman, the most populated and center of the colony's resort and commercial life; Cayman Brac, a stringbean of untamed wilderness, 89 mi/142 km northeast of Grand Cayman; and Little Cayman, the smallest, most remote of the group, 5 mi/8 km from the western end of Cayman Brac. The islands are on the edge of the North American tectonic plate, which was lifted by the Caribbean plate from a depth of over 6,000 ft/1,830 m below sea level to form a mostly submerged mountain range, known as the Cayman Ridge, that runs from the Sierra Maestra of Cuba west to Belize. On the south side of the range is the Cayman Trench, an ocean trough reaching to a depth of 24,720 ft/7,535 m, the deepest part of the Caribbean. In the millions of years that followed the uplift, the limestone sea bottom, composed of sediment from skeletons of plankton and other sea creatures, rose to the surface to form the Cayman Islands. In time, coral reefs grew in the shallows around the islands. Sand, coral, and lagoonal mud at the edge of the coasts solidified into a rock-hard limestone, known as ironshore, which characterizes parts of the islands today. The islands' limestone cores, mainly composed of dense crystalline karst with honeycombed pinnacles and sinkholes, became overgrown with vegetation. Rainwater, averaging 30 to 60 in/76 to 152 cm annually, seeps through the porous limestone to lie below the surface in freshwater lenses, providing water for vegetation and wells.

GRAND CAYMAN

Only 60 ft/18 m above sea level at its highest, Grand Cayman is made up largely of lagoons and dense mangrove swamps and is almost completely surrounded by fringing reefs. Drier areas are covered with secondary woodlands of red birch, thatch palm, logwood, and dry scrub, and pockets of the original hardwood forests of mahogany, red birch, and ironwood remain. Seagrapes grow along the beaches and coconut palms and almond

Stoplight parrotfish can range in color from blue-green to yellow to red. At night they rest on the bottom of the reef, hidden among rocks and coral branches.

trees shade the shores. Throughout the settled areas exotic flowering bushes such as oleander and poinciana were introduced for ornamentation and fruit-bearing trees, such as mango and breadfruit, were added for food.

GEORGE TOWN, SOUTH SOUND, AND BODDEN TOWN

On the west side of Grand Cayman, stretching along the main harbor, George Town is the Colony's neat, clean capital and a prosperous international banking center. Outdoor enthusiasts are unlikely to linger here as they will find much more to their liking outside of town.

Directly south of George Town are the manicured residential areas, where coastal roads are shaded by tall Australian pine, or casuarina, and brightened with masses of pink- and red-blossomed coralita, a vine that climbs up to 40 ft/12 m along fences, bushes, and trees. On the back roads yellow elder, a bright yellow-flowered shrub that grows to the size of a tree, is common. In full bloom in December, it is known as the Christmas flower. Two roadside flowers noticeable in the spring are the unusual milk-and-wine lily, whose descriptive name comes from its large, heavy-scented, red-and-white-striped trumpet blossom, and a wild, orange lily, known here and in Barbados as Easter lily. Few Cayman houses are without aloe vera near the kitchen door because of its many uses as an antiseptic for cuts and a healing agent for burns.

South Sound, protected by shallow-water reefs, is a popular swimming, snorkeling, and dive location where elkhorn corals crown labyrinths of limestone caves and grottoes house groupers and giant blue parrotfish. The South Sound Swamp is home to the least bittern, herons, snowy egret, purple gallinule, American coot, and black-necked stilt. Spotts Bay Landing, east of South Sound, is used as an anchorage when the west side of Grand Cayman is experiencing rough weather and high seas. Several roads between South Sound and Spotts Bay cross a mile or so of wetlands to North Sound, the huge expanse of mangrove-edged lagoons and shallows between the eastern and western arms of Grand Cayman. On this island and on Little Cayman, four species of mangroves thrive: red mangrove, black mangrove, white mangrove, and buttonwood.

Heading east beyond the settlement of Savannah, a detour of about 0.25 mi/0.4 km leads south to Old Jones Bay and to Pedro's Castle, a lookout built on the bluffs in 1780 that is now a restaurant. It is the best place on the coast to observe the white-tailed tropicbird. Almost anywhere along the coast one is likely to spot royal terns and magnificent frigatebirds. In the pastures of Savannah and Lower Valley, cattle egrets perch on the backs of cows; American kestrels, merlins, and black-crowned night-heron, as well as the nocturnal West Indian whistling-duck, an endangered species, populate the area.

The small seafaring village of Bodden Town, hard by a long stretch of the white sand beaches, was the first capital of Grand Cayman. The town has several historic sites that the newly organized Cayman National Trust has earmarked for preservation. The Pirates Cave, a privately run cave in town, is large enough for a ten-minute walk. Cannonballs and bones have been found here, indicating the cave was inhabited, perhaps by pirates.

MEAGRE BAY POND

East of Bodden Town on the south side of a large expanse of mangroves is Meagre Bay Pond, a bird sanctuary that attracts large flocks of pied-billed grebes, a common breeding resident found on all three islands. There are northern shovelers, American wigeons, lesser scaup, black-bellied plover, yellowlegs, sandpipers, and willets. Flocks of the snowy egret, the national bird, are seen from the roadside. Farther along the road, about 1 mi/1.6 km beyond Breakers, where an old lighthouse is a popular restaurant for local food, Frank Sound Road cuts north across the island to Old Man Bay. A more scenic route continues to follow the crescent of white sand overlooking Frank Sound and loops around the eastern end of the island to the north shore.

AROUND THE EASTERN DISTRICT

East of Half Moon Bay the shoreline is marked by the spiky rock known as ironshore. Beyond Ironshore Point at the edge of Half Moon Bay, blowholes carved by the relentless sea spout water 15 ft/5 m or more into the air. The village of East End, the first recorded settlement on Grand Cayman, has a public beach with shaded picnic tables. Farther north, in the waters off Gun Bay, there are many wrecks. A famous group is the Wreck of the Ten Sails, the remains of a convoy of merchant vessels, led by the British Royal Navy's *Cordelia*, that went down in 1785. When she hit the reefs, the *Cordelia* fired her cannons to warn the others of the danger but they did not understand the signal and, one by one, ran onto the reefs. At least 350 ships are known to have met their end on Cayman reefs; some (particularly those near George Town harbor) are popular dive sites. North of the wrecks is Colliers Pond, a bird sanctuary, richly populated with waders. The northeast corner of Cayman Island is a popular snorkeling area, but currents here are strong; one should be a good swimmer and not venture far from shore.

THE NORTH SHORE

The Queens Highway crosses an uninhabited, protected area of the north coast where tropical flowering and fruit trees grow wild. Prior to the construction of the road in the early 1980s, there were only trails here. Although the trails are not maintained, they are accessible and allow scenic

Half Moon Bay is characterized by ironshore, spiky rock formed when sand, coral, and lagoonal mud solidified into limestone.

hikes along the rocky cliffs overlooking the north shore. The cliffs, which rise about 40 ft/12 m above the sea, contain caymanite, an indigenous rock of beige, rusty, and brown hues, often used to fashion jewelry. Offshore is the North Wall, which has some of the most dramatic dives in the Caribbean; diving excursions to the North Wall depart from Cayman Kai and Spanish Cove.

Some trails go inland and can be used for birding and searching for the rare Cayman iguana, native to the area. A highly endangered lizard, no more than fifty are thought to remain. In the woods and fields of unpopulated areas one may glimpse a rare spotted agouti, known locally as the Cayman rabbit. The fuzzy-haired, short-eared animal about 15 in/38 cm in length was hunted for its meat; some are raised domestically now.

The north-shore region is the best place to see endemic land birds. Perched on low tree branches might be La Sagra's flycatcher, a common breeding resident on Grand Cayman, absent from its sister islands. The rare Caribbean dove and the migrant yellow-billed cuckoo and mangrove cuckoo are seen here. (Surprisingly, the resident mangrove cuckoo is not found in the mangroves in the Caymans; it prefers a dry inland habitat.)

Inland 0.5 mi/0.8 km from Old Man Bay—the northern terminus of the Frank Sound Road—and hidden in the dense brush are caves that the National Trust plans to make accessible to the public. The cave to the west of the road is inhabited by bats. North Side and Hutland are the most likely places to spot the Cayman Islands form of the Cuban parrot, distinguished by its red throat and white forehead.

RUM POINT AND NORTH SOUND

At the northeastern tip of North Sound is Rum Point, a sleepy little community of private houses and condominiums overlooking a palm-shaded beach where one can enjoy the island's most spectacular sunsets. North Sound, with its cays, shallows, reefs, and mangroves, is, in effect, an enormous marine and avian refuge extending west and south for 7 mi/11 km and separating the two arms of Grand Cayman. The mouth of the Sound is protected by a reef that stretches from Rum Point on the east to Barkers on the west. Never more than 12 ft/3.6 m deep, the Sound's many spits of land and lagoons are ideal for wading, birding, boating, snorkeling, and diving. Only Little Sound, a protected cove on the east side directly south of Rum Point, is off limits to all sports and commercial activity.

Just inside the barrier reef is one of the most unusual sites in the Caribbean, dubbed "Stingray City" for the number of ray that populate this spot. This strange fish has eyes on the top of its body and a 5-ft/1.5-m wingspan. Here, in only 12 ft/3.6 m of water, divers can see, touch, feed, and photograph friendly stingrays, a half-dozen at a time.

East of Rum Point on the north coast, Cayman Kai is a large resort with a dive operation serving this area of the island. In addition to boats from Rum Cay and Cayman Kai, day excursions for snorkeling and swimming in North Sound and for diving along the reef and walls of the north coast leave from various marinas and water-sports centers on the west side of North

Stingrays, usually hidden in the sand with only eyes and spiny tail exposed, are unusually friendly in North Sound, where one can feed and photograph them.

Sound and Seven Mile Beach. The drive from George Town to Rum Point via East End covers almost 40 mi/64 km one way and takes at least three hours, more with stops. A new ferry service crossing North Sound leaves twice daily except Sundays from the Grand Pavillion dock, north of George Town, and from Rum Point; the ride is fifteen minutes one way. Check locally for times and to be sure it is still operating.

SEVEN MILE BEACH

The western arm of Grand Cayman is a narrow strip of land running north from George Town along the island's main resort area centered around Seven Mile Beach, a magnificent crescent of powdery white sand edged by tall casuarinas bending gently over a quiet turquoise sea. North of the Holiday Inn, where most of the water-sports facilities are located, a public beach has small cabanas and tables with seats. A frequent companion on the beach, ready to steal a sandwich from a picnic basket, is the Greater Antillean grackle, known locally as chinchin. Another large black bird, the smooth-billed ani, is seen on trees and fences. Scrounging for food in the hotel grounds and picnic areas are doves, and around homes in West Bay and almost any village is the West Indian woodpecker, one of the island's most common species. The bananaquit is ubiquitous but hummingbirds are nowhere to be seen, making the Caymans the only major West Indies group without a single hummingbird species. Man o' War Cay, east of the Holiday Inn, has large colonies of roosting snowy egrets and other herons, as well as magnificent frigatebirds.

TURTLE FARM

In 1503, on his fourth voyage, Columbus came by chance upon "two very small islands full of tortoises," which he called "Las Tortugas," the Spanish word for "turtles." Historians have identified the islands as Cayman Brac and Little Cayman. Over the centuries that followed, green, hawksbill, and loggerhead turtles were hunted almost to extinction by sailors who found them a fine source of fresh meat for their long voyages across the Atlantic and by others who made use of their skins and shells. In 1973, the world's first sea-turtle farm successfully bred captive turtles for the first time. Today, the Turtle Farm, which is also a research station, breeds the green sea turtle commercially at the rate of 50,000 a year and has contracts to restock the waters of countries around the world. Visitors can observe turtles at various stages of development in their breeding pans. For a nominal fee, one can sponsor a turtle for release to the ocean. There is a museum and gift shop, but visitors should be aware that sea turtles are on the endangered-species list and tortoiseshell is not allowed into the United States. The Turtle Farm is open daily.

HELL

A short distance east of the Turtle Farm is a field of ironshore that was officially named Hell in the 1930s. The Caymanians, never ones to miss a business opportunity, turned a tiny hut here into a post office in 1962. Since then, every visitor to Grand Cayman has felt compelled to send at least one postcard from Hell. More recently, a boardwalk was added to provide better access for viewing the ominous-looking rocks. Signs are posted on the main road.

BARKERS

Barkers takes its name from the reef that fronts more than a mile of white sand beach between Spanish Cove and Palmetto Point. Its mangrove-bordered headland overlooking North Sound is an excellent place for birding. Approximately half of the 180 species recorded on the three islands have been spotted in the Barkers vicinity. The West Indian woodpecker, northern flicker, Yucatán vireo, stripe-headed tanager, and Cuban bullfinch breed only on Grand Cayman. The area also has the 12-in-/30-cm-long terrapin, a freshwater and brackish-water turtle known here as higgity; it might be spotted crossing the road. Barkers is the center of the Caymanian fishing industry.

Grand Cayman has three nonpoisonous snake species, usually seen in swampy areas; one is called the "lazy snake" because it hangs on tree branches and rarely moves. The underside of any piece of coral or log is likely to conceal the world's smallest reptile, a 1.5-in/3.8-cm lizard known locally as the wood slave. A small, photogenic lizard, the lion or curlytail, has distinctive markings and a characteristic way of curling its tail.

CAYMAN ISLANDS MARINE PARKS

The Caymans Portfolio for Development and Natural Resources, a government agency responsible for the marine environment, has divided the shores and lagoons of the three islands into three zones: marine park, replenishment, and environmental. Specific conservation laws govern the use and fishing activity in each zone, and violations carry heavy penalties. On Grand Cayman, the whole western shore with its twenty or more dive sites, Spanish Cove on the northwest coast, and a small area east of Rum Point on the northeast coast are *marine parks* where water sports are permitted but the taking of marine life, alive or dead, is prohibited (except for line fishing from shore and beyond drop-offs). All anchoring must be at fixed moorings or else follow certain prescribed conditions. South Sound, Half Moon Bay, Gun Bay, Spotter Bay, Barkers, and approximately the eastern half of North Sound, except for Little Sound, are less-restricted

Seven Mile Beach, which fronts the Caribbean Sea along Grand Cayman's narrow western peninsula, is the island's main center for watersports and swimming.

replenishment zones where anchoring is permitted and fishing for certain kinds of fish is allowed. Little Sound is an *environmental zone*, the most restricted category, where no taking of marine life or any in-water sports activity is allowed. There is a bird sanctuary within Little Sound too.

THE CAYMAN WALL

The Cayman Islands are famous for wall diving. All three islands are surrounded by walls which collectively have come to be referred to as the Cayman Wall. It is something of a misnomer. In actuality, the walls are an extensive and enormously complex system of cliffs, slopes, canyons, and valleys of submerged mountains which might be likened to the Grand Canyon under water. They have no particular pattern. In some places, the walls are vertical drop-offs at the edge of the coral reefs close or fairly close to shore, beginning in water only 20 to 50 ft/6 to 15 m in depth and plunging to 6,000 ft/1,828 m. Other places have short drop-offs, followed by shelving that might extend a few hundred yards/meters or several miles/kilometers before the wall drops again, shelves again, and finally drops into the abyss. Another characteristic is a recession in the wall immediately under the coral fringe at the top, creating the shape of an inverted "s." In other places, the terrain slopes and dips, rises again, and plunges to great depths in the same way a mountain range has peaks and valleys of varying height and breadth.

Throughout, the most outstanding feature of the walls is that their creviced and ridged faces are so densely encrusted with coral that it is impossible to see the basic rock on which it grows. Forests of elkhorn, black coral, and other hard corals, and rainbows of giant sponges, sea fans, sea whips, and other soft corals of every size and description, appear. There are caves and endless labyrinths. Attracted to this magnificent underwater display are vast numbers of fish as colorful and exotic as the food on which they feed. Only recently, with the use of submersibles, have scientists and others been able to drop below the areas where sunlight reaches and the rock outcroppings appear. An unexpected revelation has been the appearance of volcanic rock, bringing into question the long-held theory that the Cayman Islands are made up entirely of planktonic material.

On Grand Cayman, the dramatic North Wall runs 20 mi/32 km or more along the north coast, beginning at 50 ft/15 m in some places and dropping almost vertically thousands of feet. Dive operators limit divers' depths to 80 to 100 ft/24 to 30 m, but the water is so clear that divers enjoy visibility to 200 ft/60 m and more. The most convenient, popular sites are found on the western half of the North Wall between Conch Point and Rum Point where divers see a series of high coral cliffs and ravines covered with staghorn and black corals and a great array of gorgonians and sponges. Such places as Gale's Mountain—an enormous coral formation approximately 250 ft/75 m across at the base, flanked by canyons and covered with diverse hard and soft corals, including pink vase sponges—attract large schools of jacks and other fish. At Grand Canyon, another huge formation, two gigantic corals about 150 ft/45 m apart jut out from the wall; between them is clear blue water that seems to drop to infinity. In addition to the two main departure points of Spanish Cove and Cayman Kai, dive operators based on Seven Mile Beach visit the North Wall several times weekly; the trip takes approximately an hour. The eastern part of the North Wall, no less spectacular, is not as easy to reach, with some of the popular sites being 2 mi/3.2 km or more from Cayman Kai; it is more often explored from live-aboard dive boats, of which there are several based in the Caymans. Similarly, the east and south coasts are largely unexplored beyond the reefs and are visited mostly by live-aboards.

On the west coast, wall formations are more frequently characterized by sloping and shelving; in some places the shelf extends for 3 mi/4.8 km. The area of wall most commonly visited by recreational submersibles is south of George Town, where the wall drops about 600 ft/180 m or so before it begins to shelve.

CAYMAN BRAC

Although Grand Cayman's diving is better known, its sister islands offer spectacular walls as well. Cayman Brac is considered to be one of the last virgin areas of the Caribbean. Located 89 mi/142 km east-northeast of Grand Cayman, Cayman Brac is known to a handful of pioneering divers but it has yet to be discovered for its other attractions—birding, hiking, fishing, and caving. Its name, Brac, from the Gaelic word for "bluff," refers to the island's most striking feature, a limestone plateau that runs between the north and south shores, starting at about 6 ft/ 2 m elevation in the west and rising to 140 ft/44 m at the eastern end where it plunges to the sea.

The rugged island, 12 mi/19 km in length, is a strangely beautiful wilderness covered with dry woodlands of red birch, aloe, cactus, and a great variety of orchids. There are papaya, mango, and other tropical fruit trees growing wild and displays of exotic flowering trees such as poincianas, which one sees on the road upon leaving the airport at West End. The lush vegetation around the lagoon and bird sanctuary south of the airport is quite different from the rocky seascapes farther along the south shore.

The flat roads and light auto traffic make the island a good place for hiking and biking. One can walk on the main north road that runs almost the length of the island connecting the tiny coastal settlements where most of the people live; or one can travel a road of lesser quality along the less-developed south coast. But the most interesting route is the new west–east dirt road down the center of The Bluff where there are almost no cars. It intersects the main north–south road at about midpoint and gives access to dozens of footpaths across the high plateau.

The Bluff is covered with a great variety of vegetation reflecting the presence of macroclimates and soil variants, including an unusual reddish clay similar to that found in the American Southwest. The eastern area is to be made into a national park. Cactus, thorny bush, and sharp, knee-high eroded limestone pinnacles poking through the underbrush make many areas difficult to cross, except where roads and footpaths have been cut. Hikers should wear slacks, long-sleeved shirts, and sturdy shoes to protect against the jagged limestone and spiny vegetation, and against maiden plum, a plant with a shiny leaf that causes a reaction similar to poison-ivy rash when it brushes the skin. Recent growth on some trails might have to be cut by machete.

From Spot Bay, the largest settlement on the northeast, a trail of a mile or so ascends the steep hill and leads to the easternmost end of The Bluff where there is a year-round colony of brown boobies. From January to August, white-tailed tropicbirds nest in caves and crevices in The Bluff's northeast face. Cayman Brac is a major flyover point for migratory birds and a refuge for some rare species including the elusive Cayman Brac parrot, a form of the Cayman parrot. The Caribbean elaenia is abundant and the yellow-bellied sapsucker, a winter resident, is found in the palm trees.

The Brac, as the island is known, is honeycombed with caves, many yet to be explored. Legend has it that pirates of old hid their loot in these caves. Over the years, islanders have kept the legends alive by clearing land and searching newly discovered caves where they have found coins, goblets, and other artifacts. Because foliage on The Bluff is so dense, cave openings only a few feet away are often unnoticed by hikers. Indeed, there is a real danger of falling into an opening if hikers are not careful.

Cayman Brac's marine parks are found on the north coast between Buccaneer's Inn and White Bay, and on the south coast from Brac Reef to Beach Point and from Jennifer Bay and Deep Well. Spot Bay on the northeast and small shoreside strips at Dennis Point and Salt Water Point on the southwest coast are replenishment zones. While formations are similar to those of Grand Cayman, the Brac provides greater variety of diving on virgin sites closer to shore.

On the north coast where the water is normally calm, wall formations are close enough for diving from shore. The area also has some of the best snorkeling, with patches of coral heads and small fish in water shallow enough for snorkelers to stand. On the south shore, where the water is normally rough, diving is by boat. As divers approach the walls, over 300 ft/ 90 m from shore, they will see a series of canyons formed by long fingers of coral reaching down 75 to 100 ft/22 to 30 m and more. Magnificent stands of elkhorn, staghorn, brain, and other hard corals are mixed with sponges and other soft corals in much better condition than those on Grand Cayman, where there are many more divers. Protection of the corals from dive-boat anchors was improved recently by the addition of moorings. The island has two fully equipped dive centers, both offering underwater photography instruction and facilities for certified divers.

LITTLE CAYMAN

Little Cayman, even less explored than Cayman Brac, is the most preferred of all by experienced divers, not only for its pristine qualities but because its drop-offs start in only 20 ft/6 m of water. The 10-mi-/16-km-long island has two dozen residents and two tiny hotels. A low-lying wilderness of scrub and limestone forest, Little Cayman, like Grand Cayman, has large expanses of mangroves and lagoons. Virtually the entire south coast is protected either as a bird sanctuary, marine park, or replenishment zone.

At Tarpon Lake, a miniature version of ocean tarpon has adapted to fresh water, making it an unusual species. The island is known also for bonefish-

ing, which is particularly good in the shallow lagoon on the southwest. Almost any place on the island is good for bird-watching. Great blue herons, tricolored herons, black-necked stilts, and egrets are abundant. Directly behind South Town is 1-mi-/1.6-km-long Booby Pond, whose north side is fringed with mangroves that are home to one of the largest breeding colonies of red-footed boobies in the Caribbean, estimated to number as many as 4,000. It also has a sizable colony of magnificent frigatebirds. At Tarpon Lake are found blue-winged teal, a common winter resident on all three islands, and West Indian whistling-ducks, the Caymans' only resident duck whose numbers, greatly reduced by hunting, have now been stabilized through enforcement of protection laws.

In addition to its long white sand beaches that seldom see a footprint, Little Cayman is surrounded by extensive fringing reefs and spectacular walls. On the north shore, the marine park stretches for 3 mi/4.8 km along Bloody Bay from Spot Bay to Grape Tree Bay. Bloody Bay Wall and Jackson's Point at the edge of the reef begin in 20 ft/6 m of water and plunge down a sheer escarpment. Lacy pink and blue sponges hang on huge black coral trees in water 60 to 100 ft/18 to 30 m deep. Along the upper edge of the wall sloping back into the shallows is a reef of soft coral and sponge, teeming with small tropical fish. Among the prize species is red basket-star coral. Usually seen below 100 ft/30 m in the Caribbean, it is abundant here at 50 ft/15 m. Another 3-mi/4.8-km stretch on the northeast between Mary's Bay and East Bay is a replenishment zone.

From the airstrip on the western end, there are two tracks—each about a mile—across the island's western tip. One leads to West End Point; the other, known as the Nature Trail, crosses to Spot Bay on the north coast.

Left: Sea fan coral grows at a right angle to the current. Right: Yellow tube sponges, usually bright yellow, turn black when removed from water. Cayman Brac and, in the distance, Little Cayman offer superb diving along the underwater, coral-encrusted cliffs, walls, and canyons that encircle each island.

Outdoor Activities

HIKING: On Grand Cayman, almost any beach or road is suitable for walking, except perhaps main arteries around towns and resorts. Tracks along the canals of lagoons and mangroves maintained by the government's Mosquito Research and Control Unit are particularly useful for birders. Excellent maps of the wetlands showing bird species distribution are available from the Lands and Survey Department. Cayman Brac's and Little Cayman's dirt roads and tracks make good hiking paths. Sturdy shoes or boots for protection against the jagged limestone are essential.

CAVING: The Bluff on Cayman Brac is honeycombed with caves—as many as 170 have been counted, although many are difficult to reach due to dense foliage and rough terrain. Some of the most interesting caves open on the sides of The Bluff facing the north- and south-coast roads. Little Cayman has small caves on the northwest coast. For divers, caves are an attraction of the Cayman Islands' underwater terrain.

SWIMMING: Fine white sands to be shared with no more than a few birds characterize the three islands; Seven Mile Beach on Grand Cayman is one of the most celebrated crescents of sand in the Caribbean. Surprisingly few of the Caymanians, who have always been seafaring people, use the sea for recreational swimming or diving, so even public beaches are quite private.

SNORKELING AND DIVING: The Cayman Islands comprise one of the main diving locations in the world, best known for its walls, which are thickly encrusted with an incredible array of marine life. Because there are no rivers to carry silt to the sea, visibility is better than 200 ft/60 m. Grand Cayman offers seven diving areas: Seven Mile Beach and George Town on the west coast; South Shore; East End; and West Bay, North Sound, and the North Wall on the north coast. Seven Mile Beach and George Town, where most of the dive operators are located, have the most accessible, convenient locations with the calmest waters year-round. The variety ranges from freestanding coral heads up to 30 ft/9 m high, to canyons, caves, walls, and shipwrecks. Shallow-water coral heads at the north end of Seven Mile Beach, Soto Reef north of George Town harbor, and several shipwrecks near the harbor are popular locations for snorkelers and novice divers. One of the best-known dive sites, Trinity Caves off Seven Mile Beach, is so vast it's like being in a cathedral.

South of George Town harbor, at Hogsty Bay, is a complex system of underwater tunnels connecting coral heads that extends from 5 ft/1.5 m to 40 ft/12 m below the surface. Fish life is abundant, with schools of yellowtail snapper and blue tang, and an occasional moray or stingray. Although most diving in the Caymans is made from boats, the southwest coast has several locations that can be dived from shore. The south shore from South West Point to East End has many dive and snorkeling sites with huge gardens of elkhorn and staghorn corals. Cayman Brac and Little Cayman are practically virgin territory. Diving in Little Cayman, where fantastic wall formations start in only 20 ft/6 m of water, is rated by some experts as the best in the Western Hemisphere.

Divers can choose from more than two dozen operators equipped for all levels of diving proficiency. They provide every type of dive activity, including night diving, underwater photography instruc-

---

Clockwise from top left: surgeonfish, arrow crab, blackbar soldierfish, bristleworm, calico crab, octopus, spotted scorpionfish.

tion, and marine biology courses. The Caymans also have a large fleet of live-aboard dive boats. There are also hotels geared to divers, although almost any hotel on the three islands is only a few minutes away from excellent diving. The Cayman Islands Department of Tourism publishes a seasonally updated list of the dive operators, their equipment, rates, and other pertinent information. The largest firms have toll-free numbers for advance reservations. The Tourism Department has publications that describe various dive sites, but one should not be set on going only to a particular place; dive operators choose their sites based on weather, currents, and the level of experience of the participants. Because of the competition among dive operators, prices are about the lowest in the Caribbean. However, there is a trade-off. Many operators herd passengers in the manner of organized tours. Experienced divers find the practice frustrating and are usually more satisfied with diving in Cayman Brac and Little Cayman where there are fewer people. Finally, all dive boats have instant radio access to the recompression chamber in Grand Cayman.

Grand Cayman pioneered the use of submersibles as recreational submarines to provide a way for those who do not dive or swim to experience the extraordinary underwater world. The choices range from vessels that float just under the surface of the water to those that plunge several hundred feet. The *Atlantis*, designed specifically for undersea recreation, makes day and night dives of about one hour to a depth of 150 ft/45 m along the wall south of George Town. RSL (Research Submersibles Limited) offers the *PC-8*, a small craft accommodating two passengers, which dives to 800 ft/240 m and gives passengers the rare opportunity to see the changing character of the wall and the various

strata of sea life. Although they are expensive, *PC-8* dives are so popular they must be reserved a month or more in advance. Reservations can be made through Aqua Adventures in New York City (212-686-6210). For photographing from the submersibles, high-speed film (ASA 400) and normal lenses are advised.

DEEP-SEA FISHING: Enthusiasm for deep-sea fishing in the Cayman Islands takes on the fervor of a national sport. Among the big catches are marlin, blue-fin and yellowfin tuna, wahoo, dolphin, tarpon, groupers, snappers, barracuda, and an occasional shark. Local fishermen say the prime game-fishing season runs from November through March, but in fact, fishing is good year-round. In June, the Cayman Islands stages a Million Dollar Month sport-fishing tournament with prizes awarded in many categories. The grand prize of one million dollars goes to the angler who breaks the current world record for Atlantic blue marlin. The Caymans also calls itself the bonefishing capital of the world. Grand Cayman has five well-equipped sport-fishing operators; fishing excursions are available through hotels on Cayman Brac and Little Cayman.

SAILING AND BOATING: On Grand Cayman one can rent Sunfish and Hobie Cats or just as easily charter a 60-ft/18-m catamaran with crew. The most popular area for small boats is Seven Mile Beach. Safe anchorages are to be found in North Sound, Spotts Bay, and Gun Bay, but boats must first register at the Port Authority in George Town for passengers to come ashore. A yacht race around Grand Cayman is held annually in spring for local and visiting yachtsmen. Dive boats and fishing boats for charter are available on the sister islands, but sailboats are not.

WINDSURFING: The gentle waters along Seven Mile Beach are the favorite area for beginners and recreational windsurfers. South Sound and Cayman Kai offer more of a challenge for experienced surfers. Water-sports operators on all three islands can provide equipment.

EXPLORING THE ISLANDS

Grand Cayman is only 22 mi/35 km in length and 1 to 8 mi/1.6 to 13 km in width, but an excursion around the island is a more lengthy adventure than one might imagine. Grand Cayman can be described as two peninsulas joined at the base, forming a right angle. The two arms are separated by North Sound, a large body of shallow water bordered by mangroves, sprinkled with cays and sandbars, and protected by a barrier reef. The only way to get from one arm to the other is through George Town on the southwest coast; there is no other land connection between the two arms. Hence, to tour the island, one needs to plan two separate itineraries—one to the east side, another to the west. From George Town, several roads lead south to meet the coastal route that skirts the eastern peninsula to Rum Point. North of George Town the main artery runs via Seven Mile Beach to West Bay where the highway meets a network of secondary roads between North West Point on the west and Barkers on North Sound.

Public buses operate about hourly along Seven Mile Beach; bus stops are clearly marked. Taxis are readily available in town and at major resorts, although their rates tend to be high. Taxis do not have meters; one should negotiate the fare in advance and be sure the sum is understood to be in either Cayman Islands dollars or United States dollars.

Rental cars are reasonable in price and preferable to taxis for touring. Grand Cayman rental companies deliver cars to any location on the island; in the winter months, cars should be reserved in advance. Scooters and mopeds are adequate around George Town and nearby beaches, but a car is more practical for longer drives. A valid driver's license and visitor's permit are required; the latter can be obtained when one rents a car or moped. Driving is on the LEFT. Maps are available at the Tourist Office, Lands and Survey Department, and bookstores. Local travel agencies offer island tours. On Cayman Brac, a limited number of rental cars and mopeds are available; on Little Cayman, vehicles of any kind are very limited. One must walk or arrange transportation through an island hotel.

INFORMATION: In the U.S.: Cayman Islands Dept. of Tourism, 420 Lexington Ave., New York, NY 10170; 212-682-5582. Offices also in Atlanta, Baltimore, Boston, Coral Gables, Chicago, Dallas, Houston, Los Angeles, Miami. In Canada: % Earl B. Smith, Travel Marketing Consultants, 234 Eglinton Ave. East, Toronto, Ont. M4P 1K5; 416-485-1550. In the U.K.: Trevor House, 100 Brompton Road, Knightsbridge, London SW3 1EX; 71-581-9960. In the Cayman Islands: Cayman Islands Dept. of Tourism, Government Harbor Center, P.O. Box 67, Grand Cayman, Cayman Islands, BWI; 809-949-0623. National Trust for the Cayman Islands, Box 10, Georgetown, C.I.; 809-949-0121; fax 809-949-7494. *Birds of the Cayman Islands* by Patricia Bradley (1985) is indispensable for birding.

HAITI

DOMINICAN REPUBLIC

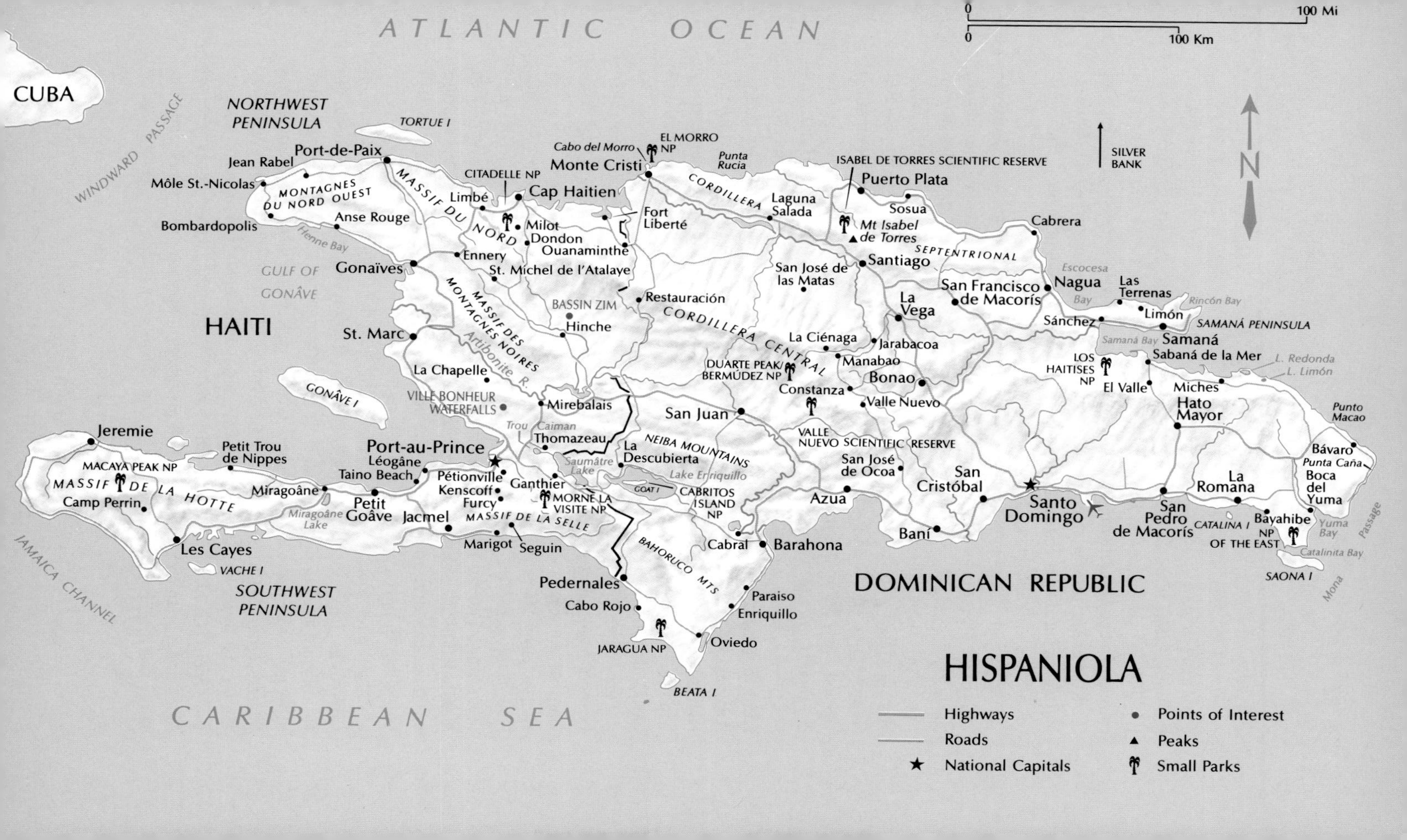

CUBA

ATLANTIC OCEAN

WINDWARD PASSAGE

TORTUE I

NORTHWEST PENINSULA

Jean Rabel
Môle St.-Nicolas
Port-de-Paix
MONTAGNES DU NORD OUEST
Bombardopolis
Anse Rouge

Cabo del Morro
EL MORRO NP
Monte Cristi
Punta Rucia
Fort Liberté
CITADELLE NP
Cap Haïtien
Milot
Dondon
St. Michel de l'Atalaye
Ouanaminthe

MASSIF DU NORD
Limbé
Ennery
Gonaïves
GULF OF GONÂVE
Hinche
BASSIN ZIM
MASSIF DES MONTAGNES NOIRES

Restauración

Punta Rucia
Laguna Salada
Puerto Plata
Mt Isabel de Torres
ISABEL DE TORRES SCIENTIFIC RESERVE
Sosúa
Cabrera

Escoсesa
SEPTENTRIONAL
San José de las Matas
Santiago
La Vega
CORDILLERA

SILVER BANK

Rincón Bay
Las Terrenas
Limón
Nagua
Sánchez
Sabana de la Mar
Samaná
SAMANÁ PENINSULA
J. Redonda
L. Limón
Punto Macao
Bávaro
Punta Cana
Boca del Yuma
Yuma Bay
Bayahibe
NP OF THE EAST
CATALINA I
SAONA I
Catalinita Bay
Mona Passage
MONA I

Samaná Bay

La Ciénaga
Jarabacoa
Manabao
Bonao
Constanza
Valle Nuevo
DUARTE PEAK
BERMÚDEZ NP
CORDILLERA CENTRAL
VALLE NUEVO SCIENTIFIC RESERVE
San Juan
NEIBA MOUNTAINS

San Francisco de Macorís
LOS HAITISES NP
El Valle
La Vega
San José de Ocoa
San Cristóbal
Baní
Azua
Bani

Miches
Hato Mayor
La Romana
San Pedro de Macorís
Santo Domingo

DOMINICAN REPUBLIC

HISPANIOLA

La Chapelle
VILLE-BONHEUR WATERFALLS
St. Marc
Léogâne
Taïno Beach
Mirebalais
Thomazeau
Sumatre Lake
Trou Caïman
Artibonite R.
La Descubierta
GOÂT I
Lake Enriquillo
CARRITOS ISLAND NP
Cabral
Barahona
Paraiso
Enriquillo
Oviedo
BAHORUCO MTS
Cabo Rojo
BEATA I
JARAGUA NP
Pedernales

Fond Parisien
Ganthier
Pétionville
Kenscoff
Furcy
Port-au-Prince
Jacmel
Petit Goâve
Miragoâne
MASSIF DE LA SELLE
MORNE LA VISITE NP
Marigot
Seguin

GONÂVE I

Petit Trou de Nippes
Miragoâne Lake
MASSIF DE LA HOTTE
MACAYA PEAK NP
Camp Perrin
Les Cayes
VACHE I
Jérémie

HAITI

SOUTHWEST PENINSULA

CARIBBEAN SEA

JAMAICA CHANNEL

N

100 Mi
100 Km

ATLANTIC OCEAN

● Points of Interest
▲ Peaks
☗ Small Parks

── Highways
── Roads
★ National Capitals

HAITI

CLOAKED IN MAGIC AND MYSTERY, marvelously creative and miraculously resilient, Haiti is not simply different from other places in the Caribbean. It's like no other place in the world. The master of her fate longer than any country in the Caribbean, Haiti has emerged from its French, African, and Caribbean heritage with the most distinctive culture in the region. Indeed, Haiti's cultural texture is so fascinating, it tends to overshadow the country's other attractions.

Eighty percent covered by mountains, Haiti has a landscape as dramatic and diverse as any in the region. Its peaks tower to heights second only to those of its neighbor, the Dominican Republic, with which it shares the island of Hispaniola as well as many natural features and birds. Haiti occupies the western third of Hispaniola, stretching west from the Gulf of Gonâve and the broad Cul-de-Sac Plain in two mountainous peninsulas shaped like the open pincers of a crab. The Northwest Peninsula extends northwest to the Windward Passage only 50 mi/80 km from Cuba; the Southwest Peninsula reaches southwest to a point about 100 mi/160 km from Jamaica. Haiti, meaning "land of high mountains" to the native Arawaks, is traversed by three great ranges that cross the border into the Dominican Republic. Two lie northwest–southeast and are separated by wide plains. The third runs east–west across the Southwest Peninsula and has Haiti's highest peaks, which rise to almost 9,000 ft/2,750 m.

The island of Hispaniola is part of the Greater Antilles, which were formed from an uplifting of the sea floor and a movement away from Central America. Millions of years ago the mountain ranges covering Hispaniola were separated by sea channels that passed through the areas that today are the central plains and the depression between the high mountains. During eons of geographic isolation, different fauna and flora developed in the separate mountain ranges, making Hispaniola fascinating for botanists and zoologists. New species of plants and animals are still being found, particularly in remote regions.

Christopher Columbus discovered the island in December 1492 and on Christmas Day, in the vicinity of Cap Haitien on the north coast, he established La Navidad, Spain's first settlement in the New World. But after gold was discovered in the eastern part of the island, the Spaniards largely ignored the west, enabling France to acquire it a century later. Under the French, the country prospered and a wealthy plantation society took root. But after two hundred years the Haitians, whose ancestors had been brought from Africa to work as slaves, expelled the French, making Haiti the first European colony in the Caribbean to shed its colonial yoke and the first black republic in the Western Hemisphere. Unfortunately, freedom brought neither peace nor harmony, and down through the decades the country has had a succession of brutal leaders. The ouster of the Duvalier regime in 1986 closed another bloody chapter in Haiti's turbulent history, but tranquility continues to elude Haiti. Its instability severely hampers travel.

PORT-AU-PRINCE

The capital of Haiti, Port-au-Prince, is a vast metropolis stretching from the Gulf of Gonâve across the Cul-de-Sac Plain to the foothills of the Massif de la Selle. At the heart is the domed National Palace, the residence of the president, surrounded by spacious lawns and gardens. It is flanked on the north by the Place du Marron Inconnu with a statue that symbolizes the black struggle for freedom, and on the east by the Place des Héros de l'Indépendance, a beautiful flowering park shaded by royal palms and flowering trees, and the futuristic building of the National Pantheon Museum which contains exhibits on the Arawaks (and the anchor from Columbus's flagship, *Santa María*). Within walking distance on the south along streets lined with trees and gingerbread houses are the Musée d'Art Haïtien, the Centre d'Art, where the Haitian art movement began, and several leading hotels.

PÉTIONVILLE, KENSCOFF, AND FURCY

East of the city, the Avenue Panamericanine (Route de Delmas is an alternate road) makes for a pleasant drive as it climbs the mountains to Pétionville, an affluent suburb of beautiful homes and gardens. Perched on the mountainside, the town provides grandstand views of Port-au-Prince stretching to the Trou d'Eau Mountains. At the hamlet of La Boule, a dirt road leads west along the crest of Morne l'Hôpital, the mountain framing the south side of Port-au-Prince, to a wooded rural area at about 3,100 ft/ 950 m that is one of the last broadleaf forests within easy reach of the capital. The road continues down the mountainside, returning to the south edge of Port-au-Prince.

Up the mountain from Pétionville, the main road winds up the canyons of the Massif de la Selle to the town of Kenscoff, nearly a mile above sea level. As soon as the road begins the climb, the temperature drops and the vegetation changes. At Fermathe there are spectacular views overlooking the Rivière Froide, a gorge carved from the mountainside, and the patchwork of green cultivated fields where dense forest once grew. The Baptist Mission here has a gift shop, farm produce shop, and snack bar. From Kenscoff the pine forest begins, occurring on the steep slopes in patches of

The cultivated slopes between Pétionville and Kenscoff, south of Port-au-Prince, yield an agricultural bounty in a country where 80 percent of the terrain is rocky.

Hispaniolan pine, escaped mimosa, bracken fern, and garrya. Deforestation here is obvious. At the turn of the century, many wealthy residents of Port-au-Prince escaped to cool "summer" homes in Kenscoff; Haitians traditionally prefer the mountains to the seashore, which partly explains the limited seaside development along this country's long coastline.

Furcy, the end of the paved road, is the usual turnaround point. The drive from Port-au-Prince to Kenscoff (17 mi/28 km) takes about an hour; to Furcy, another fifteen minutes. However, if the dirt road to Seguin and the Morne La Visite National Park is open, the additional 10 mi/16 km or so to Seguin are well worth the time. Along the way the sharp peaks of Morne (or Mount) d'Enger, Morne La Visite, Morne Bois Pin, and Morne Kadeneau—all in the Massif de la Selle—come into view on the south; their slopes have patches of natural pine forests. Where the Furcy road breaks over the top into the national park, the higher slopes are covered with pine and broadleaf humid forests.

Motor vehicles are few. Farmers from Seguin and other nearby communities use the Furcy road from Kenscoff to Seguin to bring their vegetables to market, and one will see Haitians, particularly women, walking along the road with mounds of produce on their heads. Except for areas that are extremely arid, farming is practiced throughout Haiti, even at 6,500 ft/ 2,000 m elevation, on almost any land that can be planted including some plots that appear to be solid rock. Over the past century, lumbering and clearing of the land for agriculture have resulted in terrible, often irreversible, erosion, compounding the problems of this impoverished nation.

Morne La Visite National Park

Only a few of Haiti's national parks are readily accessible. Among the newest, Morne La Visite National Park (Parc National Morne La Visite) and Macaya Peak National Park in the southernmost mountain ranges have the least-altered vegetation and fauna. Endemic plants are common in both parks; indeed, an estimated 30 percent of the species are plants found only in Haiti. Visitors need permission from the Port-au-Prince office of ISPAN (Institut pour la Sauvegarde du Patrimoine National) to enter either park.

Morne La Visite National Park is on the crest of the Massif de la Selle, south of Port-au-Prince, at 6,234 to 7,546 ft/1,900 to 2,300 m elevation. The 1,000-acre/405-hectare park is covered with Haitian pine woodland and montane broadleaf forest (and transition zones) where the growth includes trembling panax, lyonia, Picard's bayberry, podocarpus, Buch's senecio, tree ferns, dendropanax, and fuchsias, all on limestone. There are very few streams through the park, because rainwater seeps through the shallow soil and porous limestone to flow underground. Birdlife on the Massif de la Selle is abundant; the high elevations above Furcy are populated with Hispaniolan parakeet, Hispaniolan parrot, black swift, Hispaniolan emerald hummingbird, Hispaniolan trogon, narrow-billed tody, pine warbler, green-tailed ground warbler (found in Haiti only in the Massif de la Selle), golden swallow, and rufous-throated solitaire.

Pic La Selle (8,824 ft/2,674 m), the highest peak in Haiti, is slightly east of the national park near the Dominican Republic border. There is no road to the summit, but experienced hikers with compass, altimeter, and topographic maps can climb it. People who live in the vicinity do not climb the peak, hence there are no local guides.

The most direct access from Port-au-Prince to the park is a four-hour drive via Seguin (34 mi/55 km); however, landslides along the steep route above Furcy often make the road impassable. An alternate route is via Jacmel on the south coast to Marigot, where a mountain road turns north to Seguin. The drive takes four to six hours from Jacmel, depending upon road conditions, and requires four-wheel-drive. Hikers must bring all their food and water; there are no accommodations of any kind in the area. One can camp on flat land outside the park, but there are no facilities and no electricity. There is a park cabin near Seguin; inquire at ISPAN if the cabin is being attended by a warden or can be used for shelter.

JACMEL

Sitting on a hillside overlooking a palm-fringed bay of the same name, Jacmel and the surrounding countryside are the tropical landscape of a Haitian painting. Dating from the seventeenth century, Jacmel flourished under the French as a port from which sugar, coffee, and cotton were shipped. The town retains its colonial character in colorful houses with wrought-iron balconies. After a road, completed about 1980, cut driving time from Port-au-Prince to only two hours, Jacmel became a tourist destination enjoyed for its unspoiled setting by the sea and its delightful small hotels. Directly east of town are white sand beaches with coral gardens. In the mountains to the west is Bassin Bleu, a triple-stage cascade with rockbound pools hidden in dense tropical foliage. It can be reached on a footpath about 1 mi/1.6 km from town. Hikers need a local guide to find the way, since the path is obscured by vegetation.

MIRAGOÂNE LAKE

South of Port-au-Prince through the dense suburbs of Thor and Bizoton, the highway follows the coast of Gonâve Bay into the countryside lush with banana groves and mango trees, passing through Léogâne and Petit Goâve. In many places the coast is edged with swamps of red mangrove and salt bush. The rural area is densely populated, mostly with small farmers and people who work at small sugarcane plantations that have their own *trapiche*, or sugar mill.

After Petit Goâve the highway cuts inland slightly, skirting the north side of Miragoâne Lake (Etang de Miragoâne), a large freshwater lake and marshland of 3 sq mi/8 sq km about a mile outside the town of Miragoâne, two hours from Port-au-Prince. The northern and eastern shores of the lake are edged with cattails, water lilies, nelumbo, rushes, sedges, water hyacinth, and other aquatic plants. The area, abundant with water birds, is one of the main locations within reach of the capital to observe pied-billed grebes, brown pelicans, magnificent frigatebirds, snowy egrets, little blue herons, glossy ibises, white ibises, white-cheeked pintail, blue-winged teal, and purple gallinules. The north shore of the lake is a few minutes' walk from the highway, and although it is difficult to penetrate the deep marshes even with high boots, being there to see birds at dawn and sunset is rewarding. A dirt road at Chaloner (south of Miragoâne on the highway to Les Cayes) enables automobiles to go almost to the edge of the lake; however, this area is less marshy and parts are cultivated. The nearest lodgings are in Petit Goâve and Taino Beach on the Gulf coast; one should inquire locally to find out if the hotels are open before planning an overnight stay. Beyond Miragoâne, a gravel road continues along the north shore only as far as Petit Trou de Nippes. Jeremie, farther along the Southwest Peninsula, is difficult to reach because of the condition of the roads, but it is a historic port and the main town of the area. Still an active port for local trade, it has pastel houses in a lush setting that make a visit rewarding, if one can get there. There are tourist lodgings and restaurants.

The main highway across the peninsula to Les Cayes runs through the low green hills of the Massif de la Hotte, covered with banana, coffee, and cacao plantations and shaded by large breadfruit trees. At the small town of Fond-des-Nègres on the north side of the road there are two rare endemic Attalaya palms, which resemble royal palm. The fruits are red with seeds that are the size of dates and look like miniature coconuts, including even the three "eyes" similar to those on a coconut. Only fifteen specimens of this endemic tree are known to exist in the wild.

MACAYA PEAK NATIONAL PARK

About 1,000 acres/400 hectares on the summit of Macaya Peak (6,236–7,700 ft/1,900–2,347 m) in the Massif de la Hotte comprise Macaya Peak National Park (Parc National Pic Macaya). It is covered with forests similar to those of Morne La Visite Park and parts are cultivated. The peak's montane broadleaf forest, which ends at 6,600 ft/2,000 m, has parrot tree, weinmannia, garrya, and avocado; in the pine forest above there are bracken fern, agave, baccharis, gyrotaenia, and wild holly.

The park is difficult to reach even in a four-wheel-drive vehicle though it is only 22 mi/36 km northwest of Les Cayes. Camp Perrin north of Les Cayes is the starting point of a gravel road that crosses Rivière l'Acul to Le Petre and climbs a steep mountainside to the hamlet of Les Platons, the site of an old fortress at 2,297 ft/700 m. The vehicle road ends here and the hike to the summit is 6 mi/10 km on a footpath used by the local villagers. It takes more than five hours to reach the tiny hamlet of Ville Formon on the south side of the park where there is a park cabin. There are no facilities of any kind.

SAUMÂTRE LAKE

East of Port-au-Prince on the Dominican border is Saumâtre Lake (Etang Saumâtre), a large lake situated at 33 to 50 ft/10 to 15 m above sea level. Crocodiles inhabit the lake and may be seen occasionally along the shores. Many birds live among the sedges, cattails, buttonwood, and pond-apple at the edge of the lake. Among them are the least grebe, pied-billed grebe, tricolored heron, glossy ibis, roseate spoonbill, greater flamingo, West Indian whistling-duck, blue-winged teal, northern jacana, and least tern. The west end of the lake is low, sloping ground with some cultivation. On the south, the foothills of the Massif de la Selle rise directly from the lake in some places. The north shore's rugged terrain is inaccessible except by boat on the lake. Saumâtre Lake (25 mi/40 km east of Port-au-Prince) is reached by taking the dirt road to Ganthier or Fond Parisien, where there are tracks leading to the lake. The northwestern edge can be reached by road via Caiman and Thomazeau. At Caiman, Trou Caiman is a spring-fed freshwater lake of about 3 sq mi/8 sq km, with marshes where the abundant birdlife includes many of the species found at Saumâtre Lake.

VILLE BONHEUR WATERFALL

The waterfalls (saut d'eau) of Ville Bonheur, southwest of Mirebalais, are a favorite destination for Catholic pilgrims in Haiti. The falls, fed by a stream, drop about 100 ft/30 m and form a pool at their base. A small wooded area of silk-cotton, or kapok, trees and red mountain palms is found along the stream and falls, about 0.6 mi/1 km from town. Usually, visitors park their vehicles on the road above the falls and walk to the base. An easy day's outing from Port-au-Prince, the falls can be reached by a dirt road south of Mirebalais that turns west to Ville Bonheur (6 mi/10 km), or by a road that turns south at La Chapelle to Ville Bonheur (3.7 mi/6 km). Soft drinks and beer are available in Mirebalais and Ville Bonheur, but no food.

The Anse d'Azur, on the less traveled southwest peninsula, is known for its clear water. The nearest town is Jeremie, an active port in a lush setting that is difficult to reach by land. Facing page: The waterfall (saut d'eau) of Ville Bonheur.

Artibonite River Valley

North of Port-au-Prince, the highway skirts the coast, passing several beach resorts and small towns en route to St. Marc. On the east, the dry hills are covered with acacia, mesquite, and tall cacti, indicating the dryness of the region. Occasionally, one sees plantations of sisal, whose fiber is used for making rope and crafts. After St. Marc the road descends to a wide plain with large expanses of rice fields watered by the Artibonite River. Where the river meets the bay, there are large marshes populated with roseate spoonbills, greater flamingos, white-cheeked pintail, masked ducks, and tawny-shouldered blackbirds.

Gonâve Island

In the center of the Gulf of Gonâve is Gonâve Island (Ile de la Gonâve), 31 mi/50 km long, Haiti's largest offshore island. Mostly limestone affected by karstic action, the island is dry and mountainous with peaks up to 2,552 ft/ 778 m elevation. It is surrounded by mangroves and coral reefs, making access difficult but also making for good diving—the best in Haiti within reach of west-coast beach resorts and the capital. The island is also a haven for birds, including the palmchat, yellow warbler, chat tanager, gray-crowned palm-tanager, brown pelican, magnificent frigatebird, green-backed heron, great blue heron, little blue heron, yellow-crowned night-heron, greater flamingo, red-tailed hawk, clapper rail, and royal tern. Ferryboats go to Gonâve from St. Marc and Gonaïves, but there are no boats specifically geared for tourists. The island has an airstrip, but no paved roads or tourist accommodations.

North Range

From Gonaïves the main highway turns northeast to Cap Haitien, crossing two mountain ranges and passing through three types of vegetation. The Gonaïves vicinity is surrounded by spine-shrub forests and cactus, particularly pereskia cactus with pink rose-like flowers. After Gonaïves, the highway enters a small, forested, and densely populated river valley. Near Ennery on a side road to St. Michel de l'Atalaye, there are enormous silk-cotton, or kapok, trees with small pink flowers; and sabile or rattlebox, known elsewhere in the Caribbean as sandbox, distinguished by its thorny trunk. Another large tree, mapou, with large creamy lily-like flowers and spiky skin, is an endemic species.

From Ennery the road winds up the Massif du Nord where scattered remnants of the native vegetation are visible on the cliffs along the ridge. There is a noticeable change in the climate, with cooler temperatures and moisture on the ascent. After passing over the crest, the road descends rapidly on hairpin curves to Plaisance, a fertile, intensively cultivated valley. On the north side of the valley, the road rises again over the mountains and descends to Limbé where it crosses the flat western end of the Plaine du Nord, a major agricultural region. There are a few native trees such as sabile, bois doux, and Hispaniolan royal palm scattered about the farmlands.

CAP HAITIEN

Second in size and population to Port-au-Prince, Cap Haitien on the Atlantic coast is no runner-up in history or charm. The town is a medley of colorful colonial buildings and Victorian gingerbread houses at the foot of Haut du Cap, a mountain rising directly from the coast. Behind the town rise green foothills covered with groves of mango and, beyond, the rugged Massif du Nord where coffee grows. From Cap Haitien east to the Dominican Republic, the plains are covered with sugar and sisal fields. Plantation Dauphin was once the largest sisal plantation in the world. At Fort Liberté, the road turns south to Ouanaminthe, a border-crossing point. The gravel road is badly deteriorated but can be traversed by automobiles.

CITADELLE NATIONAL PARK

The Citadelle, a mighty fortress crowning the summit of Pic Laferrière (2,870 ft/875 m), was built by Henri Christophe, a young Haitian soldier who had fought in the American Revolution and who, after the French had been expelled in 1803, proclaimed himself king. The colossal fortress is not only Haiti's main historic attraction but one of the most important and impressive sites in the Western Hemisphere, included on the UNESCO World Heritage List. A major restoration was completed in 1988.

Located at the south end of Chaîne du Bonnet à l'Evêque, a forested ridge southwest of Cap Haitien, Citadelle National Park (Parc National Historique Citadelle–Sans Souci–Ramiers) covers an area of several square miles rising from about 660 ft/200 m to 2,870 ft/875 m. In addition to the Citadelle, the park includes Ramiers, a battery site immediately south of the Citadelle, and the ruins of Sans Souci, a palace built by Christophe to resemble Versailles, located in the village of Milot at the foot of the Citadelle. West of Sans Souci there is a wooded slope with large old trees (including bois blanc, bois chêne, Hispaniolan royal palm, bois rouge, and pois doux) laden with giant tillandsias, a bromeliad. The slope is watered by two streams which once were diverted to flow under the marble floors of the palace to cool it and water the gardens.

A resort on the outskirts of Cap Haitien, Haiti's second largest city, affords a wide view of the Atlantic and is not far from Haiti's historic Citadelle.

The trail to the Citadelle is a very steep climb on a rough, stony path of about 0.6 mi/1 km on the east side of the promontory. The strenuous hike, with the massive fortress always in view, helps bring into focus the monumental, ten-year effort to build the Citadelle, in which 20,000 of the 200,000 laborers lost their lives. There are magnificent views from the summit; the parapet on the north side overlooks the Chaîne Bonnet à l'Evêque and Cap Haitien and the Atlantic coast in the distance.

The round trip from Cap Haitien to the Citadelle takes about five hours. Local travel agencies arrange trips or one can hire a taxi, but there are no car rental agencies in Cap Haitien. The drive (12 mi/19 km) over a paved road from Cap Haitien to Milot takes about thirty minutes. Taxis or jeeps can drive another fifteen minutes over a cobblestone road to a parking area directly below the Citadelle. The final forty-five-minute climb can be made on foot, a more enjoyable means than the bone-crunching ride, which most tourists take, on one of the scruffy horses or mules available for rent at the parking area.

In addition to the Citadelle trail, there is hiking throughout the park and along the Chaîne Bonnet à l'Evêque on footpaths used by local residents. Hikers should enlist the aid of the ISPAN office in Cap Haitien to locate a nature guide, because paths are hard to follow; anyone venturing off the main road should carry a topographic map and compass. (Regular tour guides who take tourists to the Citadelle are not familiar with trails.)

One trail leaves from the south side of the Citadelle. At first a rigorous climb up steep, rock-strewn slopes, it descends through farm fields and coffee and banana plantations south to the Grand Gouffre River where the river disappears into a vertical cave and resurfaces on the other side of a small hill. The trail leads to a road just north of the village of Dondon. A trail of special interest to birders starts behind the chapel of the Sans Souci palace ruins and heads south, eventually connecting with another path that also leads to the Dondon Road. The surrounding valley is wooded with native trees and watered by a stream that runs through the valley.

BASSIN ZIM

On the Central Plain northeast of the town of Hinche is Bassin Zim, a pool at the bottom of a dramatic waterfall that emerges from a heavily wooded area and cascades in two large drops almost 100 ft/30 m down the mountainside. The water is very calcareous, leaving lime deposits and fossilizing vegetation and organic matter that falls into it. People do swim here, however. Some bird species in the area are red-tailed hawk, Antillean nighthawk, Antillean mango hummingbird, and cave swallow. A dirt road from Hinche leads 5 mi/8 km via the village of Savane Papaye to Bassin Zim, but one should ask locally for directions as there are no road signs or markers. Food and rustic lodgings only are available in Hinche.

NORTHWEST PENINSULA

In all Haiti, the area that has remained the most natural is the Northwest Peninsula, but the lack of roads and tourist facilities makes travel here an adventure only for experienced, intrepid travelers willing to forgo all creature comforts. Travel by four-wheel-drive jeep or pickup truck is essential, too.

From the main highway at Gonaïves, a road westward skirts the south coast of the peninsula along desert-like terrain with mesquite, acacia, and bois vert (*palo verde* in Spanish). The road passes through salt plains with salt bushes in one area. After heavy rains the road and low-lying coastal areas often are covered with water that conceals potholes and ditches and makes driving extremely hazardous.

After Anse Rouge, the road—although it may not appear to be one—continues as a dirt track another 10 mi/16 km west to Baie de Henne (Henne Bay), passing through a dry scrub forest on limestone. The rough road wanders a great deal, and progress is slow, often at no more than 6 mph/10 kph. Near the village of Petit Paradis the track cuts through a river valley with a small stream bordered by buttonwood. At Henne Bay the road turns inland and climbs to Bombardopolis, a village resting atop a

plateau at 1,524 ft/500 m elevation. Among the birds of the area are the sharp-shinned hawk, American kestrel, and mourning dove.

From Bombardopolis, the route descends through the Rivière du Gorge to Môle St.-Nicolas, a town on the northwestern corner of the peninsula believed to be the site of Columbus's first landfall. The panoramic views on the ascent to Bombardopolis and the descent into Môle St.-Nicolas are superb. The terraces formed by the rising of the land and lowering of the ocean level are pronounced. The vegetation along the route changes from the dry thorny scrub of the coast to seasonal deciduous forest on the higher plateau.

From Môle St.-Nicolas, a trail leads to the ruins of an old fortress and onto the Presqu'ile Môle St.-Nicolas, a small peninsula and one of the few uninhabited places in Haiti. The finger is covered by a dry dwarf forest of birch gum or gumbo limbo (known in Dominica and St. Lucia as gommier rouge), acacia, lantana, tamarind marron, and mesquite. Two common birds here are the double-striped thick-knee and laughing gull.

A tree-like species of prickly pear cactus grows in a desert forest in the Artibonite River Valley on the road between Cap Haitien and Port-au-Prince.

The vehicle road east from Môle St.-Nicolas runs along ancient ocean terrace formations and after about 2 mi/3.2 km turns inland a short distance to the village of Jean Rabel by a river of the same name. From here the road (in better condition than the south-coast road) continues inland across farmland, followed by desert areas of mesquite, acacia, and cacti. The road also passes through a wetland with large patches of mud and is hazardous in the rainy seasons of spring and late summer. At Trois Rivières, a river southeast of Port-de-Paix, the main town of the Northwest Peninsula, vehicles must cross the riverbed; there is no bridge. The river is wide but not deep except after a heavy rain. Trucks, jeeps, and other high-bottom vehicles are able to cross the river most of the year.

To travel in the Northwest Peninsula, one must carry all food and water, tent, and extra fuel. There are no gas stations, and supplies in such towns as Anse Rouge or Môle St.-Nicolas are limited or nonexistent. From Gonaïves to Port-de-Paix, there are neither restaurants nor lodgings, and only the most meager of food resources are to be found in Bombardopolis or Môle St.-Nicolas.

TORTUE ISLAND

Known as a buccaneers' island during the early days of Spanish exploration, Tortue Island (Ile de la Tortue) off the north coast at Port-de-Paix is Haiti's second largest island. Mostly covered by woodland, it is home to the white-tailed tropicbird, thick-billed vireo, Greater Antillean bullfinch, and bananaquit. Boats to the island leave from Port-de-Paix, but security at the military-police station and port is heavy due to Tortue's history as a staging base for invasion forces attempting to overthrow the Haitian government. Lodging on the island is very basic and one must bring food. The island has a Catholic mission which is connected to the wharf by a motor road—the only such road on the island.

OUTDOOR ACTIVITIES

HIKING: There is no organized hiking, but in this impoverished country walking is still the principal mode of travel for the majority of the people. The hinterland is honeycombed with donkey tracks and footpaths that hikers can use too. Enlisting the guidance of local villagers is not only prudent but necessary. Away from main towns language can be a problem; educated Haitians speak French and usually English; uneducated ones speak neither, and the patois is incomprehensible even to French speakers. In the past Haiti has been a safe country for foreign travelers, but recent instability has created an atmosphere that requires caution. The best source of advice is ISPAN.

SWIMMING: Leading hotels in Port-au-Prince and Cap Haitien have swimming pools. The most convenient beaches are found at seaside resorts about an hour's drive north of the capital en route to St. Marc, south of the capital in the vicinity of Petit Goâve, on the Caribbean coast at Jacmel, and on the north coast west of Cap Haitien.

SNORKELING AND DIVING: Traditionally, seaside resorts have provided the venue for water sports, but one would need to inquire in advance about the availability of equipment, particularly for snorkeling and scuba diving. The main diving location is Gonâve Island.

EXPLORING THE ISLAND

Haiti, covering an area of 10,710 sq mi/ 27,750 sq km, is a difficult country for travel due to its mountainous terrain and limited roads and tourist facilities. Two paved highways traverse the country north and south from the capital, and some paved secondary roads provide access to areas not usually traveled by visitors. The main highway north from Port-au-Prince skirts the Gulf of Gonâve to Gonaïves, the main town of central Haiti. Here the road turns northeast, climbing and descending two mountain ridges en route to Cap Haitien on the north coast. The drive from Port-au-Prince to Cap Haitien takes 4–5 hours.

Gonaïves is also the junction for a secondary road west along the south coast of the Northwest Peninsula. At Anse Rouge it peters out into track that cuts inland to Môle St.-Nicolas on the west coast and rounds the peninsula to Port-de-Paix. A more direct secondary road cuts northwesterly across the peninsula from Gonaïves to Port-de-Paix.

The major highway south from Port-au-Prince runs along the north coast of the Southwest Peninsula, branching at Léogâne directly south over the mountains to Jacmel, a resort town on the Caribbean coast; or continuing from Miragoâne southwest through the low hills of the Massif de la Hotte to Les Cayes, the main port and commercial center of the peninsula. The drive from Port-au-Prince to Jacmel takes about two hours; to Les Cayes, four hours. From Les Cayes, a gravel road cuts northwest to Roseaux and Jérémie, the main town at the western end of the Southwest Peninsula.

Directly east and southeast of Port-au-Prince, the Massif de la Selle, the ridge with the highest mountains in Haiti, rises quickly behind the city. Two arteries from Port-au-Prince run east (7 mi/12 km) through the densely populated foothills and meet in Pétionville (985 to 1,640 ft/300 to 500 m). The paved road winds up the mountains another 7 mi/12 km to Kenscoff (5,085 ft/1,550 m) and ends at Furcy (7,120 ft/2,170 m). Above Furcy, a gravel road subject to frequent mud slides crosses the Massif de la Selle to the south coast.

The main public transportation is the *tap-tap*, either a pickup truck with a brightly painted wooden cover or—in its larger version—a flatbed truck with a wooden superstructure. Both, crowded with passengers and goods, careen about town and countryside at heart-stopping speeds. Port-au-Prince also has shared taxis that travel set routes in town and to Pétionville, stopping to pick up and discharge passengers en route. One can be hailed anywhere along the route.

INFORMATION: As this book goes to press in early 1994, Haiti has no tourism offices abroad. Before planning a trip, check with your country's foreign ministry about travel advisories that may be in effect. In the U.S.: State Department Travel Advisory Office, 202-647-5226. In the U.K.: Foreign Office, 71-270-3000. Other addresses: ISPAN (Institut pour la Sauvegarde du Patrimoine National), P.O. Box 2484, Ave. John Brown 86, Port-au-Prince, 509-1-25286, restores and manages historic sites and national parks. Service de Geodesie et de Cartographie, Cité de l'Exposition, Harry Truman Blvd., Port-au-Prince, is the source for topographic maps. Bibliothèque Nationale, Rue du Centre, and Bibliothèque Haïtienne, Collège St. Louis de Gonzague, Rue du Centre, Port-au-Prince, are good library collections on Haiti.

DOMINICAN REPUBLIC

THE DOMINICAN REPUBLIC has long promoted itself as the best-kept secret in the Caribbean, and, despite an enormous increase in the numbers of visitors in recent years, most of the country's wonderful and extensive natural attractions continue to remain something of a secret—to most Dominicans as much as to their visitors.

Although the country is in the subtropics, it has extremes resulting in vastly different vegetation: from harsh, arid terrain covered with thorn forests and cacti to areas of lush forests dense with ferns and epiphytes where up to 100 in/254 cm of rain fall each year. Between these extremes, however, there is enormous diversity. From the flatlands and rolling terrain of the southern and eastern parts of the country, filled with acres of sugarcane plantations and grazing cattle, the land rises toward the central region in two tree-covered spines—Cordillera Septentrional on the north and Cordillera Central, which include the highest peaks in the Caribbean. These mountains are extensions of the ranges of Haiti, with which the Dominican Republic shares the island of Hispaniola. Along the north coast, from Puerto Plata to Cabrera, a ribbon of golden sands between the mountains and the Atlantic Ocean has become the tourists' playground, purposely developed over the last decade for mass tourism. On the south side of the Cordillera Central and west of the capital of Santo Domingo, the mountains drop low to Bani before being intercepted by another range of mountains and the Azua plain, the gateway to the sparely settled Barahona peninsula.

Following the discovery in 1492 of Hispaniola, as Columbus named it, the Spaniards established several colonies on the island and made Santo Domingo their capital from where men like Cortés and Velázquez set out to explore and conquer Mexico and the New World. From early times the land was used primarily for agriculture and much of its lowlands was cultivated in sugarcane or other cash crops or used for pasture as it is today. Remote parts and less populated mountains remained more natural, at least until the early 1900s when commercial logging changed many areas.

Still, the natural heritage remains throughout the land and in great diversity. Flowering plants and ferns alone number a staggering 5,500 species—now being catalogued for the first time. The abundance of flora and fauna is partly a result of the island's geologic history. The Greater Antilles (Cuba, Jamaica, Hispaniola, and Puerto Rico) are considered to be

Visitors come to the remote Samaná Peninsula on the Atlantic coast for its renowned sport fishing, seasonal whale-watching, excellent birding, and for the secluded sands of Playuela Beach.

an archipelago that spun off from the Central American landmass millions of years ago and moved into the area now called the Caribbean Sea. The island of Hispaniola may have formed from several landmasses—the predecessors of Haiti's southwestern peninsula and the Massif de la Selle which extends into the Dominican Republic as the Bahoruco Mountains. These elements joined more extensive masses and, finally, through the uplifting of lower areas, a single island resulted. The various landmasses share many species in common, but, at the same time, are extremely rich in endemic flora and fauna.

Santo Domingo

Santo Domingo is the country's capital and has over a million people. Combining the attractions of a cosmopolitan city with the charm of the Old World, the town sprawls from the Caribbean Sea across 10 sq mi/26 sq km to the east, west, and north. The drive from the airport takes one along a 10-mi/16-km route bordering the Caribbean Sea and a park lined with coconut palms, Australian pine, tall seagrape, West Indian mahogany trees, and flowering shrubs; this arrival route is a fine introduction to the town's beauty and the country's flora. From the Mirador de Sur, a limestone bluff on the north side of town, there is a panoramic view of the city that helps visitors get oriented. At the heart of Santo Domingo is the Old City, where one can walk through the colonial history of the New World.

National Museum of Natural History

A visit to the Museum of Natural History (Museo Nacional de Historia Natural) gives an overview of the huge variety of the Dominican Republic's natural environment. Centrally located in a complex known as the Plaza de la Cultura, the museum has exhibits on geology, zoology, and space. Particularly spectacular are the three-dimensional dioramas showing native animals in their natural habitats, including those of coral reefs. Exhibits are labeled in Spanish only.

The geology section graphically displays the country's complex composition. The amber collection is a recent addition. Gemstones unique to the Dominican Republic are Dominican amber, a rock-like resin deposit from the West Indian locust tree which is mined from caves in the north, and larimar, a light-blue rock similar to turquoise which is found in a small area in the Bahoruco Mountains. Both are mined commercially and are available in most jewelry and gift shops. Buyers should be aware that amber embedded with plant and insect fossils is considered national property, and by presidential decree in 1987 its exportation requires a permit from the Museum of Natural History.

National Botanic Gardens

At the northwest corner of Santo Domingo, spread across more than 0.33 sq mi/0.85 sq km, is the National Botanic Gardens (Jardín Botánico Nacional), whose tree-shaded open lawns are a favorite location with capital residents for relaxing and picnicking.

From a central plaza, a short path leads to the Aquatic Plant Pavilion which has displays of submerged, emergent, and floating plants in tanks at eye level and in pools with cattails, water lilies, azolla, marsilea, pickerel-weed, and horsetails, among other plants. One also sees West Indian mahogany, whose tiny, inconspicuous blossoms are the national flower, seen in the design on Dominican money. The tree, which blooms from February to April, shades many streets in Santo Domingo and Santiago.

Further along is the Gran Cañada, a cool and shady environment with trees, palms, and climbing philodendrons. The stream, lined with wild ginger and heliconia, is stocked with fish and ducks, and where the stream widens, rowboats are available for rent.

The national herbarium has a small reference library and displays of Dominican medicinal and poisonous plants. These include the poisonous euphorbias, jatrophas, and solanums and medicinals such as lemon grass, epazote, mint, achiote, and oregano. The Bromeliad Pavilion exhibits the herbaceous perennials of the pineapple family. The specialty collections include succulents such as *Agave*, *Opuntia*, *Nopalea*, *Euphorbia*, and *Stapelia*. Unfortunately, very few plants are labeled.

National Zoo

The National Zoo (Parque Zoológico Nacional), located on 400 acres/162 hectares on the north side of town, features animals, including elephants and hippos, in simulated natural settings. Taking advantage of the site's hilly terrain, the designers were able to shape the land and provide areas without cages for most animals. There is a large walk-through aviary with exotic and native birds, including the endemic Hispaniolan parrot. One might also spot the endemic Hispaniolan palmchat, or palmthrush, perched in the palm trees in the park. A common species known as *cigua palmera* in Spanish, it was declared the national bird in 1987. It lives in flocks in open areas, especially around royal palms at low elevations, and builds its nest high on the palm's trunk. The nests are remarkable: up to 6 ft/1.8 m long and 3 ft/0.9 m wide, with many compartments.

At the serpent and reptile house one can see such unusual species as the native American crocodile; the Hispaniolan hutia, a rodent found in the semiarid regions; and the Hispaniolan solenodon, an endemic insectivore

Limestone pools are characteristic of Los Tres Ojos Park, which gets its name, meaning "three eyes" in Spanish, from three large sinkholes.

found in the Los Haitises region. Two native species of iguana—the rhino iguana and Ricord's iguana—are exhibited in the children's zoo.

PASEO DE LOS INDIOS AND THE MIRADOR PARK

A pretty tree-lined boulevard and park, the Paseo de los Indios runs 5 mi/ 8 km from the central residential area of Mirador to the outlying industrial area of Herrera and provides a scenic view southward over the city and the Caribbean Sea. The park, with its expansive lawns and shade trees, is used by city residents for walking, jogging, picnicking, and cycling.

The Cueva del Paseo de los Indios is the biggest of several caves in the park formed by the dissolution of the underlying limestone rock of the park's terrace. A large domed room in the cave, located under the roadway of the Paseo de los Indios, has bats occasionally. Entrance to the cave is restricted to the daytime hours. Another chamber on the face of the overlook houses Mesón de la Cava, a restaurant and nightspot.

LOS TRES OJOS PARK

Los Tres Ojos Park, one of the city's most frequented natural attractions, is part of the Parque Mirador del Este bordering the road to the airport. It derives its name, meaning park of the three eyes, from the three cenotes, or large sinkholes, in the coastal limestone terrace that borders the sea. The water in each cavern is different: one has fresh water, another salt water, and the third sulphuric water. At the entrance, a stairway leads down through thick tropical vegetation to a cavern with a small pool and stalactites and stalagmites that sparkle under the artificial lighting. The largest cavern, with a small lake at the bottom, is inaccessible.

CORDILLERA CENTRAL

Carretera Duarte, the main highway between Santo Domingo and Santiago, provides access to the Cordillera Central, which contains two contiguous National Parks with the country's highest peaks and most challenging treks. There are excursions to be enjoyed by car and others that require four-wheel-drive, as well as a variety of hikes through heavily forested mountains and along rivers to pretty waterfalls. In addition to their beauty, the mountains of the Cordillera Central contain the headwaters of the country's principal rivers, which are essential to its agriculture and as a source of hydroelectric power. The humid forests of the mountains are home to the Hispaniolan parrot, known locally as the *cotorra*, protected by recent law from hunting, capture, or possession. Common birds of the high mountains are the La Selle thrush, rufous-throated solitaire, Greater Antillean elaenia, and Greater Antillean pewee.

DUARTE PEAK; BERMÚDEZ AND RAMÍREZ NATIONAL PARKS

At least three of the Dominican Republic's peaks—Duarte, La Rucilla, and La Pelona—are over 10,000 ft/3,048 m and several others are between 8,000 and 9,000 ft/2,438 and 2,743 m. It was not until 1944, as part of the celebrations for the country's independence centennial, that organized teams first climbed the highest summits. Since then, the trek to Duarte Peak, 10,370 ft/3,160 m, has become a national and international favorite for mountain climbers.

The route is very scenic and goes from a river valley of broadleaf forests, to a montane forest with epiphytes and tree ferns, up into the pine forests of the higher slopes which continue to the peak and give the mountains their alpine look. There is no treeline. For the most part, the trail is ascending, with brief respites that may be level or even descending. At the top there is a monument with the bust of Juan Pablo Duarte, the father of the Dominican Republic, after whom the peak is named.

Most climbers ascend the peak during the winter months, December through March; this is the driest part of the year when the narrow trails are least likely to be muddy. The climb takes a minimum of two days, but it can take four, depending upon one's pace. Trekkers do not need ropes but they do need to be in tip-top form. And they must bring all their own provisions for overnight camping plus clothing for cold nights when the temperatures drop to near or below freezing at higher altitudes.

The principal route leaves from La Ciénaga of Manabao, a village at about 4,500 ft/1.4 km west of the town of Jarabacoa in the heart of the Cordillera Central. About 9 mi/14.4 km up the mountain from La Ciénaga at La Compartición, there is a single wooden cabin where climbers may spend the night. The climb from the cabin to the top of Pico Duarte takes at least two to three hours (longer for those on a slower pace) of almost constant uphill hiking. The usual practice is to return to La Compartición for another night and continue the next day to La Ciénaga. The return trip from La Compartición to La Ciénaga is downhill most of the way and takes about seven hours.

At La Ciénaga hikers can hire local guides (who are not park employees) and a mule to carry them and/or their equipment on the 12-mi/19.3 km trek to the summit. The National Park staff can help hikers locate a guide and muleteer. Hikers should plan to arrive in La Ciénaga one day in advance in order to make arrangements for an early departure the following day. The nearest lodgings and restaurants are in Jarabacoa, which is about an hour's drive over a bad road. It is possible to camp in farm fields or pastures in La Ciénaga outside the park, but there are *no* campgrounds or facilities— only a river near the village.

For their own safety, hikers must inform the National Park staff at La Ciénaga when they are going up the trail. Whether hikers go on foot for the entire route or take a mule, they must go with a local guide who knows the route since there are several side trails on which it is easy to get lost. There are, unfortunately, plenty of true stories about people who tried— even as recently as January 1988—to climb the trail on their own, got lost, and never returned.

JIMENOA WATERFALL

The Jimenoa Waterfall (Salto de Jimenoa) on the river of the same name is the most accessible one in the country. The beautiful cascade drops over 100 ft/30 m from the upper part of the river into a pool where one can bathe. To reach the falls, one must drive south of Jarabacoa en route to Constanza for about 6 mi/9.6 km to El Salto, a hamlet of only a few houses by the side of the road. A trail leaves from the edge of the road and heads down to the falls. No signs mark the trail entrance; ask locally for directions. The descent is easy and not hazardous, but the return hike is very rigorous.

Constanza

High in a mountain valley at 4,000 ft/1,219 m is one of the Dominican Republic's biggest surprises—a farming community that might have been plucked from around Mount Fuji. In the 1950s, the country's infamous strongman, Rafael L. Trujillo, brought fifty Japanese farm families to the Dominican Republic, giving them land to cultivate while they taught local people new farming techniques. Today, the region supplies Santo Domingo with most of its strawberries, fresh vegetables, and other temperate-zone produce, and more recently it has become the main center for export flowers. Descendants of the Japanese immigrants still live and work here.

The area around the town is one of the prettiest in the country, green with forests and fresh with streams and waterfalls and invigorating mountain air. From a high escarpment on the south side of the valley one can look back to see the pine-covered Cordillera Central with its jagged peaks shrouded in thick clouds, giving the appearance of snow. The road between Jarabacoa and San José de Ocoa via Constanza and Valle Nuevo is the only way to cross the highest part of the Cordillera Central by car.

Constanza can also be reached more directly from the Carretera Duarte on a winding, muddy road from Bonao in an hour's drive. The first part of the road climbs into the mountain along a ridge overlooking Lake Rincón, one of six man-made lakes here, popular for fishing and bird-watching.

White Water Falls

From Constanza, the dirt road south to Valle Nuevo follows the Rio Grande river valley and climbs into the pine forests; along the route, small areas of montane forest can be seen. About 6 mi/9.6 km south of town, looking in the distance to the west, one sees White Water Falls (Aguas Blancas), a spectacular cascade that drops in two big stages down the face of a very steep mountain. The route to the falls passes several farms and leads to a hillside called El Convento (it is seldom marked on maps) and the turn-off for the falls. With four-wheel-drive one can motor to the base of the falls on a very narrow, steep, winding track. (If a vehicle is coming from the other direction, the ascending jeep will most likely have to back out of the way.) Alternatively, hikers can leave their vehicle at the turn-off and walk to the falls. It is less than a mile, although it is likely to seem much farther. One can bathe in the pool by the falls but the water is very cold. One might see in the region of Constanza and the falls the sharp-shinned hawk and the endemic gray-headed quail-dove and Hispaniolan trogon.

Pages 94 and 95: The Rio Yaque del Norte in the Cordillera Central.

VALLE NUEVO SCIENTIFIC RESERVE

In 1983 several areas of the country were designated as scientific reserves. The one at Valle Nuevo begins near the Valle Nuevo Military Post and extends south to the Pyramids, a monument about 24 mi/39 km south of Constanza that represents the provincial boundaries. The forest here, at almost 7,000 ft/2,134 m, is one of the most natural woods in the Dominican Republic. Some of the species, such as holly and lyonia, are of particular interest since they are found nowhere else in the Caribbean; related species usually only grow in the northern United States and Canada. Scientists speculate that their seeds were dispersed by migrating birds and they have been able to thrive in the tropics because of the temperate climate in the highlands here. Side roads, usually old logging roads, provide trails for walking into the forests in the higher areas. Some roads are passable with motor vehicles but the condition of any side road may deteriorate quickly, especially in the rainy months.

The route south zigzags through dense pine forest and more open expanses of pine savannah, both areas populated by the Greater Antillean elaenia, Greater Antillean pewee, palm crow, and Antillean siskin. The highest part of the road reaches almost 8,000 ft/2,438 m, passing through rock-covered mountaintops. The descent into Peravia Province passes by a small remnant of montane cloud forest, then breaks out into the Ocoa River Valley and continues to San José de Ocoa. Reforestation has begun to help conserve the soil in this area, but even in the headwaters of the Ocoa River there is agriculture. Except for the bad and often muddy roads and the likelihood of rain even in the dry season, the drive from Constanza to San José de Ocoa, passing through one of the most beautiful mountain regions in the Caribbean, is well worth the effort for those who yearn to travel far from the beaten path.

Among the birds of the area are Ridgway's hawk, the Antillean euphonia, the black-crowned palm tanager, and the endemic narrow-billed tody and Hispaniolan woodpecker; look also for white-winged warblers in the low trees and golden swallows in the area of Rancho Arriba. Slightly north of San José de Ocoa, the region becomes drier and south of town there is a forest of mesquite and acacia along with mahogany trees. The return to Santo Domingo takes about two hours.

EL MORRO NATIONAL PARK

In the extreme northwest of the country near the Haitian border is El Morro National Park (Parque Nacional El Morro), a large land-and-sea park northeast of the town of Monte Cristi. The park's most prominent feature is the mesa, El Morro, which rises dramatically at the edge of the sea. The mesa and its associated small hill, called La Granja (the farm), are covered with windswept shrubs and trees on the ocean side and a desert shrubland on the island side. One reaches El Morro from Monte Cristi on a road that runs through a commercial salt-production area to the coast and directly up the side of the mesa. At the end of the road, between El Morro and La Granja, there is a sweeping view of the Atlantic Ocean and the coast.

The area has no nature trails, but there are numerous goat paths which, though very steep, are walkable. Some lead down to sandy beaches that are good for bathing. Alternatively, a road at the base of El Morro goes eastward through dry woodland to another beach area. Offshore, between Monte Cristi and Punta Rucia, is one of the largest and best reefs on the Dominican coast, within swimming distance in many places. The inner reef is in 7 to 10 ft/2 to 3 m of water; the depth of the outer reef ranges from 10 to 40 ft/3 to 12 m. Ten wrecks have been identified in the vicinity of Monte Cristi and many more await discovery. Among the birds of the region are the wood stork and the American oystercatcher, which breeds on the offshore Los Siete Hermanos islands. Here, too, as along most of the Dominican Republic coast, one might spot the magnificent frigatebird, osprey, American kestrel, plovers, ruddy turnstone, willet, gulls, brown noddy, and five species of terns. Food and lodging are available in Monte Cristi.

PUERTO PLATA AND MT. ISABEL DE TORRES

The main town of the newly developed resort area of the north coast is also one of the country's oldest ports, laid out in typical colonial Spanish fashion around a plaza with a Victorian gazebo and houses with gingerbread trim. Local legends hold that Columbus himself named the town, which means silver port. The Amber Museum near the central plaza (61 Duarte St.; tel: 586-2848) has the country's largest collection of amber on public display and includes many rare pieces; guides are available. On the waterfront, Fortaleza de San Felipe, a sixteenth-century fort with a moat of sharp coral rock, has been restored as a museum and park to honor Juan Pablo Duarte who was imprisoned here. Playa de Long Beach, a sandy public beach, is located at the eastern end of the ocean boulevard.

Loma (or Mount) Isabel de Torres, the lofty mountain behind the town, can be reached by the only suspended cable car in the Caribbean. It climbs

Pages 98 and 99: The high forests of the Valle Nuevo, a scientific reserve off the beaten path, can be explored on foot via a network of old logging roads.

from the sultry tropical heat of the coast up the mountainside to the peak where the temperature may be cooler by 30°F/15°C and a sweater is needed. At the top there is a small park with a statue of Christ the Redeemer (similar to the one overlooking Rio de Janeiro) surrounded by the heavily wooded mountains of the Cordillera Septentrional. From the terrace one can enjoy a spectacular view of the town, the coast, and the mountains brightened in winter with the orange blossom of immortelle, or amapola. Isabel de Torres, like Valle Nuevo, is a scientific reserve. Among the birds of these mountains are the Hispaniolan trogon and the rufous-throated solitaire, as well as such widespread species as the red-tailed hawk, smooth-billed ani, common barn-owl, and the Caribbean martin.

The resorts of Playa Dorada and Sosúa are east of Puerto Plata and easily reached by taxi, rental car, tour, or public transportation.

SAMANÁ PENINSULA AND BAY

On the northeastern corner of the Dominican Republic is a 30-mi-/48-km-long peninsula extending into the Atlantic and forming a bay whose waters and shores hold a great deal of interest for naturalists. The main town, Samaná, is located on the south side of the peninsula overlooking the bay where there are several tiny islands with some of the prettiest beaches in the country. Rincón Bay at the northeast corner of Samaná peninsula can be reached by road from Samaná town; few roads outside the town are paved. Tourist development has started here and more is planned. Rincón Bay and Cayo de Levantado in Samaná Bay have shallow-water snorkeling. Little of the lush vegetation that covers Samaná peninsula is original; much of the land has been given over to coconut and banana production, but the relatively remote area is attractive to those who want to get away from crowded resorts.

The north coast of the peninsula is reached more easily by boat; but parts of it are accessible from Sánchez where a paved road leads over the mountains to the beaches of Las Terrenas and Portillo, which are suitable for swimming. In the low swampy areas near these beaches, birders are likely to see rails, plovers, herons, terns, sandpipers, ibises, roseate spoonbills, and purple gallinules. Along the coast are white-tailed tropicbirds, brown boobies, and wood storks. From Samaná town another dirt road leads to Limón on the Río Limón in the center of the peninsula; from here a footpath takes one to a magnificent waterfall, all but hidden amidst the savage beauty of the thickly forested mountains. The falls drop 165 ft/50 m with such force that, standing 100 ft/30 m away, one can get wet from the spray. Information and a local guide—essential to finding the way—are available from the navy guard post in Limón, where hikers may leave their cars. Here visitors can ask about renting horses if they do not want to walk the steep trail of 1.2 mi/2 km, which takes about one hour. The trail crosses the river twice and hikers must get wet to their knees.

WHALE-WATCHING AND SILVER BANK SANCTUARY

From January to late February whales can be observed at the mouth of Samaná Bay. No organized excursions are available, but arrangements to go whale-watching can be made with local boatmen at Samaná town harbor; one must obtain permission in advance from the Naval Station in Samaná.

Silver Bank (Santuario de Ballenas Jorobadas del Banco de la Plata), a marine sanctuary of the humpback whale, is located 50 mi/80 km off the coast, directly north of Cabrera (70 long., 21 lat.). The lagoon, 100 ft/30 m below sea level, attracts herds of up to 3,000 migrating humpback whales from late December to early March. Here, the whales give birth and nurture their young in an underwater world which they share with large schools of fish and marine turtles; there are large coral formations, too.

During the mating season, occasional expeditions by ship are made by scientists to Silver Bank to observe the whales. The trip takes seven to twelve hours depending on the weather. One might contact the National Parks Office in Santo Domingo or Centro de Investigaciones de Biología Marina (CIBIMA) at the University of Santo Domingo (tel: 688-8633) on the chance that a trip might be planned. MAMMA (Fundación Dominicana Pro-Investigación y Conservación de los Recursos Marinos, Inc., Av. Anacaona No. 77, Apto. C-4, P.O. Box 21449, Santo Domingo), a nonprofit organization protecting marine mammals, can assist in arranging trips from Puerto Plata and Samaná. It is also involved in projects to save the manatee and preserve the country's marine environment.

LOS HAITISES NATIONAL PARK

On the south side of Samaná Bay is Los Haitises National Park (Parque Nacional Los Haitises), a karst region comprising about 100 mi/160 km of land and adjacent mangrove estuaries. Ordinarily, rocky terrain like this would be semidesert, but because of the heavy rainfall—more than 90 in/230 cm per year—and frequent cloud cover, the small limestone knolls, some up to 1,000 ft/300 m and more in elevation, and the narrow valley bottoms are densely covered with trees. The area brings together montane plants such as begonias and mountain palms with lowland forest species such as balata, copey, and almacigo (gumbo limbo, or birch gum).

Along the coast of the bay there are many tiny, rocky islands, or cays, that were once part of the mainland. Bird Island (Isla de los Pájaros) has a small

forest atop the rock where brown pelicans, snowy egrets, roseate terns, and other seabirds roost in the trees and soar overhead. Among other birds of the region are Ridgway's hawk, narrow-billed tody, least grebe, white-cheeked pintail, and ruddy duck. From Boca de Inferno (near Bird Island) and San Lorenzo Bay (Bahía de San Lorenzo), and stretching 15 mi/24 km west to the mouth of Río Barracote at the west end of Samaná Bay over 78 sq mi/208 sq km, Los Haitises is fronted with dense red mangrove forests. One can take a boat into the swamps to see excellent examples of vegetation typical of tropical swamps. At low tide the oysters, mussels, and various crustaceans growing on the mangrove roots are clearly visible in many places. Further up the river the birdlife includes the great blue heron, coot, northern jacana, ibises, and the rare double-crested cormorant. Inland on the south side one might see the northern bobwhite and killdeer as well.

Access to Los Haitises National Park is by sea from the north or south side of Samaná Bay. The trip is best made in the morning when the bay is calm; sometimes, afternoon winds make the water choppy. The easiest, most convenient way to visit the park is on a day excursion from Samaná town, a resort on the north side of the bay with several first- and tourist-class hotels. Travel agencies offering the trip can be contacted through them. Another option is to hire MAMMA's deepsea fishing boat anchored at Samaná town harbor after securing permission from the local Navy Office.

From Sabana de la Mar, the main town on the south side of the bay, there are occasional guided tours (usually in Spanish) organized by the National Park office. They depart from Sabana de la Mar dock, and arrangements must be made in advance through the National Park office in Santo Domingo (tours originating in Santo Domingo include transportation to Sabana de la Mar). Alternatively, the venturesome can hire a small boat—usually with an outboard motor—after securing permission from the National Park office in Santo Domingo. The park office in Sabana de la Mar can help locate a boatowner. Be sure the boat has two oars before leaving the dock for emergency use if the motor fails. Those who wish to camp overnight at the park ranger cabin at Sand Cave on San Lorenzo Bay or at El Naranjo (about 3 mi/4.8 km farther west) must take all their own provisions, including water and insect repellent. Sabana de la Mar has one pension and a modest hotel.

A passenger boat that will transport motorcycles and bicycles usually crosses Samaná Bay between Samaná town and Sabana de la Mar twice daily, each way. It is thus possible to visit the north and south sides of the bay in one day.

Along the east coast of the Barahona Peninsula between Paraiso and Enriquillo there are dramatic views of the limestone that characterizes most of the peninsula.

NATIONAL PARK OF THE EAST

In the southeastern corner of the Dominican Republic, a portion of the mainland and the island of Saona comprise the National Park of the East (Parque Nacional del Este), a tropical deciduous or seasonally dry forest on limestone rock, generally with very little soil. The terrain varies from flat to gently rolling hills, with terraces near the seacoast.

At the park's western entrance near Bayahibe, there is a park ranger cabin and office and a marked trail leading inland to a cave frequented by bats and owls; park employees can guide visitors there. The eastern entrance near the town of Boca del Yuma also has a ranger's cabin at the start of an inland trail that parallels the coast. The park's few sandy beaches are accessible only by boat. On the south coast is Catalinita Bay, which is bioluminescent.

Saona Island, which is about 14 mi/22 km long and 3 to 4 mi/5 to 6.4 km wide, has two tiny villages, Punta Gorda on the west coast and Adamanay on the southwest coast, connected by a dirt road. The latter is the docking location for the Coast Guard and other boats. The island has sandy beaches, and several trails that cut across the island can be used for hiking. The island is home to the endemic Hispaniolan lizard-cuckoo, the wood stork, and the black-crowned palm tanager. Other birds include limpkins, Antillean palm swift, red-legged thrush, palmchat, black-cowled oriole, and village weaver. The American oystercatcher inhabits the area of Punta Algibe on the mainland in front of Saona, and the endemic Antillean piculet is found in the dry coastal areas as well. There are bottled drinks, but no food, shelter, or other visitors' facilities on Saona. Mosquitoes have a constant and disturbing presence here.

BARAHONA PENINSULA

West of Santo Domingo, the main highway, Carretera Sánchez, leads to San Cristóbal and Baní, crossing an area of extensive sugarcane fields. The region becomes more arid and takes on a desert look from Baní westward to Azua and south to Barahona. The desert areas are covered with short thorn forests of acacias and mesquite trees interspersed with organ-pipe cactus, jumping cholla, and prickly pear. Where irrigation is possible, there are highly productive vegetable farms. Lodging and restaurants of varying quality can be found in Baní, Azua, and Barahona. (At Cruce de Ocoa, the junction of the road to San José de Ocoa, a paved road ascends gradually into the foothills of the Cordillera Central; from here the route continues north to Constanza via a dirt road that is negotiable by jeep.)

LAKE ENRIQUILLO AND GOAT ISLAND NATIONAL PARK

Directly west of Santo Domingo, almost to the Haitian border, is Lake Enriquillo, an inland saltwater lake about 21 mi/34 km in length and 90 ft/ 27 m below sea level, the lowest place in the Caribbean. Rising abruptly out of the basin are the Neiba Mountains (Sierra de Neiba) on the north and the Bahoruco Mountains (Sierra de Bahoruco) on the south. In the center of the lake is a 5-mi-/8-km-long island given over to Goat Island National Park (Parque Nacional Isla Cabritos), a reserve to protect the native American crocodile that lives and reproduces there. Clapper rails and small flocks of greater flamingos, herons, terns, sandpipers, and roseate spoonbills are found along the lakeshores and on the island. The lake is encircled by a road at sea level; the terrain slopes downward to the lake, which is below sea level.

The hills surrounding the arid Enriquillo basin are covered by short, dry thorn scrub, acacia and mesquite trees, and cacti. Goat Island has similar vegetation. Some areas are almost impenetrable because of the thorny plants and in many places, especially in the areas above sea level, the limestone rock is exposed. In many road cuts along the lakeside, large accumulations of marine coral branches visible in the rock indicate that the Enriquillo basin and Lake Etang Saumâtre in Haiti were under water at one time. There are several sulphur springs in the lake's vicinity.

The forested high mountains on either side of the valley—Neiba Mountains on the north and Bahoruco Mountains on the south—are rich in birdlife. The endemic gray-headed quail-dove, Hispaniolan parrot, Hispaniolan trogon, and Antillean siskin are found here. Others common to the area are the mangrove cuckoo, yellow-billed cuckoo, collared swift, Greater Antillean elaenia, golden swallow, palm crow, La Selle thrush, stripe-headed tanager, and grasshopper sparrow. The rufous-collared sparrow and least pauraque are found in the northern range; the yellow-bellied sapsucker, rufous-throated solitaire, black-crowned palm tanager, and chat tanager live in the southern range.

The drive from Santo Domingo to the lake via the seaside resort town of Barahona takes almost three hours, and even with the recent completion of a new road around the north side of the lake, another hour is needed to circle it. About 0.5 mi/0.8 km before the village of La Descubierta, in the northwestern corner of the lake, there are wonderful petroglyphs on a cliffside north of the road; a steep five-minute climb is required to reach them.

A visit to Goat Island must be arranged with the park office in La Descubierta. But first, visitors must get permission at the National Parks Department headquarters in Santo Domingo to go to the island and to learn if the park's motorboat is operating. Even when they are told the boat is operating, they should not be surprised to arrive at the lake and find that it is not. The trip to the island by motorboat takes forty-five minutes; by rowboat, two hours. The area is very hot, even in winter; an early-morning start is recommended, and one should carry ample drinking water at all times. There are no tourist facilities beyond Barahona; a small shop in La Descubierta sells cheese, bread, and local fruit, but travelers are better advised to bring their own food.

JARAGUA NATIONAL PARK

In the southwest corner of the country, Jaragua National Park (Parque Nacional Jaragua), named for a Taino Indian chief, extends from Oviedo westward to Cabo Rojo over the southern parts of the Pedernales Province and the small islands of Beata and Alto Velo. It covers about 520 sq mi/1,350 sq km, of which 270 sq mi/700 sq km are sea. The region is extremely arid and usually hot, with winds coming from the Caribbean and from the Bahoruco Mountains to the north. Most of the area is covered by compact limestone rock, much of which is "dogtooth" limestone caused by the weathering of the rock. Walking among the spiny and thorny trees, shrubs, and cacti and on the dogtooth is difficult. The coast is a limestone shelf with several white sand beaches that can only be reached by long walks or by boat.

The park includes Lago Oviedo, a large saltwater lake about 6 mi/9.6 km in length, situated east of the town of Oviedo and a short distance from the road. Flamingos frequent the lake and the sandy barrier between the lake and the Caribbean Sea, while the common potoo, known here as *Don Juan Grande* for its rather imperious stance, may be spotted in the areas of the mangroves. Brown pelicans, boobies, and other water birds are found here and along the coast, which is also a turtle nesting area. Beata Island off the southernmost tip is a breeding ground for the willet and home to Ridgway's hawk and the endemic green-tailed ground warbler, a bird of Hispaniola normally found in mountain areas. There are greater flamingos, burrowing owls, Antillean palm swifts, and pearly-eyed thrashers, too. Among the animals—mostly lizards and reptiles—there are two species of iguana, the rhino iguana and Ricord's iguana.

The park can be reached by taking the road from Barahona to Pedernales on the Haiti border. Access to the interior of the park is limited and requires a truck or jeep. There are no facilities: anyone planning to leave the main road must have an ample supply of water and be prepared for hot and very dry weather. The small town of Pedernales has very meager services.

Palm-fringed Playa Goleta, near Puerto Plata, is typical of the north coast beaches.

OUTDOOR ACTIVITIES

HIKING: With a good map and some knowledge of Spanish, hikers can ramble about on any back-country road. In the high mountains, however, one should never venture off the main roads without a local guide. The National Park Service organizes guided excursions (in Spanish) from time to time; trails in the parks are neither marked nor maintained.

HORSEBACK RIDING: Several north coast resorts offer horseback riding, but the most extensive layout is at Casa de Campo in La Romana in the southeast, which has a ranch of several thousand horses for trail riding and polo.

SWIMMING: In a country known for beautiful beaches, it is hard to select the best, but the Samaná area tops the list. Cayo de Levantado in Samaná Bay is an idyllic islet fringed with palm-shaded white sand beaches surrounded by turquoise waters, easily reached by ferry from town. Las Galeras on Rincón Bay is a half-hour drive from Samaná town.

The 20 mi/32 km of beachfront on the north coast east of Puerto Plata has been the center of resort development for the past decade. On the east coast, a 15-mi/24-km stretch of palm-fringed, white sand Atlantic beaches from Macao to Punta Caña has resorts at Bávaro and Punta Caña, both with a wide choice of water sports for their guests.

Much of the coastline, particularly on the south, is coastal limestone shelf with no sandy beaches. In the vicinity of Santo Domingo, however, there are several: Guibia, popular for surfing; Boca Chica, east beyond the airport, with tranquil, shallow water; Juan Dolio and Guayacanes, popular with Dominicans and crowded on weekends. Further east, Bayahibe is the best beach near the 7,000-acre/2,833-hectare resort of Casa de Campo. Saona Island on the southeastern tip has pretty beaches but no fresh water or facilities.

The south coast west of Santo Domingo has few sandy beaches that are safe for bathing. Playa Monte Río south of Azua, and La Saladilla and Los Quemaditos south of Barahona are readily accessible. Further south of Barahona, one must be cautious as some of the beaches such as Playa San Rafael have strong waves, undertows, or sharp drop-offs. All beaches in the Dominican Republic are public property, including those fronted by resorts and hotels.

SNORKELING AND SCUBA DIVING: Reefs border the Dominican Republic in places along all three of its coasts, but the sport of scuba is only in its infancy, and generally is available through resorts rather than independent dive operators. The north coast at Monte Cristi is one of the prime locations due to the large reef and wrecks, but the area is not suitable for diving from December to March because of the strong northerly winds. The main interest for divers is an area near the mouth of Samaná Bay north of Miches where the wrecks of the seventeenth-century Spanish galleons *Tolosa* and *Guadalupe* lie. The east coast from Samaná Bay to Punta Caña is primarily a snorkeling location when the Atlantic waves are not too strong.

Catalina Island at La Romana is the main dive location for the southeast coast. The island has a wall on its north side starting at 40 ft/12 m and good reef. To reach the island one must take a boat from the marina at La Romana. With permission from the Naval Station in La Romana, one may camp on the island but it has no facilities and no fresh water. East of Casa de Campo, Bayahibe offers good diving in clear water.

In the immediate vicinity of Santo Domingo, near the airport, La Caleta Marine Park (Parque Nacional Submarino La Caleta) was created in 1987 to protect an area of 3 mi/4.8 m along the coast to a depth of 350 ft/107 m and varying in width according to the contours of the coast. The wreck of the *Hickory*, the vessel of Tracy Bowen who discovered *Tolosa* and *Guadelupe*, was sunk here to create an artificial reef to attract fish and so restock the waters depleted by local fishermen. The park has no facilities or equipment as yet; divers must bring their own gear or make arrangements through their hotel or a dive shop in town. La Caleta's calm, clear Caribbean waters are particularly popular with underwater photographers. The reef slopes very gradually from 50 to 80 ft/15 to 24 m and then drops rapidly to 120 ft/36 m. A similar artificial reef has been created in Bahía de Ocoa, west of Santo Domingo.

FISHING: The southeast coast at Bahía de Yuma along the Mona Passage is the prime area for deep-sea fishing. The town of Boca del Yuma at the mouth of Yuma River has a marina for yachts and fishing boats. An annual marine fishing tournament is held here. Cabo Rojo and the southwest tip are good fishing grounds too. Fishing in the man-made lakes in the mountains for bass and carp is available but anglers must provide all their own equipment.

SAILING AND BOATING: Recreational boating on lakes is uncommon. Local fishermen who fish for a living use rowboats or small motorboats on the reservoirs and lakes. There are marinas on the south coast at La Romana near Casa de Campo and Boca del Yuma. The Sailing Club of Santo Domingo (Club Náutico de Santo Domingo; 809-566-4522) is located at Boca Chica about forty-five minutes east of Santo Domingo.

SURFING: Playa Grande at Río San Juan and, sometimes, Sosúa on the north coast and Macao on the west coast are the best areas for surfing. All three locations are washed by Atlantic waves, which are strongest during the winter months.

WINDSURFING: Most seaside resorts offer windsurfing and have boards for rent, but Cabarete, 2 mi/3.2 km east of Sosúa, is the best site in the Dominican Republic and has gained an international reputation among windsurfing enthusiasts. The entire Atlantic east coast is popular too; winds can be quite strong depending on the time of the year.

EXPLORING THE ISLAND

Major towns have taxis and bus transportation and are connected by private, regularly scheduled bus or minibus service. Rental car companies have offices at airports and in major tourist cities. Jeeps sometimes can be rented from Budget Rent a Car and a few other agencies. In addition to the international airports of Santo Domingo and Puerto Plata, there are airfields at La Romana, near Casa de Campo; Punta Caña; and Samaná. The government plans to upgrade the latter to an international jetport. There is no regularly scheduled internal air service, but flights on chartered craft are available.

The Dominican Republic has a large network of roads. Major highways are usually in acceptable condition, but most other roads have potholes, broken pavement, or dirt-and-gravel surfaces that become mud tracks after a heavy rain. Travel these roads slowly and carefully. Service stations in towns are not open late; drivers should always fill their fuel tanks because there are often no stations in outlying areas. Road maps, sold in gift shops and bookstores, give an overview of the highway system, but are often much out of date; secondary roads may well be impassable. A topographic map, available from the Instituto Geográfico Universitario (Universidad Autonoma de Santo Domingo, Calle de Las Damas, Old Santo Domingo; 682-2680) is essential for driving on all but major arteries. There are very few road signs; drivers will need to ask for directions frequently, making some knowledge of Spanish necessary.

Food, bottled water, and other provisions can be obtained in stores and markets, but do not expect to find packaged provisions in the countryside. Always carry bottled water on excursions; it is safer to drink factory-bottled beer and soda than local water. Plan overnight stays in provincial capitals where there are hotels and restaurants. Visitors should be aware that "motels" with rooms for rent by the hour and recognizable enclosed courtyards are for short-term amorous pursuits, not overnight travelers.

INFORMATION: In the U.S.: Kahn Travel Communications, 4 Park Ave., New York, NY 10016; 212-679-5055; 800-752-1151. In Canada: 29 Bellair St., Toronto, M5R 268; 416-928-9188. There is no tourist office in the U.K. In Santo Domingo: Consejo de Promocion Turistica, Calle Desiderio Arias #24, Bella Vista; 809-535-3276. Government office hours are 7:30 A.M.–2:30 P.M.. daily (except Saturdays, Sundays, and holy days). Permission to enter national parks in the countryside must be obtained from the National Parks Department, Calle Las Damas No. 6, Old City; 809-685-1316. Most rural parks are open to 5 P.M. and have no facilities, guides, or marked trails. Frequently there is a small fee.

National Museum of Natural History, Plaza de la Cultura, Calle César Nicolás Pensón; tel. 809-689-0106. National Botanic Garden, Avda. República de Colombia at Avda. de Los Próceres; tel. 809-567-6211. Wild Life Office (División de Vida Silvestre), Secretaria de Estado de Agricultura, La Feria; tel. 809-533-0049. For hunting, fishing, or collecting of any animals (including birds), permits are required and enforcement is strict. Correspondence in Spanish rather than English is likely to produce better results. Visiting scientists should visit the Museum of Natural History and the Botanic Garden to meet with staffs regarding field work.

There are no popular guidebooks on the flora of the Dominican Republic, only technical ones. For bird watchers, *Aves de la República Dominicana*, by Annabelle Stockton de Dod (Museo Nacional de Historia Natural, Santo Domingo, 1978), and a pocket version by the same author, *Guía de campo para las aves de la República*, are excellent field guides available at the Museum of Natural History and some bookstores.

PUERTO RICO

PUERTO RICO

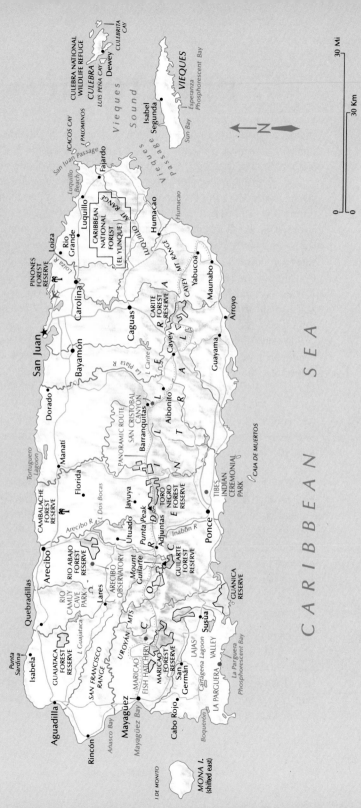

Highways — Highways

Roads — Roads

★ National Capitals

● Points of Interest

▲ Peaks

∩ Caves

🎋 Small Parks

ATLANTIC OCEAN

CARIBBEAN SEA

Vieques Sound

Vieques Passage

San Juan Passage

N

30 Mi

30 Km

CULEBRA NATIONAL WILDLIFE REFUGE
CULEBRA
CULEBRITA CAY
LUIS PEÑA CAY
Dewey

VIEQUES
Isabel Segunda
Esperanza
Phosphorescent Bay
Sun Bay

ICACOS CAY
PALOMINOS
Luquillo Beach
Fajardo

Luquillo
Río Grande
Loíza
CARIBBEAN NATIONAL FOREST (EL YUNQUE)
MT RANGE
LUQUILLO

Humacao
Humacao

PIÑONES FOREST RESERVE
Carolina
San Juan
Bayamón
Caguas
CARITE FOREST RESERVE
CAYEY MT RANGE
Yabucoa
Maunabo
Cayey
Arroyo
Guayama

Dorado
Manatí
La Plata R
L Carite

Florida
PANORAMIC ROUTE
SAN CRISTÓBAL CANYON
Barranquitas
Aibonito

Tortuguero Lagoon
Dos Bocas
CAMBALACHE FOREST RESERVE
Arecibo R
Javuya
Jayuya
TORO NEGRO FOREST RESERVE
Punta Peak
Adjuntas
Inabón R
Ponce
TIBES INDIAN CEREMONIAL PARK
CAJA DE MUERTOS

Quebradillas
Arecibo
RÍO CAMUY CAVE PARK
RÍO ABAJO FOREST RESERVE
Lares
ARECIBO OBSERVATORY
L Guajataca
Utuado
Mount Guilarte
GUILARTE FOREST RESERVE
GUÁNICA RESERVE

Punta Sardina
Isabela
GUAJATACA FOREST RESERVE
SAN FRANCISCO RANGE
UROYÁN MTS
MARICAO FISH HATCHERY
MARICAO FOREST RESERVE
LAJAS
Susúa
San Germán
LA PARGUERA
Cartagena Lagoon
LA PARGUERA VALLEY
La Parguera Phosphorescent Bay

Aguadilla
Rincón
Mayagüez
Mayagüez Bay
Añasco Bay
Cabo Rojo
Boquerón

I DE MONITO
MONA I. (shifted east)

PUERTO RICO

FOR MOST PEOPLE, Puerto Rico conjures up images of beach strips set against an urban skyline. Or sophisticated casinos, nightclubs, and international restaurants. Or cruise ships pulling up alongside a city steeped in history. Puerto Rico does offer all this, but it has another side.

More than 300 miles of coastline surround the island—the rough Atlantic on the north, the calm Caribbean on the south. Cliffs and mangroves, palm groves and sand dunes give the beaches wide diversity. Tropical vegetation covers the north from the Atlantic to the central mountains; semiarid landscapes predominate in the south. Rolling hills brightened here and there by flowering tropical trees rise into the lushly green, cloud-tipped Cordillera Central, the backbone of this 110-by-35-mi/176-by-56-km island. Rural communities tucked away in the mountains, still rich with colonial and agricultural traditions, are little touched by the cosmopolitan air of the capital city of San Juan.

For centuries, Puerto Rico was the Spanish gateway to the West Indies. Tradewinds flowing in a southwesterly direction guided wind-powered ships into the heart of the Caribbean. This natural phenomenon made Puerto Rico important as a military outpost for Spain for four centuries— from the time of its discovery by Columbus in 1493 and the first Spanish settlement by Ponce de León in 1509 to the Spanish-American War in 1898.

But by the nineteenth century, Spain had lost most of her empire and needed revenue more than military strongholds. She began to develop Puerto Rico's agriculture, clearing the native vegetation to make way for sugar and coffee plantations. After World War II the United States, which had claimed Puerto Rico at the end of the Spanish-American War, embarked on an ambitious industrialization program. Factories and pharmaceutical plants replaced plantations, and tourism grew.

Puerto Rico's strong infrastructure enabled it to bounce back from the damage of Hurricane Hugo in 1989. However, check with the tourist office before journeying into the rain forest or to Culebra and Vieques.

SAN JUAN

The island's capital is a large metropolis by the ocean, more oriented to urban life than to nature. Here, being outdoors means walking along the cobblestone streets and ramparts of Old San Juan, beautifully restored and alive with street fairs, strolling musicians, art galleries, and museums. But San Juan is an ideal base for exploring the many natural attractions on the outskirts of this sprawling city or less than an hour's drive away.

Botanical Garden

Before leaving San Juan, one can have an introduction to the enormous variety of the island's flora by visiting the Agricultural Experiment Station Botanical Garden, a delightful 140-acre/57-hectare oasis in the San Juan suburb of Río Piedras and home of the Institute of Tropical Forestry. In a park-like setting one can stroll along paths shaded by such native trees as the Puerto Rican royal palm and the ausubo, a strong termite-proof wood used for centuries for house beams. A wide variety of trees common to the rest of the Caribbean can be seen here, including breadfruit, Indian almond, African tulip, and mammee; there are also tropical fruit trees and herb bushes from around the world. Paths bordered by beak-shaped, red-to-yellow heliconia blossoms and giant philodendron leaves wind through the garden, past a lotus-filled lagoon and a bamboo chapel. Highlights of the garden include an orchid display of small native species and showy hybrids numbering in the thousands, and a new palmetum (to the left of the main entrance) with 125 species.

Several buildings house libraries—one for tropical agriculture and another used by the U.S. Forest Service and the Institute, which conducts research on tropical trees and wildlife. Considered among the best in the hemisphere, the libraries are open to the public during weekdays.

Caribbean National Forest (El Yunque)

In the Luquillo Mountains only a thirty-minute drive east of San Juan is the Caribbean National Forest, the best place on the island to explore tropical vegetation. More commonly known as El Yunque, it protects the largest expanse of forest in Puerto Rico. As part of the U.S. Forest Service system and its only tropical rain forest, El Yunque has long been a center for research on tropical flora and fauna; 240 species of trees and more than 200 types of fern have been identified there.

El Yunque's vegetation falls into four forest types. Tabonuco forest, which grows on the lower elevations, most closely resembles the rain forests found in other parts of tropical America. It is named for a common native tree and contains the greatest variety of trees. Many of them reach 150 ft/45 m; vines and roots dangle from their branches. Palo colorado forest, known as humid montane or montane rain forest elsewhere in the tropics, dominates higher elevations. Trees here tend to be short and gnarled, often decked with bromeliads; the undergrowth is dense. A third type, sierra palm, also known as the mountain, or cabbage, palm, adds a lush, tropical cover to steep slopes and gullies where most other trees cannot grow. Dwarf, or elfin, forest grows on high peaks and ridges where

wind-stunted trees resemble elves and branches drip moss. Tree ferns resembling lacy parasols, including *Hemitalia,* are found in the more protected parts of dwarf forest.

As many as sixty species of birds inhabit El Yunque, including the Puerto Rican parrot, which, thanks to biologists, is slowly rebuilding its numbers from the twenty-two left in 1975. It is spotted often in the picnic area behind the visitors' center and from the patio next to the restaurant, where one can also see the broad-winged hawk. Look for the elusive endemic elfin woods warbler (found only in the Caribbean National Forest and Maricao Forest) in the dwarf forest and along the El Toro Trail; the green mango hummingbird can sometimes be seen by La Coca Falls. Other endemic birds include the Puerto Rican lizard-cuckoo, Puerto Rican woodpecker, Puerto Rican tanager, Puerto Rican bullfinch, and the Puerto Rican screech-owl.

A portion of El Yunque is a recreation area where trails are clearly defined and well maintained. *La Mina/Big Tree Trail* (two hours round trip) is actually two trails in one. The paved path of La Mina begins in the picnic area behind the visitors' center and parallels La Mina River, named for the gold once found there. Beyond La Mina Falls, *Big Tree Trail* journeys through the stately trees of the tabonuco forest to Road 191.

Bromeliads are epiphytes and absorb nutrients dissolved in the water trapped among their leaves. Facing page: Sierra palms are the only trees that can grow on the steepest slopes of El Yunque, but they in turn support lianas and epiphytes.

El Yunque Trail (four hours round trip) starts in the Caimitillo Picnic Area. The steep path ascends through palo colorado and sierra palm forests, then branches off to the cloud-enshrouded dwarf forest of Mt. Britton and El Yunque and to lookout peaks such as Los Picachos, Roca Marcas, and Yunque Rock from where on a clear day there are great views down the north and east slopes to the Atlantic coast.

The best of the usually weathered trails outside the recreation area are El Toro and La Coca. *El Toro/Tradewinds Trail* (6 mi/9.6 km, one way) connects Road 191, which goes through the heart of the forest, with Road 186, which skirts its western edge. This trail, the longest on the island, is muddy in places but always distinct and passes through the four forest types to reach El Toro, 3,532 ft/1,076 m, the highest of the forest's peaks. Here and in dwarf forest elsewhere the elfin woods warbler might be seen.

La Coca Trail, just below the Yokahu lookout tower on Road 191, descends into a rain-forest area crisscrossed by several streams where hikers must take care not to get disoriented. It is popular with those who like to rock-hop in search of their own remote pools and waterfalls. But the uninitiated should be aware that rock-hopping in the damp undergrowth of a rain forest can be very slippery and dangerous. It is also a good idea to wear long trousers and long-sleeved shirts in spite of warm weather because poisonous plants along the paths can give painful stings and cause rashes.

For those who want simply to take a drive through El Yunque, a tarmac route (Road 191) leads from the main highway (Road 3) deep into the rain forest, passing ferns the size of trees, trees up to 120 ft/37 m tall, waterfalls, lookout towers, picnic areas, and a restaurant. At the northern border of the forest, the National Forest's field office (open only during the week) sells a topographical map and offers trail orientation. Camping in the park is permitted; campers should inquire about the safest place to leave their car. At the foot of the mountains is the majestic coconut-bordered Luquillo Beach, a half-moon stretch of sand and calm. It is the island's most popular *balneario* (public bathing area) and is crowded on weekends.

PIÑONES

Even closer to San Juan than El Yunque is the Piñones Forest Reserve, a marshland with several lagoons and the largest mangrove forest on the island. The shrub-like mangroves, with their small green leaves and branch networks, prevent erosion and foster fish and bird life. From Boca de Cangrejos marina at the mouth of the Torrecilla Lagoon, a ten-minute drive on Road 187 from the San Juan suburb of Isla Verde, a boat takes visitors on weekend tours through the mangroves during which they will see crabs, fish, and an occasional mongoose in and under the finger-like mangrove roots. Above, in the mangrove branches, may rest a magnificent frigatebird, common tern, green-backed heron, little blue heron, tricolored heron, spotted sandpiper, or black-necked stilt.

A new paved road on a strip of land between the ocean and the Piñones marshland winds through 6 mi/9.6 km of an old coconut plantation and skirts uninterrupted beach whose firm flat sand is favored by joggers. One end of the beach is framed by a promontory created millions of years ago by barrier sand dunes being "cemented" together during periods of glaciation. The road continues to the Loíza River and the town of Loíza, the home of Puerto Rico's largest concentration of African descendants. Their culinary and musical heritage is displayed vividly during a colorful traditional festival held in July.

Piñones is one of fourteen Commonwealth Forest Reserves located throughout the island—some along the coast, others in the karst country and in the mountains where the vegetation resembles that of El Yunque. They are operated by the San Juan Department of Natural Resources and have trails (many made, as were those in El Yunque, by the U.S. Civilian Conservation Corps in the 1930s). Unfortunately, the trails of the reserves are generally not well maintained, thus only those who are experienced in tropical bushwhacking—or are accompanied by a local guide—will find their way along the trails. Inquire at the Department of Natural Resources for orientation if you are serious about completing one of the less-well-maintained trails.

Espíritu Santo

The only navigable river in Puerto Rico is the Espíritu Santo, whose headwaters are in the Luquillo Mountains. Upstream, it travels steeply down the mountains—like all the island's rivers—through a boulder-crammed course, but downriver near the coast and the town of Río Grande, it spills into marshland where there are several miles of navigable water. La Paseadora launch, moored off Highway 3 at km 25.2, makes weekend river journeys from that point through open fields and mangrove forests down to the river's mouth on the Atlantic. Occasionally one will see green-backed herons skirting the water, and a sharp-eyed birder might spot a *carpintero*, as the native Puerto Rican woodpecker is known, or the short-eared owl, which breeds in Puerto Rico.

Pages 118 and 119: Rocky Sardina Point, on the Atlantic Coast near Isabela, is just around the corner from a beach called the Shacks, which attracts snorkelers and divers. Nearby Jobos Beach has wave action strong enough for surfing.

THE CORDILLERA CENTRAL

In the background as one travels around the island is the lush Cordillera Central, ever-present, ever-cloud-cloaked. The Panoramic Route follows the Cordillera Central as it makes its mostly mountainous progress from the southeast town of Yabucoa to Mayagüez on the west coast. Forty different roads make up its total of 165 mi/266 km. Not all crucial intersections are marked, so travelers will need to come armed with a good map and a strong sense of humor. The reward is a drive through spectacular panoramas, four forest reserves, and rural towns seemingly plucked from the last century.

CARITE FOREST RESERVE

Entering from the east coast, the Yabucoa-to-Cayey section starts in a valley once covered with sugarcane, then loops along the coast via Maunabo through dry, hilly terrain resembling Mediterranean countryside and brightened with cotton-candy pink *roble* blossoms and showy red flowers of the flamboyant tree. The route rises into hills where farmers still plant yuca, or cassava, an edible tuber that was cultivated centuries ago by the Taino Indians, who inhabited the island before the Spaniards. It then ascends into the 6,000-acre/2,428-hectare Carite Forest Reserve along the Sierra de Cayey with views of Guayama, a south coast town, and the Caribbean Sea on the south. Sierra palms, with their arching fronds and pencil-like prop roots, predominate among the dozens of tree species; higher altitudes contain dwarf forest. The endemic Puerto Rican tanager, which inhabits the higher mountain forests, is common among the fifty species of birds that live here. Also common is the Puerto Rican bullfinch, once found on St. Kitts but now endemic to Puerto Rico; the bird has the curious name of *come ñame* in Spanish, presumably because it eats *ñame*, a tuber. This and the other three reserves along the route are managed by the Department of Natural Resources; all have picnic areas and campsites.

In the eastern section of the Carite Forest at the Charco Azul picnic site (on Road 184) a shaded path with eucalyptus and royal palms leads to Charco Azul, a natural spring-fed swimming hole, and continues to Cerro la Santa, 2,730 ft/832 m, the highest peak in the reserve. Although well defined and less than a mile in length, the path to the pool crosses a stream half a dozen times and must be forded at each crossing; the path to the peak is little used and overgrown. On the western side are the bluish green waters of Lake Carite, a man-made lake built a half-century ago along with other reservoirs to harness the rivers' waterpower. (There are no natural lakes in Puerto Rico.) Stocked with bass and other fish, these lakes make exotic fishing holes, but one must bring all equipment.

SAN CRISTÓBAL CANYON

Between the old tobacco towns of Aibonito and Barranquitas lies the 6-mi-/ 9.6-km-long San Cristóbal Canyon, the island's deepest gorge, which drops more than 400 ft/122 m in places. Climbing bamboo, shortleaf fig, guava, and other trees, shrubs, and grasses hug its steep walls, and such birds as American kestrels and hawks swoop over the Usabón River flowing through the canyon. Before the canyon was acquired by the island's Conservation Trust in the late 1970s, it had been a convenient dump for local residents and, here and there, hikers will still come upon debris whose removal was too difficult or costly. Natural growth now covers most of it.

Northwest of Aibonito a road skirting the eastern side of the canyon provides glimpses of the upper canyon walls; another road parallels the Barranquitas side. The canyon has not yet been developed for visitors but there are at least two places from which to make a descent. Few, if any, signs mark the route; one will need to ask locally for directions. Off Road 7725 between Aibonito and Barranquitas a short, steep, ill-defined path leads to the canyon floor and a 100-ft/30-m waterfall, the highest in Puerto Rico. It is a thirty-minute hike down, and it takes longer to return.

From Road 156, in Barrio San Cristóbal of Barranquitas, a steeper trail switchbacks down to a deeper section of the canyon, from where one can explore the canyon floor. The descent takes at least an hour; on the floor one must scramble around and over room-size boulders, slip down mossy ledges, and pause frequently to decide the best way to continue. The tops of boulders provide views of pools, waterfalls, and the face of the canyon rising more than 400 ft/122 m. These cascading waters join the Aibonito and Barranquitas rivers and all merge with the Río de la Plata on their journey to the Atlantic Ocean.

TORO NEGRO FOREST RESERVE

Farther along the Panoramic Route, the 7,000-acre/2,833-hectare Toro Negro Forest Reserve straddles the highest peaks of the Cordillera Central in the center of the island, protecting the lush forests and headwaters of several main rivers. The climate is cool and damp from the frequent rain clouds that shroud these peaks. Puerto Rico's lowest temperature—40°F/ 4.4°C—was recorded here at Lake Guineo, the island's highest lake. It is located off the road, hidden from view, just beyond Divisoria where Road 143 meets Road 149 and divides the Toro Negro forest into its eastern and western sections. Road 143 is a winding, scenic cross-island route through mountain slopes dominated by sierra palm.

A short, paved, but very steep unmarked road of several hundred yards

Tree ferns and sierra palm trees grow in the Toro Negro Forest Reserve on the high rugged peaks of central Puerto Rico.

on the north side of Road 143 leads up the south side of Cerro de Punta, 4,390 ft/1,338 m, the highest peak in Puerto Rico. The ascent on foot takes about twenty minutes. From here on a clear day one can see much of the island's interior as well as the Atlantic and Caribbean coasts. Cerro de Punta can also be approached from its northern flank from Parador Hacienda Gripiñas off Road 527 in the town of Jayuya. From the parador a network of routes—paved and unpaved roads, jeep tracks, and eroded paths—ascends through the hillsides of former coffee plantations to the peak. Hiking time is about three hours one way. Other peaks in the Toro Negro Reserve offer hiking, too. Inquire locally.

INABÓN RIVER

The tributaries of several rivers begin in the Toro Negro mountains and take rugged routes down the mountainsides en route to the sea. The most spectacular headwaters are those of the Inabón River, which drop quickly 1,500 ft/457 m from the peaks in about fifteen cascades ranging in height from 16 to 60 ft/5 to 18 m. At lower elevations virgin forests merge with secondary forest, which has taken over lands that were once coffee plantations. River shrimp grow in the Inabón pools, and blossoms of mountain immortelle add dabs of pale orange color to the intense green of the forests through which the river flows. The lower river valley is most accessible from Road 511 north of Ponce where the road borders parts of the riverbed.

Caguana Indian Ceremonial Park

West of Toro Negro Forest Reserve is the typical mountain town of Adjuntas, which prides itself on being the world's largest exporter of citron, a knobby, lemon-like fruit whose rind is candied for use in fruitcakes and other sweets. North of Adjuntas (off Road 111) another mountain town, Utuado, is the home of the Caguana Indian Ceremonial Park where 800 years ago Tainos held ceremonial dances and soccer-like ballgames on its courts. The tree-shaded site, set in a ring of mountains next to the Tanamá River, is framed by large stone monoliths inscribed with petroglyphs. Another important Taino site, Tibes Indian Ceremonial Park, is located a few miles north of Ponce.

The final stretch of the Panoramic Route, from Adjuntas to Mayagüez, passes through the heart of coffee country. In the late nineteenth century coffee was the island's main crop, winning many honors in European coffee circles. Hurricanes and changing world markets led to the crop's decline, but today a variety of coffee that does not require shade is making a modest comeback. Once again, its deep green leaves, red beans, and white fragrant blossoms decorate the hillsides as do secondary forests rich with bananas and citrus trees. This region remains one of the most remote on the island.

On a cliffside near Maricao, farmers grow bananas and other crops to sell at local markets. Nearby, the Maricao Forest Reserve protects Puerto Rico's native vegetation; it has more species than any of the island's other forests.

Mt. Guilarte

As the route crosses the dam of a lovely reservoir lake (that seems made for a canoe or rowboat, though neither is available), Mt. Guilarte looms in the distance. The mountain is the highlight of 3,600-acre/1,457-hectare Guilarte Forest Reserve; the most scenic trail along the Panoramic Route leads to its peak, passing through rain forest highlighted by sierra palms and pink impatiens. The panorama from the top is free from the media towers that mar the view from El Yunque and Cerro de Punta. The path, found near the ranger station at the intersection of Roads 131 and 518, is steep and slick in places, but it is short (about forty minutes, one way). The start of the trail is unmarked; one must ask locally to find it.

Maricao Forest Reserve

Beyond several rural communities and the coffee town of Maricao is the Maricao Forest Reserve. Both the Maricao and Guilarte forests are appreciated most for what they do *not* have. Trails lead into seldom frequented expanses of forest. A sign pointing to Casa de Piedra, a rustic, stone mountain house, also leads to a campsite from where there is a good view of the west coast. On a clear day from a stone observation tower near the forest's highest peak, Las Tetas de Cerro Gordo (2,625 ft/800 m), there is a spectacular view of three coasts and Mona Island 50 mi/80 km away.

The region is known for its serpentine soil derived from the bluish green rock of submarine volcanic origin, which produces dry but diverse vegetation. Of the 278 tree species found in Maricao—the highest number in any of Puerto Rico's reserves—37 tree species are found only here and 123 species are found only in Puerto Rico. The area receives a large amount of rainfall, but due to the winds and the nature of the soil, a great deal of the forest resembles karst vegetation rather than rain forest as might be expected.

The Maricao forest is home to forty-four species of birds, including a large number of native species. Among them are the Puerto Rican woodpecker, Puerto Rican lizard-cuckoo, Puerto Rican vireo, Puerto Rican tanager, scaly-naped pigeon, Puerto Rican tody, the sharp-shinned hawk, which breeds here, and the rare elfin woods warbler. Others that might be spotted here and in the coffee country en route are the green mango hummingbird, Lesser Antillean pewee, and the Antillean euphonia.

A little-used trail in the Maricao.forest links the forest's main ridge with the fish hatchery, which is several miles and more than 1,000 ft/300 m down the mountain. It leads from lower montane wet forest with less dense undergrowth into subtropical wet forest dominated by tabonuco, mahogany, and laurel trees. When the trail reaches the Río Maricao valley it follows the river's course through jungle-like vegetation. There is no sign to indicate it, but the trail begins at km 14.8 on Road 120 and takes approximately seven hours to hike. Frequently along the way, the trail disappears and hikers must bushwhack their way, with compass and topographical map in hand, or with a local person showing the way; it is best to find the river and follow it. The fish hatchery, situated between the forest and the town, breeds tilapia, black bass, and the other fish that stock the island's freshwater lakes and ponds.

TROPICAL AGRICULTURAL RESEARCH STATION

At Mayagüez (about halfway along the scenic west coast) is the Tropical Agricultural Research Station, similar to the one in San Juan. One can take a self-guided tour through gardens of local and imported tropical trees, plants, and shrubs.

KARST COUNTRY

Some of the finest examples of tropical karst in the world can be seen in the region along Puerto Rico's north coast northeast of Mayagüez in the northern foothills between Manatí and Quebradillas. The terrain is characterized by haystack hills and crater-like sinkholes as well as extensive cave networks. One sinkhole cradles the 20 acre-/8 hectare-dish of the world's largest radio/radar telescope, at the Arecibo Observatory. South of the town of Florida, Road 140 passes through some especially eerie karst landscapes, full of cliffs and cone-shaped hills, which one can see easily from one's car. Two forest reserves—Guajataca and Río Abajo—lie in the heart of the karst country; all can be reached via secondary roads from Road 2.

Guajataca Forest Reserve (bisected by Road 446) in the northwest is the more remote and provides a good glimpse of the most rugged karst terrain. The reserve has some 25 mi/40 km of easy-to-follow and usually marked trails meandering through and around a large depression surrounded by haystack hills. From the ranger station (where sometimes maps of the reserve are available) a short trail leads to other trails and a lookout tower. There are inviting picnic areas tucked in next to the narrow road. Of the more than dozen man-made reservoirs that dot the reserve, 3-m-/4.8-km-long Lake Guajataca is the most accessible for boating and fishing, particularly for bass. But anglers must bring their own equipment, including the boats.

Pages 126 and 127: Lake Guajataca, a manmade reservoir in northwest Puerto Rico, is in karst country, an eerie landscape of sinkholes, cliffs, and caves.

South of Arecibo and the Arecibo River valley, the Río Abajo Forest Reserves near Utuado (Road 621, off Road 10) can be explored by a series of old lumber roads and paths. From the end of the main road, these paths lead into some of the island's most disorienting karst terrain, cloaked in dusty vegetation. The area has acres of native trees including balsa, teak, and West Indian mahogany as well as introduced species such as bamboo and blue Australian pines; this was the last natural habitat of the Puerto Rican parrot. Nearby, public launches travel along the fingery branches of Lake Dos Bocas, a reservoir that borders Road 10 and is adjacent to the Río Abajo Forest. Though primarily operated as transportation for residents who live along the lake's edge, the launches can be used by anyone.

Río Camuy Cave Park

Puerto Rico has one of the most extensive cave systems in the Western Hemisphere, the result of the region's geological formation millions of years ago when the platform-shaped island began to poke slightly out of the sea. As the island continued to rise, a mix of sediments and marine deposits such as coral surfaced above the ocean, concentrating along the north coast and becoming limestone. Eventually, plants appeared and gave off carbon dioxide that mixed with water to form carbonic acid. The limestone, which is chalky and porous, was dissolved by the carbonic acid as it seeped underground, resulting in networks of tunnels. Later, dripping water left minerals which, after eons, became the stalactites and stalagmites that give many caves their haunting beauty. As the caves grew, so too did the rivers running through them.

Erosion on the surface and collapse of some of the cave ceilings produced the valleys, sinkholes, and haystack hills we associate with karst terrain. Today, dozens of caves riddle the karst underground; some are single caverns, others form complex systems. Only 220 caves have been documented, but of them all, the Camuy caves are the largest, grandest, and best-known. At least 7 mi/11 km of passageways have been explored, including a room as high as a twenty-story building. The 9-mi/14.4-km Camuy River meanders—rages during floods—through these passageways. Some studies have indicated that it is the third largest underground river in the world, surpassed only by subterranean rivers in Yugoslavia and Papua New Guinea.

The Río Camuy Cave Park (Road 129 near Lares), covering a surface of 268 acres/108 hectares, was opened in 1986 as the first major showcase of Puerto Rico's outstanding caves and tropical karst country. A bilingual tram tour takes visitors through karst forest and into a rain-forested basin where there is profuse vegetation—graceful ferns, tall mahogany trees, delicate pink impatiens, and tupa, a sumac-like poisonous plant.

A species of fish—totally blind—was discovered in a subterranean pool and named *Alaweckelia gurneei* in honor of speleologists Russell and Jeanne Gurnee who first explored the Camuy caves in 1958 and brought them to worldwide attention. Open Wednesday to Sunday, the park is much less crowded on weekdays. (*Note:* Visitors should not mistake a sign to "La Cueva de Camuy" in the town of Camuy as being the government park. It is a small, privately owned cave fifteen minutes from the park.)

CABO ROJO

South of Mayagüez, the Cabo Rojo peninsula offers rugged views from an old lighthouse, where 200-ft/60-m limestone cliffs are the backdrop on the seaward side, while the landward view takes in a mosaic of bays and beaches, lagoons and glistening salt pools. The dry lowland of the Lajas Valley lies to the east and the Cordillera Central rises in the distance on the north. Two lighthouse keepers and their families once lived in the neoclassical base of the lighthouse but the light is now automated and the doors and windows of the house are cemented shut. Ponce de León gathered salt from this spot when he came to settle the island in 1508; the flats are now a favored haunt of the snowy plover.

CARTAGENA LAGOON

Bird watchers should be sure to visit Cartagena Lagoon in the southwest corner, which, with Tortuguero Lagoon in the north, is one of two freshwater lagoons on the island. Almost entirely overgrown with grasses, and more of a swamp than a lagoon, Cartagena remains the best place on the island to view water birds. Its duck population includes fulvous whistling-ducks, West Indian whistling-ducks, white-cheeked pintails, ring-necked ducks, and the ruddy duck, which is common. Also common are the northern mockingbird, cave swallow, common ground-dove, and herons including the black-crowned night-heron. The sora, a marsh bird that is uncommon in the Caribbean outside Puerto Rico, can be spotted, as can the American purple gallinule, which is rarely seen elsewhere on the island.

LA PARGUERA PHOSPHORESCENT BAY

South of San Germán, the island's second oldest town, and west of Guánica near La Parguera is one of Puerto Rico's bioluminescent bays. The luminescence is caused by microorganisms in the water that light up like shooting stars with any movement. This fragile phenomenon occurs on this scale in few places in the world—a handful of shallow tropical bays surrounded by mangroves. Phosphorescent Bay is the most famous example of this phenomenon, although many consider Esperanza in Vieques to be more spectacular.

GUÁNICA RESERVE

West of Ponce lies the most interesting of the coastal mangrove forests in the Commonwealth Forest Reserve system. The Guánica Reserve, comprising the coastal areas and nearby low-lying hills, is a mecca for bird watchers; half of all Puerto Rico's terrestrial bird species as well as a number of migratory birds can be seen in Guánica's dry forest. Birders take to its dirt roads early in the morning, looking for such native species as the Puerto Rican emerald hummingbird, the most common small hummingbird on the island, Puerto Rican tody, Puerto Rican bullfinch, and Puerto Rican nightjar, a native bird that was thought to be extinct and now has a population of more than 900. This reserve is the nightjar's most popular habitat, as it is of the troupial, a South American species now established here. Birders might also spot Adelaide's warbler or the orange-cheeked waxbill, a native of West Africa introduced to Puerto Rico, and common species of the Lesser Antilles such as the Caribbean elaenia.

Guánica has been named a World Biosphere Reserve by UNESCO (along with the Carribbean National Forest). In addition to birds, the reserve protects over 700 tree and plant species, including a large number of lignum vitae, or wood of life, so named because of the tree's many uses. Its leaves remain green even in times of drought, making it stand out against the thorny beige and olive vegetation. Road 334 northeast of the town of Guánica leads into the heart of the forest, site of a ranger station and primitive picnic area. It is the hub of several dirt roads that are closed to vehicles and provide some of the best early-morning bird-watching. Road 333 skirts the southern coastal edge of the forest. A trail connects it with the ranger station; ask locally for its location.

CAJA DE MUERTOS

Ponce is Puerto Rico's second largest city, located on the southern, or Caribbean, coast. A ferry at the Ponce pier takes passengers on weekends on an hour's boat ride to Caja de Muertos, a 1-mi-/1.6-km-long island that has the only regular guided nature walks on Puerto Rico's offshore islands. The one large hill there is covered with scrub forest, and a narrow isthmus, bordered by back-to-back beaches, connects it to a smaller hill overlooking a pancake-flat cay. Guides point out aloe, century plants, and other species of arid island vegetation. The terrain is rocky and harsh and the isthmus has few shade trees; sturdy shoes and protection from the sun are essential for walking. The coral reefs surrounding the isthmus are intact and crowded with fish. An underwater trail here is being planned.

The northern jacana's long toes help it walk across floating leaves.

CULEBRA AND VIEQUES

Located off the east coast between Puerto Rico and the U.S. Virgin Islands, Culebra and Vieques are members of a vanishing breed—tranquil islands rich in natural resources but not yet overly developed for tourism. Their dry landscapes are more typical of low-lying islands like Antigua than of Puerto Rico. Bone-white beaches, often deserted, scallop their shores, and two of them—Flamenco on Culebra and Sun Bay on Vieques—rank among the most beautiful in Puerto Rico.

The 5-mi-/8-km-long island of Culebra is actually a miniature archipelago of one main island and some twenty surrounding cays. The Culebra National Wildlife Refuge encompasses most of the cays and a small section of Culebra proper. Offering excellent year-round birding, the sanctuary protects approximately eighty-six bird species, including marine birds such as tropicbirds, boobies, and gulls, that stop here to nest. Most common of the marine birds is a black-backed, white-bellied sooty tern; thousands of them can be seen hovering over the grasses and thickets during nesting season in late spring. One may also see the Sandwich tern, bridled quail-dove, and Puerto Rican screech-owl among many other birds.

The refuge protects nesting sites for four endangered sea turtles—hawksbill, green, loggerhead, and leatherback. It is one of only two nesting locations in the U.S. for the leatherback, one of the largest marine reptiles alive today. Earthwatch, a nonprofit organization that recruits volunteers for scientific expeditions, sends teams from April through July to patrol the nocturnal egg-laying along Brava and Resaca beaches.

Water-sports centers, primarily part-time, family-run businesses, charter boats to take passengers around these cays (two of them, Culebrita and Luis Peña, can be visited during a day's outing) and to outstanding coral reefs that fringe Culebrita, Luis Peña, and beaches on Culebra proper. Camping is permitted. Windsurfing and limited deep-sea fishing can also be arranged from Dewey, the island's sole community.

Vieques is bigger and a bit more cosmopolitan than Culebra, but only a bit. Isabel Segunda, the port town, has the last fort built by the Spaniards in the New World and archaeologists are currently studying remains from Indian settlements that date back to 200 B.C. Today, the U.S. Navy owns two-thirds of Vieques; much of that land is used for cattle grazing and a small part is reserved for military maneuvers. When there are no maneuvers, one can enter the Navy land, site of some of the most unspoiled beaches in Puerto Rico. Sun Bay (also written Sombe) lies near the village of Esperanza; it is a *balneario*, and camping is permitted.

From Esperanza, boats make nightly visits to the nearby bioluminescent bay, more spectacular than the better-known Phosphorescent Bay near La Parguera.

MONA ISLAND

Puerto Rico's most intriguing place for adventure lies 50 mi/80 km off the coast at Mayagüez. Mona Island is a 7-mi-/11.2-km-long, heart-shaped island located halfway between Puerto Rico and the Dominican Republic in the notoriously rough Mona Passage. Its history is the stuff of romance: Taino Indians using it as a stopover in their trans-Caribbean canoe journeys, pirates hiding themselves and their booty in the many limestone caves, guano miners working in sauna-like conditions, women living in caves, farmers dying of poisoned liquor. Vestiges of some of the history remain, from rocks marking Taino ball courts to narrow-gauge railroad tracks once used to haul guano (bat manure, used as fertilizer) out of the caves.

Today the island is a nature refuge; Mona enthusiasts consider it a miniature Galápagos. A tabletop mesa covers most of the island, and is in turn covered with barely penetrable, cacti-studded shrub forest topped by a lone lighthouse. Limestone cliffs 200 ft/60 m high on the north coast plunge down to the ocean in some places and to beaches in others. Labyrinthine caves riddle the cliffs. Huge iguanas plod across the island, and the endangered hawksbill turtle nests on its beaches. The north side is the nesting place of the red-footed booby. Colonies of white-tailed tropicbirds, magnificent frigatebirds, and other seabirds nest here and on the Isla de Monito nearby. The pearly-eyed thrasher is the most common land bird; and Puerto Rico's endemic yellow-shouldered blackbird is found here, too. The pristine coral reefs offshore are considered the best in Puerto Rican waters, with visibility up to 150 ft/45 m.

No permanent residents inhabit the island; visitors camp on Sardinera and Pájaros beaches in the west and east, respectively, but must bring all supplies, including water. A couple of indistinct but marked trails penetrate the mesa, and a road—Camino del Infierno meaning "hell road"—connects the beaches. Cueva Liria, once mined for guano, is just east of the lighthouse and still has tram tracks and rusted carcasses of equipment used in the century of mining that ended in 1927.

Private boats or planes, usually chartered from Mayagüez, are the only means of getting to Mona. The trip from Mayagüez by boat takes six hours to Playa Sardinera. Permission is needed from the Department of Natural Resources, which maintains the island.

OUTDOOR ACTIVITIES

HIKING: Puerto Rico has some of the best and most convenient hiking in the Caribbean. In addition to El Yunque's trails are the 14 Commonwealth Forest Reserves (Natural Resources Department, Box 5887, San Juan 00906; 809-722-1726), which have trails ranging from those for birding in the Guánica mangroves to those for high mountain trekking in the Cordillera Central.

CAVING: Warm subterranean temperatures and miles of explored and unexplored passageways and caverns make Puerto Rico a caver's paradise, but caving here is for the experienced, not the learner. Spelunkers swim and climb and rappel and even scuba dive their way through the blackness. Rivers like the Camuy and Encantado run their most spectacular stretches underground. The active Puerto Rican Speleological Society (Box 31074, 65th Infantry Station, Rio Pedras, PR 00929) requires extensive training before its members enter caves—a wise precaution, for spelunkers travel through passages that can fill up during a flash flood and openings that demand long free-fall descents.

HORSEBACK RIDING: Farmers in the mountains still ride horses along rural roads, but horseback riding for visitors is limited. Hacienda Carabalí east of San Juan near Luquillo offers group riding along the coast and in the foothills of El Yunque; and the stables at Palmas del Mar, a resort community near Humacao, has rides along beach trails and into nearby hills. In other areas, arrangements can be made more casually with local horse owners. The paso fino is a small horse bred by Spanish settlers from Arabian and other stocks to produce a horse with a smooth gait for traveling over the rough countryside. Guayama holds the world-renowned annual Paso Fino horse show in March.

SWIMMING: The hundreds of miles of coastline mean beaches of all shapes and sizes. Those along the north coast get the Atlantic's large waves and strong currents, especially in winter; promontories break the surf in many places. The coasts facing the Caribbean have calmer waters. The most popular beaches, particularly for families, are the *balnearios* run by the Department of Sports and Recreation. Open daily except Monday, they provide showers and changing facilities, lifeguards and protected waters, snackbars and parking areas. Some *balnearios* have cabins and campsites for rent. Three lie in the San Juan area; the other ten are scattered around the island. Most detailed maps mark the *balnearios*. Luxury resorts in San Juan and elsewhere are situated on beaches, and normally accommodate day visitors. Most other beaches around the island are undeveloped and unguarded, semideserted during the week and popular with local residents on weekends. The highest concentration of pretty, tranquil beaches lies on the west coast, where one can swim all day, then watch the sunset from a local seafood restaurant.

Puerto Rican lizard-cuckoo.

SNORKELING AND DIVING: The finest snorkeling is found at Fajardo, at the offshore islands of Vieques and Culebra, and along the drier stretches of Puerto Rico's south coast where fewer rivers empty their muddy waters into the sea. A series of complex ribbon coral reefs extends for a couple of miles out from La Parguera in the southwest, where tropical fish brighten the turquoise water and numerous mangrove cays add an exotic touch. Boats can be rented at La Parguera dock, but one must bring snorkeling or diving equipment. A lagoon coral reef with an unusually high number of fish species edges Caja de Muertos off Ponce.

Charter boats make daily trips along the northeast peninsula and to tiny coral-fringed islands like Icacos and Palominitos. Trips can be arranged in Fajardo or San Juan at water-sports centers in resort hotels; most rent diving equipment to certified divers. The centers also offer diving courses to obtain certification, and many of these courses conduct their final classes in Fajardo.

Red-footed booby.

The Mona iguana, a subspecies of the rhino iguana.

The north coast has one good snorkeling and diving spot near Isabela, off a beach called the Shacks. A ring of sanddune rocks topped with coral, dotted with caves, and visited by fish makes for intriguing exploration, particularly in summer when the ocean is calmer. A dive shop in Isabela rents equipment.

Most experts agree that the best coral in Puerto Rican waters lies off Mona Island. The pristine reefs are visited by a great variety of fish, turtles, and even whales that pass through the Mona Passage during their winter migration. The island is difficult to reach, which accounts, in part, for the reefs' pristine state. To reach the dive sites, one must charter a boat or plane in Mayagüez and take all necessary equipment.

DEEP-SEA FISHING: In less than an hour from San Juan Bay, there is excellent fishing in deep-sea waters. Such large fish as blue and white marlin, sailfish, and tuna follow the currents as they flow past Puerto Rico. Prestigious tournaments held here have resulted in more than thirty world records. Tarpon and bonefish abound in the shallower waters around the bay. Charter boats at Club Náutico in San Juan provide half-day and full-day fishing trips with all equipment included. Puerto Real in Mayagüez offers deep-sea fishing in the Mona Passage.

BOATING: The island's undisputed boating capital is Fajardo on the northeast coast. Thousands of boats, from native sloops to luxury yachts, moor in its marinas and bays. Some can be rented privately or as part of a group to explore the coral-bordered cays and tiny islands that lie offshore. Water-sports centers in major San Juan hotels can make arrangements for boating in Fajardo. Several other marinas around the island, most notably those at Palmas del Mar near Humacao on the east coast and Puerto Real in Mayagüez on the west coast, have boats for rent or charter. At La Parguera on the southwest coast, small motorboats can be rented to explore the numerous mangrove-topped cays offshore. San Juan has marinas, mainly catering to deep-sea fishing.

SURFING: On the west coast north of a palm-fringed *balneario* at Añasco is the picturesque town of Rincón at the western corner (*rincón*) of the island. Here mango-shaded Maria's Beach marks the start of outstanding surfing (and windsurfing) that continues up the coast to Aguadilla and around the corner east to Jobos Beach in Isabela. Twice in the last two decades, the World Surfing Championships were held here, attesting to the area's outstanding surfing conditions. Rough water and submerged rocks make this an area for experienced surfers. In winter, 10-ft/3-m waves are common. On any given day surfers walk, hitchhike, or drive through palm groves to the spot where the waves are best. Local surf shops provide some equipment, but surfers should bring their own boards. Farther east on the north coast, another good surfing spot is Los Tubos by Tortuguero Lagoon in Vega Baja. The San Juan vicinity has three sites: Pine Grove (for gentle surfing) in Isla Verde, Aviónes in Piñones, and Luquillo, east of the *balneario*.

WINDSURFING: A relatively new sport on the island, windsurfing has become immensely popular, and on weekends dozens of colorful sails skim the calm waters of Condado Lagoon and the rougher waters of the sea from Condado to Isla Verde, all in the metropolitan area. San Juan has hosted an international windsurfing contest, capitalizing on its excellent windsurfing conditions. Water-sports centers at major hotels rent equipment, and most provide instruction if desired. Dozens of beaches around the island make excellent places to windsurf; among the most popular are the Shacks (Isabela), Crash Boat (Aguadilla), Añasco, and Boquerón.

EXPLORING THE ISLAND

The best way to explore Puerto Rico is on one's own, preferably by car. Those with plenty of time (a knowledge of Spanish helps, too) can use public transportation for part of the travel. San Juan in the north and Ponce in the south make good bases from which to make excursions into the countryside.

San Juan has city bus service as well as bus service to Mayagüez. A list of bus numbers and routes can be found in the monthly guide, *Qué Pasa*. The island also has a system of *públicos*, minibuses whose routes include airports and points in and between major towns. Inquire locally. Taxis operate on meters and are comparable in price to those in stateside cities. They can be hired by the hour or half-day, but *settle the price in advance*. All major U.S. car rental firms are represented in San Juan and many are in the other major cities as well. Ferries leave frequently in San Juan, Ponce, and Fajardo to nearby places of interest.

Puerto Rico has some of the best roads in the Caribbean; almost any place can be reached within three hours from San Juan. Many but not all places of interest are indicated by road signs. Drivers should remain alert, not only for potholes (roads weather rapidly in this climate), but for other drivers who do not subscribe to the rules-of-the-road school of driving.

There are any number of ways to explore Puerto Rico—one area at a time from San Juan, or by circling its coastal regions and traversing its central highland along the Panoramic Route. A complete circle along Roads 1, 2, and 3 covers approximately 270 mi/432 km and could conceivably be completed in a day. However, these are main arteries with heavy traffic and in many places buildings take precedence over scenic views. To enjoy the natural attractions along the circuit, one should allow at least three days and get off the main highways as much as possible. Dozens of beaches lie just off the smaller roads. They range from the public, government-run *balnearios* to semideserted beaches shaded by the palm trees of abandoned coconut plantations. Be sure to lock your car and don't leave valuables unattended.

Drivers should carry a detailed road map, available at drugstores and some gas stations, and a copy of *Qué Pasa*. Gas stations and *colmados* (small grocery stores) can be found virtually everywhere on the island; in the countryside, plan to pay by cash.

The overwhelming majority of tourist accommodations are in the San Juan area, but there are also good hotels in main cities such as Ponce and Mayagüez. Or, plan to stay in one of the Paradores Puertorriqueños (800-443-0266; 809-721-2884), which are a network of country inns around the island sponsored by the government tourism company. They are modest, clean, and respectable hotels— and not to be confused with local "motels" that cater to extramarital affairs. Paradores are set attractively in such places as a former mountain coffee plantation, a converted sugar mill, next to thermal waters used by the Taino Indians, or at the foot of the rain forest. A list of paradores appears in *Qué Pasa*.

To visit Culebra and Vieques, small planes operate scheduled flights from the Isla Verde and Isla Grande airports in San Juan and the airport in Fajardo, and ferries link the islands with Fajardo on the east coast. Simple accommodations are available as are restaurants specializing in seafood and local dishes.

INFORMATION: In the U.S.: Puerto Rico Tourism Company, 575 Fifth Ave., 23rd fl., New York, NY 10017; 212-599-6262 and 800-223-6530. Also, there are offices in Miami and Los Angeles. In Canada: 2 Bloor St. West, Suite 700, Toronto, Ontario M4W 3RI; 416-969-9025; 800-223-6530. There is no European office. In Puerto Rico: Puerto Rico Tourism Company, La Princesa Building, Paseo de la Princesa, Old San Juan, PR 00902; 809-721-2400; it opens at 8:30 A.M. from Monday to Friday. Other offices are at the airport and Ponce.

Qué Pasa, the Puerto Rico Tourism Company's free guide, is an invaluable resource. For detailed information about specific towns, contact the town hall *(alcaldía)* in each town; it is usually located off the public plaza in the center of town. The magazine *Puerto Rican Living* focuses on sports. *The Other Puerto Rico* by Kathryn Robinson (Santurce, PR: Permanent Press, 1984) details the flora, fauna, and natural attractions. Herbert A. Raffaele's *Guide to the Birds of Puerto Rico and the Virgin Islands* (San Juan: Fondo Educativo Interamericano, 1989) is useful for birders. Elbert L. Little Jr. and Frank Wadsworth, *Common Trees of Puerto Rico and the Virgin Islands*, Agriculture Handbook No. 249, three vols. (Washington, D.C.: U.S. Department of Agriculture, 1964 and 1974) is the most complete reference on flora available. The Natural History Society (GPO Box 1036, San Juan, PR 00936) is a bilingual organization offering monthly lectures and field trips. Fondo de Mejoramiento (Box 4746, Correo Central, San Juan, PR 00936; 809-759-8366) schedules biweekly visits to places around the island and occasionally organizes hikes. Tours are in Spanish, but there are always people ready to translate into English when necessary.

Topographical maps are available from the Department of Transportation, Minillas Building, Santurce, PR 00908; 809-721-8787.

UNITED STATES VIRGIN ISLANDS

BRITISH VIRGIN ISLANDS

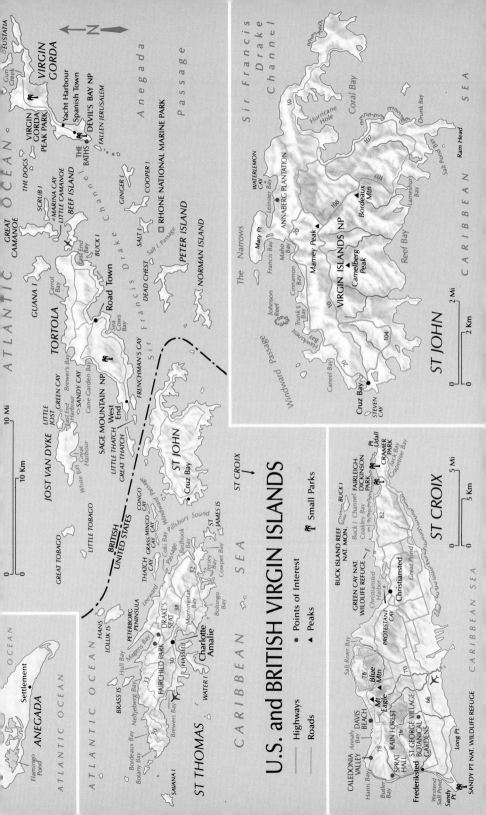

U.S. and BRITISH VIRGIN ISLANDS

- • Points of Interest
- ▲ Peaks
- Highways
- Roads
- ⚓ Small Parks

VIRGIN GORDA

- VIRGIN GORDA PEAK PARK
- Yacht Harbour
- Spanish Town
- DEVIL'S BAY NP
- THE BATHS
- FALLEN JERUSALEM
- THE DOGS
- MARINA CAY
- LITTLE CAMANOE
- BEEF ISLAND
- GREAT CAMANOE
- SCRUB I
- Gun Creek
- o EUSTATIA

TORTOLA

- Road Town
- Sea Cows Bay
- Brewer's Bay
- Cane Garden Bay
- SAGE MOUNTAIN NP
- West End
- FRENCHMAN'S CAY
- East End Bay
- BUCK I
- GUANA I
- Carrot Bay
- GREEN CAY
- SANDY CAY

Anegada Passage

- Anegada
- Sir Francis Drake Channel
- RHONE NATIONAL MARINE PARK
- COOPER I
- GINGER I
- SALT I
- Salt I. Passage
- DEAD CHEST
- PETER ISLAND
- NORMAN ISLAND
- Drake Channel

JOST VAN DYKE

- LITTLE JOST
- East End Harbour
- Great Harbour
- White Bay
- LITTLE TOBAGO
- GREAT TOBAGO

ATLANTIC OCEAN

ST JOHN

- Cruz Bay
- LITTLE THATCH
- GREAT THATCH
- CONGO CAY
- MINGO CAY
- GRASS CAY
- THATCH CAY
- Pillsbury Sound
- Windward Passage

BRITISH / UNITED STATES

ST THOMAS

- Charlotte Amalie
- FAIRCHILD PARK
- Drake's Seat
- PETERBORG PENINSULA
- Magens Bay
- Hull Bay
- Neltjeberg Bay
- Bordeaux Bay
- Botany Bay
- Brewers Bay
- Morningstar Bay
- Jersey Bay
- Bolongo Bay
- Cowpet Bay
- Red Hook
- WATER I
- HASSEL I
- BRASS IS
- SAVANA I
- SABA I
- LOLLIK IS
- HANS LOLLIK IS
- ST JAMES IS
- 30
- 32
- 33
- 35
- 38

CARIBBEAN SEA

ANEGADA

- Settlement
- Flamingo Pond
- ATLANTIC OCEAN

ST CROIX

- Christiansted
- Frederiksted
- BUCK ISLAND REEF NAT. MON.
- GREEN CAY NAT WILDLIFE REFUGE
- FAIRLEIGH-DICKINSON PARK
- CRAMER PARK
- Pt Udall
- BUCK I
- Buck I. Channel
- Coakley Bay
- Christiansted Harbor
- Great Pond
- Robin Bay
- Grapetree Bay
- PROTESTANT CAY
- Salt River Bay
- CALEDONIA VALLEY
- Annaly Bay
- DAVIS BEACH
- Mt Eagle ▲
- Blue Mtn ▲
- RAIN FOREST
- ST GEORGE VILLAGE BOTANICAL GARDENS
- SPRAT HALL
- Hams Bay
- Butler Bay
- Westend Salt Pond
- Sandy Pt
- SANDY PT NAT. WILDLIFE REFUGE
- Long Pt
- 66
- 70
- 75
- 76
- 78
- 82

ST JOHN (inset)

- VIRGIN ISLANDS NP
- Mamey Peak ▲
- Camelberg Peak ▲
- Bordeaux Mtn ▲
- ANNABERG PLANTATION
- WATERLEMON CAY
- Leinster Bay
- Mary Pt
- The Narrows
- Maho Bay
- Francis Bay
- Cinnamon Bay
- Trunk Bay
- Johnson Reef
- Hawksnest Bay
- Caneel Bay
- Cruz Bay
- STEVEN CAY
- Hurricane Hole
- Coral Bay
- Drunk Bay
- Ram Head
- Salt Pond Bay
- Lameshur Bay
- Reef Bay
- Sir Francis Drake Channel
- CARIBBEAN SEA
- Windward Passage
- 10
- 20
- 104
- 107
- 108

Scale bars

- 10 Mi
- 10 Km
- 5 Mi
- 5 Km
- 2 Mi
- 2 Km

UNITED STATES VIRGIN ISLANDS

STEEP MOUNTAINS AND ROLLING HILLS carpeted in green rise out of a sapphire sea. The hillsides are colored by a rainbow of flowers with such names as catch-and-keep, jump-up-and-kiss-me, and clashie-melashi, and easy breezes carrying a hint of jasmine and frangipani cool the air. License plates proclaim the islands to be the "American Paradise," and those who come here find it easy to agree.

The U.S. Virgin Islands are situated in the northeastern corner of the Caribbean astride the Anegada Passage, a strategic gateway between the Atlantic Ocean and the Caribbean Sea where the Greater Antilles end and the Lesser Antilles begin. They are an archipelago of about fifty islands and cays and comprise a U.S. territory. Like their British neighbors, the islands are volcanic in origin. Only the three largest are populated: St. Croix, the largest, lies entirely in the Caribbean; 35 mi/56 km north of St. Croix is St. Thomas, the most populated and developed, touching both the Atlantic Ocean and the Caribbean Sea; St. John, 3.5 mi/5.6 km east of St. Thomas, is the smallest and is mostly reserved as a national park. All three islands are ringed by porcelain-white beaches, magnificent coral reefs, and spectacular seas; otherwise, no three islands in the Caribbean are more different from one another than this American trio.

The steady breezes that keep temperatures between 75° and 85°F/23° and 29°C year-round are the trade winds responsible for much of the Virgin Islands' early history. The winds powered the ships of European explorers and traders on one of the major sailing routes between the Old and New Worlds. The islands' jagged coastlines have good harbors that made them havens for pirates and privateers.

Columbus first sighted the Virgin Islands in 1493, on his second voyage. He arrived at an island known to the Caribs as *Ay Ay*; he named it Santa Cruz, or Holy Cross, and history has called it by its French name, St. Croix. The English, Dutch, and French made futile attempts to colonize the islands; finally, in 1672, the Danes succeeded in establishing a colony on St. Thomas. They added St. John in 1718, but St. Croix, coveted for its agricultural potential and fought over by five other nations, eluded the Danes until 1733. The islands were prosperous for Denmark until slavery was abolished in 1848 and the sugar-based economy declined. With the advent of World War I, the islands took on strategic importance that led the U.S. government to purchase them from Denmark in 1917.

Idyllic as the islands are, they are not immune from today's problems. Like lonely city streets in urban areas, secluded beaches and isolated roads are places of easy prey. Visitors should seek local advice before heading off to isolated areas not described here.

ST. CROIX

Rising abruptly from the sea to forested hills on the northwest, St. Croix rolls south and east over low-lying hills to plains that were once intensively cultivated, leveling out in the south in mangroves, salt ponds, and terrain covered with thorny scrub and cactus. Within its 85 sq mi/220 sq km are natural attractions unmatched on its mountainous sisters and often unnoticed by visitors. They include wildlife refuges for birds and leatherback turtles, botanic gardens, a rain forest, three nature preserves, and three parks—one under the sea.

Frederiksted, overlooking a deepwater harbor on the west end, is one of the island's two landmark towns. The Visitors Bureau by the town pier has a map for a self-guided walk. The 0.25-mi/0.4-km pier is often labeled the most interesting pier dive in the Caribbean. Its pilings have become an underwater forest at about 35-ft/11-m depth with sponges, plume worms, and great numbers of tiny yellow, orange, and red sea horses.

St. Croix was hit hard by Hurricane Hugo in September 1989. Check carefully with the USVI tourist information office when planning a trip to St. Croix.

THE RAIN FOREST

North of Frederiksted, the hilly northwest corner is covered with dense woods, quite different from the rest of the island. Although commonly called the Rain Forest, the area does not actually receive enough rain to be classified as one. The most accessible road traversing the woods is *Mahogany Road* (Routes 76/763/765), which takes its name from the stands of huge mahogany trees through which it passes. There are also enormous silk-cotton, or kapok, trees; gumbo limbo, or red birch, also known as turpentine tree; samaan, or rain tree; and, along the guts or gullies, swamp fern and strap fern. Where the road crosses former estates, breadfruit, sweet lime, mammee apple, mango, hog plum, and other tropical fruit trees are common.

Farther north, *Creque Dam Road* (58/78) and *Western Scenic Road* (63/78) in the west and *Scenic Road* (78) in the east traverse the most remote areas in the forest. These roads are narrow, winding, often unpaved, and most easily traveled by jeep; the westernmost segments are

also well suited for hiking, birding, and horseback riding because traffic is light. Footpaths—seldom marked on maps—veer off to dry beds and guts that become pools, streams, and waterfalls after a heavy rain.

Creque Dam Road. From the west coast, Route 58 cuts through the 200-year-old Sprat Hall Estate for about a mile to the Creque Dam and forest where the canopy reaches 100 ft/30 m or more. Kapok, mahogany, turpentine, and white cedar trees are wrapped in huge philodendrons and resplendent with epiphytes and bromeliads.

Western Scenic Road. At the junction of Creque Dam Road and Scenic Road, hikers can turn north, and then west, on Western Scenic Road to ascend the ridge overlooking the north coast and Hams Bluff, marked by a lighthouse, where large waves break against the shore. The south side of the ridge, the Caledonia Valley, is a popular birding location and the only ravine with a year-round stream. The rock-strewn riverbed, dense with trees entwined with vines and vanilla orchids, has pools and a waterfall after a heavy rain. Western Scenic Road ends (or begins) at Hams Bay on the northwest coast. One can return along the coast road (63) via Butler Bay, a private nature preserve of the St. Croix Landmarks Society, open to the public. It is a popular birding area with huge trees decked out with dangling vines and bromeliads. A track inland along a gut has abundant strap fern and, after a rain, a pretty waterfall.

Scenic Road (78). From the heart of the Rain Forest, the road winds east through hills beautifully wooded with pink and white cedars where there are very steep tracks (sometimes they are difficult to follow) used by local birding groups to reach Annaly Bay and other shoreside locations. Out of more than 200 species of resident and migrant bird species recorded in St. Croix, three dozen are nesting and seen most of the year. Those common throughout the island are the Zenaida dove, green-throated carib, Antillean crested hummingbird, gray kingbird, pearly-eyed thrasher, yellow warbler, bananaquit, and black-faced grassquit. Those found in the upland forests of Creque Dam, Scenic Road, Caledonia Valley, Butler Bay Nature Preserve, and Eagle Ridge are West Indian red-tailed hawk, scaly-naped pigeon, bridled quail-dove, mangrove cuckoo, Caribbean elaenia, black-whiskered vireo, and Lesser Antillean bullfinch.

Scenic Road continues east to Eagle Ridge; there are tracks to its summits—Blue Mountain (1,096 ft/334 m) and flat-topped Mount Eagle (1,165 ft/355 m), which are the island's highest points. Eagle Ridge can be approached more directly from the eastern end of Scenic Road between River Road (69) and Canaan Road (73).

Mingo Cay, Grass Cay, and Thatch Cay are three of the many unpopulated islets that stretch like forested green stepping-stones between St. Thomas and St. John.

SANDY POINT NATIONAL WILDLIFE REFUGE

South of Frederiksted along 3 mi/5 km of white sand beach is Westend Saltpond, one of the island's main birding locations, and Sandy Point, the southwestern end of the island where the Sandy Point National Wildlife Refuge protects one of only two nesting grounds of the leatherback turtle in United States waters (the other is Culebra, off Puerto Rico). Hawksbill and green turtles come here too. From March through June, the enormous leatherback females—up to 6 ft/1.8 m in length and 1,000 lb/453 kg in weight—come ashore to dig their holes in which each lays as many as eighty eggs. They cover the eggs with sand, then lumber back to the sea, returning to repeat the ritual as many as six times during nesting season. Approximately two months later, after sunset and before dawn, the hatchlings emerge from the hidden sandpits and dash to the sea. Earthwatch, a nonprofit organization that recruits volunteers for scientific expeditions, has a monitoring program here. Inquiries should be made to the St. Croix Environmental Association (809-773-1989).

Sandy Point is also a nesting area for least terns and a site for viewing white-tailed tropicbirds, brown pelicans, American oystercatchers, and Caribbean martins, which nest elsewhere on the islands. They can also be seen at Frederiksted Harbor and other locations along the north and south coasts. Westend Saltpond attracts a great variety of resident and migrant shorebirds and waders. Among the nesting species are herons, black-necked stilts, and white-crowned pigeons. A stretch of dry scrub between the south end of the pond and Sandy Point is a unique habitat for an orchid known as the Sandy Point orchid, a ground-dwelling species that grows throughout the Caribbean in a variety of colors and is known by various local names. Here, it is seen in shades of lavender and brown.

ST. GEORGE VILLAGE BOTANICAL GARDENS

East of Frederiksted on the north side of Centerline Road, the island's main east–west highway, is the 16-acre/6.5-hectare St. George Village Botanical Gardens. It is landscaped around the ruins of a workers' village on a Danish sugar plantation of the eighteenth and nineteenth centuries. Beneath the ruins, an Arawak settlement inhabited from A.D. 100 to 900 has been discovered. Privately supported and volunteer-managed, the gardens began in 1972 when the site, which had been an eyesore, was chosen as a clean-up project of the local garden club. Members soon realized it was more than a derelict site. Over the years Arawak artifacts had been found here by people cultivating the fields, but it was not until 1976, when the area was excavated by archaeologists, that its historic significance as the largest of ninety-six Indian villages on St. Croix was established.

Now brightened by poinsettias, hibiscus, bougainvillea, and other flowering bushes and trees, the gardens combine natural growth, landscaped plantings, and open land with signposted walkways and paths for self-guided tours. Some buildings have been restored; others are used as backgrounds for botanical collections. Approximately 500 species of trees and plants were found *in situ* and another 350 species have been added. One of the club's ambitious goals is to have samples of all of St. Croix's endangered endemic plants. Another project is to collect samples of the five dozen or so plants that the Spanish botanist Gonzalo Fernández de Oviedo listed in his *Natural History of the West Indies*, a report on New World flora presented to Queen Isabella in 1526. The present collection has two endemics: St. Croix agave and a touch-me-not. There are two large sago palms, which are not true palms, although they resemble them; they are cycads, a group that has grown on the earth since the dinosaur age. The cactus garden is outstanding. The gardens are open daily; the library is open on Thursday or by special request.

BUCK ISLAND REEF NATIONAL MONUMENT

Set against green hillsides, Christiansted, with its yacht-filled harbor and historic waterfront of pastel buildings, is one of the prettiest towns in the Caribbean. The Visitors Bureau has maps for self-guided walks. The town is the island's water-sports center, convenient to north-coast reefs, and also the departure point for Buck Island, 3.5 mi/5.6 km off the north coast. By the harbor, beautifully restored Fort Christian houses the U.S. National Park Service, which is responsible for Buck Island.

Buck Island is a volcanic islet of 300 acres/121 hectares surrounded by 550 acres/223 hectares of underwater coral gardens. It offers shallow-water snorkeling on the inner reef and deepwater diving on the outer barrier reef. The island is a rookery for brown pelicans; frigatebirds roost here too. A circular underwater trail of 750 ft/229 m on the easternmost tip has arrow markers to guide viewers along the inner reef; signs on the ocean floor at depths of 12 to 15 ft/3.6 to 4.5 m identify the different coral formations— staghorn, elkhorn, brain, and finger corals, sea fans, feather duster worms, and sea anemones. Marine biologists say that the elkhorn coral here are among the most massive specimens in the world. The trail takes about forty-five minutes to swim. Of the more than 300 fish identified on the reef, those most commonly seen are blue tang, sergeant major, rock beauty, yellowtail snapper, foureye butterflyfish, angelfishes, parrotfishes, and grunts. Hawksbill turtles are often seen in the seagrass on the south side.

Buck Island, named for the goats that once grazed away most of the original vegetation, has white sand beaches on the southwest and west

The west coast of St. Croix north of Frederiksted is popular with birders, particularly Butler Bay, a private nature preserve, and the hilly dense woodland called The Rain Forest.

coasts. Its gently sloping land is covered with dry forest of red birch, wild frangipani, or pigeonwood, scrub, and cactus. A signposted trail of 1.4 mi/ 2.2 km starts on the south from the pier and picnic area, where there is also a salt pond with black mangroves, and loops over the island's highest point (330 ft/100 m), marked by an observation tower, to a second picnic area on the west coast. On the west side is a grove of poisonous manchineel trees. Here, too, one can see—and probably feel—the endemic touch-me-not; the underside of its shiny green leaves has yellow needles that detach easily and lodge in the skin.

Half-day excursions in glass-bottom boats and motorboats with snorkeling equipment are offered by the four boat companies and four individual boat operators authorized by the Park Service. They depart twice daily from Kings Wharf in Christiansted; the ride takes about thirty minutes, one way. A Park Service pamphlet picturing fish of the area is usually distributed to visitors. Some operators also offer diving on the outer reef; some go to Buck Island on half- or full-day sailing trips. Check with the boat captain regarding lunch; not all boats provide it.

GREEN CAY NATIONAL WILDLIFE REFUGE

Only about 0.24 mi/0.4 km off the northeast coast at Southgate Pond, an islet of about 20 acres/6 hectares has been made into the Green Cay National Wildlife Refuge under the aegis of the Virgin Islands Fish and Wildlife Service. It and Protestant Cay in Christiansted Harbor—places that have not had the mongoose—are the only locations where the endemic St. Croix ground lizard remains. Green Cay is wooded on the south end and provides a sanctuary for pelicans, herons, and least terns.

SALT RIVER BAY ESTUARY

On the north coast, a large bay at the mouth of the Salt River is an estuary and an important Arawak site. It is also the home of the *Aquarius* (formerly *Hydro Lab*), an underwater research laboratory where scientists live a week or more to study the sea. The facility belongs to the West Indies Laboratory/Fairleigh Dickinson University located on the eastern end of St. Croix. On the southeast end of the estuary at Triton Bay, the Nature

Large Turk's-head cacti typically grow in dry open scrub land such as the arid area at the eastern tip of St. Croix near Jack Bay and Point Udall.

Conservancy has a 12-acre/4.8-hectare mangrove preserve. The remainder of the estuary and adjacent mangroves are at the center of a heated debate over plans to develop the area. Salt River and other wetlands—Altona Lagoon, Southgate Pond, and Coakley Bay Pond, east of Christiansted; Great Pond and Long Point on the south coast—are some of the two dozen birding sites around St. Croix. Among the nesting species are the pied-billed grebe, green-backed heron, egret, common moorhen, American coot, Wilson's plover, willet, common ground-dove, and smooth-billed ani.

Salt River Drop-off at the mouth of the river is a prime dive location that is actually two sites—the east and west walls of a submerged canyon. The west wall begins at 30 ft/9 m and drops to a shelf at 90 ft/18 m from where it plunges vertically more than 1,000 ft/300 m. The wall has caves and deep crevices encrusted with corals and tube sponges and forests of black coral. Rays and large open-water fish are seen here. The east wall is more sloping and attracts large schools of fish. The Salt River Marina, on the west side of the bay, has fully equipped dive operators and boats can be hired for excursions into the mangroves.

CRAMER PARK AND FAIRLEIGH DICKINSON TERRITORIAL PARK

Two parks at the easternmost reach of St. Croix are popular with local residents but are seldom visited by tourists. Cramer Park, at the end of the paved road (Route 82), is a beachside picnic spot. Camping is allowed but there are no amenities, and seagrape trees provide the only shade. The tip of the island from Cramer Park to Point Udall (1.5 mi/2.4 km) is the Fairleigh Dickinson Territorial Park. A track to the east crosses a hilly, arid landscape covered with scrub and forests of cacti, some as tall as trees. Large Turk's-head cacti often have several caps or heads and are spectacular. Although one is unlikely to see them, the area is home to green iguanas, which grow up to 6 ft/1.8 m. A dirt road ascends Sugar Loaf Hill (672 ft/205 m), the highest of the area's hills, but hikers need permission to proceed to the top as access is restricted. Other footpaths lead to white sand beaches where there is good snorkeling. Point Udall, also known as East Point (226 ft/69 m), is the easternmost point of the United States. It overlooks a panorama of neighboring islands, and on a clear day the silhouette of Saba, 90 mi/27 km to the east, can also be seen. A path goes down the slope to the end of the Point where waves break high against the shore; caution is advised.

ST. JOHN

Serene St. John, the least developed of the U.S. Virgin Islands, is a quiet wonder of nature. The heavily forested, mountainous island has a deeply indented coastline rimmed with coves that protect pristine white sand beaches and some of the most beautiful aquamarine waters in the Caribbean. Beneath the sea is a tropical wonderland of fish and coral. More than half of the island and its coastal waters are protected by national park.

The land rises quickly from the shore in a series of ridges that reach their heights in a triangle of peaks—Mamey (1,147 ft/350 m), Camelberg (1,193 ft/364 m), and Bordeaux (1,277 ft/389 m)—in the center of the island. St. John is geologically complex; major rock formations millions of years old, but rearranged through faulting, erosion, and changes in water levels, are exposed in many places. The terrain ranges from the dry, cactus-covered cliffs and salt ponds of the eastern end to the moist subtropical forests of the northwestern slopes; it supports more than 800 plant species.

Birds are abundant. As many as 160 species have been recorded in and around the 12-sq-mi/31-sq-km terrestrial habitat of the park. Of these, more than twenty-five species nest on St. John. Common in the park's two campgrounds and wooded western areas are pearly-eyed thrasher (locally known as the trushee), Zenaida dove, bananaquit, and gray kingbird. Antillean crested hummingbirds and green-throated caribs often are seen hovering around hibiscus flowers along park roads. Sandpipers patrol the beaches where seagrape and seaside mahoe trees are abundant; American oystercatchers perch on rocky shores.

Other wildlife includes feral donkeys, used for transportation until the mid-1950s, and the mongoose, an introduced species that was supposed to control the rat population but instead destroyed other species—particularly lizards and sea turtles—by eating their eggs. Bats, the only mammals indigenous to the island, include cave bats that pollinate kapok and calabash trees; fruit bats that eat mangoes, avocados, and bananas; house bats that feed on insects; and fish-eating bats that are seen around the harbors. The hawksbill turtle nests on St. John beaches, and the green turtle is seen often in the island's waters, particularly at Francis Bay.

Yacht-filled Cruz Bay hugs a narrow strip of land on the west coast between the harbor and the mountains. Only three streets wide and four streets deep, the town is a pastiche of pastel buildings and West Indian gingerbread houses. Development is restricted here to Cruz Bay and the adjacent Southwest corner. In front of the ferry pier is a small park and Tourist Information Center where maps and brochures are available. On the north side is the National Park Service Visitor Center, the best place to start an exploration of St. John. Most people visit on day trips from St. Thomas, but outdoor enthusiasts will want to spend more time here.

VIRGIN ISLANDS NATIONAL PARK

The Virgin Islands National Park comprises 9,485 acres/3,838 hectares of land on St. John, of which 5,000 acres were donated by Laurance Rockefeller; it also includes 5,650 acres/2,286 hectares offshore and another 122 acres/49 hectares on Hassel Island facing St. Thomas. The Visitor Center (809-776-6201) is open from 8 A.M. to 4:30 P.M. It has literature and offers tours led by park rangers, hikes, wildlife lectures, and films; there is also a boating tour around the island. Ranger-led hikes are recommended because the guides provide information on flora, fauna, and history unavailable in general literature. A schedule is available in advance and reservations are recommended in winter. (Another Visitor Center, directly across from the Redhook marina, is at the end of the Cabrita Peninsula, the easternmost extension of St. Thomas. The spur from the Park's sign on Route 32 to the center is a popular jogging route.)

Park accommodations are limited to three choices: a deluxe resort and two camps—all smothered in luxuriant foliage on the northwest side of the island. Caneel Bay, the resort, is situated on the grounds of an old sugar plantation about a mile from Cruz Bay. Cinnamon Bay Campground, about 6 mi/10 km from Cruz Bay, is a rustic camp operated by a concessionaire. It accommodates most guests in screened canvas tents or cottages, and there are also a few bare campsites. Another mile east at Maho Bay, the deluxe, privately owned Maho Bay Campground has A-frame cottages resembling tree houses. Both camps have fourteen-day stay limits; reservations, particularly for the winter season, must be made months in advance. All three facilities offer water sports. Backpacking is not permitted in the park. There are also hotels in and around Cruz Bay.

The park has twenty-one marked hiking trails accessible from the North Shore Road (Route 20) or from Centerline Road (Route 10), the central west–east artery; they are outlined in a pamphlet, "Trail Guide for Safe Hiking." In the north, *Trails 1–9*, accessible from North Shore Road, overlook Caneel, Trunk, Cinnamon, and Maho bays on the northwest side of the island where the slopes have dense forests. Cruz Bay to Hawksnest Bay (1–6) are some of the easiest trails, ranging from ten minutes to two hours. Cinnamon Bay to Mary Point (7–9) provide the best introduction to the vegetation of the park and take fifteen minutes to an hour. *Trails 10–11*

Hiking trails explore the forested hills overlooking Trunk Bay Beach on the northwest coast of St. John, and an underwater trail follows its reef.

face the north coast between Annaberg and Leinster Bay. Each is thirty minutes and focuses on history as well as on the natural environment. They can be reached from either Route 20 or Route 10. *Trails 12–13*, on the northeast, are more difficult hikes, each taking two hours. They are reached from the eastern end of Route 10. *Trail 13* is not maintained. In the south, *Trails 14–18* cover a variety of terrain and vegetation on contiguous routes in the south-central part of the island and are the most popular routes for serious hikers. They begin on Reef Bay Trail (14), a two-hour downhill hike from Centerline Road to Reef Bay. About two-thirds of the way, Trail 16 branches southeast from Trail 14 to Lameshur Bay where it meets Trails 17 and 18. *Trails 19–21* are contiguous trails across the southeast, the island's driest region, and range from fifteen minutes to an hour. They start at the south end of Route 107, that is, the southern extension of Route 10 skirting Coral Bay; it turns inland on an unpaved track to Lameshur Bay.

Only the main trails are described below; all times are one-way unless noted otherwise:

Cinnamon Bay Trail 7. A self-guided loop trail of about an hour begins at the entrance of the Cinnamon Bay campgrounds and provides an introduction to the park's vegetation and historic landmarks, all labeled. It passes under canopies of bay-rum, mango, genip, and many other species to the ruins of a sugar mill. Starvation fruit, which resembles a mushy white potato, is abundant. Another abundant species is Teyer palm, the only indigenous palm on the island. It can be recognized by its fan-shaped fronds, once used for making fans, roofs, brooms, and fish traps. Cinnamon Bay, like Caneel Bay on the west coast, takes its name from the fragrant cinnamon bay-rum tree—*kaneel* being the Dutch word for "cinnamon." *Trail 8* also starts from the camp and uses an old plantation road uphill through the forest to Centerline Road, terminating about 1 mi/1.6 km west of the Reef Bay trail head. It takes about an hour.

Francis Bay Trail 9. Immediately before Mary Point, a steep, hammerhead shaped peninsula on the north coast, a trail beginning at the north end of Maho Bay, where the park's other camp is located, skirts a pond behind Francis Bay beach. White-cheeked pintails and wigeons are here during the winter, along with gallinules and teal. The cliffs at Mary Point are nesting sites for the brown pelican, a U.S. endangered species that flourishes in the Virgin Islands. Brown boobies colonize on offshore islands; frigatebirds soar overhead. Francis Bay is a good place to see and swim with green turtles.

Annaberg Plantation Trail 10. The partially restored ruins of an eighteenth-century estate overlooking the north coast give visitors a glimpse of life on a sugarcane plantation. A descriptive brochure for the 0.25-mi/0.4-km self-guided trail is available. Talks and demonstrations at the interpretive center describe the tropical foods, medicinal plants, and weaving and other skills the islanders once needed in order to subsist. Tours depart from the Visitor Center three mornings weekly.

Leinster Bay Trail 11. A walk from Annaberg along the shores of Leinster Bay can follow the plantation visit. This stretch, also known as Waterlemon Bay, has mangroves. Red markers warn of the manchineel tree whose sap can cause a severe skin rash and whose green fruits are poisonous. In shallow waters protected by reefs and headlands such as those of Leinster Bay, the land-forming red mangroves advance into the sea with their prop roots providing shelter for small fish, crustaceans, mangrove oysters, and insects, which, in turn, attract birds such as the mangrove cuckoo. In the muddy shores behind the red mangrove, black mangrove send up pencil-like shoots, or pneumatophores, in search of oxygen; behind them, on the mangrove's dry fringes, are buttonwood trees, a nesting ground for herons. Greater and lesser yellowlegs, gallinules, black-necked stilts, and bitterns are here too. Mangrove thickets are found also at Lameshur Bay on the south and at Hurricane Hole on the north side of Coral Bay. Waterlemon Cay, an islet in Leinster Bay, has one of the island's best snorkeling reefs. Day-sailing excursions to the reef are available from St. Thomas and Cruz Bay.

Reef Bay Trail 14. The park's most comprehensive hike starts 5 mi/8 km east of Cruz Bay on Centerline Road, and is the gateway to Trails 15–18. When taken alone, Trail 14 is a two-hour hike of 2.5 mi/4 km to Reef Bay on the south coast. The shady path winds downhill through moist forest to dry forest and the grounds of abandoned sugar plantations. Hikers pass many different kinds of vegetation, including exotic tropical fruit trees such as mango, soursop, papaya, and breadfruit—all labeled. Other species include bay-rum trees, from which a cologne is made locally, century plants whose flower attracts hummingbirds, and wildflowers. After 1.7 mi/2.7 km, Trail 14 reaches a junction with Trails 15 and 16 running west and east. On the west, Trail 15 is a fifteen-minute walk to rocks with petroglyphs and a small waterfall. Archaeologists are not certain if these were carved by Arawaks or later by African slaves. On the east is the start of Trail 16. From the junction, Trail 14 continues south for 0.8 mi/1.3 km to Genti Bay, a cove of Reef Bay. Hikers on ranger-led walks of Trail 14 are picked up at Reef Bay to return to Cruz Bay by boat.

Pages 154 and 155: Some of the best and least crowded snorkeling is done from boats along the fringing reefs at St. John's eastern end around Hurricane Hole.

Lameshur Bay Trail 16. From the junction on Trail 14, the path heads east-southeast for 1.8 mi/2.9 km through dry forest to Lameshur Bay where there is a picnic area. When hikers want to return from Lameshur Bay to Centerline, they have two choices. They can take the three-and-a-half-hour hike back over Trail 16 and Trail 14—uphill. Or, they can take the one-and-a-half-hour hike on *Bordeaux Mountain Trail 18* to Bordeaux Mountain Road, then another hour's hike to Centerline. Hikers sometimes arrange for transportation to meet them at a predetermined time at the junction of Trail 18 and Bordeaux Mountain Road.

When taken together, Trails 14, 16, and 18 form a horseshoe of 5.5 mi/8.8 km or about five hours of hiking. This becomes a loop trail by the addition of the Bordeaux Mountain Road.

Salt Pond Bay, Drunk Bay, and Ram Head trails 19–21 are three interconnecting trails from Salt Pond Bay over Ram Hill to Ram Head. The trail crosses arid terrain covered with thorny acacia, catch-and-keep, century plants, and organ-pipe cactus entwined with orchids and festooned with epiphytes. Wild goats and donkeys roam the area. In the tidal pools at the beach, one is likely to see hermit crabs, which often live in discarded snail and whelk shells. Varieties of both marine and land hermit crabs live in the Virgin Islands, the latter returning to sea only to reproduce.

The trail winds along slopes covered with gumbo limbo, tamarind, wild frangipani, nutmeg, and poison ash with leaves similar to holly. The ginger thomas with its showy yellow flowers is common; also known as yellow elder, it is the official tree of the U.S. Virgin Islands. On Ram Hill, the trail crosses a field where bullfinches feed on the pink fruits of Turk's-head cactus; it continues to ascend to Ram Head. The rocks of Ram Head, formed 100 million or more years ago, are known as the Water Island Formation; they are the earliest volcanic rock underlying St. John and can be seen throughout the southeast. A second period of volcanism, the Louisenhoj Formation, evidenced by a beautiful blue rock (prized as building material), is found on western St. John and eastern St. Thomas. Pillsbury Sound, the channel separating the two islands, is thought to have been the volcanic center. The Louisenhoj eruptions were so violent that huge chunks of rock from the Water Island Formation were tossed skyward and scattered over the hills. An example is Easter Rock, an enormous Water Island Formation near the road above Hawksnest Bay on St. John.

THE PARK UNDER THE SEA

Trunk Bay on the north shore, one of the most beautiful beaches in the Caribbean, has a Park Service snorkeling trail along its fringing reef. Unfortunately, it is becoming a lesson in overuse. The once-splendid reefs have deteriorated badly from constant use by large groups of people on day trips from St. Thomas and from cruise ships. The bay, the most heavily visited on the island, is to be avoided between 10 A.M. and 2 P.M., when the number of visitors is greatest. Snorkeling gear is available from the Park Service at the beach. Snorkelers and divers have many other reefs to explore around St. John, such as Johnson Reef and Waterlemon Cay on the north coast, Steven Cay and Fishbowl at Cruz Bay, and Horseshoe and South Drop on the south coast, to name a few. At Honeymoon Beach, one of the sandy coves of Caneel Bay, snorkelers can observe spotted eagle ray at very close range. These "flying saucers of the deep" are attracted to the bay by yachtmen and snorkelers who feed them, although the Park Service strongly discourages the practice.

The fringing, or patch, reefs that are typical of the area are composed of hard corals—staghorn, elkhorn, brain, and star—and soft corals including willowy sea whips, lacy sea fans, and feathery sea plumes. Lacking the calcium carbonate necessary to form hard skeletons, soft corals fasten themselves to the sea floor and sway with the currents, capturing plankton with the tentacles of their polyps. Schools of colorful parrotfishes, snappers, blue tang, and surgeonfishes passing with the water's ebb and flow are dazzling. The long, slim trumpetfish hanging vertically in the water is one of the sea's most curious sights.

ST. THOMAS

From a deep turquoise sea St. Thomas rises dramatically to steep mountain peaks that frame an irregular coastline of fingers and coves sheltering idyllic bays and providing spectacular views at every turn. This grand terrain combined with extensive development—many would say overdevelopment—makes St. Thomas seem larger than its 34 sq mi/88 sq km. Despite the bustle, the island is attractive for its sports facilities and because the conditions there are among the best in the Caribbean for deep-sea fishing, sailing, diving, and windsurfing. Those who want to flee the bustle need only take a short boat ride to uninhabited Hassel Island or a twenty-minute ferry to St. John.

Charlotte Amalie (pronounced Ah-MAHL-ya) is the capital of the U.S. Virgin Islands and the business center of St. Thomas. A notorious pirates' den in the early decades of exploration, it was first settled in 1672 under Denmark and served for two hundred years as a major trading port. Set in an amphitheater of green mountains on a deep horseshoe bay, the historic port is still one of the busiest in the Caribbean, filled with yachts and cruise ships from around the world.

A walking tour of Charlotte Amalie combines history and colonial architecture behind hedges of bougainvillea and oleander and under umbrellas of jacaranda and flamboyant. Emancipation Garden, a small park in the center of town, commemorates the end of slavery in 1848. The hillsides behind the town were so steep that roads were difficult to build. Instead, the lower and higher parts were reached by a series of stone stairs. They connect flower-filled lanes and summits with old Danish watchtowers, where history is spiced with pirates' lore and the views are spectacular.

In mango trees and among the hibiscus on St. Thomas, one is likely to see iguanas. Bright green when young, their color deepens to black with age. Unlike most Caribbean islands, where the iguana is shy and elusive, hunted and endangered, here it is something of a pet, often remaining still to be photographed. The lizards frequent the grounds of Bluebeard's Castle Hotel, Coral World, and Lime Tree Beach, in particular.

MAGENS BAY

Hardly a desolate strand, Magens Bay is often on lists of the world's ten most beautiful beaches. Situated on the north coast, the bay is 2 mi/3.2 km deep. Its long crescent of white sand is shaded by seagrapes and tall coconut palms and framed by wooded hills. From the beach one can walk along dry woodlands of genip, cashew, lignum vitae, and other native trees to the Peterborg Peninsula, which forms the north side of the horseshoe

Deep Magens Bay on the north coast of St. Thomas is sheltered by coconut palms and seagrapes and is near tidal pools teeming with hermit crabs and shorebirds.

bay. Farther west along the Atlantic side of the coast, the rocky shores have tidal pools where legions of hermit crabs and small fish are a great attraction for herons, terns, and other shorebirds. Neltjeberg and Botany Bays are nesting grounds of the leatherback sea turtles.

DRAKE'S SEAT AND FAIRCHILD PARK

Some of the island's most spectacular views can be enjoyed along Skyline Drive on the north coast, particularly at Drake's Seat and Fairchild Park. According to local lore, the English marauder Sir Francis Drake, who claimed the Virgin Islands for Britain, used the strategic lookout above Magens Bay to eye his fleet pursuing Spanish treasure galleons. The panorama from Drake's Seat stretches from the uninhabited Hans Lollik Islands north of Magens Bay to the British Virgin Islands and St. John in the distance on the east. Directly below, the cliffs on St. Thomas's northeast coast drop almost straight to the sea, and offshore lie Thatch Cay and other islets, popular for diving and deep-sea fishing.

Fairchild Park, a wooded mountaintop oasis at about 1,200 ft/360 m, is one of the prettiest spots on St. Thomas, with splendid views of both the north and south coasts. Nearby, too, there are spectacular vistas to be seen at Mountain Top (1,500 ft/450 m), the highest accessible point on the island but commercialized as a tourist attraction.

HASSEL ISLAND AND WATER ISLAND

Charlotte Amalie harbor has two small forested islands. The smaller, Hassel Island, was connected to the mainland until 1865, when a channel was cut for easier ship passage in the harbor. Most of the island is now part of the Virgin Islands National Park. It has a few trails but no tourist facilities. Cultivated in the seventeenth century and used as a coaling station in the nineteenth century, Hassel Island has not been altered since the United States purchased the Virgin Islands. The rockbound island has gentle hills with dry woods, century plants, and cactus. The western shore has small beaches shaded by seagrapes. Hikers can explore old fortifications and other ruins at nine locations. There is no public transportation to the island but one can hire a boat at the Charlotte Amalie waterfront for the short ride, agreeing with the captain on a pickup time for the return trip. Two hours is probably adequate; the island has little shade and no provisions. One should carry drinking water.

Water Island, west of Hassel Island, is private land with homes and one hotel overlooking a pretty beach. Day visitors may use the beach and the facilities of the water-sports center. The Water Island ferry leaves frequently from Crown Bay dock on the west side of Charlotte Amalie.

OUTDOOR ACTIVITIES

HIKING: All three islands offer hiking. The best is on St. John, in the Virgin Islands National Park's excellent trails; also recommended are the unpaved roads and tracks of St. Croix's Rain Forest.

CAMPING: The two campgrounds in the National Park on St. John are among the best in the Caribbean. St. Croix has campsites at Great Pond and Cramer Park but there are no facilities and one must provide all equipment.

HORSEBACK RIDING: Trails over rolling hills and through the Rain Forest make St. Croix delightful for riding. Jill's Equestrian Stable (809-772-2880) at Sprat Hall Estate and nearby Seahorse Stables (809-772-1264) offer trail rides daily and moonlight rides five nights prior to the full moon. Buccaneer Hotel has riding over trails on 300 acres/121 hectares of private land. All facilities require advance reservations.

SWIMMING: The U.S. Virgin Islands are famous for their beautiful beaches, and although many are occupied by private resorts, all beaches are public. Local visitors' guides list the main beaches with their changing and other facilities, water-sports rental equipment, and fees. In addition to sports facilities, resort beaches normally offer greater security than isolated ones. On St. Thomas the most celebrated—and most crowded—is Magens Bay on the north coast; normally, there are fewer people in the morning. Others are Coki Bay on the northeast; Morningstar and Limetree on the south; and Cowpet, Sapphire, and Secret Harbor on the southeast. These beaches and many places in between are frequented by snorkelers and divers as much as by swimmers. Brewers, south of the College of the Virgin Islands, has good shelling.

SNORKELING AND DIVING: Dive experts consider the U.S. Virgin Islands to be one of the three best dive areas in the Caribbean, with great variety for novice and experienced divers alike. Visibility ranges up to 150 ft/45 m; water temperatures are a warm 82°F/27°C in summer and 78°F/25°C in winter. Dive operators with excellent facilities are plentiful; a list is available from the U.S. Virgin Islands Tourist Office. Arrangements can be made directly with operators or through any hotel. While all operators have their favorite sites, choices are made daily on the basis of weather, sea conditions, and the level of experience of divers.

St. Croix is almost completely surrounded by coral reefs. The most accessible sites with the greatest variety of coral and fish are found in the 6 mi/9.6 km of barrier reef that protects Christiansted harbor and the north shore. In some places, the reef is only 1,500 ft/450 m from the coast in water 35 ft/11 m deep. There are operators on the wharf in Christiansted, in Frederiksted, and at the Salt River Marina.

St. Thomas has thirty-four dive sites within a twenty-minute boat ride from shore. Off the southeast coast, two places suited to snorkelers and novice divers are Cow and Calf, two rocks in Jersey Bay with corals, caves, and large schools of fish in depths of 5 to 25 ft/1.5 to 7.5 m. The St. James Islands have rocky shelves, tiny caves, and sea whips in a large sweep of coral reef. On the northeast coast, Coki Beach next to Coral World offers good snorkeling from shore, but it is used by dive classes and therefore is usually busy. Experienced divers go to St. Thomas's north side where the Atlantic and Caribbean meet and rushing waters carry tremendous numbers of fish. Congo Cay has huge boulders and lava archways only 30 ft/9 m under the sea. Thatch Cay has a series of tunnels through which divers can swim. St. Thomas has a Buck Island, too, off the southeast coast. Its main attraction is the coral-encrusted wreck of the *Cartanser*, a WWI cargo ship. It can be seen by snorkelers as well as

An Antillean crested hummingbird feeds on the flowers of a century plant.

divers, and recreational subs visit the surrounding reef.

About a dozen dive operators are based in St. Thomas, offering two and three dives daily and instructions for certification; one has a resort exclusively for divers. For those who neither swim nor dive, glass-bottom boats and *Atlantis II*, a recreational submarine, have tours from Charlotte Amalie. Coral World, an underwater observatory at Coki Point, enables viewers to walk down into the sea to watch the fish. At 11 A.M. daily, divers can be seen feeding fish, including sharks.

Dive excursions starting from St. John visit locations off the island's north coast and on the east end of St. Thomas. In front of Cruz Bay, Steven Cay is a beautiful reef crowned with sea fans and star and mountain corals and abundant with angelfishes and triggerfishes. Waters tend to be rougher on the south side of St. John and are rarely dived.

DEEP-SEA FISHING: The Virgin Islands offer superb fishing for blue marlin, with many world records to prove it. Among the most prestigious competitions is the Blue Marlin Fishing Tournament in August. Dolphin, kingfish, sailfish, wahoo, tuna, and skipjack are plentiful too. No deep-sea fishing is allowed in National Park waters, but rod-and-reel fishing is allowed from St. John's beaches. Redhook at the east end of St. Thomas is the main center for boat operators. American Yacht Harbor (809-775-6454), the St. Thomas Sport Fishing Center (809-775-7990), and a dozen or so independent boat operators offer half- and full-day fishing expeditions with bait, tackle, ice, and beer provided. The waters northeast of St. Thomas are the premier fishing grounds. In St. Croix, most boat operators are based in Christiansted; sport-fishing is best at Lang Bank off the north coast. Anglers who want to fish from shore go to Hams Bay.

SAILING AND BOATING: Magnificent seas, year-round balmy weather, and countless coves and sheltered anchorages have made the U.S. Virgin Islands a boating mecca. Regattas are held year-round; the Rolex Cup Regatta in March and the Caribbean Ocean Racing Triangle in April are major events. Every type of craft from sailfish to oceangoing yacht is available. Boats can be chartered bareboat or fully provisioned with crew. Many operators have Stateside offices and toll-free numbers. Yacht Haven Marina, the largest facility on St. Thomas, is home to the V.I. Charter Yacht League (809-774-3944) whose hundred or so member boats are available by the day, week, or longer. Many boats offer daily half- and full-day sailing trips to uninhabited islands for snorkeling and swimming. Some of the same operators have powerboats for deep-sea fishing. Similar boating facilities are available on St. John, where operators are based in Cruz Bay and Coral Bay, and on St. Croix, where the main center is Christiansted. Annapolis Sailing School (809-773-4709) operates a school here.

SURFING: During winter the sea rolls in at Hull Bay on the north coast of St. Thomas with enough force to attract surfers.

WINDSURFING: The three islands, well aligned to the trade winds, offer excellent conditions for windsurfing. In St. Croix, the relatively tranquil west shore is a good place for beginners. Favored spots for experienced sailors are Grapetree Beach near the east end, and Buck Island. John's Sports at Mill Harbor rents boards by the week. On St. John, all north-shore beaches are excellent locations. Strong winds, whipping down the Sir Francis Drake Channel north of St. John, are funneled by two hills through the Narrows to the Windward Passage. They pass the north side of Johnson's Reef about 0.5 mi/0.8 km north of Trunk Bay, creating some of the best surf-riding in the Virgin Islands. Windsurfers also sail across Pillsbury Sound to St. Thomas.

St. Thomas windsurfing is best at the eastern end where winds peak during the midday—when, also, the sun is hottest. Sapphire and Virgin Grand beaches on the east end are prime locations. Morningstar on the south has gentle winds. Hull Bay on the north offers the roughest waves. Windsurfing St. Thomas/School of Boardsailing at Pt. Pleasant and another operator at Sapphire Beach offer two-hour lessons, with the first hour on a simulator.

EXPLORING THE ISLANDS

St. Croix: Major arteries and an extensive web of narrow winding roads provide access to almost all parts of St. Croix. Centerline Road (Route 70) connects Frederiksted on the west with Christiansted on the northeastern coast, from which point East End Road (Route 82) continues to the east end. These highways are crossed by many north–south roads. Regular taxis are plentiful but expensive. The St. Croix Taxi and Tour Association (809-772-2828), however, runs specific tours and has set prices. Inexpensive shared taxis or minivans

travel between Frederiksted and Christiansted. The best way to see the island is self-drive car, touring the scenic routes that wind through the northern highlands (76, 58, 78). All major U.S. car rental firms are here, but car availability in peak season is uneven. Drivers must be twenty-one years of age and have a valid U.S. license. Those who do not have a major credit card must leave a large deposit. Driving is on the LEFT.

St. John: The island is only 9 mi/15 km long, but the mountainous terrain and winding roads make distances seem farther than they might appear on a map. Centerline Road (Route 10) connects Cruz Bay on the west with Coral Bay on the east, winding along the high ridges of the island's spine where there are grand views of St. John and neighboring islands. North Shore Road (20) is a corkscrew route along the north coast to Leinster Bay. Southside Road (104) goes only 3.2 mi/5.1 km south to Rendezvous where it turns inland through the hills for 3.5 mi/5.6 km to Centerline Road. St. John has secondary roads and tracks negotiable by jeep, but the Park Service strongly advises visitors not to strike off on their own without first being briefed by a ranger at the Visitor Center. Cars, jeeps, and taxis with driver guides can be hired in Cruz Bay. Jeeps and mopeds are the most popular rentals. The best days to visit St. John from St. Thomas are Mondays and Fridays when cruiseship passengers are fewest; Wednesdays are the most crowded. Transportation from St. Thomas is available by seaplane and ferry.

St. Thomas: The island is only 13 mi/ 20.8 km long but distances are greater due to the mountainous terrain; traffic is heavy. The island is crisscrossed by good roads, and there is good public transportation. Generally, roads are well marked but they are very winding and fork frequently, requiring the driver's close attention. It is easy to be distracted by the views. Drivers need good maps, available at tourist offices and shops. Some car rental firms offer free pickup and delivery service. Jeeps are available for rent too, but unless drivers are experienced with left-hand driving on narrow mountain roads, it is safer to rent a car on St. Thomas. A similar warning applies to moped and motorbike rentals.

Emancipation Square, the waterfront, and Market Square in Charlotte Amalie are hubs for taxis, buses, ferries, and seaplanes. Taxi rates are based on destination rather than mileage and are set by the government; a copy of the rates should be available from drivers. Taxis with driver-guides can be hired for touring. Regular bus service runs on different routes to Redhook on the east end where ferries leave for St. John, and to Bordeaux at the west end. For schedules, telephone 809-774-5678. Daytime service to Redhook is also provided by jitneys or open-air buses. Ferries depart hourly from Redhook for St. John, 8 A.M. to 11 P.M.; from St. John, 7 A.M. to 10 P.M. The trip takes twenty minutes. Less-frequent ferries depart from Charlotte Amalie beginning at 9 A.M. and return from the National Park Dock in Cruz Bay at 3:45 P.M. Ferries to Tortola also leave from Charlotte Amalie and take forty-five minutes; some continue to Virgin Gorda. Passengers need passports or proof of citizenship. Virgin Islands Seaplane Shuttle (809-773-3590) leaves about every twenty minutes from its downtown harborside locations in St. Thomas and St. Croix on flights between the two islands.

INFORMATION: In North America: USVI Office, 1270 Ave. of Americas, Suite 2108, New York, NY 10020; 212-332-2222. Offices in Atlanta, Chicago, Los Angeles, Miami, Washington. In the U.K.: 2 Cinnamon Row, Plantation Wharf, York Place, London SW113 TW; 71-978-5262. In St. Croix: Christiansted, Box 4538, USVI 00822; 809-773-0495; Frederiksted, Custom House Bldg., Strand St., USVI 00840; 809-772-0357. In St. John: Cruz Bay, Box 200, USVI 00830; 809-776-6450. In St. Thomas: Charlotte Amalie, Box 6400, USVI 00804; 809-774-8784. Virgin Islands National Park, Box 7789, St. Thomas, USVI 00801; 809-775-6238 in St. Thomas; 809-776-6201 in St. John.

Books: *Exploring St. Croix* by S. Imsand and R. Philibosian (1987). *Priceless Heritage* by Benjamin Kesler (1980). *Virgin Islands Birdlife* by S. and N. Scott (U.S. National Park Service, Univ. of the Virgin Islands, 1988). *Cruising Guide to the Virgin Islands, 1989–90*, Cruising Guide Publications.

BRITISH VIRGIN ISLANDS

THE BRITISH VIRGIN ISLANDS is an archipelago of about fifty islands, cays, and rocks spread over 59 sq mi/153 sq km of sapphire seas. All of the islands but one are volcanic in origin; most are mountainous and green, with scalloped coastlines of small coves and white sand beaches that are idyllic hideaways for yachtsmen and vacationers.

The islands make a virtue out of their lack of a glittering nightlife and sophisticated resort facilities, boasting that they do not appeal to everyone. Instead of golf courses and casinos, they offer a fantastic display of marine life for divers, remoteness for those yearning for privacy, and some of the most beautiful sailing waters in the world for those who prefer to cruise under canvas. The seas are appreciated also by anglers and windsurfing enthusiasts. For naturalists, there are colonies of seabirds, a wide range of flowering trees, and even a rare iguana or two. The pleasant year-round climate, with temperatures ranging from 77° to 88°F/25° to 31°C, and balmy tradewinds are as pleasing to sailors of today as they were to buccaneers of yesteryear.

The BVI, as they are known locally, are 60 mi/96 km east of Puerto Rico, neighboring the U.S. Virgin Islands. They nestle protectively along both sides of the Sir Francis Drake Channel, slightly west of the Anegada Passage, a major northeast corridor between the Atlantic Ocean and Caribbean Sea that separates the Greater and Lesser Antilles.

Most of the BVI are green uninhabited islands frequented by yachtsmen for their pristine beaches and good anchorage. The largest of the populated islands are Tortola, the capital; Virgin Gorda, 8 mi/13 km to the east; and Anegada, 15 mi/24 km to the north. The main islands south of Drake Channel and Tortola are Norman, Peter, Salt, Cooper, and Ginger. Those northwest of the capital are Jost Van Dyke, Great Tobago, and Little Tobago; on the northeast are Guana, Great Camanoe, and Scrub. North of Virgin Gorda lie Mosquito, Prickly Pear, Necker, and Eustatia.

Spain and the other European powers had no interest in the islands initially, but pirates who roamed the territory in the early 1600s found the secluded bays and defensible peaks lying astride a major thoroughfare of the sea entirely to their liking. Almost overnight, the islands became bustling centers of illicit commerce, intrigue, and buccaneer revelry. In-

---

Off Peter Island, just south of Tortola, divers can see the sunken ship Fearless *and explore the underwater hulk of the RMS* Rhone *in the Rhone National Marine Park.*

credible treasures were exchanged, fought over, and buried, some never recovered to this day. The heyday of piracy lasted only about thirty years but the islands' role as an entrepôt continued after they were settled by the Dutch and, later, by the British. The BVI remains one of Britain's few Crown Colonies to this day.

TORTOLA

The biggest island and capital of the BVI is also the center of commerce, government, and tourism, particularly as the home base for the largest number of yacht charters in the Caribbean. Road Town, the main town, is the only sizable residential center in the BVI, and, like everything else on Tortola, it is fairly uncomplicated. Main Street, the commercial center of pastel wood-frame shops, takes only fifteen minutes to stroll.

Tortola is mostly an island of mountain greenery and well-sheltered harbors, with only a narrow band of land separating the mountains from the coast. Along Tortola's southern shores are low-lying scrub and frangipani trees, while the north side is a sparsely inhabited refuge for beachcombers and seabirds, with beautiful white sand beaches washed by Atlantic surf and fringed by stands of palm trees and banana and mango groves.

The name, Tortola, is the Spanish word for turtledove and the recovery of these birds from near extinction by hunting is symbolic of the interest the government has shown since the 1960s in preserving the BVI's land and marine environment. Sage Mountain on Tortola, along with Spring Bay and Devil's Bay on Virgin Gorda, was a gift from Laurance Rockefeller to the BVI government in the 1960s. His action led to the creation of the BVI National Parks Trust, which has since brought eleven of twenty-three proposed areas under its management. Those realized include the Rhone National Park and the Botanic Gardens, both firsts of their kind for the BVI.

BOTANIC GARDEN

The Botanic Garden was opened in January 1987 when a neglected 5-acre/2-hectare site, formerly the BVI Agricultural Station, was transformed into a fragrant living museum. The gardens, which occupy about 3 acres/1.2 hectares, were created by the Trust and a phalanx of volunteers from the Botanic Society and Garden Club. They comprise about twenty collections of rare and indigenous tropical plants. Visitors should be aware that there are no identifying signs or pamphlets, although both are forthcoming.

The entrance leads to a three-tiered fountain that serves as the central axis of the garden from which landscaped walks radiate in four directions, each leading to different sections. At the end of one walk, for example, after passing under a blossoming trellis, one crosses over a lily pond by way of a small bridge that leads to an orchid house and miniature rain forest. Areas are reserved for fern and philodendron propagation, a flowering plant nursery, and a birdhouse.

Generally, plants are grouped according to environmental habitat. Two of the most interesting sections are the cactus garden and palm grove, both with varieties surprising in their difference and abundance. A standout is the century plant, which takes many years to mature, hence its name. A full adult plant can grow leaves up to 6 ft/1.8 m long; after eight to twelve years, it sends up a tall flowering center stem—perhaps as high as 40 ft/ 12 m—that dies after only a single blooming. Cut and dried, the stems are used locally as Christmas trees.

Reflecting the islands' profusion of flowers, the gardens are festooned with blossoming shrubs, particularly pink, red, and white oleander, hibiscus, and bougainvillea, as well as frangipani and scarlet-flowered flamboyant trees. There are examples of the eighteen species of edible fruits native to the BVI and of others introduced from Africa and South America. One will find here guava, sugar-apple, and breadfruit—all staples of the islanders' diet—and avocado, mango, papaya, banana, and guava berries.

SAGE MOUNTAIN NATIONAL PARK

The 92-acre/37-hectare Sage Mountain National Park, where reforestation has been under way for the past twenty years, is situated on peaks that form a volcanic backbone down the center of Tortola and climb to 1,780 ft/542 m, the highest elevation in either the U.S. or British Virgin Islands. The vegetation is characteristic of a rain forest and is thought to be similar to the island's original growth.

Developed hiking trails wind through huge elephant ear and other philodendrons, hanging vines, and delicate lacy and prickly ferns as well as a variety of hard- and softwood trees such as kapok, West Indian mahogany, broadleaf mahogany, and white cedar, the BVI's national tree. Flowering plants often seen are the mountain guava, identified by its small white blossom and edible green fruit; the cocoplum, a member of the rose family; and the red palicourea, a stunning plant of contrasting black fruit and small red flowers on a yellow stalk.

Two trails are open and more are planned. The paths are neatly graveled and posted with directional signs; labels now identify some of the plants. An unsurfaced road leads to a parking area and the park entrance, from where there are the best unobstructed panoramic views. Allow at least a half-day to explore the park.

Pages 168 and 169: Coconut palms, whose tall, slender trunks tend to bend and buckle, guard the white-sand Atlantic beaches on the north shore of Tortola.

Mahogany Forest Trail, beginning to the left of the main gate, winds upward toward the peak and takes about an hour to walk. The trail leads through a mahogany forest where planted trees are mixed with some natural species. Trees and, frequently, mist restrict the view at the peak. An alternative return trail across an open field passes a small group of tree ferns, which are typical of the rain forests of the Windward Islands but uncommon in the Virgin Islands. Along the way, one is likely to spot a pearly-eyed thrasher, mockingbird, or Antillean crested hummingbird among the trees, or see a Caribbean martin or American kestrel hovering overhead.

The Rainforest Trail leads from the main gate northward into the lusher, more popular area of the park and also takes about an hour. A small loop trail off to the north passes through an area with some of the island's largest trees, including the bulletwood, which grows to 100 ft/30 m. The straight trunk with thick brown fissured bark can be as large as 4 ft/1.2 m in diameter. The forest here is rich with ferns and bromeliads and a variety of anthurium on the ground.

RHONE NATIONAL MARINE PARK

Salt Island, southeast of Tortola, is less well known for its salt ponds than as the site of the wreck of *The Rhone*, the most famous dive site in the BVI, if not in the entire Caribbean. *The Rhone*'s legend began in 1867, when the 310-ft/94-m steamship sank during one of the worst hurricanes ever to strike the Virgin Islands.

Less than two years old at the time, *The Rhone* was anchored in calm seas outside Great Harbor on Peter Island, taking on stores and passengers for its return trip to England, when a howling storm suddenly blew in. The captain, puzzled by the ferocity of the storm and knowing that the hurricane season had already passed, had planned to sail to a safer anchorage during a lull in the storm but was thwarted when a cable parted, dropping the ship's 3,000-lb/1,360-kg anchor and chain into the sea. No longer able to anchor safely and her rigging torn by the winds, *The Rhone* steamed at top speed for open water to ride out the storm. She had navigated the rocky channel and was rounding the last point when the hurricane struck again, this time from the other direction, forcing her onto the rocks at Salt Island. She split apart and sank rapidly with almost total loss of life.

The wreck lies in 20 to 80 ft/6 to 24 m of water west of Salt Island in a marine park spread over about 800 acres/324 hectares. It is usually visited in two dives, the first one to the bow section in the deepest water. The great ship lies on its starboard side; swimming inside the steel shell, once shelter for so many souls but now sprouting with feathery gorgonians and soft corals, is an eerie, poignant experience. Large schools of grunts lurk in the shadows, and sometimes the park's friendly resident 300-lb/136-kg jewfish cruises by. The second dive is in shallower water and usually follows the upright stern. One's companions here are red squirrelfish with large black eyes, and the ship's winches, gear boxes, and prop shaft are readily seen. Snorkelers can enjoy this section most easily, along with nearby Rhone Reef where two coral caves are found in about 25 ft/7.6 m of water.

The park also includes 34 acres/13.7 hectares of Dead Chest Island on the west. The island, which reaches its highest point at 214 ft/65 m, is faced on its southwest side with tall cliffs where bridled tern, noddy, and other seabirds nest. Cactus scrub, trimmed by the constant wind, clings to the steep slopes along with stunted frangipani, organ-pipe, and Turk's-head cactus, sage, and sea spurge. Dry forest covers the northern slopes. A flat area on the north has salt ponds fringed with black mangrove and manchineel trees, whose fruit is poisonous.

East of Dead Chest there is an underwater pinnacle known as Blonde Rock which is only 15 ft/4.6 m below the surface of the water. A popular site, better suited to experienced divers due to the strong currents and swells, its top is covered by pale-colored fire coral. It descends in a series of ledges to 60 ft/18 m and hosts a variety of corals and fish.

NORMAN ISLAND

Across Drake Channel from Tortola is Norman Island, deserted by all but seabirds and small wild animals. The island has some old ruins, a salt pond that is a good birding spot, and several footpaths. The one to Spy Glass Hill is a thirty-minute hike up a steep hill from where one gets a fabulous view in all directions. Pirates once used this vantage point to sight Spanish treasure ships and the island is apparently still used for illegal activity. Boats smuggling drugs have been seized here recently.

The island's caves at Treasure Point are partly submerged and of interest to snorkelers. Countless small crustaceans, banded coral shrimp, and arrow crabs live under a nearby coral shelf hardly more than 20 ft/6 m deep, and millions of tiny silversides dart to and fro through the water near the caves like a waving, glittering cloud.

VIRGIN GORDA

Possibly the best known of all the BVI is Virgin Gorda. Legend has it that the Spaniards called the island "fat virgin" because it resembled a reclining, slightly pregnant woman. If so, this illusion is best appreciated by those who arrive by yacht and anchor on the south coast, just offshore the huge rock formations known as The Baths, a place frequently photographed to capture the romantic seclusion and serenity of the BVI's quiet bays.

Virgin Gorda Peak Park

The island slopes upward from south to north, rising from the huge scattered boulders on the sandy beach to a hillside atop the "belly" of the woman, 1,370-ft/417-m Gorda Peak. Generally speaking, everything above 1,000 ft/300 m is considered national park in the BVI. The 265-acre/107-hectare park at the forested peak near the island's center has a self-guided hiking trail leading to an observation point. This lookout is actually the end of a paved road leading to Little Dix Bay, where Laurance Rockefeller built a sister resort to one at Caneel Bay on St. John. Both resorts have been designed in a way that is mindful of the ecology and protective of the environment, setting a standard for the region that has seldom been equaled after three decades.

The Baths and Devil's Bay National Park

In the southwest corner of the island, gigantic boulders, many the size of houses, are piled willy-nilly along the beach. Worn smooth by wind and water over the millennia, the enormous rocks have fallen in such a way as to

In an area called The Baths on the southwest tip of Virgin Gorda, unusual rock formations create small bathing pools when the sea rushes in. Facing page: The Baths' huge granite boulders, worn smooth by the incessant action of wind and sea, also form labyrinths that invite exploring.

create countless caverns, passages, and labyrinths illuminated by sunlight filtering between the rocks. They are fun to explore, although they are not real caves, of course. Where the sea rushes in and out, the formations near the shore catch the water, creating pools of shimmering crystal-clear water that are ideal for a refreshing splash—hence their name, The Baths.

Speculation abounds as to the origin of the granite boulders, a stone not as common to the Caribbean as the ubiquitous volcanic rock. The Baths are part of a granite layer which for the most part lies beneath the surface, but also crops out on Tortola. Some experts believe the formation was hurled to the surface during a volcanic cataclysm. The vegetation around The Baths includes trees such as white cedar, turpentine, frangipani, and pitch apple (whose green fruit was boiled to produce pitch for caulking boats), and shrubs such as aromatic wild sage, box briar, wild tamarind, and a variety of cactus.

South of The Baths is the Devil's Bay National Park, a secluded coral sand beach, which can be reached by a fifteen-minute walk through a natural setting of boulders and dry coastal vegetation.

OTHER NATURE REFUGES

Many other islands have been or are being studied as possible protected areas, particularly for nesting seabirds common to the region. Immediately south of Virgin Gorda is Fallen Jerusalem, a 30-acre/12-hectare island made up of enormous granite boulders. Now that the removal of wild goats has enabled the vegetation to return, the island is settling into a new life as a bird and wildlife sanctuary. Among the birds here are Zenaida dove, common ground-dove, scaly-naped pigeon, and pearly-eyed thrasher. Fallen Jerusalem and its tiny rocky neighbors, Broken Jerusalem and Round Rock, provide nesting sites for red-billed and white-tailed tropicbirds, brown boobies, noddies, terns, brown pelicans, and laughing gulls.

A group of tiny islands due north of Virgin Gorda, known as The Dogs and comprising 165.5 acres/67 hectares of land and 4,435 acres/1,795 hectares of sea, has been proposed as a sanctuary for gulls and the roseate and other terns to protect the natural vegetation on the land and the coral reefs in the surrounding waters, which are particularly attractive for divers. The 24-acre/9.7-hectare West Dog, in fact, has already been declared a refuge for a colony of laughing gulls and nesting doves. On Great Tobago Island, the most westerly of the BVI, 210 acres/85 hectares have been designated as a sanctuary for the magnificent frigatebird colony, the only one to be found north of Barbuda and east of Mona Passage. These islands can only be reached by private or chartered boat.

On Guana Island just north of Tortola, the Guana Island Wildlife Sanctuary has eight Caribbean or greater flamingos, which were brought from Bermuda in 1986 with the hope of initiating a breeding colony. According to historical records, thousands of native flamingos once nested in the British Virgin Islands.

ANEGADA

Anegada, the most northerly of the BVI, is the exception to nearly everything that characterizes the group. Where the others are mountainous and lush, Anegada is slateboard flat, dry, and bare of foliage. With a maximum elevation of only 28 ft/8.5 m, a simple tide change can dramatically affect the island's contours. Little wonder the Spanish name for it means "flooded."

Unlike the other islands, which are of volcanic origin, Anegada is 15 sq mi/39 sq km of emerged coral atoll fringed by treacherous horseshoe-shaped reefs. In pirate days of yore, the island was especially appreciated as a haven since its low-lying reefs were almost certain to pierce the hulls of unwary pursuers. Indeed, an estimated 200 ships met their watery end here. Today the area is a magnet for divers who through their discoveries have provided most of the underwater archaeological knowledge available.

Anegada's wildlife is another anomaly. The island has about 2,000 wild goats, cattle, and donkeys, outnumbering the human population about eleven to one. The forebears of the animal population probably swam ashore during shipwrecks. But there is no such simple explanation for why the rock iguana, endemic to and once found throughout the BVI, survives today only on Anegada, one of the least hospitable of the local environments. This endangered reptile, of which an estimated 400 remain, can grow 5 ft/1.5 m long and weigh 20 lbs/9 kg. It struts freely around the island, eating food plants and annoying the other creatures.

Recently, a few rock iguanas were taken to Guana Island ostensibly to prevent the lizard's extinction should its population on Anegada be decimated by disease or habitat loss. The National Parks Trust hopes to establish an iguana sanctuary on Anegada to propagate the species, similar to its bird sanctuary at Flamingo Pond where 1,100 acres/445 hectares were set aside for waterfowl and other birds to feed and breed in the salt pond and mangroves. Among the birds seen here are nesting willet, snowy plover, little blue heron, green-backed heron, tricolored heron, and Antillean nighthawk. Anegada has the great blue heron and an occasional osprey, and during summer it is home to the roseate, Sandwich, and gull-billed terns.

French grunts tend to swim close together in schools when an intruder is present.

OUTDOOR ACTIVITIES

CAMPING: The BVI has campgrounds at Brewer's Bay on Tortola and on Jost Van Dyke. Both have about fifteen campsites, a small restaurant or snack bar, and a grocery. Brewer's Bay is more remote and is best reached by jeep. The camp on Jost Van Dyke is directly next to the ferry landing, which is fortunate because the tiny island has no taxis or car-hire service. One must bring cooking and bedding supplies; a few erected tents are available but the rest are bare sites. Camping here is very popular, and one should write ahead to reserve a site. Facilities and prices vary considerably at each location.

HORSEBACK RIDING: The BVI have no riding stables for tourists but one can sometimes arrange to visit Tortola's Sage Mountain on horseback through Ellis Thomas, the Tortolian owner of BVI's only racetrack, who occasionally leads a trek. From the racetrack at Sea Cows Bay, a few miles southwest of Road Town, riders meander up the hillside through valleys and meadows, pausing here and there to enjoy magnificent views or to take in the ruins of an eighteenth-century plantation. Equestrian skill is not essential, but paying attention is, lest one miss the guide's commentary on the local history, flora, and fauna. Like many other activities in the BVI, however, this excursion is an impromptu affair. Those interested will need to make inquiries locally; the racetrack owner has no phone.

SNORKELING AND DIVING: After sailing, scuba diving and snorkeling are the most popular activities. Marine life is abundant and the reefs healthy; the BVI's relative remoteness and low tour-

Longspine squirrelfish.

Porcupinefish.

ist profile have limited the flow of divers. There are no dramatic drop-offs or sheer walls as in the Caymans; rather, most reefs here range from 30 to 50 ft/9 to 15 m deep, with many at only 10 to 30 ft/3 to 9 m. The wreck of *The Rhone*, at about 80 ft/24 m, is one of the few deep dives available.

A brittle star.

In general, sites are spectacular for their color, variety, and good condition, rather than their physical drama. Some, such as The Indians or Blonde Rock, have tunnels to swim through and caves swarming with copper sweepers. Carrot Rock near Cooper Island is a granite slab fronted by large pillar corals that reach toward the surface from 100 ft/30 m below.

Banded coral shrimp.

Divers will find an abundance of colorful fish common to the Caribbean, such as wrasses, grunts, damselfishes, and parrotfishes, along with less frequently seen species such as queen angelfish. The variety of sponges and soft corals is enough to send an underwater photographer into a shooting frenzy. One purple tube sponge at Norman Island is more than 4 ft/1.2 m long and as thick as a man's thigh. Off Peter Island on the wreck of the *Fearless*, which lies between two coral heads in about 80 ft/24 m of water, one can find relatively rare and beautiful purple and white tunicates, their delicate semitransparent bulbs clustered on a strand of a big, healthy black coral tree. This new dive site was created by sinking a 97-ft/30-m ship originally built as a mine sweeper.

The best visibility in Tortola's waters is normally found in the area between Norman and Ginger islands, an area accessible from Tortola on day trips offered by dive shops, charter sailboats, or live-aboard dive boats. Since destinations on day trips depend largely on weather and sea conditions, itineraries are not set far in advance. But normally one can learn the next day's plan by phoning the dive operator a day ahead. Most operators are associated with hotels with which they offer combination packages; some have pickup services for those living aboard sailboats. Glass-bottom boat tours are available too.

Remote Anegada offers superb diving, particularly for visitors who enjoy exploring wrecks. At least sixty wrecks have been charted on the reefs fringing the island. Regrettably, Anegada has limited access; it is reached most easily by a live-aboard dive boat, small plane, or chartered sailboat.

FISHING: Sport-fishing is relatively undeveloped in the BVI, despite the fact that it is surrounded by some of the richest game-fishing waters in the world, including the 50-mi/80-km Puerto Rican Trench near Anegada. Sailfish, bonefish, tuna, and marlin abound throughout BVI waters. Charter operators on Tortola, Virgin Gorda, and Anegada offer pickup service from one's hotel for half-day, full-day, or long-term trips.

SAILING: The BVI are blessed with some of the finest sailing waters in the world. Tradewinds blow steadily from the northeast, and the islands are closely situated in a double line along the Drake Channel, shutting out heavy seas. Boats can sail from one island to another in a few hours and almost always in view of land, which makes navigation easy. Charterers based at Tortola's seven marinas offer some of the world's highest-quality, best-equipped sailing yachts for hire—bareboat or with crew—for a day, a week, or longer. Motorboats are available too. There are sailing schools that offer learn-to-sail weeks. Most BVI operators will not allow charterers to sail to the U.S. Virgin Islands for insurance reasons, and night sailing is forbidden for safety reasons.

West of Tortola, Jost Van Dyke has beautiful anchorages at White Bay, Great Harbour, and East End Harbour, all within an hour's sail. It is also a single tack from St. John's. Great Harbour, palm-fringed and one of the BVI's most popular anchorages, is likely to be filled with yachts. The island has trails and a resident, Ivan Chinnery, conducts nature walks; inquire locally. Offshore are the soft white beaches of Sandy Cay. On Tortola's west end, Little and Great Thatch are favorite stops too. Each harbor has its partisans.

SURFING: Cane Garden Bay and Apple and Carrot Beaches on the northwest coast of Tortola are favorite and well known locations.

WINDSURFING: Although equipment is available at many of the resorts, the sport has not been seriously developed here. A school, Boardsailing BVI, at Trellis Bay on Beef Island, offers lessons.

Most visitors arrive first in Tortola where they charter a boat or connect with onward transportation to reach any of the small resorts scattered about the other islands. But even getting to Tortola requires a certain amount of determination and good humor. There are no direct flights from the U.S.; passengers fly via San Juan, St. Thomas, or St. Croix to connect with one of the feeder lines serving Tortola or Virgin Gorda. Charter and scheduled air service is also available between Tortola and Anguilla, Antigua, St. Kitts, and St. Martin. Beef Island, the site of Tortola's main airport, is separated from the island by only 300 ft/91 m of one-lane highway. Interisland aircraft carrying up to forty passengers are the largest planes that land there.

Large ferryboats, some with topside sun decks and bars, are an alternative mode of transportation. There is frequent service between St. Thomas and St. John, USVI, and Tortola's West End and Road Town. Most cross in about three hours and are competitively priced; tickets may be purchased at the dock. In high season, one should buy a round-trip ticket and be at the dock early to ensure a seat. Service on a less frequent schedule is available from St. Thomas or Tortola to Virgin Gorda, Anegada, and Jost Van Dyke.

The three points of entry to Tortola—Road Town, the ferry landing at West End, and the airport at Beef Island/East End—are linked by paved road. Secondary roads, also paved, wind over the mountainous interior and link these centers with Brewer's Bay, Cane Garden Bay, and other resort regions along the northwest coast. Other roads are unpaved, and access to more remote areas requires four-wheel-drive. Taxis are abundant on Tortola and can be hired by the day from stands at Beef Island Airport and on the waterfront in Road Town. Rates are fixed according to distance traveled.

Although there is a 3,000-ft/914-m airstrip for private planes on Virgin Gorda, most visitors arrive by sea. Hence, shoreside activity centers in Spanish Town and its large marinas, minimizing the need for auto transportation. Four- to six-passenger jeeps, mopeds, and bicycles can be rented on a daily basis at Yacht Harbor.

Organized sightseeing on Tortola and Virgin Gorda is typically a half-day tour by minivan; taxis and travel agencies offer these tours. On Virgin Gorda an open-air jitney makes shuttle stops at the main bays, Spanish Town, and The Baths. By taking the service, one can see most of the island in under three hours. On either island, it is almost impossible to get lost while sightseeing on one's own. Major car-rental firms as well as independent ones have offices in Tortola; two companies rent cars on Virgin Gorda; no car-hire service is available on the other islands. Remember, in this British Colony driving is on the LEFT.

INFORMATION: In North America: British Virgin Islands Tourist Board, 370 Lexington Ave., Suite 313, New York, NY 10017; 212-696-0400, 800-835-8530. In the U.K.: % FCB Travel/Marketing, 110 St. Martin's Lane, London, WC2N 4DY; 71-240-4259. In the BVI: BVI Tourist Board, Box 134, Road Town, Tortola; 809-494-3134. National Parks Trust, Fishlock Road, Road Town, Tortola; 809-494-3904.

ANGUILLA

ST. MAARTEN/ST. MARTIN

ST. BARTHELEMY

SABA

ST. EUSTATIUS

ST. KITTS AND NEVIS

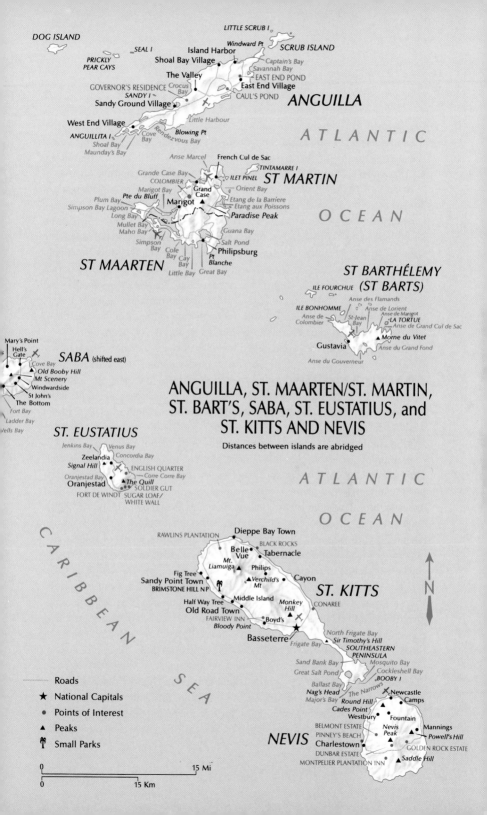

DOG ISLAND

LITTLE SCRUB I.

SEAL I.

PRICKLY
PEAR CAYS

Windward Pt
Island Harbor
Shoal Bay Village
The Valley
Captain's Bay
Savannah Bay
East End Village
EAST END POND
CAUL'S POND

SCRUB ISLAND

GOVERNOR'S RESIDENCE
Crocus
Bay
SANDY I.
Sandy Ground Village

ANGUILLA

West End Village
ANGUILLITA I.
Shoal Bay
Maunday's Bay
Cove
Bay
Blowing Pt
Rendezvous Bay
Little Harbour

ATLANTIC

Anse Marcel
French Cul de Sac
Grande Case Bay
COLOMBIER
Marigot Bay
Pte du Bluff
Marigot
Plum Bay
Simpson Bay Lagoon
Long Bay
Mullet Bay
Maho Bay
Simpson
Bay
Cole
Bay
Cay
Bay

ST MARTIN
TINTAMARRE I.
ILET PINEL
Grand
Case
Orient Bay
Étang de la Barriere
Étang aux Poissons
Paradise Peak
Guana Bay
Salt
Pond
Philipsburg
Pt
Blanche

ST MAARTEN
Little Bay
Great Bay

OCEAN

ST BARTHÉLEMY
(ST BARTS)
ILE FOURCHUE
Anse des Flamands
ILE BONHOMME
Anse de Lorient
Anse de Marigot
Anse de
Colombier
St-Jean
Bay
LA TORTUE
Anse de Grand Cul de Sac
Morne du Vitet
Gustavia
Anse du Grand Fond
Anse du Gouverneur

Mary's Point
Hell's
Gate
Cove Bay
Old Booby Hill
Mt Scenery
Windwardside
St John's
The Bottom
Fort Bay
Ladder Bay
Wells Bay

SABA (shifted east)

ST. EUSTATIUS
Jenkins Bay
Venus Bay
Zeelandia
Concordia Bay
Signal Hill
ENGLISH QUARTER
Corre Corre Bay
Oranjestad
The Quill
SOLDIER GUT
FORT DE WINDT
SUGAR LOAF/
WHITE WALL

ANGUILLA, ST. MAARTEN/ST. MARTIN,
ST. BART'S, SABA, ST. EUSTATIUS, and
ST. KITTS AND NEVIS

Distances between islands are abridged

ATLANTIC

OCEAN

C
A
R
I
B
B
E
A
N

S
E
A

RAWLINS PLANTATION
Dieppe Bay Town
Belle
Vue
BLACK ROCKS
Tabernacle
Mt.
Liamuiga
Philips
Fig Tree
Verchild's
Mt
Cayon
Sandy Point Town
BRIMSTONE HILL N.P.
Half Way Tree
Middle Island
Monkey
Hill
CONAREE
Old Road Town
FAIRVIEW INN
Bloody Point
Boyd's
Basseterre
Frigate Bay
North Frigate Bay
Sir Timothy's Hill
SOUTHEASTERN
PENINSULA
Mosquito Bay
Cockleshell Bay
Sand Bank Bay
Great Salt Pond
BOOBY I.
Ballast Bay
The Narrows
Newcastle
Nag's Head
Round Hill
Camps
Major's Bay
Cades Point
Westbury
Fountain
BELMONT ESTATE
Nevis
Peak
Mannings
PINNEY'S BEACH
Powell's Hill
Charlestown
DUNBAR ESTATE
GOLDEN ROCK ESTATE
MONTPELIER PLANTATION INN
Saddle Hill

ST. KITTS

NEVIS

N

Roads
★ National Capitals
• Points of Interest
▲ Peaks
⛺ Small Parks

0   15 Mi
0   15 Km

ANGUILLA

LIMESTONE HILLS honeycombed with water-sculpted caves, seawalls alive with nesting birds and coral reefs hosting thousands of bright tropical fish: these are some of the features that make this quiet, little-known spot in the northeastern corner of the Leeward Islands a delight for nature lovers.

Anguilla, 10 mi/16 km north of St. Martin, is a low-lying island of limestone and coral with a scalloped white-sand coastline bathed by clear turquoise and cobalt blue waters that have attracted fishermen for centuries and yachtsmen for decades. Measuring 16 mi/26 km long and 3 mi/4.8 km wide at its largest bulge, it rises above the sea from the Anguilla Bank only 130 ft/40 m below the water's surface. Compared with other islands in this corner of the Caribbean, Anguilla is dry and flat, except for some hills and limestone ridges on the north side—an intriguing matter when one learns that geologists believe Anguilla and the neighboring mountainous islands of St. Martin and St. Barts formed one landmass only 7,000 years ago.

Whether Anguilla was once covered with forests like her neighbors is debated by scientists. But for certain in modern times, the harvesting of white cedar for boatbuilding and to make charcoal for cooking, together with periodic destruction by hurricanes and long periods of drought, have left most of the island covered with low scrub or degraded evergreen woodland. There are a few patches of mangroves and several freshwater swamps and saltwater ponds where birdlife is plentiful.

A complete study of Anguilla's flora has yet to be made, but a preliminary survey lists sixty-two species of trees. Although few in number, the most common fruit trees of the tropics, such as mango, soursop, and avocado, and flowering trees, such as flamboyant and frangipani, are here. Over the past decade changing agricultural traditions combined with a seemingly altered weather pattern marked by higher levels of rainfall are making the island unusually green for long periods of the year.

The Dutch began mining salt on Anguilla in 1630, and the first European settlers—landless English farmers and freed indentured servants from St. Kitts—arrived in 1650, but Malliouhana, as Anguilla was known to its former Arawak inhabitants, was inhabited as early as the fifth century, and possibly as early as 2000 B.C. Anguilla formally became a British colony in the early nineteenth century but was left to its own resources, making the islanders independent and self-reliant—characteristics they have kept to this day. Only in the 1970s did the island get its first paved roads, electricity, and telephones. It remained the place time left behind, appealing to yachtsmen and true beachcombers for its unspoiled qualities, until the 1980s when resort development began. Since 1983 in particular, with the overnight success of a very posh new resort, building has continued at a gallop and brought with it a boom that could barely have been imagined a decade ago. So far, however, there are no golf courses, casinos, or shopping arcades, and there are still as many goats and sheep as people.

Anguilla's tiny main town, The Valley, is a hodgepodge of shops, offices, government buildings, and colorful houses of West Indian architecture, vaguely bounded by four nameless roads that form a rectangle. It is located about midisland, a mile north of the airport and 4 mi/6.4 km from Blowing Point, where ferries from St. Martin dock.

CROCUS BAY

After rising steeply to Crocus Hill, one of the highest points on the island, the main road descends precipitously to Crocus Bay, a popular fishing area. Boats can be hired here to take one to coves east of the bay for snorkeling. The limestone cliffs to the east and west of Crocus Bay are favorite nesting areas for the tropicbird. Laughing gulls, boobies, magnificent frigatebirds, and brown pelicans can usually be seen here too. The royal tern and brown noddy nest here in summer. The setting is magnificent at sunset.

West of Crocus Bay old footpaths cut by islanders and their sheep and goats meander along the top of the ridge above Katouche Bay to Sandy Ground and can be used for hiking. Hikers will need to ask locally for directions, however, since the paths are becoming less defined with each passing year as their use by Anguillans diminishes.

FOUNTAIN CAVE

About 0.25 mi/0.4 km before reaching Shoal Bay on the northeast coast, a dirt track on the left (west) leads to The Fountain, a large dome-shaped limestone cavern on a ridge about 70 ft/21 m above sea level. It contains Anguilla's most important archaeological site, discovered in 1979, where extraordinary petroglyphs of Arawak deities are carved on stalagmites. The most important represents Jocahu, known as the creator of cassava and hence the supreme god of the Arawaks. The nature of these petroglyphs has led researchers to speculate that the cave may have been an Arawak religious or ceremonial center, perhaps one of the most important in the Caribbean. The only other petroglyph of Jocahu ever found was discovered in Cuba and is now in a museum in the United States. That the petroglyphs had not been vandalized or damaged is all the more remarkable

Pages 184 and 185: Low-lying Anguilla's popular Shoal Bay beach, located on the northern coast, is two miles long and is more isolated at its eastern end.

since the cave contains a source of fresh water often used during droughts.

The cave entrance, 60 ft/18 m above the cavern floor, is very small, allowing in little natural light. Growing out of the opening is an old banyan tree, known locally as a monkey mango, whose long, exposed roots were once used like ropes for shinnying down to the cavern floor. A steel ladder was added in 1953 for easier access. The government plans to develop 4.75 acres/2 hectares of land surrounding the cave as a national park, but meanwhile, the cave is closed to prevent damage.

The site for the park, extending from the shoreline to the highland behind the cave opening, already has a representative cross section of the island's flora. Seagrape and coconut palms can be seen along the beach. Inland, the dense growth includes buttonwood, torchwood, mawby, black chink, ironwood, loblolly, and Anguillan frangipani trees (called pigeon-wood here). The highest point is marked by turpentine trees.

Shoal Bay, one of the island's most beautiful beaches, is losing the ecology race to beach bars and condominiums, but Upper Shoal Bay, the eastern side of the coast, has so far been spared. Here, a sand spit is often populated by seabirds rather than tourists.

CAUL'S POND AND EAST END POND

On the main road to Island Harbor at the sign for Clynton's Hidden Rainbow Bar and Restaurant, a dirt road leads south to Caul's Pond, a large area of brackish water that attracts huge flocks of black-necked stilts and white-cheeked pintail ducks at sunset. Among the other birds seen here are the great white heron, the belted kingfisher, and the endangered peregrine falcon, which can knock down its target in flight at speeds of up to 175 mph/280 kph, making it the world's second fastest bird.

One can walk easily along the flat, gravelly north shore of the pond for closer viewing, but the birds' favorite gathering place, the southwest corner, is more difficult to approach because the road peters out in a thickly wooded area where footpaths, such as they are, are overgrown. The vegetation around the pond is typical of the island. There are some particularly good examples of Turk's-head cactus (also known as pope's crown) and native Anguillan frangipani, whose leaf is much narrower than the cultivated frangipani, although the flower is similar. Curiously, this tree is called pigeonwood on the east end of Anguilla and frangipani on the west end.

On the south side of the island, in the direction of Savannah Bay, the main road skirts East End Pond, another bird-watching area, particularly for two types of egret and a variety of warblers.

ISLAND HARBOR

From Island Harbor, a lilliputian fishing village on a horseshoe bay on the northeast coast, most of the island's fleet sets out each day for the catch that supplies the markets and restaurants of St. Martin as well as Anguilla. By afternoon the fishermen have drawn their colorful boats onto the beach and can be seen mending their nets, repairing their boats, or relaxing after the day's work. Many fishermen still build their boats by hand without a blueprint by methods handed down from one generation to another. The most colorful is a racing vessel used on special holidays and raced annually on the first Thursday in August in the middle of Carnival, the most important regatta of the year.

CAPTAIN'S BAY AND WINDWARD POINT

East of Island Harbor, rough dirt roads, best negotiated by jeep or by foot, lead to several locations on the eastern end of the island. The most notable are Captain's Bay on the north coast, where a secluded, romantic beach of beautiful white sand is bracketed by limestone cliffs, and Windward Point at the tip, the most isolated area with untamed landscape and a rough seascape of Atlantic waves breaking against the rocky coast. Porpoises and dolphins can often be spotted offshore.

SANDY GROUND

Located on the northwest side of the island, 2.5 mi/4 km west of The Valley, Sandy Ground is the principal cargo and yacht harbor where visitors in their own yachts and cruise ships usually dock. It has a spit of land known as Road Bay which is fringed by a pretty beach on one side and salt ponds on the other. Sandy Ground was once Anguilla's salt-mining center; today, it is an area of small resort development and the most convenient location for hiring boats and equipment for water sports. Sandy Ground's salt ponds and the ridges and beaches along the north shore—Long Bay, Mead's Bay, Barnes Bay, West End Bay—attract a variety of birds and are popular locations at sunset for watching gulls, pelicans, and other birds dive for their food and soar over the sea in the light of the setting sun.

CAVANAH AND KATOUCHE CAVES

Midway between Sandy Ground and The Valley a paved road branches north from the main highway to Old Ta where Government House, the residence and office of the governor of the island, is located. In a field directly east of the house, footpaths lead to two caves: Cavanah Cave, a former phosphate mine, and Katouche Cave, which takes its name from the

A small coral arch on the southern shore of Anguilla faces St. Maarten and the Caribbean.

bay below. The latter is home to many bats. Both sites are an easy twenty-minute walk from the main road, but one would need a local person to show the way since the paths have been lost to new growth. What's more, a large tree grows out of the opening of Katouche Cave; it marks the entrance but at the same time helps to obscure it. Spelunkers will need lights to explore the caves as very little light penetrates beyond the entrance. Both caves have some minor stalactite formations. The vegetation along the way is typical of the island: there are tamarind trees and good examples of Turk's-head cactus, and occasionally one may see wild orchids.

In 1883 the Smithsonian Institution published an account of the discovery in the Cavanah Cave of the skeleton of *Amblyrhisa inundata*, an extinct rodent as large as a goat or deer. Anguilla and St. Martin are the only places where traces of the species have been found.

South Coast Beaches and Ponds

The south coast facing the Caribbean, with the outline of mountainous St. Martin in the distance, is fringed by one long, magnificent beach after another. Little Harbor, a sheltered cove with a modern resort and some residential development, has a small patch of mangrove and a shallow-water reef that is popular with snorkelers.

West of Blowing Point lies the almost perfect arc of Rendezvous Bay, one of Anguilla's most beautiful beaches. Fringed by rolling sand dunes, this quiet beach is usually studded with pretty seashells and oddly shaped driftwood as well as coconuts that have fallen from the palm trees that shade the sands. Farther west, Cove Bay, Maunday's Bay, Shoal Bay (not to be confused with Shoal Bay on the northeast coast), and Sherrick's Bay are magnificent stretches of powdery white sands, some of which have been taken up by new resorts.

The entire western tip of Anguilla is interlaced with ponds that have had birdlife in the past. But resort construction is altering this terrain. Some ponds have been partially filled in; others have been opened to the sea. It remains to be seen if the birds will return to these feeding grounds after construction stops. Gull Pond, at the western end of Maunday's Bay, has some mangroves; the owners who are developing the resort on this bay plan to make the pond into a sanctuary for local and migratory birds. Maunday's Bay also has some of the largest seagrape trees on the island.

Seagrape grows on the northeast coast around Fountain Cave, an important archeological site, as well as around Maunday's Bay on the south shore.

OFFSHORE ISLANDS

Off Anguilla's westernmost tip, tiny Anguillita is an islet popular for snorkeling. Sandy Island, off the northwest coast, is another islet with pretty beaches; it has good snorkeling for beginners. Unfortunately, the pristine quality of this once idyllic spot is being eroded; a beach bar has set up shop and day-trippers from St. Martin have discovered the island in more numbers than old salts like to see. Prickly Pear Cays, also off the northwest coast, are pretty atolls surrounded by reefs with huge elkhorn coral.

Dog Island, farther to the northwest, holds interest for both archaeologists and naturalists. Ten pre-Columbian sites have been uncovered here, and the middle of Dog Island's three cays is a nesting ground for brown pelicans and one of the few places in the Caribbean where the masked, or blue-faced, booby nests. All can be reached by boat from Road Bay.

Off Anguilla's eastern tip lie Scrub Island and Little Scrub, sparsely covered, unpopulated islands that are popular for picnicking and snorkeling excursions from Island Harbor. Little Scrub has interesting coral formations and flocks of seabirds.

OUTDOOR ACTIVITIES

SWIMMING: Anguilla boasts thirty-two beaches of powdery white sand washed by spectacular turquoise waters. Two of the island's most secluded, deserted beaches can be reached by road from Crocus Hill north of The Valley: Little Bay, a cove with a sliver of sand encircled by some of the highest cliffs on the island, is reached by a steep descent from the edge of the road; Limestone Bay awaits at the end of a dirt road toward the northeast. Other secluded beaches are at Savannah Bay and Mimi Bay on the southeast coast, both reached by dirt roads. Among beaches with facilities and places to rent watersports equipment, Shoal Bay in the north has one of the island's most beautiful stretches of beach; it faces a large reef that is within easy swimming distance for snorkelers.

SNORKELING AND DIVING: Off Anguilla's west and northwest coasts lie two large reefs, one behind the other, where enormous coral formations grow to the surface of the sea. The gardens have a great variety of species that include sea fans, star coral, and flower coral, but the most dramatic are the huge elkhorn and staghorn corals. Darting about in this majestic setting are striped squirrelfishes, torpedo-headed wrasse, butterflyfishes and angelfishes, sergeant majors and damselfishes, trumpetfishes, garfish, and tiny metallic squids, to name a few.

Beautiful and fascinating as the reefs are today, they were treacherous territory for trading captains of yore, judging by the variety of wrecked ships and undelivered cargo that went down off Anguilla's shores. At least two dozen shipwrecks have been identified off the south coast, on northern reefs, and near Dog, Sandy, and Scrub islands. Many others await exploration.

A water-sports center on the beach in Road Bay is a PADI training facility and offers scuba-diving courses as well as snorkeling excursions and a variety of water sports. The center has trips to different islands each day.

Out beyond the reefs, humpback and sperm whales migrate northward from the Caribbean in March and April and return on their southward journey in September and October. Often they can be sighted off Anguilla's coast. The slower-moving humpbacks are easier to spot since they tend to stick closer to the shore.

BOATING AND FISHING: Slick yachts or humble fishing boats are available to take visitors to nearby offshore islands for a picnic and a day of snorkeling or deep-sea fishing. Arrangements can be made in Road Bay, Crocus Bay, or Island Harbor.

WINDSURFING: Most beachfront hotels and water-sports centers have windsurfing equipment. The calmer south and west coasts are best for beginners, while the north and east coasts where the waters are rougher offer more challenge.

EXPLORING THE ISLAND

Anguilla has no public transportation system. But car and jeep rentals, which are the most convenient means for exploring the island, are plentiful and reasonably priced. Main roads are good; secondary ones are dirt tracks and some are suitable only for high-mounted four-wheel-drive vehicles. Driving in this British Colony is on the LEFT.

Roads do not have names or numbers, and there are almost no road signs. Rather, Anguillans refer to places by their location on the island ("East End," "West End") or by their proximity to the nearest bay or beach. Hence, one should approach sightseeing in the same manner, that is, by exploring one end or one area of island at a time. Main roads run east-west from The Valley and branch north or south to principal locations; no road makes a complete loop around the island. At Mahogoney Tree Corner, the main stoplight in The Valley, two roads lead east to the fishing village of Island Harbor on the northeast shore. After 3 mi/4.8 km the northernmost of the two forks left to Shoal Bay.

Finding one's way is not as difficult as it may seem since reasonably good maps are available. The Land and Survey Department's topographical maps show some footpaths and tracks and are suggested for hikers. The Department as well as the Anguilla Tourist Office are located in a group of government buildings midway between The Valley and the airport.

Taxis are available at the airport and ferry landing. Reputable car rental companies can be counted on to have new cars in good condition, and they usually offer free pickup and delivery, road map, unlimited mileage, and emergency road service. Upon presentation of a valid driver's license, car rental companies issue customers a local driving permit, which is required; there is a small fee. Motorbikes are available for rent, too.

INFORMATION: In North America: Anguilla Tourist Office, % Medhurst & Assoc., The Huntington Atrium, 775 Park Avenue, Huntington, NY 11743; 516-271-2600; 800-553-4939. In the U.K.: Windotel, 3 Epirus Road, London 3W6 7UJ; 01-937-7725. In Anguilla: Anguilla Department of Tourism, The Valley, Anguilla, WI; 809-497-2759. Anguilla Archaeological and Historical Society, P.O. Box 252, The Valley, Anguilla, BWI. The Society's report on archaeological sites, with maps of their locations, is on sale at local stores.

ST. MAARTEN/ ST. MARTIN

THE LARGEST OF THE DUTCH WINDWARD ISLANDS, Sint Maarten shares the island, roughly half and half, with French Saint Martin. The combination of two cultures in so small a space is one reason for the island's popularity with tourists. The pretty scenery—green mountains, scalloped bays, long stretches of powdery white sand beaches, and turquoise seas—is a further attraction. For these reasons, and because it is a major air and sea gateway to the northeastern Caribbean, the island has enjoyed a nonstop boom for twenty years. Though naturalists are likely to find too much development for their liking, they should not dismiss this island. The creature comforts it offers—excellent hotels and French restaurants, a pleasant climate with low humidity—make it a relaxing base from which to explore the more rugged islands of Saba and St. Eustatius. Anguilla, St. Barts, St. Kitts, and Nevis are also a short plane or ferry ride away. St. Maarten's own beaches are gorgeous and there are quiet country roads for strolling; the sports facilities here are excellent, and many small boats take visitors to offshore islands and cays for snorkeling, diving, or picnicking. With some creative planning, one can be a pampered tourist one day and a curious explorer the next.

The two halves of St. Maarten/St. Martin are quite distinctive. Before Columbus found the island in 1493 and claimed it for Spain, it had been inhabited by Arawaks and Caribs. Over more than a century, it changed hands between the Dutch, French, and Spaniards, but in 1648 the Spaniards abandoned their claim to Holland, and the French agreed to divide the spoils with the Dutch. Local legend has it that land was divided between the Dutch and French by having a Dutchman and a Frenchman walk in opposite directions around the island from the same starting point; when they met, the starting and finishing points were connected and that line formed the border. Apparently, the Frenchman's stride was faster: the French side of 21 sq mi/54 sq km is slightly larger than the Dutch area of 16 sq mi/41 sq km. Today there are no real boundaries or border formalities between the two.

PHILIPSBURG

The main town of St. Maarten, Philipsburg, is situated on a thin stretch of land separating the deepwater harbor of Great Bay on the south from Salt Pond on the north; hills anchor the town at either end. Two thoroughfares—Front Street and Back Street—run east–west and between them, running north–south, are little lanes, or *steegjes*, that are crowded with boutiques and restaurants. Wathey Square, the heart of the town where the Sint Maarten Tourist Board office is located, is a good place to start a stroll around town. Several old buildings of West Indian architecture with gingerbread trim remain.

Boats and ferries to neighboring islands depart from marinas at the eastern bend of the bay. Near the south end of the hilly finger separating Great Bay and Little Bay are the ruins of Fort Amsterdam with a view east over Philipsburg and the cliffs of Point Blanche and north to Fort Hill and the ruins of Fort William. A walkway crosses over the western hills between the two bays.

Cole Bay and Cay Bay

A series of hills—Fort Hill, Cay Bay Hill, and Cole Bay Hill—separates Philipsburg from the west end of the island where many resorts and some of the best beaches are located. North of town along Salt Pond, roads leading west to the airport skirt the north side of Cole Bay Hill, where the Scottish adventurer John Philips lies buried on the hill overlooking the town he founded. From the summit, a wide view overlooks Great Bay and Little Bay and extends to neighboring St. Barts on the southeast, with Saba, St. Eustatius, St. Kitts, and Nevis farther out to sea. Cay Bay has one of the more secluded beaches on the Dutch side. A hike between Cole Bay and Cay Bay takes less than an hour and follows a trail used by early-morning equestrians from a nearby riding center.

The West End

Landlocked Simpson Bay Lagoon, one of the best hurricane anchorages in the eastern Caribbean, is a center for water sports. Two cuts spanned by bridges—on the south side at Simpson Bay and on the north side at Marigot Bay—enable boats to enter the lagoon. At the east end, the main road forks north directly to Marigot, the main town of French St. Martin, and crosses the boundary between the two countries. The fork west skirts the south side of the lagoon, paralleling the airport. Maho Bay and Mullet Bay, two beautiful beaches with large resorts, are at the western end of the runway. At the west end of the lagoon the main road turns north but secondary roads wind through the hills of the peninsula that forms the western end of the island. The area is pleasant for hiking because the traffic is light, and there are pretty views of the coast, access to magnificent beaches, and vantage points for watching gorgeous sunsets.

Cupecoy Bay, at the western end of the national boundary, has a dramatic setting of sandstone cliffs with small caves where Arawak artifacts have

been found. Footpaths provide public access to the beach from a dirt road west of the Cupecoy Beach Resort. West of the cliffs is Long Bay, one of the finest white sand beaches in the Caribbean. It begins at La Samanna, a cliffside luxury resort smothered in bougainvillea and tropical gardens, and curves over 1 mi/1.6 km around a crescent of beach to Plum Bay, marked by a lighthouse. Any spot along the way makes a fine perch for watching a Caribbean sunset. Long Bay and Plum Bay beaches have topless bathing.

The wooded northern slopes of the peninsula overlook Baie Rouge, or Red Bay, one of the most secluded of St. Martin's beaches. From here, cliffs of multihued rocks extend north to Pointe du Bluff, a finger of land that anchors the northwest end of Marigot Bay, one of St. Martin's widest, prettiest bays with exceptionally clear aquamarine waters. La Belle Creole, a deluxe resort built to resemble a Mediterranean village, commands a superb view of the bay from the Point. A road around the bay skirts the north side of Simpson Bay Lagoon to the town of Marigot.

MARIGOT

Marigot is a St. Tropez in the tropics, complete with sidewalk cafés, fishing boats, and topless beaches. Only a twenty-minute drive from Philipsburg, it is so unmistakably Gallic that one does not need the signs or khaki-clad gendarmes to know this is France. Despite recent development, the little village has retained enough of its old character to make a stroll through town a delight. The harbor, always full with fishing boats and ferries departing for Anguilla, has an outdoor fruit and vegetable market that is particularly lively on Saturday mornings. The recently restored Fort Marigot on a hilltop north of the harbor commands a nice view of the town and bay and the island of Anguilla.

COLOMBIER AND PARADISE PEAK

There are several places to stop for short hikes along the road between Marigot and Grande Case, the main town of the north. About halfway to Grande Case a country road leads inland through tranquil green pastures that seem light-years away from the resorts and casinos of the coast. One can walk or drive the mile to Colombier, a rural area of traditional houses set in gardens of poinsettias, bougainvillea, and hibiscus where humming-birds dart among the blossoms. Behind Colombier rises the spine of mountains that crosses the island from north to south.

About 0.2 mi/0.3 km beyond the turn-off to Colombier, another country lane turns inland from the main road and winds up Paradise Peak (1,378 ft/

Turk's-head cactus grows on a slope overlooking Guana Bay on the east coast of St. Maarten.

420 m), the island's highest hill. Off this lane a dirt road on the left can be traversed by car to the peak; the hike is pleasant, too. Paradise Peak receives more rainfall than most other parts of St. Martin and is one of its most verdant areas. As the road ascends, the vegetation becomes more dense and lush with ferns and other tropical vegetation. At the parking area, a short loop path goes to a viewpoint looking out to Philipsburg, Salt Pond, and Great Bay on the south; Anguilla on the north; and Oyster Pond and the Atlantic coast on the east. From a radio tower on the southwest side, there are views of Marigot and the bay. The ascent by foot to the peak takes about an hour.

GRANDE CASE AND FRENCH CUL DE SAC

Pretty little Grande Case enjoys an international reputation as a haven for gourmets. The main road through town forks at the north end where a dirt track turns west to Grande Case Beach and a small resort whose well-equipped water-sports center serves this part of the island. The fork on the east cuts across the island to French Cul de Sac, Orient Bay, and the Atlantic coast. The hilly, wooded northern end of St. Martin is still its least developed, most isolated part, but probably not for long—several resorts are under construction. A steep country road winds up through the hills to Anse Marcel, a beautiful cove with French St. Martin's largest resort, a marina, and a riding stable nearby.

ORIENT BAY AND FLAMAND BAY

At the north end of Orient Bay on the Atlantic coast, Etang de la Barrière is a pretty cove surrounded by barren hills with pockets of woods. The beach's sandbanks contain thousands of ancient shells. Just offshore are the tiny islands of Petite Clef on the south and Ilet Pinel on the north; both have fine beaches and reefs ideal for snorkeling. Ilet Pinel has wild goats that browse on its vegetation of scrub and cactus; one can walk around the island in about an hour. Arrangements to reach the islands can be made with a local fisherman in Cul de Sac; one can also go there on boat excursions from Marigot and Philipsburg or with residents on weekends. Green Cay on the south end of Orient Bay is a nesting ground for pelicans. It is surrounded by beautiful turquoise water with some of the best coral reefs in St. Martin. Orient Beach, which stretches for 1 mi/1.6 km along the bay, is the island's official nudist beach; a small naturist resort is located on the south side. No roads go directly to the beach; rather, one must park on tracks off the main road at the north or south end of the beach and walk a few hundred feet to the water.

South of Orient Beach at the foot of Paradise Peak a lagoon, Etang aux Poissons, is separated from the Atlantic by a spit of land skirting Baie de l'Embouchure, or Flamand Bay, where a long, beautiful beach has only a small resort at the north end. The lagoon is edged by mangroves and is the most natural part of the coast; the easiest access is via a road east from Orleans. Farther south, the main road passes rural areas where life seems to have changed little for centuries. The national boundary comes up about a mile beyond French Quarter and from there the road returns to Philipsburg or detours east to Oyster Pond.

OYSTER POND AND GUANA BAY

On the Atlantic coast immediately south of the Dutch–French border is Oyster Pond, an almost landlocked anchorage with new development on the encircling wooded slopes. South of the pond, a long white sand beach, protected by extensive coral reefs, stretches to Guana Bay where Atlantic waves large enough for surfing break against Guana Point. The northern stretch, known as Dawn Beach, is occupied by a large resort, but the southern end by Guana Point is still natural. Several roads lead down to and around the shore; some badly rutted ones are more pleasant for walking than driving. A winding road over Naked Boy Hill, which offers some wonderful views of the coast, connects St. Maarten's Atlantic side with Philipsburg.

OUTDOOR ACTIVITIES

HIKING: The island has no marked trails or organized hiking, but it has many rural roads and tracks with little or no traffic which hikers can use to see the hilly interior.

BIKING: The French pay homage to the Tour de France by staging an around-the-island event. For most people, though, the island is too hilly and the roads too narrow and rutted for biking. Bikes can be rented at some resorts, mainly for use around the property.

HORSEBACK RIDING: Crazy Acres Riding Center, Cole Bay (599-5-42061), offers a beach ride weekdays at 9 A.M. for groups of up to eight people; reservations must be made two days in advance. Riders must wear jeans or long pants, but should wear a swimsuit under them. The trail, starting from the Wathey Estate at Cole Bay, climbs the hillside overlooking the south coast and descends in easy stages to Cay Bay. Caid & Issa, a stable at Anse Marcel on the north end of French St. Martin, offers two daily excursions over the hilly countryside to a secluded beach.

SWIMMING: St. Maarten is famous for its beaches, some busy with people and activities, others deserted. Some beaches on French St. Martin permit nude or topless bathing; those on St. Maarten do not. If one takes a taxi to a secluded beach, arrangements should be made for the taxi to return at a specific time; agree in advance on the fare for the round trip. The alternative is to walk to the nearest town or bus route for transportation. In addition to the mile-long strand of beach on Great Bay in Philipsburg, Little Bay is within walking distance from town and has excellent water-sports facilities. The west end of Cupecoy Beach has bathing in the buff but no facilities. Secluded Plum Bay and Rouge Beach are more easily reached by boat than by car; they have no facilities. Orient Bay on the northeast side of French St. Martin is a nudist beach.

Feather duster worm.

SNORKELING AND SCUBA DIVING:
St. Maarten offers ideal conditions for learning to snorkel or dive, with shallow reefs in calm waters accessible near shore and visibility to 150 ft/46 m. Dive operators offer a one-day resort course to teach the basics; one can book directly with the operator at Simpson Bay Lagoon or through a hotel.

St. Maarten's seascape is characterized by coral reefs set in descending series of gentle hills and valleys associated with the many small offshore islands. Forests of soft corals in shallow, protected waters are abundant. Dives are made from boats because the best sites are a mile or more offshore. South of Great Bay lies one of many wrecks, the British man-of-war H.M.S. *Proselyte*, sunk in 1801. The wooden hull is gone, but divers see coral-encrusted anchors, cannons, and metal fittings; a large school of French grunts feeds here. Off the northeast coast, Spanish Rock, about 1 mi/1.6 km off North Point, is one of the island's best dive locations for experienced divers who are accustomed to large swells. A small hill of rock and corals that starts at about 7 ft/2 m, it attracts lobsters, nurse sharks, and large numbers of angelfishes.

About 2 mi/3.2 km southeast of North Point is Tintamarre Island (also known as Flat Island), which attracts day-trippers and small cruise ships, as well as divers. It has a tugboat that was sunk to create a dive site. On the southeastern tip is a forest of 8-ft/2.4-m elkhorn coral

in shallow water that snorkelers can enjoy. Marine life around the island includes large schools of reef fishes as well as rays, eels, snappers, groupers, and barracuda. North of Tintamarre, a site known as The Dolphins has caves and arches that are home to dolphins and a variety of other fish. Dive boats from St. Maarten/St. Martin also go to reefs west and north of Anguilla.

In French St. Martin, the dive shop at the Grande Case Beach Club is operated by Americans with U.S. instruction and equipment; others use French equipment and standards. Just outside of Grande Case Bay there is an area of reef covering about 2 acres/0.8 hectare starting at a depth of 20 ft/6 m where one can see moray eels and large eagle rays.

Underwater Adventures (Maho Water Sports; 599-5-44387) has a novel excursion for those who cannot swim, dive, or snorkel. It involves a headpiece that completely covers one's head (it looks like an astronaut's headgear) and allows participants to walk with an escort on the ocean floor, observing fish and coral at close range.

Tentacles of orange coral.

DEEP-SEA FISHING: Sport-fishing is a big attraction here. Half- and full-day boat charters with tackle, bait, and snacks are readily available at Bobby's Marina, Great Bay, Simpson Bay, and Port La Royale Marina. The season for dolphin, kingfish, and barracuda is December to April; tuna is fished year-round.

Beautiful water hyacinths have an important ecological function: they can filter toxins from polluted water.

BOATING: St. Maarten offers excursions on two types of boats: large catamarans holding twenty-five or more passengers that sail to St. Barts for the day where passengers have two to three hours for sightseeing, lunch, or the beach; and small sailboats for six to ten passengers that sail to a secluded beach or deserted island for a swim, snorkel, and picnic. Boats leave from Bobby's Marina and Great Bay Marina in Philipsburg, Simpson Bay Lagoon, and Port La Royale Marina at Marigot Bay. Port Lonvilliers is a new marina at the north end of French St. Martin. Members of the St. Maarten Charter Boat Association are licensed boat operators offering daily excursions and charters under safety regulations set by the Netherlands Antilles government.

WINDSURFING: The island's calm, shallow waters, especially at Simpson Bay Lagoon, provide ideal conditions for learners. Beachfront resorts and watersports operators usually offer parasailing, waterskiing, and other water sports as well.

EXPLORING THE ISLAND

Self-drive car is the best way to tour. Most car rental companies have pickup and delivery service and offer unlimited mileage. One should book in advance, particularly in high season, but do not be surprised if a confirmed reservation is not fulfilled. Driving is on the RIGHT. Mopeds and motorbikes are available but are not recommended because the roads are hilly and replete with blind curves and potholes. Often drivers must stop dead without notice for a cow or goat that has strayed onto the road. The northeast side of French St. Martin is rural and animals have the right-of-way.

Taxis do not have meters and are expensive. Rates must have government approval; they are based on destination and allow for two passengers per trip. Taxi drivers usually quote prices in U.S. dollars, but be sure to have the currency agreed on *in advance* in order to avoid misunderstandings. Inexpensive public buses run between Philipsburg and Marigot throughout the day. Hourly buses connect Mullet Bay, Simpson Bay, Cole Bay, and Grande Case. Bus stops are marked *Bushalte* on the Dutch side, *Arrêt* on the French. One can also flag them to stop. In Philipsburg, Wathey Square is the station for taxis, buses, and car rentals. In Marigot, a taxi service is located at the port near the Tourist Information Board. After 9 P.M. 25 percent is added, and after midnight, 50 percent.

From St. Maarten's Queen Juliana Airport, Winair has daily flights to Saba, St. Eustatius, and St. Barts; in Philipsburg, inquire at Bobby's Marina for seasonal ferries to these and other islands. From St. Martin's Espérance Airport, Air St. Barts flies daily to St. Barts; ferries depart from Port La Royale Marina in Marigot. From Marigot, St. Barts is a 90-minute sail and Anguilla is a 20-minute ferry ride.

INFORMATION: In the U.S.: St. Maarten Tourist Office, 275 Seventh Ave., 19th fl., New York, NY 10001; 212-989-0000. French West Indies Tourist Board, 610 Fifth Ave., (628 Fifth Ave. for walk-in info), New York, NY 10020; 900-990-0040. In Canada: St. Maarten Info. Office, 243 Ellerslie Ave., Willowdale, Toronto M2N 1Y5; 416-223-3501. French Government Tourism Office, 1981 Ave. McGill College, Montreal H3A 2W9; 514-288-4264; and 30 St. Patrick St., Suite 700, Toronto, M5T 3A3; 416-593-4723. In Europe: St. Maarten Tourist Board, Cabinet of the Plenipotentiary, Badhuisweg 173-175, The Hague, Holland. Maison de la France/F.G.T.O., 178 Piccadilly, London, W1V 0AL; 71-493-6694. In the Caribbean: Sint Maarten Tourist Bureau, Imperial Bld., Walter Nisbeth Rd., 3rd fl., Sint Maarten, NA; 599-5-22337. St. Martin Tourist Board, Port de Marigot, 97150 St. Martin, FWI; 590-87-57-21.

ST. BARTHÉLEMY

TINY ST. BARTHÉLEMY, better known as St. Barts or St. Barth, is an island of scenic beauty where every turn in the road—and there are many—reveals a new panorama of steep green hills and miniature valleys overlooking a rocky, deeply indented coastline. The smallest of the French West Indies, located 15 mi/24 km southeast of St. Martin, St. Barts is a stylish, intimate hideaway for those with light hearts and heavy wallets.

A paradox of modern French sophistication and conservative Old World tradition, St. Barts has been something of an anomaly throughout its history. Discovered in 1493 by Christopher Columbus, who named the island for his brother, Bartolomeo, St. Barts is unlike most other Caribbean islands, where African, Asian, and European cultures have been fused. Rather, St. Barts is a droplet of ancient France, where blond farmers and blue-eyed fishermen speak a dialect most French speakers cannot understand, and shy elder women wear starched bonnets reminiscent of those worn by their sturdy Norman and Breton ancestors who began arriving in the seventeenth century when the island was the far side of paradise. Fishing boats and pirate ships used its hidden bays and protected deep harbors, but the little island was too hilly, rocky, and dry to be coveted for agriculture. Neither African slaves nor Asian indentured servants were brought here and the plantation society typical of the colonial Caribbean never developed. The island had a short tenure under the Knights of Malta and another under Sweden—the only Caribbean island the Swedes ever possessed. More recently, St. Barts has become a playground for the rich and famous from both sides of the Atlantic, creating a tourist boom that is gradually changing the island's character.

GUSTAVIA

Gustavia, named for the Swedish king Gustavus III, is the island's lilliputian port on the southwest coast. Yachts bob in the harbor, red-roofed houses climb the surrounding green hills, and boutiques and sidewalk cafés give the town a distinct French ambience. The Swedish legacy remains in street signs that are in Swedish as well as French. The normally quiet town is filled by day with visitors from St. Martin and small cruise ships. On the south side, a five-minute walk past Fort Karl leads to Petite Anse de Galet, also known as Shell Beach, where there is good shelling. St. Barts is surrounded by rocky islets with nesting birds; near Gustavia, on Gros Ilets, Les Saintes, and Pain de Sucre, one sees boobies, known locally as balaou, and brown pelicans, the symbol of St. Barts. These islets are also popular diving sites.

ANSE DU GOUVERNEUR

Uphill from the port on the east, beyond the clock tower, the steep hill climbs for about a mile to Castelets, a tiny inn perched on the side of Morne Lurin where there is a spectacular view across the island from the west coast to St.-Jean Bay on the north. Beyond Lurin, the steep, bumpy road drops south to Anse du Gouverneur, or Governor's Cove. On the descent, Saba, St. Eustatius, and St. Kitts loom on the south horizon, and at the end of the road, the terrain falls quickly to the beach, which is likely to be deserted. Bracketed on both sides by jagged cliffs, the cove's crescent of soft white sand is washed by aquamarine water with light swells that rock the lazy swimmer up and down and break gently against the shore. Local legend has it that the seventeenth-century pirate Monbars the Exterminator hid his treasures in a cave on the side of the cliff at Grande Pointe, the southernmost point of St. Barts.

COROSSOL

On the north side of Gustavia after Fort Gustav (where there is a fine view of the harbor), the road forks northeast to the airport and northwest to Corossol, the most traditional of the island's tiny fishing villages, where the old Norman dialect is still spoken. Some of Corossol's elderly women still don long blue-and-white-checked dresses and the *calèche*, a stiff-brimmed bonnet derived from a Breton style of the seventeenth century. The shy ladies hide at the first sight of strangers with cameras, but they are happy to sell them their famous handwoven straw hats and other products made from the fan-shaped fronds of latania palms. It is the finest, most supple straw in the Caribbean. The Inter Oceans Museum, devoted to a private collection of shells, is open daily from 10 A.M. to 4 P.M.

FLAMANDS

A serpentine road rises and falls on its way to the north coast and Anse des Flamands, one of the island's most beautiful coves with a wide, half-mile stretch of blinding-white sand that you sink into; the beach is fringed by latania palms and framed by weather-worn rocks washed by intensely turquoise seas. There are several small resorts here. Off the coast are two rocky islets, Ile Bonhomme and Ile Frégate, where migrating sperm whales are seen in May. Ile Bonhomme, a large cactus-covered mass also known as Ile Chevreau, has wild goats and iguanas. Low-lying Ile Frégate

From every side of hilly St. Barts one can see the rocky offshore islets where nesting birds, iguanas, and sometimes wild goats live.

is named for its colony of frigatebirds. Iguanas are found on other offshore islets and are sometimes seen on hills near the sea on St. Barts.

COLOMBIER

The northwest end of the island at Colombier has a beach that is accessible only on foot or by boat. At the end of the main road a path meanders through tropical vegetation with century plants and tall torch cactus down to Anse de Colombier. The pretty cove in an amphitheater of wooded slopes is a favorite destination for day-charter boats from Gustavia; sunsets are splendid. From April through August, female sea turtles come here—and to Flamands and Corossol—to lay their eggs. Hunting sea turtles for meat and shells is permitted in French waters from mid-September to March.

ILE FOURCHUE

About 2 mi/3.2 km off the northwest coast is the desolate island of Ile Fourchue, sometimes referred to as Five Fingers. It has stark, moonscape terrain that rises quickly from the sea to five peaks connected by steep ridges, forming a horseshoe and sheltering a bay with a small beach on the southwest. The highest peak rises to over 300 ft/90 m and overlooks wild Atlantic waves that crash against the rocks. St. Maarten/St. Martin is on the northwest, and beyond St. Barts on the south are Statia and Saba, respectively. Ile Fourchue is treeless; only Turk's-head and other cacti and brush grow among the rocks and boulders. There are wild goats and seabirds. One can easily spend a full day exploring the island but it is very hot. Hikers should bring a generous supply of water and wear sturdy shoes as protection against the sharp-needled cactus. Several boat excursions sail to Ile Fourchue for the day from Gustavia or one can hire a boat.

ST.-JEAN BAY

Mushroom-shaped Baie de St.-Jean, with its calm, reef-protected aquamarine waters, is rimmed by white sand beaches and divided at about midpoint by a half-acre mound of quartzite on which sits tiny Eden Rock, the island's first hotel. The bay is the hub of the island's resort and watersports activity. Its quiet waters are ideal for snorkelers. From Morne de Dépoudré, the hill behind Eden Rock, there are wonderful views of the bay. Just beyond Eden Rock, a road inland crosses the island to Grande Saline where salt was once mined. From the salt flat a footpath goes over a low hill to Anse de Grande Saline, a development-free cove with a half-mile beach of alabaster sand along beautiful clear waters. Although signs banning nude bathing abound around St. Barts, they are not always obeyed, especially on secluded beaches such as Saline. Topless bathing, however, is the norm.

Lorient

East along St.-Jean Bay the coastal road overlooks the palm-fringed beach with long rolling waves at the village of Lorient, the site of the first French settlement in 1648. The beach is popular with surfers and windsurfers and is used by local families, but it goes almost unnoticed by tourists. The headland between Lorient Bay and Marigot Bay has two points—Milou and Mangin—where Atlantic waves crash against the jagged cliffs. Pointe Milou, a residential area of elegant homes and resorts, was almost barren a decade ago. The road to the Point affords fabulous views over St.-Jean Bay and the north coast. East of Mangin Point, the little beach of Marigot Bay can be reached from the main route by a steep dirt and concrete road. The calm bay has good snorkeling along the rocky shore at the far end. La Tortue, a rocky islet on the east, has good snorkeling too.

Morne du Vitet

Inland from Lorient, a road to the south coast passes between the island's two highest peaks, Morne du Grand Fond (899 ft/274 m) on the west and Morne du Vitet (938 ft/286 m) on the east. Alternatively, the road east loops around Morne du Vitet to Grand Cul de Sac and the south coast, passing through small villages and meadows where cattle graze. From the main route, a road ascends Morne du Vitet, passing rural landscapes crossed by centuries-old serpentine stone walls and farmhouses tucked into the green hills overlooking Marigot Bay and the northeast coast.

Grand Cul de Sac to Grand Fond

Grand Cul de Sac, a large bay, is the resort and water-sports center of the northeast. Its shallow reef-protected waters are ideal for learning to windsurf. On the south and east sides of the bay are lagoons fringed with mangroves. There are manchineel trees here; their sap can cause rashes and their fruit is poisonous. At the adjacent bay, Petit Cul de Sac, a footpath leads to the beach where a bed of oolitic rock—a granular form of limestone cemented together—is a geological curiosity thought to be unique in the Caribbean. The less-traveled road from Grand Cul de Sac to Anse à Toiny is an interesting walk—or drive—over the mountain where volcanic slopes with patchwork fields outlined by low stone fences descend to the arid, rocky, and wilder windward shores of Toiny and Grand Fond, often likened to the rugged coast of Normandy.

Pages 206 and 207: Sunsets over Gustavia Harbor silhouette Les Islettes, Les Saintes, and Pain de Sucre, where boobies and brown pelicans nest.

OUTDOOR ACTIVITIES

HIKING: Despite its hills, St. Barts's small size, lightly traveled country roads, and many goat paths make walking and hiking a popular pastime even for those who normally prefer driving.

SWIMMING: St. Barts is scalloped with more than two dozen powdery white sand beaches with tranquil turquoise waters and no crowds. All beaches are public and free. Signs officially ban nudism but the monokini is common attire. Anse du Gouverneur and Anse de Grande Saline on the south are the most secluded beaches.

SNORKELING AND SCUBA DIVING: St. Barts is almost completely surrounded by shallow-water reefs, better suited for snorkeling than for diving. A dozen or more places are within swimming distance of shore. Snorkeling equipment is available for rent or purchase in Gustavia and at water-sports centers around the island. At St.-Jean Bay, the most accessible reefs lie northwest of Eden Rock where there is a great variety of fish, but one must be careful since sea urchins are abundant too. For more experienced snorkelers, Ile Tortue has a long, narrow reef running southwest toward Marigot Bay.

The best dive locations are on the west coast within easy reach of Gustavia at about 50 to 60 ft/15 to 18 m with visibility up to 100 ft/30 m. Just outside the harbor, Gros Ilets, a rock rising about 75 ft/22 m above the sea, attracts groupers, snappers, morays, lobsters, and barracuda as well as large schools of reef fishes. To the south, the three tiny Saintes are actually pieces of reef where parrotfishes, rays, and occasional sea turtles and dolphins are seen. Farther out, La Baleine is the top of a seamount that attracts barracuda, lobsters, and nurse sharks. At the edge of the reef in open water, Pain de Sucre, which rises about 160 ft/48 m above the sea, has some of the best diving. It starts at about 20 ft/6 m, where elkhorn coral is abundant, and drops to about 60 ft/18 m where there are colorful sponges, caverns, and tunnels. Strong currents and numerous sharks limit the windward coast at Toiny to experienced divers only.

St. Barts has one dive operator offering several boat trips daily in the peak winter season; groups are limited to six people. The staff is certified by their French federation. They are familiar with American methods and standards, and the shop maintains American as well as French tanks and regulators. During the low season, it offers free introductory sessions on the use of scuba equipment and diving safety.

DEEP-SEA FISHING: Boat charters with fishing gear are available at the harbor in Gustavia or can be arranged through one's hotel. Popular catches are tuna, bonito, dorado, marlin, and barracuda. Spearfishing is permitted, providing one is not wearing scuba gear. Equipment is available for purchase in Gustavia. Catches include grouper, amberjack, ray, and moray eel. Not all fish in the island's waters are edible; local fishermen are the best source of advice.

BOATING: St. Barts is a yachting mecca, due in part to its location between two big yachting centers—the Virgin Islands and Antigua. Gustavia's harbor has mooring and docking facilities for about forty vessels and perhaps the most extensive stock of marine supplies in the Leeward Islands. There are also good anchorages at Public, Corossol, and Colombier bays. Sunfish are a popular pastime in the gentle winds of St.-Jean and Grand Cul de Sac bays, where rentals are available. Picnic sailing excursions and boat charters for up to six passengers leave from Gustavia for nearby beaches and islets for a day of swimming and snorkeling. A full-day sail to Ile Fourchue departs Gustavia at 9:30 A.M.

SURFING: The north coast, particularly at Lorient, is the main surfing area. Boards can be rented at water-sports centers where one can also find out about water conditions.

WINDSURFING: Rentals are available at most beachside water-sports centers; conditions are ideal for learners. St. Barts Wind School and similar centers at St.-Jean and Grand Cul de Sac offer lessons.

WATERSKIING: Waterskiing is authorized only in Colombier Bay between 8:30 A.M. and 3 P.M. Equipment is available from the Association Sportive et Culturelle du Centre de Colombier (596-27-61-07).

EXPLORING THE ISLAND

St. Barts, less than 10 sq mi/25 sq km in size, can be toured by car in half a day. The sporting thing to do is to rent an open-sided, canopied Mini-Moke or jeep and wander, following one's whim. A knowledge of French is helpful. However, do not try to keep pace with the French on St. Barts's corkscrew, washboard roads.

The roads are few and easy to learn. Main roads often branch on to dirt or rocky roads that are best traversed on foot. A car can be rented at the airport and in Gustavia; advance reservations are recommended in winter. Foreign driver's licenses are honored. Not all car rental agencies take credit cards. Of the island's three gas stations, only the Shell station at the airport is open Sunday. Motorbikes, mopeds, and scooters are also available but are not advised unless riders are very experienced. Driving is on the RIGHT.

There are taxi stations at the airport and in Gustavia, and taxis may be requested by telephone (596-27-66-31). After 8:00 P.M. and on Sundays and holidays, fares have a 50 percent surcharge. Tours of an hour or two by taxi or by minibus for up to 8 passengers with the driver acting as guide are also available.

There are daily flights to St. Barts from St. Maarten on Winair and on Air St. Barts, though in peak season it is difficult to find a seat for the ten-minute flight. Air Guadeloupe flies daily from Pointe-à-Pitre and from St. Martin. Arriving at St. Barts's tiny airport is an experience not soon forgotten. Located in an area known locally as La Tourmente, the short runway is between the hills and the sea on the island's largest

piece of flat land. A strong downdraft causes the nineteen-seat STOL aircraft (Short Take-Off and Landing)—the largest plane the runway can accommodate—to drop suddenly as it glides in to land. The tiny runway is credited with saving St. Barts from further development.

Alternatively, the *St. Barth Express*, a twelve-passenger open-motorboat service between St. Barts and St. Martin, leaves on Mon., Wed., and Fri. from Gustavia at 8:15 A.M., and from Marigot at 3:30 P.M. and Philipsburg at 4 P.M. The ride takes less than an hour. *St. Barth Express* reservations can be made through Sibarth in Gustavia; 596-27-62-38. Sibarth also arranges private boat charters through WIMCO, Newport, RI; 800-932-3222 or 401-849-8012. Catamarans on round trip day excursions leave the marinas in St. Maarten daily for the ninety-minute sail to Gustavia. Skippers usually take one-way passengers when there is space.

INFORMATION: In the U.S.: French West Indies Tourist Board, 610 Fifth Ave. (628 Fifth Ave. for walk-in info), New York, NY 10020; 900-990-0040. In Canada: 1981 Ave. McGill College, Montreal H3A 2W9; 514-288-4264; and 30 St. Patrick St., Suite 700, Toronto, M5T 3A3; 416-593-4723. In the U.K.: F.G.T.O., 178 Piccadilly, London W1V OAL; 71-493-6694. In St. Barts: Office du Tourisme, Mairie de St. Barth, rue Auguste Nyman, Gustavia, 97133 St. Barthélemy, FWI; 596-27-60-08. Open Monday to Saturday, 8:30 A.M. to 12:30 P.M. Tourist desk at airport is open Monday through Friday from 3:00 to 6:00 P.M.; 596-27-63-56.

SABA

RISING ALMOST STRAIGHT FROM THE SEA to a height nearing 3,000 ft/900 m, the island of Saba is the top of a volcanic cone with a shoreline of sheer rock cliffs. It has no beaches or flat land; its lilliputian villages cling precipitously to the steep slopes. Below the sea the volcanic walls continue their sharp drop to great depths; around these underwater slopes another wondrous world lives. Hiking and diving are the two main outdoor attractions here.

Until the first road was built in 1943 the island's inhabitants and their goods were hoisted to the land from boats that rode in on the surf. To reach their villages, the islanders had to climb up 800 steep, hand-hewn stairs and trails. Today Saba has an airport whose 1,300-ft/397-m runway cut from a mountainside resembles the landing deck of an aircraft carrier.

Claimed by the Dutch and the English, Saba, pronounced "SAY-ba," was first settled in the seventeenth century by Europeans whose origins remain something of a mystery. Over the next 200 years they cleared and terraced the land in all but the most inaccessible parts and cultivated coffee, sugar, indigo, and other crops. Farming was never a profitable venture, however, and by the dawn of this century Saban men routinely left the island for better jobs elsewhere. The amount of land under cultivation dropped sharply, allowing various types of woodlands to return.

The Saba volcano was last active about 5,000 years ago. In the late stages of activity, scientists say, the crater of the volcano filled in, forming Mt. Scenery, Saba's highest peak. Other masses of slow-flowing lava settled, forming other peaks around the island. Today, the only evidence of volcanic activity is the hot springs on the west side of the island.

TRAILS FROM THE ROAD

"The Road" on Saba is 19 mi/30 km long and crosses the island from the airport on the northeast to Fort Bay on the southwest, passing through all four of the island's villages. From the airport, the first part of the oleander-bordered road, hand-built by the islanders, zigs and zags in twenty hairpin turns up the mountain through Hell's Gate, and continues to Windward-side, a neat little village of gingerbread houses and gardens that looks like a stage set for *Hansel and Gretel*, and over the mountain to descend to The Bottom, Saba's capital, overlooking the west coast. The Bottom, a village of small, white clapboard houses with red-gabled roofs, does not sit in the crater of a volcano as its name suggests. The name actually derives from

By the time they reach the 950th step of the 1064-step trail up Mt. Scenery, Saba's highest point, hikers have entered a moist, botanically rich rain forest world.

botte, the Dutch word for "bowl," which is an apt description of the contour of the land in which the village is positioned.

The Road, which climbs to 1,800 ft/549 m before dropping to sea level on the southwest coast, can be an enjoyable hike; if taken in sections, it is not exhausting. It also provides access to the hiking trails.

Sulphur Mine Track. At Lower Hell's Gate, about halfway up the hairpin turns from the airport, a track north of the road leads to the cliffsides of the north coast overlooking Green Island, whose adjacent coral reefs are part of the Saba Marine Park. The track passes Behind the Ridge, a post-volcanic formation where sulphur was mined in the last century; remnants of the mining operation can be seen. The area is covered with dry vegetation. Two species of tropicbirds nest in the cliffs near the mine, while bridled tern, sooty tern, and brown noddy nest on Green Island. Sulphur Mine Track, one of the trails to be renovated, takes about an hour round trip; it should not be attempted without a local guide, however, as footing is treacherous.

Sandy Cruz Track. From Upper Hell's Gate, a trail heads northwest to Sandy Cruz using the first part of an old path that once went all the way to Mary's Point, near the west coast. The track passes through once-cultivated fields that are returning to forest and windswept rain-forest scenery in and around a ravine known as Deep Gut. From 1,886 ft/575 m to 2,543 ft/775 m, tree ferns are abundant. These pioneer plants, which appear after the destruction of the rain forest by man or fire, provide a favorite perch for the purple-throated carib, one of three hummingbird species found on Saba. The other hummingbirds—the Antillean crested and the green-throated carib—are found around the flowers in gardens as well as in the rain forest. At about 2,625 ft/800 m, mountain palm is abundant, particularly on the steepest slopes such as those around Deep Gut. Sandy Cruz Track, one of the trails being improved, takes about forty minutes one way.

Old Booby Hill. From the tiny hamlet of English Quarter, a trail on the south leads via Spring Bay Gut to Old Booby Hill, two of the island's prime birding locations. Red-tailed hawks and American kestrels are commonly found on the lower slopes of the eastern and southeastern sides of the island. Audubon's shearwaters nest in burrows of the steep cliffs; bridled quail-doves live in the rugged sides of the ravines; Antillean euphonias might be spotted on the steep slopes here or on the north side of Mt. Scenery; and red-billed tropicbirds and terns glide over the sea. There are also wonderful views of neighboring St. Eustatius and St. Kitts on the southeast.

Mt. Scenery. At the pretty village of Windwardside, the main road reaches its highest point at 1,788 ft/545 m. The Saba Museum, situated in a century-old sea captain's house, and the Saba Tourist Bureau are here.

Windwardside is the starting point for the hike to the summit of Mt. Scenery (2,652 ft/870 m), the highest point on Saba and the main goal of serious hikers here. The trail, which has 1,064 hand-hewn steps, begins from a sign at the west end of Windwardside and climbs up through rain forest and into the misty clouds of elfin woodland at the peak. The stairs ascend through rain forest with an upper-story canopy of 30 ft/10 m, resplendent with ferns, bromeliads, lianas, and epiphytes and brightened with the flowers of heliconia. Almost year-round, hikers can find fresh mountain raspberries to eat, and in winter they will see yellow heliconia blooms and perhaps also tiny red orchids at the top, although most people need the aid of an experienced guide to find them.

The abundant tree ferns with their graceful parasol crowns give the rain forest an air of enchantment when the sunlight filters through the tiny leaves of their fronds. At higher elevations, the vegetation is more dense but little sun shines through the ever-present moisture-laden clouds. Above 2,707 ft/825 m is elfin woodland thick with lianas, mosses, and ferns. In addition to hummingbirds, the rain forest is also populated with the scaly-breasted thrasher and bridled quail-dove. Pigeons, bananaquits, and Lesser Antillean bullfinches are common.

At the summit, to the south of the radio tower, there is a wide view of the Caribbean with Windwardside below, St. Eustatius and St. Kitts to the southeast, and St. Maarten on the north. A separate trail almost at the summit passes through some of the most pristine vegetation on the island where the forest is rich with bromeliads and ferns. The hike is a thirty-minute round trip but the path is extremely slippery and impassable after a rain.

The hike to the summit of Mt. Scenery is delightful but strenuous. There are several shelters along the way where one can rest and take refuge from occasional bursts of rain. The trail from Windwardside is about two hours round trip, longer after a rain when the steps are slippery. Hikers should take clothing suitable for the cool, damp air at the high altitudes. A local horticulturist, Anne Keene, leads hiking tours to the top of Mt. Scenery and other locations around the island; inquire at the Saba Tourist Office or at Weavers Cottage, Windwardside.

Crispeen Track. From Windwardside the main road descends to the village of St. John's, which has wonderful views across the island and out to sea. From St. John's, the Crispeen Track leads northeast through a narrow gorge with dense, lush vegetation, then through terraced fields of citrus and banana, connecting with the Mt. Scenery Trail at Rendezvous. In the higher parts of Rendezvous, which are no longer cultivated, the vegetation resembles secondary rain forest, while the tops of the windswept hillocks are covered with wild mammee, anthurium, and philodendron. Hiking time

to Rendezvous is just under fifty minutes. The western part of the trail from Crispeen is part of what was once the only path from The Bottom and Windwardside.

The Ladder. At The Bottom the main road turns south to Fort Bay by the sea, where the pier and one of the island's two dive operators are located. West of The Bottom at the end of the Ladder Bay road, called The Gap, more than 500 steps—part of the original 800 steps—lead to Ladder Bay, where boats once came ashore to unload passengers and cargo when rough seas made it impossible to use Fort Bay. Today, the historic steps are part of a scenic trail that provides access to a picnicking site overlooking Ladder Bay. The walk down takes about thirty minutes, but the hike up from Ladder Bay is longer and more difficult as the steps are steep.

Wells Bay to Mary's Point. On the north side of The Bottom a road and footpath both lead to Wells Bay on the west coast, from where an old trail leads to the abandoned village of Mary's Point. The trail passes from dry coastal shrubs of wild sage, prickly pear cactus, candle cactus, and small trees of red birch, fiddlewood, and water mampoo or loblolly, to dry ever-

Crowning the peak of Mt. Scenery is an elfin woodland with the mosses, ferns, and epiphytes found on such high ridges. Facing page: Organ-pipe cactus grows in an area of arid vegetation near Behind the Ridge, site of a former sulphur mine on Saba's north cliffs.

green forest with a large stand of West Indian mahogany and occasional tamarind and flamboyant trees. At Mary's Point there is a good view of Diamond Rock, a nesting ground for brown boobies. The Rock, white with guano, and its adjacent reefs are part of the marine park. The trail, for experienced hikers only, takes about an hour one way. It is so overgrown as to be nonexistent; one needs a guide who can bushwhack a path.

SABA MARINE PARK

Around Saba's steep undersea walls there is a wonderful display of pinnacles and boulders encrusted with a spectacular variety and abundance of colorful marine life. Until recently, human impact on its marine resources was minimal, but with the current popularity of diving, the need to safeguard Saba's marine environment became pressing. With the help of international organizations, the Saba Marine Park was completed in 1988 under the direction of marine biologist Tom van't Hof, who also directed the creation of the marine parks in Bonaire and Curaçao. It is now administered by the Saba Conservation Foundation.

The park encircles the island and includes self-guided underwater trails. The waters and seabed from the high-water mark to a depth of 200 ft/60 m and two offshore seamounts are protected. A guidebook describing twenty-six dive sites is in preparation; the sites are mapped, named, and numbered 1 to 26, beginning on the west side and encircling the island in a counterclockwise fashion.

The park has four zones, each permitting different uses. The west coast from Tent Bay to Ladder Bay together with Man of War Shoals, Diamond Rock, and the offshore seamounts comprise the recreational diving zones where line, trap, and spearfishing and anchoring are prohibited, though handlining from shore and midwater trolling are allowed. From Ladder Bay north to Torrens Point is an all-purpose recreational zone that includes Saba's only "beach," a pebbly stretch of coast with shallow water for swimming, and areas for diving, fishing, and boat anchorage. Another anchorage zone is west of Fort Bay. East of Fort Bay along the south, east, and north coasts to Torrens Point is a multiple-use zone where fishing and diving are permitted.

Offshore on the west coast at the top of a seamount at about 110 ft/33 m depth are three pinnacles: *Third Encounter, Twilight Zone,* and *Outer Limits* (1–3). Two pinnacles are covered with brightly colored tube sponges, hard corals, and fan-shaped deepwater gorgonians. The sites attract sharks, rays, and turtles and hosts of large, tame groupers. *Shark Shoal*

(4), an isolated pinnacle west of Wells Bay, begins at about 90 ft/27 m and drops to 120 ft/36 m. It has caves, black coral, sharks, and groupers.

Directly off Torrens Point are two prime dive sites: *Diamond Rock* (6), a large rock that rises steeply from a sandy bottom at 80 ft/24 m where there are always stingrays, and sometimes sharks and schools of horse-eye jack. The walls of the rock are covered with sponges, gorgonians, and other soft corals, and the water teems with coneys, graysbies, glasseye snapper, barracuda, goatfishes, rock beauty, sergeant major, and more. *Man of War Shoals* (7) is a similar rock structure but is completely submerged. It has caves, colorful sponges and anemones, turtles, and fish including groupers, jacks, sharks, and rays. *Torrens Point* (9) is a shallow-water dive of 40 ft/12 m in well protected water and is suitable for snorkelers and novice divers. It begins in heavily encrusted old elkhorn that leads to a passageway through steep cliffs. Divers may continue through a tunnel that leads to shallow caves.

Nine sites (11–19) between Ladder Bay and Tent Bay comprise the park's main dive locations and range from 50 to 120 ft/15 to 36 m. *Ladder Bay Deep Reef/Customs House Reef* (11) is a deep patch reef inhabited by several dozen barracuda. *Lou's Ladder/Porites Point* (12) is named for its extensive fields of *Porites porites*, or thick-finger coral, populated with schools of blue chromis, butterflyfish, turtles, and rays. *Ladder Labyrinth* (14) is actually two dives: a deep one at about 80 ft/24 m and another through shallow alleyways between coral-encrusted boulders cemented together in a maze of beautiful coral ridges. The unusual formations include brain, pillar, and finger corals, sea fans, and barrel sponges. Between the crevices one can see shrimp and lobsters, and around the edges are barracuda. The site can be enjoyed by both snorkelers and divers. The two most visited dive sites of the park are *Tent Reef Wall* (17), which drops to 80 ft/24 m in a panoply of colorful tube sponges and black coral; and *Tent Reef* (18), a long, shallow ledge at 50 ft/15 m with overhangs, walls, big barrel sponges, barracudas, hundreds of coneys, French angelfish, margates, garden eels, and horse-eye jack. Tent Reef attracts both snorkelers and divers.

Five dive sites (20–24) are found on the multi-use south-coast zone. Two deep sites are on a long offshore reef sloping seaward in depths from 65 to 80 ft/20 to 24 m. Three shallow sites (30 to 50 ft/9 to 15 m) have elkhorn and staghorn corals and boulders encrusted with sea fans. Wrasses, grunts, queen triggerfish, blue tang, and other reef fish are abundant. Lobster are found here too. The Saba Bank, 3 mi/4.8 km southwest of the island, is a shallow-water stretch that runs 32 mi/51 km; fishing is excellent. The sea on the northern and northeastern coasts is generally too rough for diving.

Outdoor Activities

Hiking: There are trails of varying difficulty all over the island; the Saba Conservation Foundation is currently upgrading the most interesting and scenic ones. All are accessible from The Road, and many can be traversed without a guide.

Snorkeling and Diving: The waters around Saba are protected as part of the Saba Marine Park. An abundance of fish swim among the complex pinnacles, boulders, and ridges that make diving here so exciting. Saba has two fully equipped dive operators with their own dive boats, which make several trips daily. They also offer instruction and certification, and arrange fishing trips.

Red-billed tropicbirds.

Exploring the Island

Saba is 28 mi/45 km southwest of St. Maarten and 14 mi/22 km northwest of St. Eustatius; together the three islands form the Dutch Windward Islands. Saba is visited most often on day trips from St. Maarten, but for outdoor enthusiasts the island warrants a longer stay. From St. Maarten, Saba can be reached on daily morning and afternoon flights on Winair, six times weekly on luxury passenger ferry, and on frequent boat and dive excursions.

Information: There is no office in North America. In Europe: % Cabinet of the Plenipotentiary, Badhuisweg 173-175, The Hague, Holland. In Saba: Tourist Office, Windwardside, Saba, NA; 599-4-2231. Saba Marine Park, Fort Bay; 599-4-3295.

Books: *History of Saba* by J. Hartog (Saba Artisan Foundation, Saba, N.A., 1975). *Saba, The First Guidebook* (1985) and *The Saba Supplement* (1987), both by Natalie and Paul Pfanstiehl. *A Guide to the Saba Marine Park* by Tom van't Hof (in press).

Aloe plant in bloom.

At Ladder Bay on the west coast, sheer rock cliffs overlook Saba's pebbly "beach" and a water recreation zone that permits diving, fishing, and boat anchorage.

ST. EUSTATIUS

THE LEAST-KNOWN OF THE DUTCH WINDWARD trio, St. Eustatius is the sleeper of Caribbean islands for hikers and divers alike. The island has one of the most distinctive profiles of any island in the Caribbean. From a flat central plain the land rises rather abruptly at the hilly north end to 965 ft/ 294 m and drops almost directly into the sea. The south end is dominated by the silhouette of The Quill, the crater of an extinct volcano. The leeward side has limestone cliffs and some beach between the hills that fall to the sea. On the windward side the north and south ends are connected by a wide, 2-mi/3.2-km arc of golden-gray sand beach along the ledge of an ancient lava flow. Good trails with numbered signposts lead to rain forests and elfin woodland on the crater rim and down into the vegetation-smothered interior. Others traverse the hot, arid hills and gullies of the north.

Offshore, layers of history lie undisturbed among the corals. Statia, as the island is called, is haunted by its curious past. In the late eighteenth century, at the time of the American Revolution, this small island was one of the richest free ports in the Americas. But on November 16, 1776, its heyday came to an abrupt end after its Dutch garrison at Fort Oranje became the first foreign port to salute a ship flying the American flag after the United States had declared its independence. The gesture enraged the British, who retaliated by capturing Oranjestad. Once in control, they lured 150 merchant ships into the harbor, confiscated their cargoes, sacked and burned the town, and destroyed the harbor's breakwater. The island never recovered.

The neat little town of Oranjestad, which grew up around the old fort, is divided into Upper Town, situated on a cliff 150 ft/45 m high, and Lower Town, where a mile-long stretch of slate-gray sand is the island's most popular beach. The two parts are connected by the cobblestoned pedestrian Bay Path, as well as by a motor road. In Upper Town, palm-shaded cobblestone streets with West Indian gingerbread houses and flowering gardens lead to Fort Oranje, where a park brightened with bougainvillea and oleander memorializes the British attack. The St. Eustatius Historical Foundation Museum, near the fort, has displays from Indian settlements dating from A.D. 300.

From Upper Town, a road south along the leeward coast passes Queen Wilhelmina Park and leads to tiny Fort de Windt, from where one can see White Wall and Sugar Loaf, formations of ancient limestone sediment from the sea bottom that were tilted up by tectonic movements.

From Lower Town, a twenty-minute walk north along the beach (*White Bird Track/XII*) passes beneath the cliffs of Powder Hill (or Fort Royal

Hill) where tropicbirds nest. Known locally as white birds, tropicbirds are easily recognized by their two long tail feathers. They nest in crevices of the rock, laying only one egg per season. At the end of the Powder Hill cliffs at Smoke Alley, Oranje Beach has calm water for swimming. It is usually deserted during the day but draws island people and visitors at sunset. Powder Hill is private property and too dangerous to climb.

THE QUILL

Geologically speaking, The Quill, from the Dutch word *kuil* meaning "crater," is a young volcano, having erupted about 4,000 years ago. From a distance the rim appears to be a perfect cone but a closer approach reveals creviced slopes and a craggy rim that is higher on the south side than on the north. Its bowl-shaped interior is about 1,000 ft/300 m in diameter. Five trails climb up to and around the rim and down into the crater.

Quill Track/I (Nos. 1–20), the most direct trail, is a fairly easy but steep path—a forty-five minute hike—that can be slippery in places after a rain. It begins on the south side of Oranjestad on Welfare Road at a telephone pole marked "Quill Track 1" and goes up the west side of the crater rim at 1,312 ft/400 m elevation. As the trail ascends, it passes from low shrub to dry woodlands with pink poui and other trees that grow taller near the rim. At Sign No. 5, one can follow the gut, or gully, which is a straight track to the rim; or, after a short distance, one can follow another, almost parallel and less slippery track (Nos. 6–16) that veers off to the right. *Quill Track/ II*, an alternative trail, starts at the top of Rosemary Lane, crosses Pleasures Plantation, and meets Quill I at No. 14. Both tracks end at the crater rim (No. 20) where three more trails begin.

Crater Track/III (Nos. 1–16) descends on a steep, often very slippery slope through steamy thick foliage where trees, protected from winds and hurricanes, grow tall and the orchids on their trunks are as tiny as a fingertip. An alternate path to the left (at No. 12) passes an enormous silk-cotton, or kapok, tree. Over the years the crater was cultivated with coffee, cacao, and cinnamon which can still be seen; the only plantation now is of bananas. Some of the original vegetation are anthuriums, heliconias, known locally as wild banana, begonias, and some orchid species. At the crater bottom, 558 ft/170 m below the rim, it is easy to walk around without getting lost. The hike down takes about twenty-five minutes.

Mazinga Track/IV (Nos. 1–40) begins at the lowest part of the rim and climbs to 1,968 ft/600 m through vegetation that changes from dry woods to rain forest, thick with philodendrons, ferns, and epiphytes. The Mazinga Peak, the highest part, often concealed by clouds, is an eerie world of elfin woodland where water-soaked lichens and mosses dangle from dwarfed

Five trails explore the crater of The Quill, an extinct volcano where the varied vegetation includes dry woods, a rain forest, and an elfin woodland.

trees and cling to boulders. The hike takes forty-five minutes to an hour and is difficult because the track runs along a steep slope that is extremely slippery, particularly after rain. When there are no clouds around the peak, hikers enjoy a view into the crater and a sweeping panorama of Statia and its neighboring islands.

Panorama Track/V (Nos. 1–11) is a roller-coaster hike on the northeast rim of the crater. From the first peak (No. 6) there is a beautiful view north toward Zeelandia and the windward coast. The second peak (No. 8) offers a look into the crater. At No. 9, the view takes in the island from Lower Town on the west to the English Quarter on the east. Most of the trail passes through rain-forest vegetation, resplendent with epiphytes and bromeliads and lichens dangling like long gray beards from tree branches. Beyond No. 11, the path is too steep and dangerous to continue.

BEHIND THE MOUNTAIN ROAD

Behind the Mountain Road circles through the lowland of English Quarter, fragrant with lemon grass and wildflowers, to the southwestern flanks of The Quill and three more tracks. *Corre Corre Bay Track/VIII* (Nos. 1–34) turns east toward the sea at a sign—a white square with an exclamation mark (!)—painted on a large stone on the right-hand side of the road. The track crosses private property (which the owners permit) and passes the ruins of a plantation house on whose land sugarcane, cotton, and some tobacco were once cultivated. The seashore is edged with *patate bord de mer*, a creeping vine with pretty lilac flowers known locally as sweet-a vine, and offshore the waves break against an outer reef. The hike takes eighty minutes, round trip. After the Corre Corre Bay turn-off, Behind the Mountain Road is unpaved and very rutted for the last mile or so. If one walks this stretch, allow an additional twenty-five minutes, one way.

Track Around the Mountain/VI (Nos. 1–63) is a fairly easy trail along the south and west slopes of The Quill. After ascending through dry forest and bending to the west (No. 10), the track continues on a rather horizontal plane to the summit of White Wall (No. 30). The formation's chalky face cannot be seen because the trail is above it. A side path (Nos. 30A–E) leads to a lookout for a splendid view of the south coast. The main trail continues northwest, ending on Rosemary Lane on the outskirts of Oranjestad. The hike takes about ninety minutes one way.

Soldier Gut Track/VII (Nos. 1–27) follows a lower route along the southern slope and is fairly easy as far as No. 13. Here hikers can descend into Soldier Gut, but this part is recommended only for experienced mountaineers because the slope is steep and often slippery. The name Soldier Gut

Kapok, or silk-cotton, trees grow in the rain forest of The Quill's crater, sometimes to a height of 150 feet. Their pods contain a springy floss used as filling for mattresses and blankets.

derives from the soldier crab, also known as hermit crab, which is abundant here. The crabs are born in the sea, but after metamorphosis they become land crabs and climb the hills to the highest peak of The Quill. To reproduce they must return to the sea.

THE WINDWARD COAST

On the rugged windward coast, foamy Atlantic waves wash the golden-gray sands of Concordia Bay that arc along the edge of an ancient lava flow from the foot of Gilboa Hill and Zeelandia to The Quill. The 2-mi/3.2-km stretch of beach looks inviting but an undertow makes it dangerous for swimming. It is popular for sunbathing, hiking, and—after a storm—for beachcombing and shelling. A dirt road on the south just before the entrance to Maison sur la Plage, a small resort, leads down to the sea, but do not drive too close to the beach because it is easy to get stuck in the sand.

THE NORTH HILLS

Over the centuries settlers farmed the arid north hills, but now the hot, inhospitable land has been left to the goats. Three tracks depart on a jeep track at the north end of Concordia Bay, just west of Maison sur la Plage.

Venus Bay Track/IX (Nos. 1–27) is a forty-minute hike to the bay on the northeast coast over hills with thorny bushes, Turk's-head cactus, and large century plants, known locally as corrudo. From No. 11, it descends into a hot gully, passing canga, a weed with flowers like those of a tomato, and a rainwater pond; it then makes a loop (Nos. 20–26) along the bay. Venus Bay, flanked by the rough cliffs of Bomba Hill on the north and Gilboa Hill on the south, is edged by seagrapes and meran, or wild sage, along the beach. There are also some manchineel trees, whose sap causes a skin rash and whose small green fruit is poisonous. Sign No. 25 is posted on a barbasco tree, a species whose branches were used by the Carib Indians for fishing. When the leaves and branches are put in the sea, their poisonous sap, rotenone, suffocates the fish by paralyzing its breathing apparatus. The sap, however, is not poisonous to humans. Alternatively, at Venus Bay Track's highest point (No. 11), *Gilboa Hill Track/X* (Nos. 1–15) turns east to the cliffside for spectacular views across Statia to The Quill with St. Kitts on the south horizon and St. Barts and St. Maarten on the north.

STATIA UNDERSEA

Between 1493 and 1700, Statia changed hands among rivaling European powers twenty-two times. The bottom of its leeward coast is littered with an estimated 200 shipwrecks and other ruins that have lain undisturbed for centuries. Divers might find antique bottles lying side by side but a century apart in age. Atop this jumbled maze, corals grow and attract a great variety of fish and marine life. Most diving is in 20 to 80 ft/6 to 24 m of water with visibility over 100 ft/30 m; snorkeling is exceptional too.

Of the sixteen charted dive sites, the most popular, dubbed the Supermarket, is located 0.5 mi/0.8 km off the coast from Lower Town, at 60 ft/ 18 m depth. Here, less than 150 ft/45 m apart, are two shipwrecks with patches of beautiful coral and colorful purple and red tube sponges growing over them. (Usually one must descend to 100 ft/30 m to see red tube sponges.) The area is populated with cottonwick, a rare grunt indigenous to the eastern Caribbean. There are soldierfishes, squirrelfishes, spotted moray eels, sea turtles, puffer fishes, and stingrays, but the biggest thrill is the flying gurnard, a fish rarely seen by divers. About 12 in/30 cm or more in length, it is black with white spots and iridescent blue pectoral wings; it looks like a hovering bird as it swims. Off the southwest coast Crooks Reef has elkhorn corals, large sea fans, and pillar corals.

Outdoor Activities

Hiking: Twelve nature trails with sequentially numbered signposts make use of old donkey and farming tracks in three separate areas. A guide is not needed, but a guidebook is available.

Snorkeling and Diving: Untouched by commercial development, Statia's waters offer an extraordinary combination of coral reefs, marine life, and historic shipwrecks. Statia's one dive operation has its own boats, which make two or three dives daily. On the northwest coast, the shallow coral gardens of Jenkins Bay are suitable for snorkelers and novice divers.

Exploring the Island

St. Eustatius is 8 sq mi/21 sq km, with only a few roads, but getting around the island is easy. Taxis and rental cars are available from the airport and in town; donkeys can be hired for hilly treks. All motor roads leave from Oranjestad, the main town, and cross the flat part of the island. The roads also provide access to the nature trails. St. Eustatius is a ten-minute flight south of Saba, or seventeen minutes from St. Maarten.

Information: There is no office in North America. In Europe: % Cabinet of the Plenipotentiary, Badhuisweg 173-175, The Hague, Holland. In St. Eustatius: St. Eustatius Tourist Bureau, Oranjestad, St. Eustatius, NA; 599-3-82433. Offices also at the airport and pier. St. Eustatius Historical Foundation Museum, Wilhelminaweg, Oranjestad; 599-3-2288. Both have literature on nature trails.

Pages 226 and 227: Corre Corre Bay, on Statia's southeast windward coast facing the Atlantic.

ST. KITTS AND NEVIS

GENTLE ISLANDS OF GRACE and beauty, St. Kitts and Nevis have great appeal for their tranquil, unspoiled qualities. With profiles dominated by volcanic peaks, the islands are separated on the surface of the sea by a 2-mi-/ 3.2-km-wide strait known as The Narrows, but beneath the sea they lie on the same subterranean rock base on which their volcanic mountains were formed eons ago. Land connecting the two runs in shallow water—only 20 to 50 ft/6 to 15 m deep—from the southern tip of St. Kitts to the north coast of Nevis.

The first English settlers arrived in St. Kitts in 1623 and established a foothold in the middle part of the island. A year later, the French seized the north and south portions. Thus began an intense rivalry between Britain and France that raged for nearly a century, interrupted only briefly when the settlers joined forces to annihilate the Carib natives. Meanwhile, St. Kitts became the "Mother Colony," as she was known, from which the British settled Nevis, Antigua, and Montserrat, and the French laid claim to Martinique, Guadeloupe, St. Martin, and St. Barts. Finally in 1783, St. Kitts and Nevis became British colonies, which they remained until they became fully independent in 1983.

From the arrival of the first colonists, St. Kitts and Nevis were intensively cultivated, mostly with sugarcane, and the islands had the highest-yielding cane crop in the world. Today, the fields are still planted with sugarcane but the old plantation homes have been turned into gracious inns. Plantation roads are ideal for walking and horseback riding through the green countryside, and they provide access to mountain trails for hiking in tropical rain forests on brooding volcanic peaks.

ST. KITTS

St. Kitts lies on a northwest–southeast axis, with a spine of mountains comprising three separate ranges that rise to almost 4,000 ft/1,212 m: the North West Range with the island's highest peak, Mt. Liamuiga (pronounced Lee-a-MOO-ee-ga); Central Range with Verchild's Mountain; and the steep-sided South East Range. In colonial times, the mountain slopes above 1,000 ft/300 m were made Crown lands to preserve the watershed and thus some parts were spared deforestation. Today, those peaks are thick with rain forests. From these lofty heights the land slopes gently through verdant, crop-producing foothills and grasslands to the sea. Rain from the heavy clouds brought by the northeast trade winds cascades down the steep mountainsides, carving deep ravines and carrying rich volcanic soil over the foothills. Most of the coast is bordered by a band of coral rock and, in some places, black sand beaches. Different in appearance is the Southeastern Peninsula, a narrow tongue of land that stretches south toward Nevis. It is made up of a series of low hills covered with dry woodlands and scrub interspersed with salt ponds and scalloped with white sand beaches.

Poinciana, or flamboyant, which blooms from May to September, is everywhere on St. Kitts, as well it should be. The tree was named for Count de Poinci, a seventeenth-century French governor of St. Kitts and a keen botanist. Another common flower, particularly in the winter months, is a red-trumpet-blossomed plant known in the United States as amaryllis and in St. Kitts as Barbados lily (but in Barbados it is called Easter lily). The Kittitians, as the people are called, keep their houses freshly painted, and even the tiniest yard is brightened with flowering shrubs and orchids.

BASSETERRE

Despite its French name, Basseterre, the capital of St. Kitts, is unmistakably British. Sited on a wide bay on the southwest, it offers the stroller glimpses of Victorian and Georgian architecture, particularly near Independence Square, a public park with flowering gardens in the center of the town. One might walk down to the pier from where the ferry departs daily for the forty-five-minute ride to Nevis. Saturday is market day and a good time to learn about the tropical fruits and vegetables grown on the island.

A nice view of Basseterre, which means "lowland," can be seen on the west side of town from a promontory where the gardens of the Ocean Terrace Inn are sure to have bananaquits and hummingbirds feeding off the blossoms and Lesser Antillean bullfinches sneaking sugar from the tables. East of town, another fine view of Basseterre and the Caribbean climaxes a hike of about an hour to the summit of Monkey Hill (1,319 ft/400 m), named for the green monkey that lives there and elsewhere on St. Kitts and Nevis.

FAIRVIEW AND BLOODY POINT

The road north from Basseterre hugs the leeward coast most of the way and borders the tracks of the sugar train that encircles the island at the fringe of the sugar fields. In the background are the mountains with ever-towering Mt. Liamuiga in the north. Most of the coast is rockbound, except for occasional small coves with tiny golden sand beaches between Old Road Town and Half Way Tree. At the hamlet of Boyd's, a 0.25-mi/0.4-km detour inland leads to Fairview Inn, a former plantation great house on a foothill of the South East mountains. The inn is surrounded by gardens whose trees, profuse with fruits and flowers, attract several species of hummingbirds and finches; tropical mockingbirds populate the more open fields and

woods. The inn's terrace overlooking the gardens is as fine a place as any on the island for viewing a Caribbean sunset. Immediately behind the inn, a track winds up through a forested mountainside to an elevation of 1,709 ft/ 513 m, where there is a radio tower and a sweeping view of the leeward coast.

North of Boyd's, Stonefort Ravine is the place where in 1626 British and French forces massacred the entire Carib population of 2,000 who were planning an offensive against a new settlement of Europeans farther up the coast. The ravine, it is said, ran with blood for three days, hence the name Bloody Point by which it is more commonly known.

Romney Manor and Cross-island Nature Trail

At Old Road Town, the site of the first British settlement, established in 1623, one can turn inland to Romney Manor and Wingfield Estate, former plantations on the slopes of the mountains. Here and at West Farm near Fairview Inn, there are small boulders with Carib petroglyphs; the stone drawings have been reproduced as designs on the batik made at the

Strategically perched atop a spur of Mt. Liamuiga, Brimstone Hill Fortress commands a view to the north over one of St. Kitts' few flat green fields.

Caribelle Batiks workshop at Romney Manor. The seventeenth-century plantation house, surrounded by flowering gardens, is set in a grove where a huge samaan tree dominates the entrance. Known also as the raintree, the specimen is thought to be more than 350 years old. Green monkeys cavort in the surrounding woods.

At the Wingfield Estate, on a plateau at about 800 ft/240 m elevation, a paved road leads northeast through wooded hillsides for about 1.5 mi/2.4 km then meets a footpath along the southern flanks of the Central Range. The road passes through private land grazed by cattle; as a precaution and a courtesy, hikers should ask for permission locally before proceeding. A path, known as Nine Turn Gut, wanders over and around three ridges and valleys between the Central and South East ranges for approximately 3 mi/4.8 km until it meets another plateau on the windward side of the island at Philips and the Molineux Estate. The path is a moderate hike of about two hours, but from coast to coast it takes four to five hours. Experienced hikers may not need a guide, but one is recommended because the path's many twists and turns can be disorienting.

VERCHILD'S MOUNTAIN

Farther north on the coast at Middle Island, a road inland to Lambert's Estate at 800 ft/240 m elevation provides access to a trail up Verchild's Mountain (3,100 ft/939 m) to Dos d'Ane Pond set amid huge ferns and other dense tropical vegetation near the top. The hike on an undefined trail ascends up steep mountainsides through seasonal evergreen forest on the lower slopes and tropical rain forest in the higher ones. At 2,700 ft/710 m elfin woodland begins. Beyond the pond, another 0.5 mi/0.8 km of difficult hiking through the tangled growth of elfin woodland leads to the summit. Because there are no real trails on Verchild's Mountain, hikers must have a local guide to show them the way.

MT. LIAMUIGA

Known throughout colonial history as Mt. Misery, volcanic Mt. Liamuiga dominates the northern end of St. Kitts, though its peak is often obscured by a crown of white clouds. In a landscape of patchwork green, the mountain slopes up through cultivated foothills to about 1,000 ft/300 m, where rainforest vegetation begins, and rises to the lip of the crater at 2,625 ft/800 m. Mt. Liamuiga's actual peak (3,792 ft/1,156 m) is located on the east side of the crater. The vegetation at the crater rim and around the peak, where strong winds and clouds prevail, is short, tough cloud forest, or elfin woodland.

The trail to the lip of the crater is a steady ascent through rain forest under a dense canopy 50 ft/15 m high where candlewood, gommier, Spanish oak, West Indian locust, and wild plum trees dominate over huge philodendrons and ferns. The thick greenery is brightened by an occasional red and orange heliconia flower; wild orchids and other epiphytes climb the tree trunks and hang gracefully from the branches. Views down the coast are spectacular.

The ascent of Mt. Liamuiga is made from the north end of the island at Belmont Estate where a dirt road leads inland over the foothills to an elevation of about 1,500 ft/450 m. The trail begins where the road ends and continues on a gradual ascent through the rain forest and along deep ravines up to the crater rim. The hike to the rim takes about two and a half hours on the ascent and about one and a half hours on the descent. Experienced hikers may not need a guide to go only as far as the crater rim, but they should inquire locally about trail conditions before proceeding. Vegetation grows quickly, often obscuring the trail. Hikers who go on their own must arrange in advance for their return transportation from Belmont to their hotel or starting base. An alternative route to the trail starts at Rawlins Plantation, about 1 mi/1.6 km inland from the north coast.

Mt. Liamuiga also offers hikers with stamina and agility the rare opportunity to walk down—crawling might be a more accurate description—into the crater of a dormant volcano. There is no real trail; rather, hikers make their way down 400 ft/120 m from the rim to the crater floor along very steep, slippery sides, clinging to roots and vines—which are not always secure. It is an arduous trip, not to be undertaken casually. The crater floor is over 0.5 mi/0.8 km in diameter and covered with volcanic rocks, some vegetation, and, at times, a small lake. The smell of sulphur can be detected. The lack of a trail and the slippery conditions make a local guide essential; it is easy to become disoriented and lost.

Another option is to continue along the rim through the misty wonderland of the elfin forest to the east side of the crater. If the air is clear—more likely to occur in February, March, and June—one has panoramic views of St. Kitts, with neighboring Saba and St. Eustatius on the north, Montserrat and Redonda on the east, and Nevis on the south. Hikers should be prepared for rain and chilly winds and must be careful along the slippery paths; lightweight boots or sturdy hiking shoes are recommended. The peak of Mt. Liamuiga is a rocky, razorback ridge, considered too unstable and dangerous to climb.

BRIMSTONE HILL NATIONAL PARK

Brimstone Hill Fortress, one of the most massive and best-preserved forts in the Americas, is perched on an 800-ft/240-m spur of Mt. Liamuiga overlooking the west coast. Begun in 1690 by the French and completed by

the British over a period of a century, the fortress covers 38 acres/ 15 hectares. The panorama from the ramparts helps one understand St. Kitts' strategic importance. Below the fort on the north are green cultivated fields—one of the few stretches of flat land on St. Kitts—and the islands of Saba, St. Eustatius, and St. Barts in the distance. Along the south coast, green waves of sugarcane fields undulate through the foothills of the North West and Central ranges. Nevis and Montserrat peak in the distance. Behind the fortress's walls of volcanic stone looms Mt. Liamuiga. A road brightened with pink oleander blossoms leads up a steep hill almost to the fort's entrance. But hiking from the lower walls gives one a better grasp of the enormous effort that was needed to build the colossal structure. Restoration has been in progress for over a decade, and museum exhibits are installed in some of the rooms.

BLACK ROCKS

Rounding the northern tip of the island to Dieppe Bay Town, the coastline is fringed by coral and interspersed with black sand beaches shaded by seagrapes and palm groves. At the edge of the sea by Belle Vue on the windward coast are huge, weathered lava boulders that make the scenery magnificent.

Particularly dramatic formations of huge lava boulders, called black rocks, are on St. Kitts' northeast Atlantic shore. Facing page: South of Basseterre, colored cliffs frame one of the white sand beaches that attracts hikers and birders as well as swimmers and snorkelers.

SOUTHEASTERN PENINSULA

Over the hill southeast of Basseterre, a narrow tongue of land with a series of low hills is covered with dry woodlands populated by white-tailed deer, green monkeys, mongoose, and a great variety of birds. The knolls conceal pretty coves overlooking some of St. Kitts' nicest white sand beaches. Until recently, the peninsula was the most isolated part of St. Kitts, accessible only on foot or by boat. But since the late 1970s the first mile, as far as Sir Timothy's Hill and encompassing the golden sand beaches of Frigate Bay on the north and south coasts, has been the focus of resort development. Now, the rest is being opened by a new road. The government has engaged ecologists and other scientists to work with developers to help protect the natural environment and wildlife, but both are bound to be affected. Meanwhile, there are many places for hikers and birders to enjoy on foot, and for swimmers, snorkelers, and divers to reach by boat. The vegetation is quite diverse and includes wetlands and semideciduous evergreen forest in some places, acacia, scrub, and almost barren desert in others.

GREAT SALT POND

The largest of six salt ponds that dot the peninsula is located near the south end between Sand Bank Bay, a beautiful beach on the north coast, and Ballast Bay and Major's Bay on the south coast where the new road ends. Stilts, gulls, and terns are regular visitors to the pond and seashore. On the west side, a sliver of land with a track separates Little Salt Pond from Great Salt Pond. Major's Bay is a beautiful horseshoe cove with a half-mile crest of white sand where two international groups are already planning resorts. A bluff on the east side of the bay is a nesting site for the American kestrel, known here as sparrow hawk or falcon. Nag's Head, the cliffs on the southwesternmost corner, has breeding colonies of brown pelicans and magnificent frigatebirds.

St. Kitts' potential for bird watchers is only beginning to be discovered. From late July to early October of 1988, ornithologists working with the environmental survey in the Great Salt Pond area identified as many as twenty-five species, including Wilson's plovers, lesser golden-plovers, short-billed and long-billed dowitchers, black-necked stilts, roseate terns, least terns, whimbrels, red knots, and a black-tailed godwit, believed to be the first sighting of the species in this region. The surrounding woodlands have the purple-throated carib, Lesser Antillean flycatcher, pearly-eyed thrasher, trembler, black-whiskered vireo, and yellow warbler.

St. Kitts' best beaches—Major's Bay, Banana Bay, Cockleshell Bay, and

Mosquito Bay, all on the south side of the peninsula—had been accessible only by boat from Basseterre prior to completion of the new road. Banana Bay and Cockleshell Bay have cottage beach resorts with water-sports facilities operated by Ocean Terrace Inn in Basseterre. Directly in front of the resort is one of the island's best snorkeling locations. The reef is in about 15 ft/4.5 m of water and has elkhorn, star, and brain corals and a large variety of colorful fish such as queenfishes, angelfishes, and damselfishes.

NEVIS

From a distance Nevis appears to be a single, dark green mountain rising to a perfect cone from a deep turquoise sea. The island is circular in shape and has at its center a volcanic peak that swoops up to 3,232 ft/985 m. But a closer look reveals long strands of golden sand beaches fringing a lush interior, and several other mountains—Saddle Hill (1,250 ft/381 m) on the south, Round Hill (1,014 ft/309 m) on the north, and Powell's Hill (1,901 ft/ 580 m) on the west. The entire coastline is fringed with coral.

This now-quiet hideaway was the social hub of the Caribbean in the seventeenth and eighteenth centuries when its celebrated spa drew European aristocrats seeking to cure their gout and rheumatism. The once-grand Bath Hotel and Spa stands as a ruin, but Nevis still attracts travelers to its stately homes. They have been converted into some of the finest small resorts in the Caribbean, situated in rambling groves of coconut palms and banana trees and surrounded by magnificent gardens under the spreading arms of poinciana, mimosa, and fruit trees laden with breadfruit, soursop, mango, guava, and papaya. Passionfruit is so abundant here that it grows as a vine along roadsides.

As many as sixty species of birds populate the gardens, countryside, and rain forests. Three hummingbirds—purple-throated carib, green-throated carib, and Antillean crested—as well as the bananaquit, Lesser Antillean bullfinch, and a variety of finches are common in gardens. Bird lists are sometimes available from hotel managers.

Nevis is ideal for those who enjoy ambling down unnamed and unpaved country roads and along footpaths still very much used by local people. Here, doing-nothing-in-particular has been raised to a fine art that West Indians call "limin'." Those with real energy and hiking skills tackle the arduous trip to Nevis Peak.

Pages 238 and 239: St. Kitts' best beaches begin around Frigate Bay on the long thin peninsula reaching south toward Nevis.

CHARLESTOWN

Visitors who come to Nevis by ferry from St. Kitts arrive on the west side of the island at Charlestown, a delightful colonial village with a West Indian flavor—and as good a place as any to practice "limin'." A short stroll along Main Street can take in tiny shops and the Hamilton Museum, the home of Nevis's most famous native son, Alexander Hamilton, the first U.S. Secretary of the Treasury, born here in 1755. The most popular place in town is the post office where the Philatelic Society sells Nevis stamps. Although St. Kitts and Nevis are one nation, each issues its own stamps, which makes them much prized by collectors.

PINNEY'S BEACH

The road between Charlestown and Newcastle on the north side of the island skirts the coast along Pinney's Beach, an idyllic 4-mi/6.4-km stretch of palm-fringed golden sand. No one will have trouble "limin'" here—or farther up the road at Cades Point, where there is a spectacular view of St. Kitts and the Caribbean from the Cliffdwellers Resort. Dedicated hikers can make their way on foot up the steep hill to the main house perched high above the sea. Sunsets from here are breathtaking. Another sight in the late afternoon is the arrival of flocks of cattle egrets on the north end of Pinney's Beach at Nelson's Spring, a freshwater pond, where they roost. Nevis's coast is dotted with springs and seasonal lagoons that fill after heavy rains.

NEWCASTLE AND ROUND HILL

Visitors who fly in arrive at the Newcastle Airport at the base of the Nisbet Plantation, an inn that was once the estate of Frances Nisbet, the wife of Lord Nelson. Connecting the house and the beach is a magnificent lawn bordered by gardens of flamboyant and passionfruit trees and a double row of stately coconut palms. Another landmark nearby is the Newcastle Pottery, where one can watch pottery being made from Nevis's rich red clay and fired by traditional methods.

At the north end of Pinney's Beach, a road cuts inland from the coast via Westbury through rolling green hills and meadows to Fountain and then to Camps on the Atlantic coast. One can also hike from Fountain to Newcastle on a track along the east side of Round Hill. A motoring road ascends part of the way to the summit of Round Hill but the steep last half-mile must be taken on foot. It is worth the effort for the view that sweeps from Newcastle on the north coast down to Charlestown on the west coast, with Nevis Peak looming in the background. Open areas are likely places to spot yellow grass finches and tropical mockingbirds; black-whiskered vireos rustle in the undergrowth; herons, brown pelicans, laughing gulls, and royal terns enliven the shore scenes.

SOUTH OF NEVIS PEAK

On the south side of Charlestown at Bath Stream (whose water once supplied Bath Spa), great flocks of egrets arrive to roost at sunset. From Morning Star, a side road leads south to Montpelier Plantation Inn, a restored great house surrounded by magnificent gardens with a fine view of Nevis Peak. The gardens attract a host of bananaquits, Lesser Antillean bullfinches, hummingbirds, Caribbean elaenias, common ground-doves, and black-faced grassquits. South of the inn a road via Cox Village leads to a footpath up Saddle Hill (1,250 ft/375 m). From here the view of the south coast stretches from the Atlantic on the east to the Caribbean on the west. The ascent takes about an hour.

The south coast, the driest part of the island, is covered mostly with acacia and cactus, particularly Turk's-head cactus. A secondary road of about 3 mi/4.8 km, paved about halfway, follows the coast from Charlestown to the lighthouse on the island's southernmost tip. The area is popular for birding and is populated by semipalmated sandpipers, sanderlings, and ruddy turnstones. A reef offshore is one of Nevis's best diving spots.

North of the main road after Morning Star, the area known locally as Gingerland has five former plantations whose great houses or sugar mills have been converted into inns. All are situated at about 1,000 ft/300 m elevation on the southern slope of Nevis Peak, and one can hike on lanes and footpaths from one estate to the next, enjoying the panorama of the island down to the sea. Gingerland hotels can arrange visits to some of the area's magnificent private gardens; they are the most convenient starting places for hikes to Nevis Peak and the Rainforest Trail.

NEVIS PEAK

Cloud-capped Nevis Peak, rising to 3,232 ft/985 m in the center of the island, dominates the landscape from every direction. Last active in 1692, the volcano has a crater 0.5 mi/0.8 km in diameter and about 790 ft/240 m deep. Although it is dormant, it emits sulphurous gases with temperatures up to 392°F/200°C from the solfataras, or vents. The hike to the rim of the crater is as difficult as any in the eastern Caribbean and should be undertaken only by experienced hikers. A trail of about 2 mi/3.2 km begins above Dunbar Estate on a plateau at 1,528 ft/466 m, but it is so ill-defined that a guide is needed even to find the start. In some places, the climb is almost vertical and one continues by holding on to roots and vines. People both-

ered by heights should not attempt this hike. When the weather at the top is clear—which is seldom—there are superb views across the emerald fields of Nevis to the Caribbean on the west and the Atlantic on the east. A guide can be arranged through one's hotel; the hike takes a minimum of five hours round trip.

THE RAINFOREST TRAIL

A challenging but less taxing hike leaves from Stoney Hill at the top of the Rawlins Road above Golden Rock Estate and winds north through groves of cocoa, breadfruit, and nutmeg trees along the mountain overlooking the Atlantic coast. It continues up through forests of white cedar to the rain forest where the woods are full of hummingbirds, forest thrushes, yellow warblers, scaly-breasted thrashers, and tremblers. Red-tailed and broad-winged hawks soar overhead. Monkeys can be seen between Golden Rock and Stoney Hill. Golden Rock Estate has a map of the trail and will arrange for a guide for those who need one. The hike is three hours, round trip.

Clockwise from top left: purple-throated carib; tropical mockingbird; great blue heron; black-crowned night-heron. Facing page: Coconut palms overlook Nevis's Newcastle Bay.

Outdoor Activities

HIKING: With a map in hand, hikers should have little trouble finding their way in the lowlands and foothills of St. Kitts and Nevis. Walking is an important means of transport for many villagers in these quiet islands. In the mountains, however, one should hike only with a local guide because trails rapidly become overgrown. In St. Kitts, guided hiking trips are offered by Greg's Rainforest Tours (tel. 809-465-4121) and Kriss Tours (tel. 809-465-4042). On Nevis, guides can be arranged through hotels.

BIKING: Both islands are suitable for cycling on the roads that skirt the lowlands, where traffic is light. Modest bicycles are available at some hotels; inquire when making hotel reservations.

HORSEBACK RIDING: On St. Kitts half-day outings in Conaree on the windward coast are available from The Stable, Trinity Inn (tel. 809-456-3226). Rawlins Plantation offers riding on Mt. Liamuiga's foothills. Riding in the southeastern peninsula has been halted until road construction is completed; inquire locally. On Nevis, Howell's Multi-Line Services (tel. 809-469-5389) and Jan's Travel (tel. 809-469-5426) arrange horseback riding with local owners.

SWIMMING: St. Kitts' best white-sand beaches are on the southeastern peninsula—Frigate Bay, Friar's Bay, Major's Bay, Banana Bay, and Cockshell Bay, all locations slated for development with the opening of a new road.

The glistening black sand beaches on the Atlantic northeast coast are more of a curiosity than good for sunbathing. In the stretch south of Black Rock, swimmers should be careful of the strong currents and undertows. Dieppe Bay Beach on the north coast, where the water is calmer, has slate-gray sands framed by a pretty palm grove. Conaree Beach on the east coast is grayish and good for surf swimming.

Pinney's Beach, Nevis's palm-fringed stretch of golden sand north of Charlestown, is easily accessible on footpaths that cut across from the main road to the beach at intervals of about 0.25 mi/0.4 km. The beach has never been developed, although several inland hotels have locations where they take their guests. It is a delightful place to spend the day and to watch the sun set. North of Pinney's Beach, Oualie Beach on the northwest coast is a more open area with tall grass. There is surf here, too.

SNORKELING AND DIVING: St. Kitts and Nevis have yet to be discovered as dive destinations, although extensive reefs off their coasts offer walls, canyons, caves, and drift diving. Rain runoff from the volcanic mountains tends to make water near the shore murky, so the best diving is a mile or so offshore.

The reefs have abundant star, staghorn, and brain corals. There are huge crinoids and sponges in 40 to 80 ft/12 to 24 m of water and gigantic sea fans, some as big as forest trees. But the most outstanding features of these waters are the enormous schools of angelfishes, soldierfishes, trumpetfishes, squirrelfishes, and snappers. The reefs have big drop-offs, known as "white holes," that attract large schools of tropical fish. Spiny lobsters and barracudas are common. Divers are likely to see small sharks, bottlenose dolphins, and Spanish mackerel as well.

The largest reef is the Grid Iron, a long barrier reef that stretches for over 6 mi/10 km from Conaree on the east coast of St. Kitts to Newcastle Bay on Nevis at depths varying from 6 to 50 ft/1.8 to 15 m. It helps protect The Narrows between St. Kitts and Nevis where there is a large circular reef that spreads over an area about 0.5 mi/0.8 km in diameter at depths ranging from 18 to 50 ft/5 to 15 m. Here one can see large schools of angelfishes and other species common to the region. The south side of the reef, known as Monkey Shoals, at 35 ft/10 m, is thick with black coral.

Another lure of diving here is the possibility of stumbling upon one of the unexplored wrecks known to be in St. Kitts' waters. Eight wrecks have been identified, but historic records show that at least 300 ships went down here.

Arrangements to dive off Nevis can be made through water-sports operators on either island. In Basseterre, facilities for diving, jet-skiing, sailing, fishing, and windsurfing are found at Fisherman's Wharf. On Nevis, Oualie Beach is the center for water sports.

FISHING: Sport-fishing can be arranged through one's hotel, or sometimes with local fishermen at Fisherman's Wharf. Catches include kingfishes, groupers, and occasionally sailfish and blue marlin.

WINDSURFING: The best locations for windsurfing on St. Kitts are Frigate Bay and Banana Bay. Equipment is available from water-sports operators and beachfront hotels. The coast from Cades Bay and Oualie Beach to Newcastle is another popular windsurfing location; it is bordered by coral reefs within easy reach for snorkeling.

EXPLORING THE ISLANDS

Paddle-shaped St. Kitts, 23 mi/37 km long and 5 mi/8 km wide, narrows to a peninsula—the "handle" of the paddle—that stretches for about 7 mi/11 km to The Narrows and varies in width from about 3 mi/4.8 km to less than 0.25 mi/ 0.8 km. A good road completely encircles the main part of St. Kitts along the coast and a new road traverses the southeast peninsula. There are no cross-island roads through the central interior but there are footpaths. The ring road makes it easy to drive—or bicycle—around the island, and provides access to the mountains of the interior where there is splendid hiking. In addition, St. Kitts has 36 mi/58 km of rails that circumnavigate the sugar fields and a sugar train that offers special passenger excursions (tel. 809-465-8157).

Nevis has a highway of about 20 mi/ 32 km that encircles the island, but not always following the coast. The road is narrow, winding, and undulating. Traffic is light enough that one can walk along the road, which is how many islanders get around. On the south side of the island, particularly, there are many villages close together and from any of them it is easy to wander down a side road to explore the countryside, visit a plantation inn, or enjoy a nice view.

Car rentals are available and can be arranged through one's hotel or the rental company, or one can hire a taxi for sightseeing excursions. Driving is on the LEFT. Visitors with a valid driver's license can obtain a local driver's license from the police stations in Basseterre and Charlestown; there is a fee. Maps are available in a free tourist guide published by the Tourist Board. Topographic maps (1979), particularly useful for hiking on Nevis, can be purchased in the Tourist Office and local bookstores.

INFORMATION: In the U.S.: St. Kitts and Nevis Tourist Board, 414 East 75th St., New York, NY 10021; 212-535-1234. In Canada: 11 Yorkville Ave., #508, Toronto, Ont. M4W 1L3. In the U.K.: % Rosamunde Bern Assoc., 10 Kensington Court, London W85DL; 71-376-0881. In St. Kitts: Pellican Mall, Basseterre; 809-465-2620 or 4040. In Nevis: Main Street, Charlestown; 809-469-5521.

ANTIGUA AND BARBUDA

MONTSERRAT

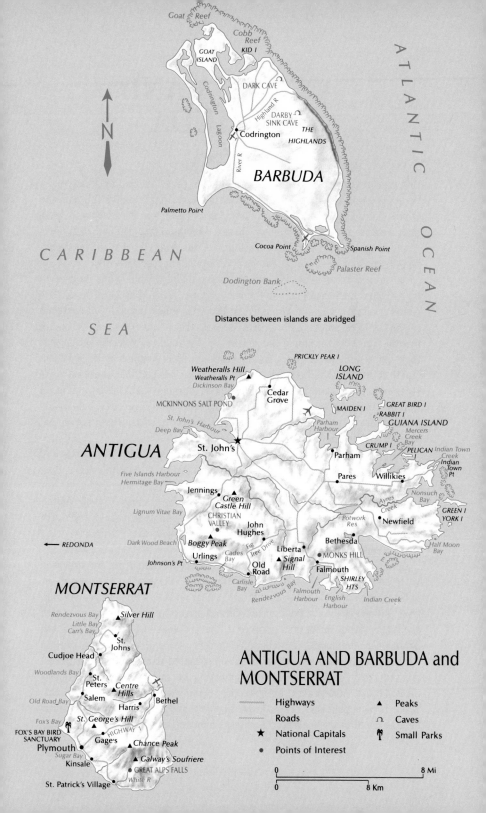

Goat Reef

Cobb Reef

KID I

GOAT ISLAND

ATLANTIC

DARK CAVE

Codrington Lagoon

Highland R.

DARBY SINK CAVE

× Codrington

THE HIGHLANDS

River R.

BARBUDA

Palmetto Point

OCEAN

CARIBBEAN

Cocoa Point

Spanish Point

Palaster Reef

Dodington Bank

SEA

Distances between islands are abridged

PRICKLY PEAR I

Weatheralls Hill
Weatheralls Pt
Dickinson Bay

LONG ISLAND

MCKINNONS SALT POND

Cedar Grove

MAIDEN I

GREAT BIRD I

RABBIT I

GUIANA ISLAND

St. John's Harbour

Parham Harbour

Mercers Creek Bay

CRUMP I

Deep Bay

ANTIGUA

★ St. John's

Parham

PELICAN I

Indian Town Creek

Indian Town Pt

Five Islands Harbour
Hermitage Bay

Pares

Willikies

Jennings

Green Castle Hill

Ayres Creek

Nonsuch Bay

CHRISTIAN VALLEY

John Hughes

Newfield

GREEN I
YORK I

Lignum Vitae Bay

Potwork Res

Dark Wood Beach

Boggy Peak

Fig Tree Drive

Liberta

Half Moon Bay

← REDONDA

Urlings

Cades Bay

Signal Hill

Bethesda

MONKS HILL

Johnson's Pt

Old Road

Falmouth

Carlisle Bay

SHIRLEY HTS

Rendezvous Bay

Falmouth Harbour

English Harbour

Indian Creek

MONTSERRAT

Rendezvous Bay
Little Bay
Carr's Bay

▲ Silver Hill

St. Johns

Cudjoe Head

Woodlands Bay

St. Peters

Centre Hills

Salem

Bethel

Old Road Bay

Harris

Fox's Bay

St. George's Hill

FOX'S BAY BIRD SANCTUARY

HIGHWAY

Gage's

Chance Peak

Plymouth

Sugar Bay

▲ Galway's Soufriere

Kinsale

GREAT ALPS FALLS

White R.

St. Patrick's Village

ANTIGUA AND BARBUDA and MONTSERRAT

Highways
Roads
★ National Capitals
● Points of Interest

▲ Peaks
∩ Caves
🎋 Small Parks

0 ——————— 8 Mi

0 ——————— 8 Km

ANTIGUA AND BARBUDA

ANTIGUA

SWEEPING WHITE SAND BEACHES and hidden coves washed by shimmering turquoise waters and fringed by colorful reefs, boats under full sail and windsurfers gliding over deep-blue waters—these are the images of Antigua, a mecca for those who love the sea. Low humidity coupled with year-round northeast tradewinds create one of the best climates in the Caribbean and make the island ideal for a variety of outdoor activities.

Antigua is an emergent island consisting mainly of limestone built up in hills around a central plain and almost entirely fringed by coral reefs. The island is shaped vaguely like a maple leaf with miles and miles of coastline to shelter bays, inlets, and natural harbors. It is about 108 sq mi/280 sq km in area. The hilly terrain of the southwest, the result of volcanic action that took place millions of years ago, reaches its highest point at Boggy Peak (1,319 ft/402 m). Unlike most islands of the Lesser Antilles, Antigua lacks steep mountains, and this relative flatness, together with the deforestation that began with the earliest settlers in the seventeenth century, have made it one of the driest islands in the eastern Caribbean, with an average annual rainfall of only 46 in/118 cm.

Except for the volcanic peaks, which contain the island's last patches of tropical forest, Antigua's terrain is made up mainly of flatlands and rolling hills once extensively planted with sugarcane and now barren, except for pockets of secondary forest and grassland used for grazing. To help revitalize the agriculture of this once-fertile island and to conserve its water resources, a series of water catchments and reservoirs was constructed throughout the island about three decades ago.

Around the shoreline, dry scrub and acacia woodland are interspersed with watery habitats—mangroves, tidal flats, salt ponds, and freshwater pools formed by rainwater runoff—that host an active birdlife year-round. Over 143 species have been observed in Antigua, of which about one-third are year-round residents, another third are seasonal visitors, and the balance are migrants. Bananaquits, grassquits, and two of the island's three hummingbird species—the green-throated carib and the Antillean crested—are frequent visitors to flowering gardens. Dowitchers, black-necked stilts, gulls, terns, herons, egrets, and warblers flock to the shores, while brown pelicans, tropicbirds, boobies, and magnificent frigatebirds nest on the limestone cliffs of Antigua's many offshore islets and cays.

Over eighty archaeological sites, one dating back 4,000 years, have been found on Antigua. Among the most extensive are those of the Arawaks who settled here from about 500 to 900 A.D. In 1493, when Columbus discovered *Yarumaqui*, as it was known to the Arawaks, or *Wadadli*, as the Carib Indians called it, he named the island Antigua after the Church of Santa María la Antigua in Seville. In 1632, after the island was occupied by English settlers from St. Kitts, Antigua became British. For the next 200 years it was Britain's most strategic Caribbean colony due to its location and protected harbor. In 1981, Antigua and her sister islands of Barbuda, 32 mi/51 km north, and uninhabited Redonda, 35 mi/56 km west, became an independent country, Antigua and Barbuda.

ST. JOHN'S

The capital, St. John's, is situated on the island's northwest Caribbean coast at the head of a sheltered inlet deep enough for large cruise ships to anchor. It had been a sleepy West Indian town until recently when it was awakened by a tourist boom. On the north side of the harbor at the tip of a 2-mi/3.2-km scenic headland is Fort James, built in the early eighteenth century to protect the harbor. Its counterpart on the south side of the harbor commanded an even larger peninsula, popular today for its white sand beaches and gentle waters. Around the peninsula to the south side is Five Island Harbour, another deep bay with any number of deserted coves and mangroves at its head, and the tiny offshore islets of Five Islands, home to blue-faced boobies, among other birds.

The most historic section of St. John's can be seen in an easy walk of an hour or so. An eighteenth-century courthouse, now the Museum of Antigua and Barbuda, houses a collection of Arawak and pre-Columbian artifacts; the Historical and Archaeological Society, which operates the museum, sponsors island tours highlighting Antigua's early natural and cultural history. On the south end of Market Street, the lively public market on Fridays and Saturdays is a good place for an introduction to Antigua's local produce.

McKINNONS SALT POND

North of St. John's en route to Dickinson Bay (the most resort-intensive beach on the island), the main road skirts McKinnons Salt Pond, a beach with brackish ponds. During the rainy months of May and June and September to November, as much as 100 acres/40 hectares might be covered with up to 4 in/10 cm of water, but during the dry seasons or droughts, the ponds can dry up completely. Of the twenty-six species of water birds recorded on the island, most were seen here, particularly in autumn. In

summer, least terns and Wilson's plover nest on the sand, and yellow-crowned night-herons breed in the mangroves on the fringe. Among the most remarkable sights are the flocks of small semipalmated sandpipers—as many as 3,000 at a time—making their short, swift flights, twisting and turning low over the water, then climbing high in the air.

WEATHERALLS HILL

On the north side of Dickinson Bay, Weatheralls Hill has a small, closed-canopy stand of trees over 30 ft/9 m in height, said to be the most mature sample of evergreen woodland in Antigua. The forest is dominated by Antigua white cedar, birch gum or turpentine, loblolly, boxwood, and ebony berry; the undergrowth has torchwood, cinnamon, and willow, among others. On the north side, at Blue Water Beach, is one of Antigua's prettiest hotel gardens crowded with brightly colored tropical flowers and fruit trees where hummingbirds dart about the blossoms. "Sugar birds" (the local name for the bananaquit) and Carib grackles busily steal sugar from the tables of the open-air dining terrace.

In addition to water sports available at resorts along Dickinson Bay, there are beaches and snorkeling areas along the fan-shaped northern crown of the island and the offshore islets. Paradise Reef, a mile-long coral garden north of Dickinson Bay, is popular for snorkeling and glass-bottom boat excursions. Tiny Prickly Pear Island, surrounded by coral gardens similar to those of the Cades Reef, is a favorite destination off the north coast for day sailors.

The incessant battering of strong Atlantic waves created Devil's Bridge, a natural formation at Indian Town Point on the eastern shore. Facing page: Hermitage Bay is a secluded cove at the mouth of Five Islands Harbour, one of several deep bays on Antigua's west coast.

Parham Harbour and Fitches Creek

The main road east from St. John's to Indian Town Point passes through the villages of Pares and Willikies from where secondary roads and tracks provide access to the irregular, deeply indented northeast coast from Parham Harbour to Mercers Creek Bay and Indian Town Point. A great number of islands, cays, and reefs shelter the coast and provide calm waters for sailing, snorkeling, and fishing. Directly east of St. John's, across the base of the island's northern crown, is Parham Harbour, the large bay that was the original harbor of Antigua. Fitches Creek, an inlet on the north side of the bay, is an area of brackish water and mangroves that attracts a variety of birdlife including whimbrels, plovers, yellowlegs, whistling-ducks, herons, egrets, clapper rails, and yellow-billed cuckoos. Farther east, Mercers Creek is also bordered by mangroves with similar birdlife.

Long Island

Less than a mile from the coast on the north side of Parham Harbour is Long Island, the private home of Jumby Bay, one of the Caribbean's most exclusive resorts. The island, flat and dry, is scalloped with long, undisturbed beaches and is densely wooded except for the resort grounds, which are festooned with oleander, bougainvillea, frangipani, flamboyant, and other tropical flowers and trees. Ponds on the island attract egrets, herons, white-cheeked pintails, and laughing gulls. Willets have been known to nest there. Nature trails and biking paths meander through the woods, beside the mangroves, and to the various beaches. Among the trees one sees are wild lantana, loblolly, tamarind, Norfolk Island pine, cordia, box briar, and gliricidia. Closer to the shore there are seagrape, Antigua whitewood, wax myrtles, and manchineel, whose poisonous sap the Amerindians used on their arrows to repel their enemies.

Pasture Bay on the north side of the island is a nesting beach for the hawksbill turtle from late May to December. Jumby Bay helps protect this endangered species with a turtle watch directed by WIDECAST, the Wide Caribbean Sea Turtle Conservation Network. The hawksbill, whose shell is the tortoiseshell used for jewelry, is the most beautiful of the sea turtles and the most valuable. Named for its beak-like upper jawbone, the reptile measures from 2 to 4 ft/0.6 to 1.2 m in length and can weigh 120 lb/54 kg or more. The female is prolific, depositing up to 200 eggs in her nest and repeating the performance in two-week intervals up to five times during the season. She takes about two hours to dig a nest 2 ft/0.6 m deep, lay her eggs, and return to the sea. Incubation takes about ten weeks.

The northeastern corner of this island has an archaeological site consisting of a floor covered with flints that may be over 7,000 years old; geologists have speculated that this island and the others surrounding Antigua were one landmass during the last ice age. Long Island can be visited on day trips by booking for lunch at Jumby Bay; the resort's ferry departs regularly from the Beachcomber jetty, north of the international airport.

GREAT BIRD ISLAND

Of particular interest to naturalists is Great Bird Island, a tiny uninhabited islet with a beach and limestone cliffs that are home to the red-billed tropicbird. These magnificent birds display and nest along the seaward side of the island. It is well worth the short climb from the beach to the top of the cliffs to observe the graceful tropicbirds gliding on the wind currents blowing in from the Atlantic. The island also has nesting colonies of sooty terns and brown noddies and is visited from April to September by laughing gulls and, occasionally, purple martins. Great Bird Island also has Antigua's only "snake," the harmless blindworm, or slowworm, a limbless lizard with minute eyes. Two islets south of Great Bird—Hells Gate and Rabbit Island—are breeding grounds of the brown pelican. Several boat operators in Antigua offer daily excursions to Bird Island by yacht and catamaran with picnic and snorkeling. The surrounding reefs are particularly good for spotting lobsters and eagle rays.

INDIAN TOWN NATIONAL PARK

Indian Town Point, the tip of a deep cove named Indian Town Creek, is a protected area of natural beauty and archaeological interest and a popular tourist attraction. At the mouth of the cove a natural formation known as Devil's Bridge has been created by the relentless waves of the Atlantic pounding against the rocks. Along the shore are several "blowing holes," where sprays of water surge noisily up through vents that are also the result of wave action. The area is covered mostly by dry scrub, known locally as cassie after the acacia tree which dominates the growth. Here, the yellow warbler makes its home. In the area of Long Bay, just west of Indian Town Creek, thirty-five different bird species have been identified. The main road ends at Long Bay, but several tracks branch to the shore and are suitable for short hikes: to Indian Town Point, 1.5 mi/2.4 km; Fanny's Cove, 0.5 mi/0.8 km; Laurys Bay, 1 mi/1.6 km; and Ledeatt Cove (also known as Emerald Cove), 1 mi/1.6 km. Long Bay offers good snorkeling in water 15 to 30 ft/4.5 to 9 m in depth.

Potswork Reservoir

Directly south of Parham or Mercer's Creek, a main artery skirts the north edge of the Potswork Reservoir. Over 1.6 mi/2.5 km long, it is one of the largest bodies of fresh water in the eastern Caribbean and the largest of Antigua's numerous man-made catchments, most of which attract considerable birdlife. The reservoir is one of the few easily accessible forested environments on the island. Potswork is noted for great blue herons in spring; nearby on the north, Collins Reservoir attracts the fulvous whistling-duck. The pied-billed grebe is at Bethesda Reservoir in the south year-round.

Ayres Creek, Nonsuch Bay, and Half Moon Bay

Farther east of the Potswork Reservoir and north of Newfield, a secondary track leads to Ayres Creek, a wooded area at the head of Nonsuch Bay on the Atlantic coast. The creek is fringed with mangroves where the West Indian whistling-duck nests. The area between Collins Reservoir and Ayres Creek is considered an outstanding example of undisturbed riverine or riparian woodland where groves of Antigua whitewood reach 60 ft/18 m in height and host large bromeliads and other epiphytes. The area is the only

York Island can be glimpsed from Friar's Head, not far from Half Moon Bay.

The very long strand at Half Moon Bay has some calm swimming areas protected by a reef; other sections have waves strong enough for body surfing.

place in Antigua where iguanas are found. A rare Antillean euphonia has been spotted here as well.

The mouth of Nonsuch Bay is rich with coral reefs; a large area on the south side of the bay is private land belonging to Mill Reef, an exclusive residential area which also owns offshore Green Island, a nature preserve. Nearby, tiny uninhabited York Island is another nesting spot of the red-billed tropicbird; roseate terns breed here in May. Peregrine falcons have been spotted here and over Mill Reef. The reef between Green and York islands is the most popular area for day-trippers on the east coast. On the south side of the Mill Reef estates is Half Moon Bay with one of the most beautiful beaches on the island—it's a thirty-minute walk from end to end—where large Atlantic breakers roll in. Southeast of Half Moon Bay, the waters of the Atlantic have carved another natural bridge rock formation.

GREEN CASTLE HILL

Southwest of St. John's and just east of Jennings, Green Castle Hill, 595 ft/ 181 m, is the remnant of a volcano with several lengthy spurs. Some say that the rock formations here—alignments of circles and columns—are an unusual geological phenomenon but others think they are megaliths of a prehistoric civilization, or had an astronomical function in the measurement of time. The climb to the top of Green Castle Hill starts at the brick factory and takes about an hour. It is well worth the effort for the spectacular view of the volcanic hills on the south and of the coast and sea in three directions.

DARK WOOD

On the southwest coast are two of Antigua's most beautiful beaches—Lignum Vitae Bay, better known as Jolly Beach for the large resort here, and Dark Wood Beach. Between the two beaches and on the south coast near Urlings are freshwater and brackish ponds fed by runoff from the nearby hills; the area is one of the prime birding locations on the island. Among the common residents of Dark Wood are grebes, herons, egrets, whistling-ducks, and blue-winged teal. The American coot comes in winter; northbound shorebirds are attracted in the spring. Glossy ibises, American wigeon, and an occasional common black-headed gull from Europe have been spotted in November.

BOGGY PEAK

One of the few areas on Antigua with vegetation similar to that of a tropical rain forest can be found on the west side of Boggy Peak, the island's highest point. In the humid environment here a small closed-canopy forest thrives with buttressed trees, abundant epiphytes and lianas, and a profusion of ferns on the forest floor. Among the dominant trees are locust, known locally as stinking breath, which can be identified by their straight gray trunks and shiny oblong leaves that resemble rabbit ears; and kapok, or silk-cotton, usually with large buttresses to support the trunk, which can grow to 8 ft/2.4 m in diameter. The trunk was used by the Arawaks and Caribs for making their canoes. This woodland, considered to be the last relic of the tropical forest that once covered Antigua's heights and slopes, attracts many birds, including the purple-throated carib, ruddy and bridled quail-doves, and scaly-breasted and pearly-eyed thrashers. The scarlet tanager is a winter visitor as is the American redstart, one of four winter-resident warblers.

Beyond Johnson's Point and Urlings, a secondary road turns inland at Cades Bay and winds its way up Boggy Peak. (A communications tower stands at the top.) The area of Cades Bay is noted for the sweet, delicious Antigua black pineapple grown here. The coastline fronts the 2.5-mi/4-km Cades Reef, a typical fringe reef dominated by staghorn and elkhorn coral and rich in colorful reef fish such as parrotfishes and blue tang. Within walking distance of the town of Old Road are three magnificent stretches of white sand beaches. Overlooking one is Curtain Bluff Hotel, where extensive gardens attract many of the same birds one is likely to see along nearby Fig Tree Drive and the adjacent woods.

FIG TREE DRIVE

A 3-mi/5-km stretch of road—bumpy in places—winds through the volcanic hills between Old Road and the village of John Hughes. It is known as Fig Tree Drive for the Antigua fig, the local name for banana, which grows here in abundance. Antiguans call the Drive a rain forest because the tropical vegetation overhanging the road is a contrast to the typical dry growth that covers the island. Bananaquits and hummingbirds can be seen dashing about the flowering hedges bordering the road.

WALLINGS WOODLANDS

On the north slopes of Signal Hill, there is a secondary forest, Wallings Woodlands, which has been protected since 1912. Less humid and more open than the rain forest on the Boggy Peak slope, the forest, when surveyed in 1977, had thirty-three species of shrubs and trees, some over 70 ft/21 m tall. A prominent species is mahogany, a typical tree of deciduous seasonal forests throughout the Caribbean. Rainwater from the slope drains via paved ditches to Wallings Reservoir, one of many catchments constructed in this area to provide water for irrigation. White-crowned pigeon, Zenaida dove, and ruddy and bridled quail-dove are seen by the water; thrashers and a rare Antillean euphonia are found in the forest. American redstart, northern waterthrush, and northern parula are among the ten species of warblers that have been spotted in the woodland in winter. Others are the Guadeloupe woodpecker, trembler, and yellow-throated vireo.

Many short hikes—not more than an hour in length—can be taken over the hills between Old Road and Falmouth; stops for swimming, snorkeling, and picnicking can be added to make a day's outing. Hikers need a topographical map and should wear sneakers for comfort and long pants as protection against the thorny bush. At Old Road, from the beach that skirts Carlisle Bay, a narrow path bears southeast to the top of the cliff along Fishers Hill. The trail (about one hour) continues east over Mt. Carmel to Farley Bay, a beautiful beach with fringe reefs and accessible only to hikers or by boat. From here, one can continue east for about thirty minutes over Tucks Point to Rendezvous Bay, a spectacularly beautiful

Pages 258 and 259: The many footpaths for hiking in the hills between Old Road and Falmouth pass through fields of organ-pipe cactus and an interesting variety of low shrubs.

beach and a good location for shell collectors. Coral gardens for snorkeling are directly in front of the beach. The hiking is not difficult, but the walk between Mt. Carmel and Rendezvous Bay, up and down steep hills, does require some stamina. From Rendezvous Bay a trail through the valley between Sugar Loaf Hill and Cherry Hill leads northeast for forty-five minutes to Falmouth where taxis are available. Rendezvous Bay can be reached from Falmouth by four-wheel-drive vehicle as well.

MONKS HILL AND FORT GEORGE

A hike from the village of Liberta to Monks Hill and Fort George leads to another spectacular view. At Liberta a road—for walking or driving—marked with a sign "Monks Hill Great George Fort" leads to the village of Table Hill Gordon. From here, a strenuous, steep hike of about a mile up to Monks Hill takes about an hour at a moderate pace. At the summit of Monks Hill is Fort George, designed as a refuge for women and children in times of attack. A panoramic view here overlooks English and Falmouth harbors from the north. For the return trip, another road on the east side of the hill leads to the village of Cobbs Cross; that hike is not difficult and takes thirty minutes.

ENGLISH HARBOUR AND SHIRLEY HEIGHTS

On the southeast coast, a small inlet known as English Harbour is one of the best natural harbors in the Western Hemisphere—deep enough for seagoing ships but barely visible from the sea and surrounded by hills that protect it from hurricanes and make excellent lookouts—all reasons that the British Navy used the harbor for two centuries as its West Indies dockyard. A naval base, later named Nelson's Dockyard after the famous British admiral who was stationed here, was built on a narrow promontory that juts into the bay and separates English Harbour from neighboring Falmouth Harbour.

To protect the port, a series of forts and other military installations was built at the harbor and on the surrounding heights. The hills on the east are known as Shirley Heights, named for the governor of the Leewards who had the positions fortified. The British Navy has long gone, but English Harbour is still very much appreciated by sailors and is one of the busiest yacht harbors in the Caribbean. The historic buildings at the Dockyard have been restored to house shops, inns, and restaurants, and Nelson's home is now a museum. The Shirley Heights installations have also been preserved and have a small museum, but the main reason to come here is for the magnificent panorama. It is a favorite place for Antiguans (and their visitors) to watch the fabulous sunsets. There are views of English and

Falmouth harbors in the foreground and the hills and coast of Antigua in the distance; on a clear day one can see as far as Redonda, Montserrat, about 30 mi/50 km to the southwest, and Guadeloupe, 46 mi/74 km to the south.

A nature walk on a developed footpath winds up the hill from English Harbour to Shirley Heights. It starts by the Galleon Beach Hotel gate at a sign reading "To The Lookout" and is marked with white tape on tree branches. From Freemans Bay, the eighteenth-century warship anchorage just inside English Harbour, the trail passes by a swampy area and continues through a wild xerophytic environment strewn with boulders. It winds up through woodlands to the gun emplacements and signal station at the summit (480 ft/144 m). A pamphlet describing the trees and plants along the trail and their historical uses is available from Carib Marina just outside Nelson's Dockyard or from the National Parks Authority in the Dockyard. The hike is not difficult and takes about forty minutes to the summit. Or, as a downhill route from Shirley Heights, the path starts on the north side of Bar's kitchen and takes about twenty minutes. One should wear sneakers.

BATS CAVE

From the north side of English Harbour, a road winds east over Dow Hill, near where Arawak and Carib artifacts have been found. The hill, used by NASA for a tracking station during the Apollo program, is now occupied by the Medical School. East of the school, a footpath leads to Bats Cave, a cavern about 50 ft/15 m in circumference that was used as late as 1645 as a Carib hideout. The name comes from the hundreds of bats that can be seen hanging from the ceiling. (A flash is needed to photograph them.) Local legend says the cave goes under the sea as far as Guadeloupe, and from nineteenth-century records, the cave's depth is known to be at least 360 ft/110 m. However, when an expedition from the Smithsonian Institution visited the cave in 1958, fallen rock prevented exploration beyond 100 ft/30 m. The cave is on private property and permission must be obtained to visit it; inquire at the Medical School.

INDIAN CREEK

On the southeasternmost tip of the island, through a rough stretch of water where the Caribbean and Atlantic meet, is Indian Creek, an inlet with a mangrove swamp where one can watch brown pelicans diving for tarpon and snook. Here was found one of the island's two most important archaeological sites, a large Arawak village occupied from about 30 to 1100 A.D. A secondary road from Dow Hill leads to remnants of a colonial fort and from here a footpath goes along Indian Creek and the sea.

The pink sand beaches of Barbuda's south shore draw swimmers and windsurfers. Offshore, the marine reserve of Palaster Reef protects reef fauna and historic shipwrecks.

BARBUDA

Located 26 mi/42 km north of Antigua, the sparsely settled island of 62 sq mi/ 160 sq km is a sanctuary of the magnificent frigatebird, whose flocks— along with the island's goats and sheep—outnumber the population. Barbuda, a coral island fringed by reefs, is flat; its highest point, the Highlands, is 128 ft/39 m above the sea. The island lies so low that early sea captains sometimes hit the shoals before they saw the land. Of the hundreds of shipwrecks off Barbuda's coast, 115 have been documented.

Largely undeveloped, the island is normally very dry and covered with low scrub vegetation interspersed with lagoons and marshes, salt- and freshwater ponds, and mangroves. It is said to host 170 species of birds that include pelicans, snipe, tropical mockingbirds, egrets, warblers, and a variety of doves, pigeons, and ducks. No bird list is available, however. Mammals include the introduced white-tailed deer and wild boar.

Barbuda has only one small settlement, Codrington, named for the plantation family that held it as its personal fiefdom for almost 200 years. In 1904 Barbuda became a Crown estate governed by Antigua. It remains politically joined to Antigua, but a locally elected council governs the island internally.

CODRINGTON LAGOON

A large brackish estuary along the west coast with an opening to the sea on the north shore is a refuge for several thousand frigatebirds. In the marshy interior, an area known as Man of War Island, every bush—or so it seems—has two dozen or more birds on it. The sight is particularly spectacular during the mating season from late August to December when hundreds of males with wingspans up to 8 ft/2.4 m display by ballooning their red throat pouches as they glide through the air a few feet above the flapping females on the bushes. Frigatebirds can fly at speeds up to 100 miles per hour. The male, who gathers nest-building materials for his mate, can be seen flying to and fro with branches and leaves. After the female lays her egg, both parents share the work of incubating it, which takes about fifty days. Both also bring food to the chick, not able to fly on its own until it is nearly five months old. Local boatmen are readily available to take visitors in their rowboats (some with small motors) the short distance from the jetty west of town into the middle part of the lagoon. With apparently no fear of humans, the birds take little notice of intruders and can be observed and photographed at very close range for hours at a time.

Barbuda's west coast is a long thin spit of land separating the Caribbean from Codrington Lagoon, whose marshy interior is a sanctuary for thousands of magnificent frigatebirds.

DARBY SINK CAVE

From Codrington, Highland Road leads about 3 mi/5 km directly east to the Highlands on the east side of the island. From here there is a panoramic view and the ruins of Highland House, the Codringtons' residence built in the early eighteenth century. On the southwest fringe of the Highlands, Darby Sink Cave, located about 5 mi/8 km inland from town, is a sinkhole about 300 ft/90 m in diameter with cliff-like sides, approximately 70 ft/21 m deep. The sinkhole has an abundance of vegetation, dominated by palmettos, providing a sharp contrast to the dry scrub of the surrounding area. The descent to the bottom is not difficult, although the path does drop precipitously at one point. On the moist "cave" floor, where only a little sunlight filters through, ferns and lianas hang from the trees; the environment is not unlike the canopied undergrowth of a tropical rain forest. Experts say this growth indicates the presence of underground water. One area of the cliff has an overhang along whose rim water drips intermittently, causing stalagmites to build; the largest is approximately 8 ft/2.4 m high and about 2 ft/0.6 m in diameter.

DARK CAVE

At the north end of the Highlands is another cave, less accessible than Darby. The entrance is located on the north side of a shallow, scrub-covered sinkhole. One must first crawl through a narrow slit that leads to the bottom of a cavern, approximately 300 ft/90 m long and 60 ft/18 m wide, and from there continue along an inclining passage for about 400 ft/120 m. The passage is difficult as one must stoop in several places to pass under huge overhanging boulders. The bottom of the cave, where there is total darkness, has several chambers and a series of five freshwater pools which contain a rare blind shrimp, otherwise known to exist only in Mona Island off Puerto Rico. Endemic to these waters are minute crustaceans called amphipods. Near the entrance to the cave, the remains of a small Amerindian settlement dating from about 800 A.D. have been found. Barbuda's limestone base apparently is honeycombed with caves, yet to be explored and mapped. Spelunkers would need to inquire locally.

SPANISH POINT AND PALASTER REEF

From Codrington, River Road runs 3 mi/5 km south to Palmetto Point and the beautiful pink sand beaches along the south coast, southeast past Cocoa Point, where the island's only resort is located, and on to Spanish Point, a half-mile finger of land that divides the strong Atlantic from the calm Caribbean. "The Castle" indicated at Spanish Point on maps of Barbuda is no more than the ruins of a small lookout. The Point is the site of the most important Arawak settlement found in Barbuda.

Just off the Point is Palaster Reef, a marine reserve established in 1972 to protect the reef fauna and the historic shipwrecks here and on the adjacent reefs. Among the numerous wrecks that have been documented are the *Payson Tucker*, a 1,000-ton/907-metric-ton American barque; the Danish brig *America*, and three cargo ships, the *Camilla*, the *Elite*, and the *Victor*. Another fifty-seven ships have been documented, including at least two warships with guns. One can swim from the beach to the reef to view its spreading elkhorn coral and abundance of staghorn coral and colorful fish, and perhaps to chance upon an anchor or a cannon in these pristine waters.

Anglers will find the lagoons of Barbuda rich in lobsters, marlins, tarpon, and bonefish, and the sea around the island has mackerels, groupers, and snappers, to name a few. But one must bring fishing equipment from Antigua. Hunting is allowed for white-tailed deer and wild boar, and for pigeons, doves, and ducks and other waterfowl at specified periods of the year. Hunting and firearm permits must be obtained in advance from the Ministry of Education in St. John's.

REDONDA

The rocky, uninhabited islet of Redonda is located about 35 mi/56 km west of Antigua, between Montserrat (15 mi/24 km) and Nevis (25 mi/40 km). It is best reached by boat from Montserrat where boat operators offer day sailing excursions. The rocky, isolated island is the remnant of a volcanic cone, the vent of which has lost its western half, leaving a small, extremely rugged piece of land about 1 mi/1.6 km long and 0.33 mi/0.5 km wide surrounded almost entirely by sheer cliffs. From the summit of the western side, the cliffs fall almost perpendicularly 1,000 ft/300 m into the sea. The island is covered with coarse grasses and sedges and several kinds of cacti. The burrowing owl is an island resident and boobies nest here. In the mid-nineteenth century the island was mined for guano, and later an American company mined for aluminum phosphate until 1914. Landing is made through surf onto rocks near the southwest extremity on the leeward side. Once ashore, one must climb a steep, rocky cleft to reach the island's few acres of level ground. Ruins of the phosphate mining operation can be seen. The island is home to a small black iguana.

The uninhabited rocky island of Redonda, a remnant of a volcanic cone, can be seen from the northwest coast of Montserrat near Rendezvous Bay.

OUTDOOR ACTIVITIES

HIKING: Antigua is crisscrossed with dirt roads, tracks, and footpaths. Hikes organized by the Historical and Archaeological Society are available once a month. Inquire at the Antigua Museum in St. John's.

HORSEBACK RIDING: Several stables and resorts with their own horses offer riding to outsiders as well as guests. Usually, one must book twenty-four hours in advance. There are riding trails through the southeast countryside and along the beach and half-day rides to Monks Hill. A trek at Half Moon Bay goes through the countryside around Mannings and overlooks Soldier Point on the Atlantic. Inquire at the Tourist Office or through your hotel.

SWIMMING: Many people would say the best reason to visit Antigua is its beaches, frequently ranked as the Caribbean's best. The Antiguan claim of having as many beaches as there are days in the year may sound like hyperbole but it is true. The island's ragged coast is scalloped with coves and ribbons of powder-fine white sand that sometimes stretch for miles. The beaches on the Caribbean side of the island, such as Runaway, Dark Wood, Callaloo, and Jolly Beach, are gentle and calm; many of the quiet coves between St. John's and English Harbour are best reached by boat or by foot from the main road, and one is virtually assured of solitude and privacy as a reward for the extra effort. Beaches on the Atlantic or windward side, like Half Moon Bay, have good wave action for body surfing. A reef at the extreme northeast end of Half Moon Bay protects the beach and forms a quiet swimming area. Indian Town Creek is a tranquil cove with a small, intimate beach ideal for a day's outing.

Barbuda's undisturbed pink sand beaches are its greatest pleasure, ideal for swimming, windsurfing, and shell-collecting.

SNORKELING AND DIVING: Antigua is surrounded by shoals and magnificent coral reefs in crystal-clear, shallow water ideal for snorkelers. With a few exceptions, diving is in shallow water, too, at sites under 60 ft/80 m in depth. Staghorn and elkhorn coral is the most characteristic formation, and small, colorful reef fish such as parrotfishes, blue tang, and wrasse abound. Occasionally divers sight turtles, eagle rays or stingrays, and oceangoing fish like dolphins.

Part of Cades Reef, a 2.5-mi/4-km virgin reef about 1 mi/1.6 km off Cades Bay on the leeward coast, has been designated an underwater park. Here, visibility ranges from 80 to 150 ft/24 to 45 m. The reef is dominated by staghorn coral, particularly in the shallows; the names of the dive locations, such as Eel Run, Snapper Ledge, and Big Sponge, are descriptive of popular sites. Along the west coast at Hawksbill Rock, there is a cave in 15 ft/4.5 m of water. Sunken Rock, which drops to a maximum depth of 122 ft/37 m, is the experienced diver's best choice for a deep dive. Along the dropoff one may see open-water fish such as stingrays, great barracudas, and occasional dolphins. The rock formation has overhanging corals that form a cleft through which divers can swim, providing the sensation of a cave dive. In the shallow areas on the outside of the coral formations, blue and brown chromis, sergeant majors, parrotfishes, and other colorful reef fish abound.

Antigua and Barbuda are only now becoming known for wreck diving. The most popular of the six wrecks close to Antigua's shore is the *Andes*, a three-masted, fully rigged merchant vessel that sank in 1905. It is located south of St. John's harbor by Deep Bay in only 20 ft/6 m of water. Famous treasure

Codrington Lagoon frigatebirds.
Top: Gliding on an 8 ft/2.4 m wingspan. Center: A nest full of young. Bottom: A new-born chick.

hunter and wreck salvager Mel Fisher has a fifteen-year salvage agreement with the Antiguan government.

Snorkeling equipment is available on Barbuda (although one might prefer to bring one's own from Antigua), but there is no dive shop on that island. Diving is best done by a chartered boat from Antigua that has scuba gear and a compressor on board.

FISHING: Although there are plenty of fish in Antiguan waters, the island is not well organized for deep-sea fishing. Hotels normally can assist guests in making arrangements. The best places to arrange a charter are the Catamaran Club at Falmouth Harbour and Crabbs Marina on the north side of the island.

SAILING: Tradewinds that blow 90 percent of the year from the east, the spectacular waters that surround the island, the variety of anchorages and sheltered coves with pretty beaches and reefs, and the splendid facilities have combined to make Antigua one of the major boating centers of the Caribbean. Charter companies offer the full range of craft from sailfish to ocean-going yachts, bareboat or with crew. Day trips to offshore islands or longer charters for trips through the eastern Caribbean are available. English Harbour, the main marina on Antigua, is headquarters for Nicholson's Yacht Charters, one of the Caribbean's oldest and most respected operations with an international reputation; its founders spearheaded the renovation of the historic port. The Yacht Club is on the southeast corner of Falmouth Harbour.

Regattas are held year-round but late April is the time for true salts to be in Antigua. Sailing Week, the most important sailing event in the Caribbean, attracts sailing greats and would-be greats from around the world. In the two decades since its inception, the annual event, in which more than 120 top-class racing yachts participate, has become for sailing what Wimbledon is to tennis.

WINDSURFING: The same tradewinds that make Antigua a sailing mecca are equally great for windsurfing. On the leeward side of the island the gentle breezes and calm sea are perfect for beginners, while on the windward side, strong winds varying from 12 to 25 knots and seas with 2- to 3-ft/0.6- to 1-m chops appeal to advanced windsurfers. There are several established international windsurfing schools and an annual Windsurfing Antigua Week, usually in January. Many of the hotels have boards available at their water-sports facility.

EXPLORING THE ISLANDS

Antigua, pronounced An-TEE-ga, can be explored by taxi or rented car, and to a lesser extent by bus. Buses do not operate on regular schedules and therefore are not useful unless one has much more time than money. Reasonably priced tours are offered by local travel agents and are recommended for a quick orientation, since the island can be confusing.

Sightseeing by taxi is expensive unless one has others with whom to share the cost. Car rental is more reasonable and recommended. During the winter season, demand is often greater than supply and cars can be difficult to obtain; reserve in advance. A local driver's license is required and will be granted upon presentation of a valid U.S. license. Driving in this former British Colony is on the LEFT.

The island has a rather extensive network of roads, and although they are in fairly good condition compared to other islands in the Antilles, they are narrow, winding, and bumpy in places. One must drive with caution to avoid unexpected potholes. The main arteries are neither numbered, named, nor well marked. Even with a good map, which is essential, one can expect to get lost a few times. People are generally very helpful, but don't be surprised if a request for directions leads to a request to ride along. Be friendly but prudent.

The basic road system fans out, more or less, from St. John's on the northwest coast across the island on the major arteries, most of which loop around a section of the island—the north, the southeast, or the southwest—making it possible for one to leave from the capital by one route and return by another. To avoid getting lost, one should know the road's principal destination. For example, the main road north from the capital along the coast runs 4 mi/6.4 km to Dickinson Bay, where many of the main hotels are located. A second road, slightly inland, runs 6.5 mi/10.4 km to the north coast via Cedar Grove. And a third goes northeast 6 mi/9.6 km to Antigua International Airport. Spurs connect the three roads, enabling one to make a circular route and return to the capital.

Barbuda, for the most part, is an undisturbed wilderness awaiting discovery by those who need no amenities and are able to make arrangements as required. A tour of the island is difficult to arrange in advance and the best-laid plans are likely to go awry. There are jeeps for rent, but the island has no paved roads, only dirt tracks, and these are not marked. One definitely needs a map. The best map is one drawn by B. S. Dyde, 1984; it shows tracks and all the main points of interest. Horses and guides are also available but, like everything else on Barbuda, they are not always easy to arrange. Inquire from the Tourist Office in Antigua or upon arrival in Barbuda.

The easiest way to visit Barbuda is on a day excursion available from local travel agents in Antigua. It will include pickup from one's hotel, a LIAT flight, lunch, and sightseeing with transportation and a driver arranged in advance. Upon arrival, if (and it's a big *if*) arrangements go as planned, one has the option of snorkeling from beautiful pink sand beaches which seldom see a footprint, visiting the bird sanctuary by boat, or roaming by motor scooter or jeep over the wilderness and perhaps stopping at a cave. One should wear sturdy shoes and long pants for hiking in the thorny bush. Be sure to include drinking water as a standard provision, because the island is very hot and dry.

Barbuda can be reached daily in a ten-minute flight via LIAT, the Caribbean airline headquartered in Antigua, or by charter of private aircraft. Charter boats are also available.

INFORMATION: In the U.S.: Antigua Board of Tourism, 610 Fifth Ave., Suite 311, New York, NY 10020; 212-541-4117. In Canada: 60 St. Clair Ave., Suite 205, Toronto M4T 1N5; 416-961-3085. In the U.K.: Antigua House, 15 Thayer St., London W1; 71-486-7073. In Antigua: Box 363, St. John's, Antigua, WI; 809-46-20029 or 20480. Historical and Archaeological Society, Museum of Antigua and Barbuda, Long St., St. John's, Antigua, WI; 809-46-24930. National Parks Authority, English Harbor, St. John's, Antigua, WI; 809-46-01379. The Parks Authority, based at Nelson's Dockyard, is a new governmental body responsible for historic sites and parkland.

Books: Multer, Weiss, and Nicholson, *Antigua, Reefs, Rocks and Highroads of History* (Leeward Islands Science Assoc., Box 103, St. John's, Antigua, WI). M. P. Weiss and H. G. Multer, *Map of Modern Reefs and Sediments of Antigua* (Dept. of Geology, Northern Illinois Univ., DeKalb, IL, 1988). *A Guide to the Birds of Antigua* by William Spencer, n.d., is available at local bookstores. *The Story of the Arawaks in Antigua and Barbuda* by Desmond Nicholson, n.d.; ask at the Museum of Antigua and Barbuda—the author is its director.

MONTSERRAT

THE CARIBBEAN as it used to be—that's the way this low-key corner of the Caribbean describes itself, appealing as it does to those who seek the tranquil, uncommercialized ambience and unspoiled natural environment that Montserrat still offers.

Located in the Leeward Islands, 27 mi/43 km southwest of Antigua, Montserrat is a mountainous volcanic island of 39.5 sq mi/102 sq km. A narrow belt of lowlands and foothills rises quickly to an interior highland green with rain forest and tropical vegetation and carved by rivers and streams. The central spine of mountains, formed as a result of three different volcanic eruptions, reaches its highest point in the south where cloud-wreathed Chance Peak rises from the Soufriere Hills and continuing volcanic activity is very much in evidence.

Because of its fertile, mountainous, and intensely green terrain, Montserrat was long ago dubbed the Emerald Isle of the Caribbean, but its physical resemblance to Ireland is only part of the story. Montserrat was settled in the early seventeenth century by Irish Catholics fleeing religious persecution in nearby St. Kitts. Those early settlers left their mark

Tall bamboo and low-growing impatiens can be seen in the dense forests of the Soufriere Hills in the southern third of Montserrat. Facing page: Between the high forested ridges of the Galway's Soufriere crater, active volcano vents leave crystalline sulphur deposits and other mineral residue.

throughout the island, in the names of people and places that hark back to their Irish origins. Montserrat is the only Caribbean island that celebrates St. Patrick's Day as a public holiday; there's a shamrock mounted on the governor's home; and, lest they forget, visitors' passports are stamped with a shamrock, too.

Hurricane Hugo caused much damage on this island in September 1989. Check carefully with the tourist board when planning a trip to Montserrat.

Montserrat was discovered by Columbus in 1493. As the story goes, the great explorer, upon seeing the island's serrated peaks, named it after the monastery of Santa María de Montserrat near Barcelona, which is surrounded by similar mountains. The Spanish apparently had no interest in the island, and the hills and forests were left to the Carib Indians until 1632 when the Irish arrived. The British and French fought over the island for a century or more, but finally, in 1783, the British acquired Montserrat and the island remains a British Crown Colony to this day.

In Montserrat's rich volcanic soil, sugarcane flourished and a plantocracy based on the labor of African slaves developed. After emancipation early in the nineteenth century and the decline of the sugar industry on the island, limes and later sea island cotton were cultivated as cash crops. Today, most of the lowlands that were once agricultural estates are covered with scrub and grassland, but in recent years cotton has made something of a comeback and the Montserrat government is committed to developing a local textile industry. Otherwise there is surprisingly little commercial agriculture, given the island's fertility and abundance of tropical fruits.

From the experience of touring the countryside and hiking through rain forests to waterfalls and volcanic peaks, it will be obvious that Montserrat has a rich variety of trees and plants typical of other islands in the eastern Caribbean. The lobster claw is the national flower, while many varieties of hibiscus, bougainvillea, anthuriums, ginger, and frangipani are common in gardens. Wild orchids, frequently found in the lower forests, can also be seen in local gardens and resort grounds, with the showiest being the yellow oncidiums. But the most impressive forms of vegetation on the island are the dense, huge tree ferns and the giant philodendrons called elephant ears in the rain forest.

In addition to vegetables grown for local consumption, the countryside is resplendent with exotic fruit trees, such as avocado, sugar apple, mammee apple, mango, guava, soursop, papaya, passionfruit, coconut palm, and breadfruit. Pineapples and bananas are plentiful. A walk through the Friday- and Saturday-morning open-air market in the capital of Plymouth is a chance to see much of this produce in one place.

The animals of the island include the agouti, a rabbit-sized, tailless rodent that was once abundant in the Lesser Antilles and is now extinct on most islands. Found here in the wooded lowlands and mountain areas, it is hunted for its meat. Montserrat's "mountain chicken" is a large frog, the legs of which are a local delicacy. Known locally by its Creole name, *crapaud*, it is hunted after rainy spells. Common are giant marine toads and tiny tree frogs called crickets, which can be heard, if not seen, after a shower. Common, too, are small lizards such as anoles and geckos and the larger ground lizards found in gardens almost everywhere. Iguanas live near the dry beach areas. Nine species of bats have been identified on Montserrat, including fruit bats and a fish-eating bat.

Birdlife on Montserrat, some of it migratory, numbers almost one-hundred species; approximately thirty species breed here. The endemic, mountain-dwelling, black-and-yellow Montserrat oriole is the national bird. The island has three species of hummingbirds: the Antillean crested hummingbird and the green-throated carib are most common in the lowlands, while the purple-throated carib is more likely to be found in higher areas. Thrashers, doves, bananaquits, and finches are common around gardens. Along the shoreline, one can see brown pelicans, brown boobies, magnificent frigatebirds, tropicbirds, and a variety of terns. The American kestrel, also known as the killy hawk from its shrill cry of *killi-killi-killi*, is a year-round resident. Occasionally one may sight a peregrine falcon; a red-tailed hawk, known in other eastern Caribbean islands as the chicken hawk; or a merlin, similar to the peregrine falcon but smaller and often confused with the American kestrel.

Plymouth, the capital of Montserrat, located on the southwest coast, is a small West Indian town of British colonial architecture interspersed with modern buildings. Two worthwhile stops on a walking tour are Tapestries of Montserrat and the Sea Island Cotton Company, both known for their high-quality local products. Government House, on a hill overlooking Plymouth, is surrounded by pretty gardens. Just north of town, the Montserrat Museum, operated by the Montserrat National Trust, is housed in what was the windmill of a sugar plantation. The museum, open Wednesday and Sunday afternoons, has an interesting collection of artifacts and exhibits related to the island's cultural and natural history. With a grant from the World Wildlife Fund (U.K.), the National Trust is guiding the establishment of a national park system.

Pages 274 and 275: Rendezvous Bay at the northern tip of the island is Montserrat's only golden sand beach. It is generally reached by boat.

Fox's Bay Bird Sanctuary

Fox's Bay Bird Sanctuary, situated on the coast 3 mi/4.8 km northwest of Plymouth, is a protected wildlife area of 15 acres/6 hectares established by the Montserrat National Trust in 1979. The sanctuary is a mangrove swamp and bog with a central pond that is the primary nesting area for coots, gallinules, kingfishers, cuckoos, and several species of heron, of which the cattle egret population is quite large. The best time to see the birds is late afternoon or early morning. A nature trail circles the sanctuary and ends at Fox's Bay beach where there are facilities for swimming and picnicking. Manchineel trees are plentiful in this area. Be aware that the poisonous sap of the manchineel can cause painful burns; its little green fruits are poisonous and should never be eaten.

Soufriere Hills

The southern third of Montserrat is dominated by the Soufriere Hills, the youngest and most southerly of the island's three volcanic formations. Several peaks are covered with dense rain forest, making them the island's most popular hiking area. Trails range in character from an easy drive to an all-day trek. Chance Peak, the highest point on the island at 3,002 ft/915 m, dominates the group; Gage's Lower and Upper Soufrieres, ranging up to 1,750 ft/533 m, comprise the western portion; Roche's Mountain, 2,778 ft/847 m, the eastern side; and Galway's Soufriere, the southeastern part.

The Soufriere Hills, as well as the forested regions of the Centre Hills, are home to the Montserrat oriole, which is most readily seen on Chance Peak and on the path to the Bamboo Forest southeast of Galway's Soufriere. Among other bird species of these forested regions are the trembler, a member of the mockingbird and thrasher family which builds its nest in the cavity of a tree or tree fern or at the base of a palm frond; and the forest thrush, which usually can be spotted atop the undergrowth.

Galway's Soufriere

A thirty-minute drive over paved road south of Plymouth leads to Galway's Soufriere, a boiling crater rising to an altitude of 1,700 ft/518 m. From St. Patrick's Village on the coast south of Plymouth, the road climbs steeply out of rolling hills and green valleys up to the rim of the crater, where the vista down the White River Valley is magnificent. In contrast to the lush green landscape of the island, the crater is a stark, grayish expanse of rock and volcanic tuff with pits of bubbling muddy water and hot springs that emit strong-smelling sulphurous vapors. The Tourist Board issues warnings to be cautious about slipping off the trail as hikers have been burned by the bubbling water. Sturdy shoes are a must.

A visit to the crater can be combined with a stop at Galway's Plantation, an archaeological project sponsored by the Montserrat National Trust and directed by specialists from the University of Tennessee and Boston University with assistance from Earthwatch and other conservation groups. The plantation was started in the mid-seventeenth century and was operated on and off for over 250 years; its ruins are among the most impressive in the eastern Caribbean. Until excavation began in 1981 the buildings could not be recognized for what they were under the cloak of dense foliage that had grown over them after the plantation was abandoned. The ruins include a windmill tower, boiling house, great house, cisterns, and other structures, many of them built of beautifully cut stone.

GREAT ALPS FALLS

Water from Galway's Soufriere forms the White River, which tumbles down the south side of the mountain to Great Alps Falls, a 70-ft-/21-m-high cascade that plunges through lush vegetation into a shallow rock pool. Depending on the time of year and the rainfall, Great Alps Falls may either gush or trickle, but the pool is usually only deep enough for wading. Nonetheless, the hike to the falls is enjoyable for the setting and as an introduction to the luxurious vegetation of a tropical rain forest.

Hikers pick up the track to the falls past Shooters Hill Village where the river nears the sea, about a mile south of St. Patrick's Village. From here an hour's hike on a narrow mountain path passes through dense foliage of lianas and giant ferns and along deep ravines of the White River to the falls. Hikers must crisscross the stream a dozen or more times, scrambling over wet, slick rocks, so footwear that provides good traction is needed.

BAMBOO FOREST

A footpath on the south side of Galway's Soufriere leads to Roche's Estate on the windward side of the island, passing through a bamboo forest with canes up to 80 ft/24 m tall. From the crater rim the trail descends to a fairly level path that runs along the forested slopes of the South Soufriere Hills to Roche's Estate. The hike to this point takes about two and a half hours, and the return is by the same path. This trail continues all the way to Long Ground and covers one of the most isolated, least developed parts of Montserrat, inaccessible to motor vehicles. Past Roche's, there is a steep path down into and across the ravine known as Ghaut Mefraimie, and from here a track leads on to Long Ground. The hike from Galway's Soufriere to Long Ground is strenuous and takes between five and six hours one way. A guide is essential. Transportation must be arranged from Long Ground for the return to Plymouth.

CHANCE PEAK

A highly rewarding hike to Chance Peak, trekking through rain and montane forests, can be done in a morning. The last part of the trip is on a very steep and narrow footpath through what is said by experts to be one of the best examples of elfin vegetation in the Caribbean. There is a transmission tower at the summit.

Organized hikes to Galway's Soufriere are available from tour companies in Plymouth, and guides to Galway's Soufriere, Great Alps Falls, and Chance Peak can be hired at the police station in St. Patrick's Village.

The second of three volcanic eruptions formed the forested, sparsely inhabited Centre Hills in the middle of Montserrat.

CENTRE HILLS AND NORTHERN HIGHLANDS

After leaving Plymouth, the cross-island highway passes over the central highlands. At Gage's, a side road on the north leads to the 1,000-ft/300-m plateau called St. George's Hill, a perfect picnic spot with a superb view of Plymouth and the Caribbean Sea. Farther east at Harris, the main village of the highlands, the highway descends along the Paradise River Valley, commonly called Pea Ghaut, to the east coast. North of Harris, tracks lead into the Farm River Valley and across Centre Hills, a deeply creviced, sparsely inhabited central mountain range, the second oldest volcanic formation of the island. Katy Hill, rising to 2,431 ft/741 m, is the highest point of this range. There are no easily found trails in the area; an experienced guide would be essential for hiking here.

Silver Hill, the oldest and most northerly of the three volcanoes that originally formed Montserrat, dominates the island's northern tip. From the tiny abandoned inland village of Rendezvous, there are tracks and footpaths which can be used to climb to 1,322 ft/402 m, the highest point of the hill. Hikers should inquire in Plymouth about a local guide for this trek.

OUTDOOR ACTIVITIES

HIKING: The Montserrat government is in the process of developing new walking and hiking trails. Inquire at the Tourist Board office in Plymouth. Visitors can generally make arrangements for a guide through the Tourist Board or their hotel manager. Indeed, several hotels have walking and hiking maps for jaunts near their hotels.

HORSEBACK RIDING: Rides can be arranged at Sanford Farms for people of all ages and levels of skill. In two hours riders are taken to the hills for fabulous views of Plymouth and the countryside. Early morning and late afternoon are the coolest times for riding. Beach rides, for a minimum of two hours, are available for experienced riders over ten years of age. Day-long picnic rides can be arranged with one- to two-days' notice. Overnight camping expeditions for two or more experienced riders must be arranged well in advance. Contact Barbara Tipson at Sanford Farms, Reid's Hill (tel. 809-491-3301).

SWIMMING: The stretch of Caribbean coast from Sugar Bay south of Plymouth to Carr's Bay north of the town has the island's best and most accessible beaches. None has been developed commercially, and most are small secluded strands of sand bracketed by rock cliffs. Isles Bay, Old Road Bay, Woodlands Beach, Carr's Bay, and Little Bay are all ideal destinations for a day at the beach with a picnic, swimming, and snorkeling. Most of the time the waters lap quietly at the black sand beaches, but occasionally storms change the character of a beach, pulling all the sand out to sea. The sand returns quickly, however, when the winds die down.

Rendezvous Bay in the far north is the only beach with golden sand. It is surrounded by an amphitheater of high volcanic cliffs and is usually reached by boat from Little Bay, the beach directly south of Rendezvous. Alternatively, one can hike on a fairly easy inland path from Little Bay to Rendezvous in about forty minutes or, from the north end of Little Bay, make a steep thirty-minute climb over the bluff separating the two bays. During the winter season, full-day picnic cruises and sunset sails are offered daily by boats that depart from Vue Pointe Hotel at Old Road Bay.

WATER SPORTS: Scuba diving, deep-sea fishing, windsurfing, and boat trips along the coast can be arranged through one's hotel or directly with boat captains and dive operators in Plymouth, but as yet water sports are not well developed. The most active water-sports center is located on the beach at Vue Pointe Hotel (tel. 809-491-5210). One can also make arrangements through the Montserrat Yacht Club at Wapping, south of Plymouth (tel. 809-491-2237).

Day-sails to Redonda, an island 16 mi/26 km northwest of Montserrat, are available. Redonda belongs to Antigua and Barbuda, but is closer to Montserrat.

EXPLORING THE ISLAND

Taxis and sightseeing minibuses are plentiful. Rental cars and jeeps are available from agencies in Plymouth and at hotels at rates comparable to those in the U.S., but for one's first visit, it might be easier to engage a taxi. Although the island has 136 mi/218 km of paved roads, they tend to be narrow mountain roads that require close attention. Taxi drivers who act as guides are animated and charming storytellers; their passengers can relax and enjoy the scenery instead of watching the road.

For those who prefer to drive themselves, a good map of the island is a must; maps are available from hotels, the Montserrat Museum, and the Montserrat Tourist Board. A temporary local license is required and is issued at the police station at the airport or at the main station in Plymouth. There is a fee, and the applicant must have a valid driving license issued in another country. Before striking out on one's own, be aware that there are very few road signs, no service stations except the two in Plymouth, and few public telephones along the way. Driving in this British Colony is on the LEFT.

The main roads are on the leeward or western side of the island. One branches in hairpin turns south from Plymouth to O'Garro's just beyond Old Fort Point and gives access to the Soufriere region; another winds north around hillsides that skirt the island's main beaches to Carr's Bay. A third artery crosses the central highlands and links the capital on the southwest coast with Blackburne Airport on the rocky east coast.

The main route north from the airport is a beautifully engineered road that took three years to build. It zigzags along the rockbound east coast overlooking spectacular views, with Antigua visible in the distance. After about 5 mi/8 km, the road bends west across the northern part of the island, cutting through the hills and valleys between Katy Hill on the south and Silver Hill on the north and joining the main north–south road at Carr's Bay. As an alternate route for the return to Plymouth, one could turn south at Old Norwood, midway across the island, onto a challenging single-lane road and proceed to St. John's then on via Cudjoehead to St. Peter's on the coast.

INFORMATION: In North America: % Caribbean Tourism Organization, 20 East 46th St., New York, NY 10017; 212-682-0435. In Montserrat: P.O. Box 7, Plymouth; 809-491-2230. There is no tourist office in the U.K.

The best source for information on the natural history of Montserrat is the Montserrat National Trust, Parliament St., Plymouth, Montserrat, WI; 809-491-3086. *Birds of Montserrat* by Allan Siegel (Montserrat National Trust, 1983) includes a list of birds sighted on the island since 1879.

GUADELOUPE

DOMINICA

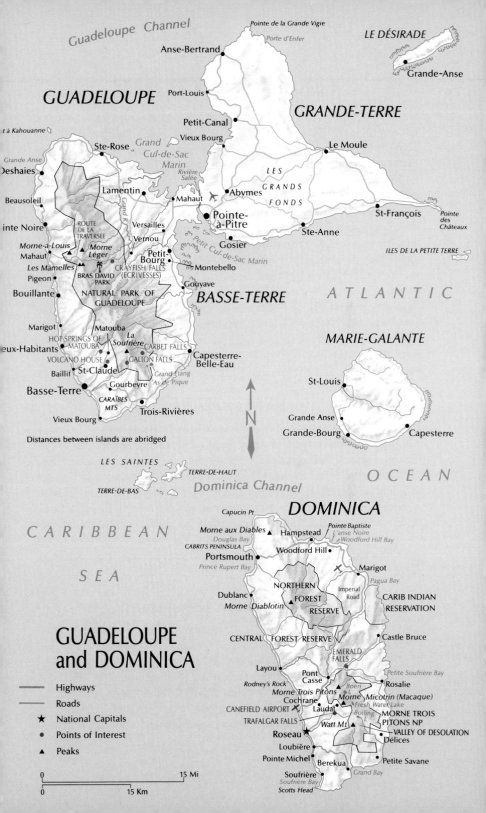

Guadeloupe Channel

Pointe de la Grande Vigie

Porte d'Enfer

LE DÉSIRADE

Anse-Bertrand

Grande-Anse

GUADELOUPE

Port-Louis

GRANDE-TERRE

Petit-Canal

Vieux Bourg

Le Moule

Ste-Rose

Grand Cul-de-Sac Marin

Rivière Salée

LES GRANDS FONDS

t à Kahouanne

Grande Anse

Deshaies

Lamentin

Mahaut

Abymes

St-François

Pointe des Châteaux

Beausoleil

Pointe-à-Pitre

Ste-Anne

inte Noire

ROUTE DE LA TRAVERSEE

Versailles

Vernou

Gosier

ILES DE LA PETITE TERRE

Morne-à-Louis

Morne Léger

Petit-Bourg

Mahaut

Les Mamelles

CRAYFISH FALLS (ECRIVESSES)

Montebello

Pigeon

BRAS DAVID PARK

Gouyave

MARIE-GALANTE

Bouillante

NATURAL PARK OF GUADELOUPE

BASSE-TERRE

ATLANTIC

Marigot

Matouba

St-Louis

eux-Habitants

HOT SPRINGS OF MATOUBA

La Soufrière

CARBET FALLS

Grande Anse

Capesterre-Belle-Eau

VOLCANO HOUSE

GALION FALLS

Grande-Bourg

Capesterre

Baillif

St-Claude

Grand Etang As de Pique

Basse-Terre

Gourbeyre

CARAÏBES MTS

Trois-Rivières

Vieux Bourg

OCEAN

Distances between islands are abridged

N

LES SAINTES

TERRE-DE-HAUT

TERRE-DE-BAS

Dominica Channel

DOMINICA

Capucin Pt

CARIBBEAN

Morne aux Diables

Hampstead

Pointe Baptiste

L'anse Noire

Woodford Hill Bay

Douglas Bay

CABRITS PENINSULA

Woodford Hill

Portsmouth

Prince Rupert Bay

Marigot

Pagua Bay

SEA

Dublanc

NORTHERN FOREST RESERVE

Imperial Road

CARIB INDIAN RESERVATION

Morne Diablotin

GUADELOUPE and DOMINICA

CENTRAL FOREST RESERVE

Castle Bruce

EMERALD FALLS

— Highways

Layou

Pont Casse

Petite Soufrière Bay

— Roads

Rodney's Rock

Morne Trois Pitons

Rosalie

★ National Capitals

Cochrane

Boeri

Morne Micotrin (Macaque)

CANEFIELD AIRPORT

Fresh Water Lake

● Points of Interest

Laudat

Boiling

MORNE TROIS PITONS NP

▲ Peaks

TRAFALGAR FALLS

Watt Mt

VALLEY OF DESOLATION

Roseau

Délices

Loubière

Pointe Michel

Berekua

Petite Savane

Soufrière

Grand Bay

0   15 Mi

Soufrière Bay

0   15 Km

Scotts Head

GUADELOUPE

NATURE'S EXQUISITE BEAUTY and excellent human design have come together to make Guadeloupe one of the most rewarding islands in the Caribbean for outdoor travelers. Nowhere else is such variety and high quality of activity so readily available. Named Santa María de Guadalupe de Estremadura by Columbus, the island was known to her pre-Columbian inhabitants as *Karukera*, land of the beautiful waters.

Guadeloupe is not one island but two, Basse-Terre and Grande-Terre, so close together it is difficult to see the separation, but so different in appearance it is easy to make the distinction. A bridge connects the two islands, which are shaped like butterfly wings. Some parts of Guadeloupe were damaged by Hurricane Hugo in 1989; ask the tourist board about current conditions.

Guadeloupe and her satellite islands, along with French St. Martin and St. Barts, 125 mi/201 km to the north, comprise a *région* of France, in the same way the Hawaiian Islands constitute a state of the United States. Martinique, farther south, is a separate *région*. Altogether, these islands form the French West Indies. People here are culturally French and citizens of France.

BASSE-TERRE

Basse-Terre, the western of Guadeloupe's two islands, is volcanic in origin and dominated by a spine of richly forested mountains that climax in the highest smoking peaks in the Lesser Antilles. Most of the mountains are parkland with almost 200 mi/320 km of superb trails through rain forests and elfin woodland, along rugged gorges, rivers, and some of the highest waterfalls in the Caribbean, tumbling from peaks where up to 400 in/1,016 cm of rain fall annually. Around the coast in the north the land flattens and the rivers flow into mangroves; in the south they wash to sea along black sand beaches. A port town on the southwest coast, also named Basse-Terre, is the capital of Guadeloupe.

NATURAL PARK OF GUADELOUPE

Covering 74,100 acres/29,988 hectares—one-fifth of Guadeloupe's total landmass—the Natural Park of Guadeloupe (Parc Naturel de Guadeloupe) protects the heavily forested mountains that run the full length of Basse-Terre. The ridge rises on the north coast at Piton de Ste.-Rose (1,171 ft/ 357 m), peaks at Les Deux Mamelles (2,519 ft/768 m) about mid-island, and reaches its highest point at the smoldering volcano of La Soufrière (4,841 ft/1,467 m) in the south. The ridge drops and rises again in the

Caraïbe Mountains (1,880 ft/573 m) at the southern extreme, but this massif is not parkland.

For some, La Soufrière, a brimstone-belching volcano, is the highlight of the park. Other visitors find pure enchantment in the rain forest, with its lacy ferns, yellow-flowered heliconias, and deep green, luxuriant foliage under a closed canopy of enormous hardwood trees thick with epiphytes and bromeliads. Throughout the park there are small exhibition centers designed to educate visitors about their particular interests: the volcanos, forests, coffee and sugarcane plantations, archaeology, and wildlife. From key centers, which are easily accessible on paved roads, well maintained and signposted trails of varying lengths lead through the forest. Those who travel as the French do will bring along cheese, bread, and wine and stop at one of the many tree-shaded picnic areas along the way. There are no accommodations in the park, but there are plenty of *gîtes*, or modest inns, in towns along the coast within easy reach of the park.

ROUTE DE LA TRAVERSÉE

The Route de la Traversée, the cross-island highway also known as Route des Deux Mamelles, is a masterpiece of French engineering traversing the central highlands of Basse-Terre through the heart of the Natural Park. Rising from sea level at Versailles, it rolls through sugarcane fields and banana plantations to about 600 ft/183 m at Vernou, a fashionable residential district overlooking the serpentine Lézarde River Valley. From Vernou the highway climbs through the lush rain forest of the Natural Park to the Deux Mamelles Pass at over 2,000 ft/610 m. Along with magnificent views and cool mountain air, the scenic drive provides easy access to more than a half-dozen walks and hikes, from a ten-minute stroll to a 10-mile trek.

CRAYFISH FALLS

About a mile from the park entrance, a walk of less than ten minutes along the banks of the Corossol River through profuse tropical vegetation and a tall canopy of gommier rouge, or birch gum, and other large trees, leads to Crayfish Falls (Cascade aux Ecrevisses), a broad waterfall that drops into a pool. One of the most accessible in the forest, this idyllic setting is popular for swimming; across the road from the entrance is a shaded picnic area. Just beyond a bridge over the Corossol River, a walk of less than thirty minutes on an asphalt forest road leads through the woods to another swimming and picnic spot. Hikers should take a minimum of cash and valuables on this popular hike. Do not leave cameras and other personal belongings unattended. It is best to hike with at least two other people, or with a local guide.

Bras David Tropical Park

The halfway point of the Route de la Traversée is marked by Bras David Tropical Park, on a river of the same name. The park has well equipped picnic grounds, trails, and an interpretive nature center, La Maison de la Forêt, with outdoor displays on the flora, fauna, and topography of the region (signs are in French only). Trails of varying duration enable hikers to penetrate the rain forest without having to go great distances. On the south side of the highway, three signposted walking paths of an hour or less offer the easiest access into the heart of the forest.

The rain forest is like an enormous greenhouse. Between 984 ft/300 m and 2,297 ft/700 m above sea level, tall trees covered with lianas and epiphytes (plants that grow on trees but are not parasitic) tower over an undergrowth of shorter trees and bushes. The principal hardwood species, 80 to 130 ft/25 to 40 m in height, are gommier or white chestnut, sweetleaf mahogany, redwood, carapite, marbri, and yellow mangrove.

Zoological and Botanical Gardens

The fauna of Guadeloupe, unfortunately, is not as interesting as the flora; earlier Frenchmen hunted many species for food and sport, often to extinction. However, there are still a good number of birds to be seen along the trails. The endemic Guadeloupe woodpecker, known locally as *le tapeur*, is almost black in appearance and lives mostly in the northeastern range; Guadeloupe's resident belted kingfisher, a larger bird than the migrant form, hunts along the rivers and waterfalls. Forest residents include the scaly-naped pigeon, ruddy quail-dove, stolid flycatcher, Lesser Antillean pewee, Antillean euphonia, and three hummingbirds—the purple-throated carib, green-throated carib, and Antillean crested. Among the forest's many insects, the most spectacular is the Hercules beetle, or *scieur de long*, with a big claw protruding from its head; at over 5 in/13 cm, it is one of the largest insects in the world. The park has no poisonous insects or snakes.

The mascot seen on the park's welcoming signs is Titi the raccoon. Abundant in North America, the American raccoon is considered endangered here, where it is called *raton laveur*. Raccoons, agoutis, mongoose, iguanas, land turtles, and other species are on view at the small Zoological and Botanical Gardens about 2 mi/3 km west of La Maison de la Forêt.

The Natural Park of Guadeloupe on Basse-Terre, whose trails are well maintained, offers hikers access to the heart of rain-forested ridges.

Morne Léger and Les Deux Mamelles

When the highway reaches the main ridge, it passes several peaks where there are roads or footpaths for hiking. On the north side a trail of relatively easy ascent (ninety minutes one way) follows an old road along the top of the northern ridge to Morne Léger (2,018 ft/615 m). From the summit there are views over the forested slopes to Basse-Terre's east coast.

On the south side are the Deux Mamelles—Petit Bourg (2,349 ft/716 m) and Pigeon (2,519 ft/768 m). The latter has a lookout at 1,969 ft/600 m and a path that is a forty-five-minute walk in cool mountain air to the peak where the vegetation is closer to elfin woodland: trees are shorter and tougher, humidity is greater, and temperatures are lower. The most abundant species are mountain mangle, bois couché, bois canon, and *palmiste montagne*, or mountain palmetto. On clear days the panorama sweeps across both slopes of the ridge: the west coast from Pointe-Noire on the north to Basse-Terre town on the south, and eastward to Grande-Terre. The Route de la Traversée winds through the pass of Les Deux Mamelles. On the north, a paved side road branches off to the top of Morne-à-Louis (2,438 ft/743 m), where there is a television tower and a vista across the northern ridge.

Trace des Crêtes

The Route de la Traversée is linked to the southern ridge by the Trace des Crêtes (Trail of the Crests), which runs along the ridgeline from the Mamelles to the Bouillante Peak and Falls (Pitons et Sauts de Bouillante). The trail continues south along the crest above the west-coast towns of Bouillante and Village to just above Marigot. Because the high mountains east of the Bouillante peaks absorb so much of the moisture brought by the trade winds, the sky over the Bouillante ridge usually is clear and the trail offers remarkable views from coast to coast over the slopes of the Natural Park, at times taking in the cloud-crowned peaks of La Soufrière. This is one of the most rewarding hikes of the Natural Park, but it is a strenuous journey of 9.5 mi/15.2 km and takes a minimum of five hours. Hikers must be in top condition to go the distance over up-and-down, rugged terrain.

The trail starts from the pass between the Mamelles and quickly ascends to the ridgeline, leaving the rain forest for the open highlands. From the ridge trail, three secondary paths trek down the mountainside to the west coast; they can be used as alternatives to walking the complete distance of the ridge. These less-frequently-used paths are not as well maintained as the main trail, however, so inquire locally about their condition. The first cutaway is about two hours south of the Mamelles and picks up a stream part of the way to the coast. The second one drops off from Pitons de Bouillante, the highest point of the main ridge, and descends to the Forêt

Espérance and the coast near the village of Pigeon. The third, about an hour's hike south of Pitons de Bouillante, drops quickly in forty-five minutes to meet a paved road leading to Bouillante on the coast. A short distance beyond the third cutaway is one of the prettiest parts of the trail where it begins a fast but comfortable descent along a narrow ridge with clear views of the coast. It meets a paved road along the Crête de Village and leads to the coast.

VICTOR HUGUES AND MERWART TRAILS

The two longest, most difficult trails of the Natural Park link the isolated central areas with the southern region of La Soufrière. In early colonial times, they were the routes of runaway slaves, who hid in the mountain forests. They were also the warpaths and even the commercial routes of rivaling European powers, since the coast—malaria-infested and always vulnerable to attack from the sea—was considered even more perilous. Today, for the most part, the summits of the mountains are barely accessible because of their many deep gorges and the impenetrable elfin vegetation, whose intertwined branches resist the sharpest machetes.

Victor Hugues Trail, the longest trail of the park, is an eight-to-ten-hour trek across the high mountain plains between Matouba, southwest of La Soufrière, and Montebello, on the east coast. It begins at the Forestry House of Matouba. *Merwart Trail*, eight to ten hours, follows the same trail from Matouba across the central range for the first six hours and branches at Matéliane for the final stretch along Morne Merwart to Vernou. The trails are slow going, the region is hours away from any help, and the weather alternates between hot sun and cold mist. Hikers must be in top condition and be accompanied by local guides.

PIGEON ISLAND AND COUSTEAU UNDERWATER RESERVE

From the cool heights of the Natural Park, the Route de la Traversée makes a steep descent to the coast under a canopy of flamboyant trees that runs for 2 mi/3 km. The sight is spectacular from May to October when the trees are aflame with blooms. From Mahaut the scenic road turns south along the west coast to Basse-Terre town. At Pointe de Malendure there are views of the gray sand beaches of Malendure and Pigeon Island, a five-minute boat ride from shore. Glass-bottom boat excursions as well as snorkeling, diving, and deep-sea fishing trips are available from Malendure Beach to the Underwater Park of Pigeon Island (Parc Naturel Sous-Marin), also known as the Cousteau Underwater Reserve.

Composed of volcanic stone and covered with scrub, Pigeon Island is actually two tiny islands with several dive locations, each with different characteristics and abundant marine life. Suitable for novice as well as experienced divers, the reef on the north side begins in shallow water and drops off to small canyons and walls. Great clusters of colorful tube sponges up to 6 ft/1.8 m and unusual green sea fans grow on the ledges of the walls; star and brain corals are abundant. Gray snappers, damselfishes, sergeant majors, and trumpetfishes are plentiful, as are spiny sea urchins.

The Golden Corniche, as the leeward coast is called, is a wild landscape of cliffs and gorges winding south along pretty little coves and across streams that run from the mountains to the sea. At Bouillante a geothermal plant captures the sulphurous and ferruginous steam emitted from thermal springs, some of which are subterranean.

GRANDE RIVIÈRE

At Vieux-Habitants, a scenic drive winds up through green, wooded mountains along the Grande Rivière, a deep gorge providing magnificent vistas of the National Park and Soufrière peak. It ends at Coffee House (La Maison du Café), an interpretive center at about 1,500 ft/450 m, and La Grivelière (tel: 590-98-48-42), a small-scale renovated coffee plantation with a tour for visitors. Just outside of Vieux-Habitants, and at Rocroy 1 mi/1.6 km south, are two of the nicest beaches on this coast. About 1 mi/1.6 km north of Baillif, a footpath leads inland on a short track to rocks bearing Carib petroglyphs.

Past vegetation such as the seagrape, a network of trails climbs the steep slopes to the summit of La Soufrière, almost always covered by clouds.

Sunlight barely penetrates through the dense, moss-covered trees near Carbet Falls on the eastern slope of La Soufrière.

Basse-Terre, St.-Claude, and Vauchelet Falls

Situated at the foot of the Soufrière Mountains, Basse-Terre is one of the oldest towns in the French West Indies; it was occupied several times by the British during the two centuries of rivalry between France and Britain for control of the West Indies. The town has suffered at the hand of nature as well, with destruction from hurricanes and volcanic eruptions, but it still manages to retain its historic character and some imposing colonial buildings. Basse-Terre is an important banana-loading port; a short walk from the harbor is the colorful town market. Farther south on a promontory is Fort St.-Charles where the Galion River, which originates on the slopes of La Soufrière, runs under the fort's ramparts on its way to the sea.

The drive from Basse-Terre town to Savane à Mulets (3,747 ft/1,142 m), a large plateau from which the cone of the Soufrière volcano rises, takes thirty minutes. The road passes through the pretty hillside town of St.-Claude, a wealthy residential community of gracious Creole houses. At Volcano House (La Maison du Volcan), there is a visitors' center with displays on La Soufrière and volcanology throughout the world. St.-Claude provides access to several mountain trails.

A walk of twenty minutes from the Relais Bleu de la Soufrière, a country inn next to Volcano House, leaves on a footpath behind the police barracks. It passes through dense forests of gommiers and ferns along the crest of a narrow gorge to a large pool at the base of Vauchelet Falls. Cascading from a height of 98 ft/30 m, the falls are formed by the Rivière Noire (Black River), which originates on the west side of La Soufrière between Morne Amic (4,406 ft/1,343 m) and Nez Cassé (4,247 ft/1,287 m).

Above St.-Claude, a steep, narrow road winds up 4 mi/6.4 km through thick tropical forest past Aire du Soleil, a mountainside picnic site with splendid views, and Bains-Jaunes, a hot mineral springs at the foot of the Morne Goyave (3,117 ft/950 m); it continues to Savane à Mulets, where there is a large parking area and the volcano trails begin.

SOUFRIÈRE VOLCANO

Known locally as the Old Lady, and more recently dubbed the Mt. St. Helens of the Antilles after its last eruption in 1976, La Soufrière continues to boil, bubble, and rumble. Stirrings from the volcano had been recorded since the fifteenth century at wide intervals, with increased seismic activity in each case, but it was not until 1975 that the volcano erupted for the first time in recorded history. Composed of solidified lava, the crown has a deep north–south split through the center where two chasms, Gouffre Dupuy and Gouffre Tarissan, discharge fumes. Vegetation on the sides of the volcano is sparse due to the constant emission of sulphurous gases and the extraordinarily high annual rainfall of up to 400 in/1,016 cm.

A visit to the summit of an active volcano is a rare opportunity to be at the center of nature's strongest forces and to see the evidence of its ability to devastate. Soufrière has four well-marked trails which, when hiked together, take three and a half hours to cover. *Red Trail* is a moderately difficult path leading directly to the summit from the Savane à Mulets parking lot, gaining about 1,000 ft/300 m in forty-five minutes by a series of switchbacks. *Yellow Trail*, known as Chemin des Dames (Ladies Path), is a difficult path of one hour that enables hikers to go from the car park, around the caldera's base, and up the cone's western flank to the Grande Faille, or fault, along Fente du Nord, its north part. At the top, *Green Trail* crosses the summit area, passing a number of fumaroles. *Blue Trail* leads directly to (or from) the Col de l'Echelle along the southeast side where the lava flowed in the 1976 eruption. It can be used to return to Savane à Mulets. The Natural Park's suggested route for a complete tour is to ascend on Yellow Trail to the Grand Faille, cross on Green Trail to Col de l'Echelle, and descend via Blue Trail to Savane à Mulets.

Whatever trail hikers use, at the top they will find a fantastic moonscape with pools of boiling mud and steaming craters, heaps of weirdly shaped rocks, and steam and hot gases belching from giant, jagged fumaroles and yawning chasms. In the haunting silence, the odor of sulphur, the mist, and the swirling clouds add to the drama of the eerie setting. Hikers should wear sturdy shoes and rain and wind protection, and they must be extremely cautious around the fumaroles, faults, and mud pits at the summit. Although the peak is usually engulfed in clouds, the mist comes and goes; after a few moments the air clears enough to reveal the path or a directional sign. Vistas from the summit are often obscured by the clouds, but on a clear day—more likely between December and April—they are magnificent.

Several easy walks in the vicinity of Savane à Mulets can give one an impression of the volcanic activity and vegetation without demanding a hike to the summit. West of the parking lot at Pic Tarade (3,397 ft/1,035 m), one can see tough pioneer plant species revegetating soil that had been left barren by the eruption. From here, too, there are views of other peaks, notably l'Echelle and La Citerne to the east and the Caraïbe Mountains on the island's southern tip.

LA CITERNE AND GALION FALLS

Another alternative, easier than Soufrière, is La Citerne (3,790 ft/1,155 m), a volcano with a round crater, small lake, and lunar landscape at the summit. From Savane à Mulets a motor road leads east directly to La Citerne; or, one can reach it by a pleasant thirty-minute walk passing numerous fumaroles and hot springs and views of the Caraïbe Mountains on the south. From the crater there are views down the east coast.

A detour from the road can be made to the Galion Falls, or Chutes du Galion, on the Galion River, which originates on the south face of La Soufrière and empties into the sea beneath Fort St.-Charles. Less than a mile from its source the river forms a beautiful waterfall that drops 131 ft/ 40 m. The trail to the falls leaves via Pas du Roi (King's Way) and the Bains-Jaunes and goes down into the Galion Valley along a sometimes slippery path through dense vegetation. It is a fairly difficult hike of about an hour. From the falls, hikers can follow an ascending trail up the river valley to La Citerne and return by the motor road to Savane à Mulets.

MATOUBA

From St.-Claude another motor road branches northwest for about 2 mi/ 3.2 km to Matouba, the southernmost point of the Victor Hugues Trail. Matouba is also the location of Maison Forestière (Forestry House), at 2,234 ft/681 m altitude, where hikers can arrange for guides. West of Matouba, a thirty-minute walk through a banana grove and woods leads to

the St. Louis River and the falls—Saut d'Eau du Matouba—which drop through a narrow crevice of volcanic rock.

Northeast of Matouba, at the base of Nez Cassé (meaning "broken nose"), is the source of the Hot Springs of Matouba (Bains Chauds du Matouba). Highly regarded for their therapeutic properties, the mineral waters are used for medical treatment at the Clinique les Eaux Vives at the Thermal Spa of St.-Claude near Matouba. The source of the water can be reached on a trail of one hour that leaves from the Forestry House. It is, in fact, the start of the Victor Hugues Trail and leads toward Nez Cassé along the Rivière Rouge (Red River). About halfway, the trail crosses to the east side of the river and climbs through stunted, gnarled vegetation of mountain mangle to the springs.

CARAÏBES MOUNTAINS

On the southern tip of Guadeloupe, the volcanic Caraïbe (Carib) Mountains overlook the point where the Atlantic Ocean meets the Caribbean Sea. From these wooded, steep-sloped mountains one has expansive views of the leeward coast from Basse-Terre town on the west to Trois-Rivières on the east, the offshore islands of Les Saintes on the south, and Marie-Galante farther out to sea; cloud-capped Soufrière looms on the north. Inquire in Vieux-Fort or the hamlet of Champfleury for directions to paths in the Caraïbe Mountains.

The middle tier of Carbet Falls is the most dramatic. Facing page: The Basse-Terre coastline between Trois-Rivières and Capesterre-Belle-Eau.

Archaeological Park

At the edge of Trois-Rivières, the Roches Gravées Archaeological Park (Parc Archéologique) preserves some of the petroglyphs of the Carib Indians. An easy path winds through the park along a bed of volcanic rock and boulders with specimens of the plants—cassava, cocoa, calabash, and pimiento—that the Indians cultivated and taught the Europeans to use. The petroglyphs, thought to date from about A.D. 300, depict animal and human figures. The park is situated on the road leading to Embarcadere des Saintes, the ferry landing for the Iles des Saintes.

L'As de Pique

Less than an hour north of Gourbeyre is l'As de Pique (Ace of Spades), a lake named for its shape. Dammed by an ancient lava flow from the base of La Cisterne, the lake, at 2,454 ft/748 m altitude, covers about 5 acres/ 2 hectares. It can be reached by taking a paved road through the Plateau du Palmiste to Moscou Road, a secondary road, and finally a footpath. Another footpath links l'As de Pique to Grand Etang, a large inland lake more easily reached from the east coast.

Carbet Falls

Routes inland from St. Sauveur and Capesterre-Belle-Eau lead to the Carbet Falls (Chutes du Carbet), the tallest falls in the Caribbean. The waters drop from La Soufrière over 800 ft/240 m in three stages down the eastern slopes, forming Grand Carbet River which empties into the sea at Capesterre. The first or upper cascade drops 410 ft/125 m through a narrow, steep crevice; the middle stage falls 361 ft/110 m through a slightly wider canyon; and the third or lower falls are broad and drop 66 ft/20 m. On the volcanic heights where the waters originate, they are a boiling 203°F/ 95°C and sulphurous, but they cool and become clear as they plunge down the face of the mountain, gathering the waters of several tributaries before flowing into the sea. All three stages can be reached by hiking, but the middle falls draws the most visitors because it is the most dramatic and easiest to reach—a twenty-minute walk through lush tropical forest.

To reach the lower falls, visitors follow the Routhiers Road from Capesterre-Belle-Eau, which brings them to the entrance of a dense hardwood forest where they leave their cars. From here they walk on an easy, well-defined path for about thirty minutes, keeping to the left. The second stage is accessible from the small town of St. Sauveur on the east coast. The route is inland via l'Habituée (D. 4) to the end of the road; from here a twenty-minute walk on a marked park path leads to the foot of the falls and a picnic area. Nearby, a smaller falls drops into a pool where one can swim; there are thermal springs here as well. To reach the upper falls one follows the same road to the second stage that goes to a bridge where a marked path begins. The ninety-minute hike is steep and difficult.

GRAND ETANG

The Habituée road to the second stage of Carbet Falls skirts mirror-like Grand Etang. The largest of several ponds in the area, the basin was created when lava from a volcanic eruption blocked the St. Sauveur River. Surrounded by heavy moisture, heat, and sunlight, the 50 acres/20 hectares of wetland are like a greenhouse thick with giant philodendrons, orchids and other epiphytes, anthuriums, bromeliads, and giant ferns. Among the trees of the swamp are blood mangle and golden fern. There is a footpath around the edge; the pond is one of the park's main bird-watching locations.

On the coast a short distance beyond St. Sauveur en route to Capesterre-Belle-Eau, the road passes through Allée Dumanoir, which for more than a kilometer is lined with stately, century-old royal palms, one of the most frequently pictured settings on Guadeloupe. On the north side of Capesterre, a shorter and even more beautiful stretch is Allée des Flamboyants, a road lined with magnificent flamboyant trees that bloom from May to October.

NORTHERN BASSE-TERRE

The northern part of Basse-Terre with mangroves and miles of banana and sugar plantations along the east coast provides a contrast to the forested highlands of the Natural Park. After emerging from the Route de la Traversée at Mahaut, the road winds along the west coast to Pointe-Noire, a town known for its wood craftsmen. House of Wood (Maison du Bois) is a display center and forestry museum with labeled species of plants and trees. There is an admission fee.

North of Deshaies on the coast, Grande Anse has a long crescent of golden sand where the only commercially operated campground in Guadeloupe is located. Farther north about a mile, Plage de Cluny has unusual deep orange sand, but one should be careful about swimming here because there is a strong undertow. The north coast is popular for its Creole and seafood restaurants.

Two trails cross the northern mountains from coast to coast. One, known as the *Contrebandiers Trail*, links Pointe-Noire and Lamentin on the northeast via Duportail; it is 4.3 mi/6.9 km long and takes about three and a half hours to hike. A second trail, *Trace de Baille-Argent–Sofaïa*, crosses the main ridge between Beausoleil on the west coast and Sofaïa and Ste.-Rose on the northeast. It is a long but not difficult trail of about 7 mi/11 km. Inquire locally.

Pointe des Châteaux, a rocky headland on the easternmost tip of Grande-Terre, juts one mile into the swirling waters where the Caribbean and Atlantic meet.

GRANDE-TERRE

In contrast to Basse-Terre's lofty, volcanic heights, Grande-Terre is a flat, limestone island where rainfall averages less than 40 in/100 cm per year. Its central area has been greatly altered by karstic action and is made up of eroded hills and valleys, known locally as *montagnes russes*, French for roller coasters. More populated and more developed for tourism than its twin, Grande-Terre has Guadeloupe's largest town, Pointe-à-Pitre, which is the region's commercial capital and main port.

Directly behind the colorful fruit and flower market at the Darse (dock) in Pointe-à-Pitre is the Place de la Victoire, a graceful park commemorating the site of the British defeat in 1794. Bordered by old colonial houses with wrought-iron balconies, the square is colored by royal poinciana and African tulip, or *tulipier du Gabon*, and shaded by fine specimens of royal palm and *sabile*, or sandbox tree, planted by Victor Hugues, a national hero for whom the Natural Park trail was named.

East of the city beyond the university campus along the south coast, white sand beaches stretch to Pointe des Châteaux at the eastern tip. Here, Guadeloupe's main resort centers—Gosier, Ste.-Anne, and St.-François—offer a full range of water sports, beginning with Bas du Fort, one of the largest marinas in the Caribbean. The resorts are set on pretty beaches or on hillsides overlooking the Caribbean and surrounded by flower-festooned gardens visited frequently by hummingbirds and bananaquits. Some are situated in renovated estate houses and mills of former sugar and coconut plantations where horseback riding is available. At Gosier, about a half-mile offshore, little Ilet du Gosier is a nudist beach. Between Gosier and St.-François, white sand beaches alternate with small fishing villages. St.-François is both a fishing village and a large resort and reputedly has the island's tastiest shellfish; its local restaurants specialize in Creole seafood dishes. There is a branch of the Tourist Information Office in town.

POINTE DES CHÂTEAUX

A rocky headland reaching more than a mile out to sea, Pointe des Châteaux is bordered by miles of white sand beaches that are safe for swimming, except at the tip where the colliding waves of the Atlantic Ocean and the Caribbean Sea constantly batter the shore. Immediately before the tip of Pointe des Châteaux, two short tracks cross to the north-side beaches fringed by coral reefs. One path goes to Tarare Beach, a nudist enclave; the other path leads to Grande Saline, a salt pond where flocks of shorebirds congregate. Pointe des Châteaux and the inland stretches behind the east coast are dry with mostly xerophytic vegetation. Among the taller trees are white wood (known here as local pear), Antillean galba, birch gum or red gum, Indian almond, mapous or loblolly, and cinnamon. The thorny underbrush and cacti include campeche, black wood, monval, acacia, and *griffe chat* or cat's claw.

East of the Point, the Iles de la Petit Terre are two tiny deserted islands, ideal for day trips. Terre-de-Bas has a lighthouse and a path that runs the length of the island. A long white sand beach that seldom sees a footprint runs along the north coast; the east side is rocky. Surrounded by coral reefs, the island is covered mostly by scrub, with abundant sharp-needled cactus, and is inhabited by iguanas that scamper about in the undergrowth and small crabs that parade on the sand. It was probably once farmed, as there is evidence of rock walls used to fence in grazing livestock. Terre-de-Haut is covered with brush and cactus and is difficult for hiking, although there is a footpath across the island from a small beach on the north. The area between the two islands is a dive location. Transportation must be arranged from Ste.-Anne or St.-François by private boat.

LES GRANDS FONDS

Across the central region, from Pointe-à-Pitre and Abymes on the west to Le Moule on the east, is the roller-coaster terrain known as Les Grands Fonds where roads snake through "mornes" and "fonds," the names given locally to the hills and valleys that characterize the karst landscape. Unlike other karst regions, such as those of Jamaica and Puerto Rico, the landscape here is surprisingly soft and pretty.

Le Moule, once the capital of Guadeloupe, was also the site of fierce fighting between the Carib Indians and the early French settlers. Today, it is the main town on the Atlantic coast; in the adjacent hamlet of La Rosette is the Musée d'Archéologie Precolombienne Edgar Clerc, a museum that has a collection of Carib and Arawak Indian artifacts gathered from the islands of the eastern Caribbean. The environs of Le Moule are covered with grassland grazed by large herds of local hybrid Brahma cattle and canefields dotted with sugar-mill towers and windmills.

POINTE DE LA GRANDE VIGIE

The northernmost point of Grande-Terre is reached from the east coast via Gros Cap and Campèche, in the least populated area of the island. On the leeward coast there are secondary roads from Anse-Bertrand that are better for walking than driving. Pointe de la Grande Vigie overlooks a spectacular setting of waves crashing against the rocks and stark limestone cliffs. To the east at Porte d'Enfer (Gate of Hell), there is a grotto, Trou Madame Coco, named after a local legend that claims a Madame Coco disappeared one day walking across the waves carrying a parasol. The sea is too rough for swimming but the site offers magnificent vistas.

Between Anse-Bertrand and the small fishing village of Port-Louis there are nice beaches, all but deserted on weekdays. Down the coast from Port-Louis in Petit-Canal is the Monument to Liberty. It stands on the side of a hill at the head of fifty-seven stone steps used to torture slaves. Each slave plantation provided one step; the owners would punish the rebellious by putting them in barrels with spikes driven into the sides and rolling them down these steps.

GRAND CUL-DE-SAC MARIN

The most extensive mangroves in Guadeloupe border the Grand Cul-de-Sac Marin along the west coast of Grande-Terre. White mangrove occurs at the land fringe of the marsh; black mangrove and red mangrove stand in water. The best places for birding are the marshes north of Port-Louis and Anse de Souffleur; however, they are not as accessible as the mangroves around Petit-Canal, Vieux Bourg, and Rivière Salée, the channel separating the two parts of Guadeloupe. Other birding locations are the salt ponds at Gosier and the Pointe Canot marsh east of Gosier on the south coast.

Seven species of heron are seen in wetlands and ponds. Lesser and greater yellowlegs, stilt sandpipers, spotted sandpipers, semipalmated sandpipers, and least sandpipers are seasonal at the edge of the lagoons.

Common snipe are found in the savanna and the grass of the bog from October to April, while whimbrels come year-round. Semipalmated plovers visit the beaches from August to December, and black-necked stilts are spotted occasionally in the saline ponds. Common moorhens usually are seen in the grass and among the red mangroves from September to March. The sora, a migrant, passes through Guadeloupe from August to December. Blue-winged teal are abundant in September and October. Magnificent frigatebirds are found on the coast, particularly over Ilet Frégate de Haut in the Petit Cul-de-Sac Marin. The American kestrel is found throughout.

Among the land birds, the bananaquit and Carib grackle are ubiquitous. The resident gray kingbird is abundant in the savannas; tropical mockingbirds are found in the southeast of Grande-Terre and the offshore islands; the yellow grass finch inhabits the open fields; the streaked saltator is seen in the dry scrub and undergrowth.

ILES DES SAINTES

An archipelago of eight tiny volcanic islands, the Iles des Saintes are idyllic tropical hideaways scalloped by white sand beaches. Only the two largest, Terre-de-Bas and Terre-de-Haut, are inhabited and only the latter has hotels and other tourist facilities. Most inhabitants, descendants of seagoing Bretons, are fisherfolk who still wear the *salako*, a broad-brim, flat straw hat covered with white cloth.

Terre-de-Haut, usually referred to as Les Saintes, is a mountainous island, 3 mi/4.8 km long, with terrain rising over 1,000 ft/300 m. It has only one village, Bourg des Saintes, and one road, a bougainvillea-decorated lane that runs, more or less, from end to end. From town, it is a pleasant hour's walk to each end of the road. Taxis are available, too. East along the harbor at the edge of town, a road climbs up the hill to the seventeenth-century Fort Napoléon, which has a fine view over the island. The fort has a new botanical garden specializing in cactus species with abundant Turk's-head and candle cacti. The main road ends at the Baie de St.-Pierre, a pretty horseshoe bay with a white sand beach; there is an entrance fee. Another beach on the south side is usually too windy and rough for swimming but it has a path to a cliff for a view of the pretty seascape.

The main road west of the pier skirts Le Chameau (1,013 ft/309 m), the highest hill, which has a track to an old watchtower at the top. The trek takes about an hour and is worth it for the panoramic view of Terre-de-Haut's quiet bays and rocky coves, its sister islands, and Basse-Terre with cloud-capped La Soufrière on the north and Marie-Galante on the east. North of the main road is Le Pain de Sucre, a sugarloaf hill overlooking a

popular beach and a bay usually crowded with yachts. The main road ends at Pointe Boisjoli; the south side has a tiny bay with a nudist beach.

Daily ferry service runs from Trois-Rivières and Basse-Terre town to Bourg des Saintes in thirty minutes. There also is air service connecting Pointe-à-Pitre, Basse-Terre, and Terre-de-Haut. As a result of the frequent connections, Guadeloupeans as well as visitors often go to Terre-de-Haut for the day. In addition to its delightful surroundings, the island has good restaurants and water sports.

LA DESIRADE

Off Grande-Terre's east coast lies the little island of La Désirade, once a penal and leper colony and as yet undeveloped for tourists. Its inhabitants live a simple life from and by the sea as boatbuilders and fishermen; their daily catch of conch, sea urchins, clams, sea snails, and many varieties of fresh fish guarantees a succulent fish dish during one's visit. There are two good beaches, one with a small, simple hotel. The vegetation is dry and cacti are abundant. Iguanas inhabit the island in enough numbers that one is likely to see them at close range. Ferries leave daily from the marina in St.-François for the forty-five-minute ride. Air service is available twice daily.

MARIE-GALANTE

Situated 27 mi/43 km south of Grande-Terre, Marie-Galante is geologically similar enough to that island to suggest that it may have broken off from it and floated out to sea in an earlier geologic era. Along the west and south coasts, white sand beaches skirt green, rolling hills, while most of the east side is rockbound. Women still don colorful Creole madras dress for holidays here, and the landscape is dotted with old sugar mills still in use; carts pulled by oxen take the cane to distilleries. The slightly pear-shaped island has good roads connecting the three main towns—St.-Louis, Grand-Bourg, and Capesterre. Each has narrow streets and pastel houses that are light-years away from French sophistication or American-influenced tourism. Good roads, light traffic, and the low-lying terrain make biking a delightful way to tour the island.

A main road connects St.-Louis, the beaches of the west coast, and Grand-Bourg along a scenic drive brightened with flamboyant and other

At the northern tip of Grand-Terre, in its most secluded reaches, the limestone cliffs of Pointe de la Grande Vigie drop precipitously to the sea.

flowering trees. Another traverses the rolling hills of the interior from St.-Louis to the eastern part of the island. On the east side the road branches to Le Trou à Diable (Devil's Hole), a grotto with stalactites; a local guide is needed to show the way. South of St.-Louis on the way to Grande Anse, a marsh encircled by a road has birdlife, including white-tailed tropicbirds and brown pelicans (unusual in Guadeloupe); laughing gulls are abundant.

On the north end, a secondary road from St.-Louis and another from the beautiful beaches of Anse Canot are scenic routes along each side of La Grande Barre, a high green ridge, that divides the north half of the island into two plateaus—both with tracks that can be used for hiking. One should ask locally for directions. At the island's northernmost point, the Gueule du Grand Gouffre is a whirlpool of colliding tides at the foot of a high limestone bluff, Grosse Pointe. Anse Canot and Vieux Fort beaches have reefs for snorkeling but you must bring your own equipment as there is none to rent on the island.

Marie-Galante has numerous restaurants and small hotels and can be reached daily from Pointe-à-Pitre in fifteen minutes by air and in an hour or so by large ferries. Bikes can be taken on the ferry.

OUTDOOR ACTIVITIES

HIKING: In Basse-Terre's Natural Park there are almost 200 miles of marked trails, ranging from easy walks to arduous treks. The Tourist Office in Pointe-à-Pitre has park brochures and maps. Guided excursions for one to twelve persons are arranged by the Organisation des Guides de Montagne (tel. 590-81-45-75). Guided hikes of about four hours in the Caraïbe Mountains are available through the Organisation des Guides de Montagne de la Caraïbe (tel. 590-81-45-79). Hikers also can join scheduled hikes of the Club de Montagnards (Mountaineers' Club), which is closely associated with the park through the Amis du Parc Naturel (Friends of the Natural Park). Commentary is in French.

CAMPING: Campsites do not have amenities, except at the commercial operation, Les Sables d'Or on Grande Anse Beach near Deshaies, Basse-Terre, where tents may be rented and basic facilities are available; it is frequently very crowded (tel. 590-81-39-10). Fully equipped camping cars, sleeping four or five persons, and camping trailers are available for rent; inquire in advance at the Tourist Office in New York. The Natural Park has no camping facilities.

BIKING: Biking is popular in Grande-Terre and Marie-Galante, with their low-lying terrain and good roads. The Tour de la Guadeloupe, a ten-day international race in August, is as much a hotly contested event here as the Tour de France in the mainland and has helped to make cycling a national sport. Biking tours, with maps and bikes supplied, are available through a local tour agency; three-speed bikes may be rented in Pointe-à-Pitre, Ste.-Anne, Gosier, and St.-François. Country Cycling

Tours—140 W. 83rd St., New York, NY 10024; 212-874-5151—offers programs in February and March.

HORSEBACK RIDING: Le Criolo (tel. 590-82-79-99), a riding school at St. Félix near Gosier, has thirty horses and ten ponies and organizes riding tours and picnic excursions. Le Relais du Moulin (tel. 590-88-23-96), situated on a large spread near Ste.-Anne, takes guests riding on property trails.

SWIMMING: Guadeloupe's nicest beaches are on Grande-Terre and the offshore islands. Public beaches are generally free, though some charge for parking; a few have rustic changing and toilet facilities. Hotels welcome nonguests but may charge for changing facilities, beach chairs, and towels. Topless bathing for women is common at hotels but is discouraged on village beaches. There are several officially designated nudist beaches, the most popular being Pointe Tarare at the eastern end of Grande-Terre.

SNORKELING AND DIVING: The French pioneered the sport of diving, and CMAS (Confédération Mondiale des Activitées Subaquatiques), the national scuba association of France, has the most rigorous courses for certification. American divers should be aware that French dive tables and apparatus are different from those to which they are accustomed, and even certified divers will be checked on the use of the equipment. Pigeon Island off the west coast of Basse-Terre is the main site where two dive operators have their own boats. Other Basse-Terre locations are Grande Anse and Ilet à Kahouanne on the northwest coast, and Goyave and Ste.-Marie on the east coast. Grand Cul-de-Sac Marin has large areas of coral gardens, although this is open-water diving; Ilet à Fajou is the prime location, easily visited on day trips with dive operators from Grande-Terre resorts. One can make arrangements directly with dive operators located in a resort area or through hotels.

FISHING: Hotel desks can help guests make arrangements with deep-sea fishing boats based at the Port de Plaisance Marina in Bas du Fort (tel. 590-82-74-94) or at St.-François. One of the main areas is the west coast of Basse-Terre at Pigeon where local operators take anglers fishing for marlin, tuna, and other large game fish. One can also contact the Fishing Club Antilles in Bouillante (tel. 590-86-73-77), or Guadeloupe Chartaire in Pointe-à-Pitre (tel. 590-82-34-47). The season for barracuda and kingfish is January to May; for tuna, dolphin, and bonito, December to March.

SAILING: Yachting is a well established and challenging sport in Guadeloupe where winds and currents tend to be strong. The offshore isles of Marie-Galante and Les Saintes offer safe anchorages and are popular destinations for day excursions. Yachts and boats of all sizes with varying degrees of luxury can be chartered, crewed or bareboat, by day, week, or longer. Some offer combinations of trekking and horseback-riding excursions with sailing to Guadeloupe's satellite islands, or longer charters to Dominica, Martinique, and other nearby locations. Le Boat, a new service that operates within the French West Indies like a car rental agency, enables the renter to pick up a boat in one island and drop it off in another without extra charge. Inquire at the Tourist Office or hotels. Port de Plaisance, Bas du Fort (near Gosier), is the largest marina with 700 berths, fifty-five of which are available to visiting boats. It is one of the best in the Caribbean and can handle all types of pleasure craft up to 130 ft/40 m in length. St.-François is another boating center. In Basse-Terre, southeast of Basse-Terre town, Marina de Rivière-Sens (tel. 590-81-77-61) is the closest mooring for sailors who want to visit the Soufrière volcano. Deshaies on the northwest coast has three anchorages.

WINDSURFING: Lessons and equipment for rent are available from almost all seaside hotels.

EXPLORING THE ISLAND

Guadeloupe's 1,225-mi/373-km road network is one of the best in the Caribbean. It is possible to make a complete loop around both wings—Basse-Terre and Grande-Terre. Distances can be deceiving, however, and usually take about twice the time one anticipates. Off the tourist track some knowledge of French will be helpful.

Car rentals are readily available from agencies at the airport upon arrival, in Pointe-à-Pitre and Basse-Terre town, and at many hotels. Rates are comparable to those in the United States and Europe. Self-drive is the best way to tour the island; one needs a valid driver's license. Driving is on the RIGHT, and traffic regulations and road signs are like those in Europe. Drivers here do like to speed, but visitors unaccustomed to the roads should be more cautious.

Most people arrive by air at Raizet Airport, north of Pointe-à-Pitre, and head for the resort areas along Grande-Terre's south coast. To reach Basse-Terre from Pointe-à-Pitre, one crosses the Pont de la Gabare, the bridge over the Rivière Salée; 2 mi/3.2 km farther west, at the Destrelan traffic circle, highway N. 1 turns south along the east coast of Basse-Terre, and highway N. 2 leads north to Le Lamentin and Ste.-Rose and on around the northern tip of Basse-Terre to the west coast.

Guadeloupe has a good, inexpensive public bus system that operates from 5:30 A.M. to 7:30 P.M. Buses stop along routes at bus stops marked *arrêt-bus*, or one can signal by waving to the bus driver to stop. Buses for Gosier and St.-François leave from La Darse, the dock, near the Tourist Office in Pointe-à-Pitre. The terminal for buses to Basse-Terre is located in the Bergevin quarter on the north side of town. Taxis are plentiful, but they tend to be expensive and not all drivers speak English. Night rates, from 9 P.M. to 7 A.M., are 40 percent higher than daytime rates.

Marie-Galante, Les Saintes, and La Désirade have daily connecting air service in addition to ferries.

INFORMATION: In the U.S.: French West Indies Tourist Board, 610 Fifth Ave. (628 Fifth Ave. for walk-in info), New York, NY 10020; 900-990-0040; offices also in Dallas, Los Angeles, San Francisco, and Chicago. In Canada: French Government Tourism Office, 1981 Avenue McGill College, Suite 490, Montreal, Que. H3A 2W9; 514-288-4264. In the U.K.: 178 Piccadilly, London WIV OAL; 71-493-6694. In Guadeloupe: 5 Square de la Banque, 97110 Pointe-à-Pitre; 590-82-09-30.

Organisation des Guides de Montagne, Maison Forestière, 97120 Matouba; 590-81-45-75 (contact, Mr. M. Berry). Publications in French are available from the Natural Park: Maison des Forêts, Jardin Botanique, 97109 Basse-Terre, Guadeloupe, FWI; tel: 81-17-20. Among them are *Parc Naturel de la Guadeloupe; guide de découverte; La flore de la mangrove* (1982); *Les oiseaux de la mangrove* by B. Belbeoc'h (1983); *La forêt dense* (1981).

Clockwise from top left: heliconia, lobster claw, bougainvillea, the flower of the cannon-ball tree, oleander, frangipani, and flame of the forest, also called the African tulip tree.

DOMINICA

OF ALL THE ISLANDS of the Caribbean, Dominica tops the list for adventurous nature lovers. Covered from end to end with spectacular tropical scenery, this gift of nature is dominated by towering green mountains jungle-thick with rain forests and crisscrossed by rivers and streams. Within its boundaries are five ecological zones—each with its own flora and fauna.

Dominica, the largest of the Windward Islands, is the most mountainous of the volcanic Lesser Antilles, with peaks reaching almost 5,000 ft/1,524 m. Evidence of continuing volcanic activity abounds throughout the island, which is 29 mi/46 km long. It is washed by calm Caribbean waters on the west and pounded by Atlantic waves on the east. Ocean winds rise over the mountain peaks where they condense and release up to 250 in/635 cm of rain per year. The forests are home to rare animals and plants and more than 135 species of native and migratory birds. Two parrots—the imperial and the red-necked—are endangered species found only here. The island has one of the world's largest beetles, but there are no poisonous snakes.

Much of Dominica's lush vegetation is new as a consequence of the destruction caused by Hurricane David in 1979. In some areas loss of trees, shrubs, flowers, and wildlife was so complete that some species are probably gone forever. A new inventory of birds and plants has not yet been made, since the island is only now returning to normal. Fortunately, the hurricane did not damage many areas of true rain forest, particularly in the northern part of the island. But hurricanes or not, no island in the Caribbean is more bent on retaining its natural environment. Dominica is primarily an agricultural country, and tourism is integrated into the life of the people; it plays a secondary role in the economy. The island is free of the jarring presence of large resorts, shopping centers, and casinos.

Nothing about Dominica fits the usual image of a Caribbean island. In many places the mountains fall steeply to the sea, and the few beaches have dark volcanic sand. It is the island's interior, however, and not its beaches, that commands attention.

Known to the native Carib Indians as Wai'tukubuli, meaning "tall is her body"—an apt description of Dominica's towering mountains—the island was discovered in 1493 by Columbus, who named it "Sunday" for the day of discovery. Domination of the island seesawed for several centuries between the French and British, and a treaty in 1686 declared Dominica to be a neutral territory to be left forever to the Caribs. In practice, however, there was no end to the fighting between rival European powers. After changing hands several times, the island finally went to the British in 1805. After almost another two turbulent centuries Dominica became independent in 1978. To this day, the influence of the French is almost as strong as that of the British, particularly in the patois, or local Creole speech, in the names of people and places, and in the culture and cuisine. Dominica and St. Vincent are the only places in the region where Carib Indians, after whom the Caribbean is named, have survived.

Roseau

The island's capital, Roseau, is situated at the mouth of the Roseau River on the southwest coast. It is a typical West Indian port, looking a bit newer than most since it had to be rebuilt after Hurricane David destroyed 80 percent of the town. At the seafront the old market, once the slave block, has been renovated to house craft shops and a tourist information bureau. The colorful fruit and vegetable market is a must on Saturday mornings when it is crammed with people from the countryside selling what seems to be every exotic fruit and flower of the tropics. Two Dominican specialties available at hotels and restaurants in town are "mountain chicken," or frog's legs, called *crapauds*, and callaloo, a soup made from the heart-shaped leaves of the young dasheen plant, which can be seen growing throughout the country. Great views of Roseau and the coast can be seen from Morne Bruce, an elegant residential hillside, and further up the mountain at a cliffside hotel.

Dominica Botanic Gardens

Situated at the foot of the wooded cliffs of Morne Bruce, the Dominica Botanic Gardens were once the pride of the Caribbean. When they were laid out in 1890, they covered 110 acres/44.5 hectares, but decades of urban growth have reduced them to only 40 acres/16 hectares, and a main road passes through their heart. Even so, the gardens are still the largest tract of open space in the town. Further devastation came in 1979, when the eight-hour onslaught of Hurricane David left the gardens beyond recognition. A poignant reminder can be seen near the entrance—a yellow school bus crushed beneath the weight of an African baobab tree. The tree, which has now sprouted new branches, began flowering again in 1985.

Originally, the gardens were laid out in two sections: an ornamental section and a commercial one devoted to growing plants of economic and industrial value. The gardens contain about 150 species of trees and shrubs; the goal is to return it to the 500 species it had at its prime. Among the trees to note are Carib wood, whose bright crimson blossom is Dominica's national flower. An indigenous tree found in dry coastal areas along the leeward coast, it blooms from March to early May, and can also bloom again

Pages 310 and 311: On the western slope of Morne Micotrin in Dominica National Park the cascades of Trafalgar Falls drop to a rain forest garden below.

in October. Other unusual species are the pride of Barbados; bottle palm; African almond with leaves that resemble the magnolia; balata, used for snakebites; white cedar, which blooms with masses of lovely white flowers in autumn; and the no-name tree, so called because specialists have never been able to identify it.

DOMINICA NATIONAL PARK

Most of Dominica's prime attractions are found in the Dominica National Park, also called Morne Trois Pitons National Park after its highest peak, the "mountain with three peaks." Established in 1975 and located in the central and southern highlands, the park's 16,000 acres/6,475 hectares have magnificent scenery with a great variety of plant and animal life and five types of forests—dry scrub woodland, rain, lower montane, montane, and elfin. The park's four highest peaks from north to south are Morne Trois Pitons, 4,403 ft/1,342 m, the second highest peak on the island; Morne Micotrin (also known as Macaque), 4,006 ft/1,221 m, a young dormant volcano; Morne Watt, 4,107 ft/1,224 m; and Morne Anglais, 3,683 ft/1,122 m. These mist-shrouded mountains can be climbed, but not without a guide. Trails are difficult or nonexistent; guides will often have to hack a path through the growth with a machete.

On the north side of Roseau, a road east leads into the beautiful lush valley of the Roseau River for approximately 2 mi/3.2 km where it branches and provides access to most of the attractions in the park's central region.

TRAFALGAR FALLS

The nearest, most accessible, and prettiest excursion to the park from Roseau is a visit to Trafalgar Falls, located on the western slope of Morne Micotrin. Here three spectacular waterfalls cascade over a precipitous side of the Micotrin mountain to pools several hundred feet below. At the base of the cliff and the entrance to the trail is the Papillote Inn, a wilderness retreat and nature sanctuary with a magnificent rain-forest garden.

Begun in 1969 on the eroding mountain slope, the Papillote Rain Forest Garden is situated 1,000 ft/300 m above sea level at the edge of the park. Over the years terraces, flat areas, and footpaths were created following the slope's natural contours. Informal in arrangement, the garden groups plants in families within small ecological niches and blends them in with the indigenous vegetation. There are several special collections of plants— begonias, bromeliads, ferns, gingers, orchids, and heliconias—in addition to herbs, teas, and fruit trees. More than fifty species of nesting birds frequent the general area. Among those most likely to be seen from the inn's dining terrace are the bananaquit, purple-throated carib, green-throated carib, Antillean crested hummingbird, pearly-eyed thrasher, Lesser Antillean bullfinch, trembler, and great blue heron.

The hike to the main falls on a well-maintained trail takes about ten minutes through magnificent tropical vegetation and makes an ideal introduction—or finale—to a Dominica visit. The three falls are quite far apart, but at one point on the trail, all three are in view. At the inn there are warm sulphur water pools where, after a fatiguing trek in the nearby mountains, guests may soak their aches away. The inn organizes guided nature walks and treks to the Boiling Lake and other nearby attractions.

FRESHWATER AND BOERI LAKES

The most northern branch of the Roseau Valley road winds northeast along the mountainside for 3 mi/4.8 km to the village of Laudat at the base of Morne Micotrin from where the excursion to two freshwater lakes in the national park begins. Freshwater Lake, 2,779 ft/847 m altitude, and Boeri Lake, 2,800 ft/853 m altitude, were a single body of water in the crater of an old volcano until Morne Micotrin, a young volcanic cone, formed and divided the water.

Freshwater Lake, the largest of Dominica's five lakes, is shaped like two intersecting rectangles and has park trails that follow the irregular shoreline along its north and east sides through montane, or higher, forests which cover most of the area. Here, hikers will see large, showy bromeliads, large-leaved anthuriums, and delicate ferns. A common shrub is the blue wax flower; more open areas have brightly colored, red-and-yellow heliconias. Floating on the lake are purplish-blue-flowered water hyacinths. Adjacent to them are various sedges rooted in the muck of the lake's bottom. Around the lake's edge the most common trees are the mangle rouge and the mangle blanc, whose prop roots extend well up their trunks to give them support in the waterlogged soil. To explore other areas of the lake hikers would need to bring an inflatable boat or they can hire a canoe at Roxy's Mountain Lodge.

Among the birds—the most conspicuous wildlife in montane and elfin forests—most often seen are the Antillean crested hummingbird, the purple-throated carib hummingbird, and the rufous-throated solitaire, or mountain whistler. The first-named, often seen feeding on heliconia flowers, can be recognized by its brilliant blue-green forehead feathers which shimmer like iridescent gems in the sunlight. The ridge to the east of Freshwater Lake is actually part of the rim of an inactive volcano; it overlooks numerous peaks and ridges formed by various volcanic eruptions, reflecting the island's violent origins. The view is splendid.

The trail up the mountainside to Boeri Lake, one of the largest lakes in

Dominica, starts by a rushing stream where the mineral-rich water has turned the rocks a rust color. The man-made stream is being used to divert water from Boeri Lake to raise the level of Freshwater Lake. The route to the lake takes hikers past a forest of giant tree ferns and various other fern species, hot and cold springs gushing from the side of the mountain, and finally through montane forest and elfin woodland. The trees dominating the montane forest here are mahot cochon; palmiste, which is endemic to Dominica; mountain cabbage; and gombo montaigne, a relative of the hibiscus. Some trees support plants such as wild anthuriums, bromeliads, orchids, and, occasionally, red-and-yellow heliconias and the similarly colored apoplexi flower. Many plants of the montane forest can also be seen in the elfin woodland, which becomes clearly visible as one approaches higher elevations.

The walk up the ridge to Boeri Lake offers wonderful panoramic views. To the east one can see the villages of Grand Fond, Morne Jaune, and Rosalie near the Atlantic coast, and an old mountain track used by villagers before new highways were constructed. To the south is Freshwater Lake and further south is Morne Nicholls, which overlooks the Valley of Desolation and the Boiling Lake.

Along the trail small birds, particularly the Antillean crested hummingbird, can be spotted frequently. The lovely song of the small, shy mountain whistler can be heard and occasionally a migratory waterfowl is seen on the lake. Other than birds and butterflies, the most conspicuous wildlife in the Boeri Lake region are small tree lizards (zandoli), which have a different color pattern from those at the low elevations. The black-and-yellow siwik, or river crab, often makes its home between the boulders along the shores of the lake.

Boeri Lake has a beautiful setting between Morne Micotrin on the south and Morne Trois Pitons on the north. While large slippery boulders block direct access to the lake from the trail, it is easy to scramble over the rocks to dangle one's feet in the cool water or jump in for a swim.

The trail to the lakes begins just before the village of Laudat with a steep 1.5-mi/2.4-km dirt road (too rough to negotiate except by Land Rover or truck or on foot) that rounds the south side of Micotrin mountain on its way to Freshwater Lake. By foot the hike takes about thirty minutes. From Freshwater Lake, the more difficult 1.25-mi/2-km trail to Boeri Lake takes forty-five minutes for experienced hikers, an hour or more for those less fit.

Freshwater Lake, formed in the crater of an old volcano, is the largest of the island's five lakes. The wide-leafed plant, called z'ailes mouches (carludovica insignis) is used to line baskets and sometimes to make the roof for an overnight shelter.

TITOU GORGE, BOILING LAKE, AND VALLEY OF DESOLATION

Beyond the village of Laudat the road leads south for 0.25 mi/0.4 km to the Titou Gorge and the trail through the Valley of Desolation to the Boiling Lake, the world's second largest solfatara lake and a highlight of the park. As the crow flies, the Boiling Lake is 6 mi/9.6 km directly east of Roseau, but to cover that distance and reach the lake requires four hours and some of the most arduous trekking in the Caribbean. A new easier, shorter trail was opened in 1993; inquire locally.

The Titou Gorge, a very narrow, deep gorge where the trail begins, was formed by volcanic action, not cut by a river. Its undulating sides indicate that as the molten lava was cooling, it split and pulled apart, similar to the way a drying mud puddle splits and cracks. The first part of the trail tracks southeast to Morne Nicholls where it winds along the mountainside through one of the island's best stands of resinier montaigne, also known as laurier de rose, a tree typical of montane forest and the only native gymnosperm, or evergreen (conifer), in Dominica. The upper regions of Morne Nicholls are covered with elfin woodland species, their branches and trunks hidden by the mosses and lichens growing on them.

The trail continues down through and across the Valley of Desolation and then ascends to the Boiling Lake on the far side (one and a half hours). Once a lushly forested area, the Valley of Desolation now appears lifeless due to destruction caused mainly by the sulphuric fumes in the region. The valley floor is covered with a thick mat of mosses and lichens and occasional yellow-and-white-flowered wild thyme and grasses that can survive in the harsh environment. Wildlife, too, is limited by the harsh conditions to lizards, cockroaches, stoneflies, mayflies, and ants.

Scattered throughout the purple-green valley floor are brightly colored hot springs—blue, white, black, and orange—whose colors come from the minerals washed and deposited by the water. Some rocks are covered with yellow sulphur crystals. Trekkers are advised by their guides to stay on the trail at all times to avoid breaking through the thin crust covering the hot lava below.

The Boiling Lake, approximately 210 ft/61 m across, looks like a huge caldron of bubbling grayish blue water enveloped in a cloud of vapor. The sides of the caldron are a mixture of clay, pumice, and small stones. The lake is not thought to be a volcanic crater but, rather, a flooded fumarole, a hole in a volcanic region from which hot gases and vapors "boil" or escape at regular intervals from the molten lava below. Rainfall from the surrounding hills collects in the basin of the fumarole to form the lake; the water then seeps through the porous bottom to the hot lava below where it is trapped and heated to the boiling point. The Boiling Lake was first sighted in 1870 by Mr. F. Watt and Dr. H. Nicholls for whom the nearby mountain peaks were named. An 1875 study showed the water temperature along the edges to range from 180° to 197°F/82° to 92°C, and the depth of the lake to be greater than 195 ft/60 m. Its current depth is unknown.

The trail to the Boiling Lake is a constant up-and-down climb and is often slippery from water runoff even in the dry season. It is toughest during the wet season when the ground becomes even muddier and more slippery. Approximately a half-mile from the Valley of Desolation, the trail becomes a very narrow, twisting muddy path, and in the elfin woodland areas the waist-high foliage is often so thick that hikers cannot see their feet to know where to step. The return hike, though no less rugged, can be made in about two and a half hours. Trekkers should bring food, a change of clothes, and, of course, a camera. Experienced guides recommend lightweight tropical hiking boots for better support and ankle protection, rather than sneakers or running shoes, which are adequate for most hiking in Dominica. Those in less than tiptop shape may want to hike only as far as the Titou Gorge, where they can have a swim in a pool of warm water, or they can go about halfway on the trail to the edge of the Valley of Desolation, a hike of two to two and a half hours.

A more convenient place to see bubbling mud and sulphur fumes rising from pockets in the earth is the Sulphur Spring at Wotten Waven, reached via the most southern branch of the Roseau Valley road.

MIDDLEHAM TRAILS

At a point 2 mi/3.2 km north of Roseau the road to Pont Casse turns east into the mountains. It zigs and zags through a deeply indented valley, passing Springfield Estate, an old plantation at 1,200 ft/366 m elevation, and skirting the Middleham Estate on the northwest boundary of the Morne Trois Pitons National Park. Here, the Park Service trails were cut through a 950-acre/384-hectare tract of rain forest donated to the park in 1975 by the American owner of Springfield Plantations, Ltd. The Middleham area is considered to have one of the best examples of rain forest in Dominica. Access to the trails can be gained from three sides: Sylvania on the north, Cochrane on the west, and Providence (via the Laudat road) on the south. The trails were recently upgraded and can usually be hiked without a guide. They may be impassable in the rainy season, however.

From Sylvania, 2 mi/3.2 km north of the Springfield Estate, the trail (a one-hour hike) first passes through an area of secondary growth before entering true rain forest. There once was a coffee plantation here.

From Cochrane, situated between the Laudat and Pont Casse roads, the

route passes several estates and cultivated areas before it enters true rain forest. Here the forest is dominated by gommier and chataignier trees. The trail passes by Tou Santi (meaning "stinking hole"), a collapsed lava tube that emits hot air and houses several species of bats and an occasional snake. Its name derives from the smell of the bat droppings. At this point the Cochrane trail intersects a footpath that leads back to Sylvania, a hike of one to two hours, depending on one's interest and pace.

Alternatively, one can continue to Providence for a hike of about two hours. The trail leads to a viewpoint overlooking the 150-ft/46-m Middleham Falls, one of Dominica's tallest waterfalls, and continues through rain forest to Providence. Another choice at the falls is to take an upper trail that tracks back to Sylvania on a hike of about two and a half hours.

The birdlife of the Middleham area, best observed in the early morning and late afternoon, includes the Caribbean elaenia, the ruddy quail-dove, several species of thrush, the scaly-naped pigeon, and the trembler. Among the wildlife one might see is opossum, known as manicou in Creole, and agouti, a tailless rodent that grows to about 20 in/51 cm in length. It resembles a rabbit but is more closely related to the guinea pig.

Yellow sulphur crystals cover rocks in the Valley of Desolation. Facing page: The delicate scarlet flower called Bâtard la Pite in Dominica can grow near boiling sulphur pools, whose waters are heated by the hot lava below, though it is usually found along the roadsides.

EMERALD FALLS NATURE TRAIL

East of Pont Casse 2.5 mi/4 km, past a quarry on the right, an unmarked road on the left turns north to Castle Bruce through the beautiful L'Or River and Belle Fille River valleys, an area laced with ferns, bordered by banana plantations, and backed by jungle-thick mountainsides. Shortly after the turn-off, a sign on the west side of the road points to the Emerald Falls Nature Trail, the easiest, most accessible trail in the National Park.

The trail, located on the northern end of the park, is a thirty-minute walk on a well-defined footpath that meanders for a half-mile through lush forest to a beautiful cascade where the water drops 20 ft/6 m into a pool of black rock surrounded by a greenhouse of ferns, orchids, and trees—hence the name, Emerald Falls. (Bring a towel, since the pool is large enough for a swim.) Technically, the trail passes through a transition zone of vegetation between true rain forest and montane forest. It has two lookouts: the first offers views of a wild stretch of the east coast at St. David's Bay and Castle Bruce; the second overlooks the upper part of the Belle Fille Valley with Morne Laurent (also known as Nègres Marron) on the north. A short paved section of the trail, after the second lookout, is part of the old road used by the Caribs before the main road to Castle Bruce was built in the 1960s.

Among the birds common to the area are hummingbirds, Caribbean elaenia, and rufous-throated solitaire. Other birds that can be heard or spotted are the scaly-naped pigeon, ruddy quail-dove, house wren, scaly-breasted thrasher, trembler, forest thrush, black-whiskered vireo, plumbeous warbler, bananaquit, and Lesser Antillean bullfinch.

CENTRAL FOREST RESERVE

North of Dominica National Park are the conservation areas of the Central Forest Reserve, which includes a small diversified forest dominated by the gommier tree; and the Northern Forest Reserve, a huge area covering much of the northern half of the island.

The Central Forest Reserve (and gommier forest) is traversed by the Imperial Road, a 20-mi/32-km stretch between Pont Casse and Marigot on the northeast coast. The gigantic gommier tree, which grows to heights of 120 ft/36 m, is a beautiful and durable hardwood used to make furniture. For centuries it has been used by the Caribs to make oceangoing canoes. The tops of the gommier are favorite nesting places for the rare imperial parrot, known locally as the sisserou. With commercial logging, however, the trees were being cut at an alarming rate, causing soil erosion as well as loss of the parrots' habitat. Since the creation of the national parks and forest reserves in 1975, the Forestry Department has exerted some control by selecting the areas to be logged, but it is not able to stop poaching entirely.

From the gommier forest, the road drops into lime and banana plantations along the Pagua River to Pagua Bay, a beautiful crescent of golden sand where the Atlantic surf rolls in against the rocky shores. On the north side of the bay a sweep of the vegetation bent and shaped by the wind hugs the cliffside. The bay marks the northern boundary of the Carib Indian Reservation, an area of 3,600 acres/1,457 hectares held in common by the over 3,000 descendants of the Caribs, who inhabited the island at the time of Columbus's discovery.

Alternatively, the road east from Pont Casse skirts the northern end of the national park and leads to Rosalie, a small village surrounded by banana plantations and notable for a lovely waterfall that plunges into the Atlantic. From Rosalie there are secondary roads to the beautiful, rocky coast of Petite Soufrière Bay where more waterfalls cascade into the sea. One can continue north along the coast to the fishing village of Castle Bruce, the southern boundary of the Carib Indian Reservation.

NORTHERN FOREST RESERVE

The huge Northern Forest Reserve, covering the mountains of the northern half of the island, is dominated by Morne Diablotin, the island's highest peak at 4,748 ft/1,447 m. It is named for a bird (presumably the black-capped petrel) which, it is said, the French hunted to extinction in this region. Today, the reserve is the last refuge of the imperial parrot and its smaller relative, the red-necked parrot, known locally as the jacquot. Said to have numbered in the millions in the late fifteenth century, only an estimated fifty imperial parrots and a hundred red-necked parrots remain.

Dublanc, on the west coast highway about 5 mi/8 km south of Portsmouth, is the turn-off for the best parrot-viewing site on the island. The road snakes up the mountain to the Syndicate Estate on the edge of the reserve. Here a track cuts through banana and grapefruit plantations for a mile or so, from where hikers leave their jeeps or trucks to scramble over an ill-defined, overgrown path through a grove of banana trees to the lookout facing the slopes of Morne Diablotin. The trail for climbing to the summit of Morne Diablotin is also in this area and takes about three hours.

Making this excursion usually means leaving Roseau by 4:00 a.m. in order to be at the viewing site by sunrise when the chances for seeing the famous birds are best. Patience and complete silence will pay off, and before long the distinctive "waak waak" of the parrots will be heard. The birds are difficult to spot but the guides are expert at helping viewers find them.

Parrot-viewing areas in the reserve can be approached from the north coast, too. Beginning at Woodford Hill, a logging road goes into the mountains for 4 mi/6.4 km through coffee, banana, and grapefruit plantations. A short walk from the road takes hikers to a clearing where jacquots can be seen. Another location is Governor Estate, also on the north coast, near Marigot and Melville Hall Airport.

INDIAN RIVER

At the mouth of the Indian River on the south side of Portsmouth, Dominica's second largest town, barges ply back and forth ferrying boxes of bananas out to the cargo ships of Geest, the British company that buys all Dominica's banana production for European markets. Small row boats can be rented for a trip upriver through mangroves so thick that they form a tunnel over the river; only rays of light filter through. After about thirty minutes of rowing, the boatman, who also acts as a guide, lands his party at a clearing for a hike in the countryside, identifying the birds and flora along the way. A plant particular to the savannah is citronnelle, or lemon grass, a sharp-edged grass that when rubbed gives off a strong lemon scent. It is quite astringent and can cause a temporary rash. It is used locally to make a tea for colds or chills. Here, too, one can see many tiny Antillean crested hummingbirds close enough to photograph.

CABRITS HISTORICAL AND MARINE PARK

On the northwest coast, the 1,060-acre/429-hectare Cabrits Historical and Marine Park, which is part of the Dominica National Park, encompasses a 260-acre/105-hectare peninsula joined to the mainland by a freshwater swamp and a marine reserve of 800 acres/324 hectares. The park takes its name from the Cabrits peninsula which is dominated by two steep hills, the remnants of two volcanoes separated by a narrow valley. Behind the peninsula towers the massif of Morne Diablotin. The name "Cabrit" is a corruption of the word for goat in several European languages, and was used to name the area by sailors of various fleets who, in the early days of exploration, left goats here so they would have fresh meat on future visits.

The peninsula overlooks Portsmouth and Prince Rupert Bay on the south; on the north is Douglas Bay, the site of the marine reserve. From 1770 to 1815, on a promontory of the Cabrits, the British built Fort Shirley, one of their most impressive military installations in the Caribbean, to protect Prince Rupert Bay, a strategic source of fresh water drawn from the rivers that empty there. Today, the extensive ruins are being restored following the original plans, which had been preserved in England. In addition to the battlements, a museum has been installed in two restored

At the northern end of Dominica National Park, Emerald Falls cascade 20 ft/6 m into an inviting pool where one can swim surrounded by a lush forest of trees, ferns, and orchids.

powder magazines, and trails using the old tracks of the British garrison have been opened. One trail leads to the commander's house, a ghostly shell of a mansion now strangled in the gigantic roots of ficus trees.

The Cabrits and adjoining wetlands contain the most impressive area of dry scrub forest and the most extensive area of wetlands on the island. More than forty species of trees have been identified. These include savonnet, a tall, straight tree with a smooth gray bark and small purple flowers; bayleaf tree, whose leaves have a strong lime odor; white cedar, whose leaves are used locally for the treatment of pain; and l'epine, silk-cotton, and sandbox trees, whose trunks are covered with spikes. Before the area became a national park, the Forestry Division introduced teak, blue mahoe, and mahogany trees on an experimental basis. At an earlier time, fruit trees such as lime, mango, grapefruit, guava, soursop, and custard apple were added.

The east side of the peninsula is flanked by 89 acres/36 hectares of swamp and marsh and is the only area in Dominica where three typical swamp tree species have been identified: pond-apple, a close relative of soursop; white mangrove; and bwa mang—or mangrove tree—the largest of the swamp species, growing up to 2 ft/0.6 m in diameter and 90 ft/27 m in height.

Among the wildlife, birds are the most numerous and include herons, plovers, sandpipers, terns, hummingbirds, kingfishers, swifts, and warblers. Of Dominica's five species of snakes, three are found at the Cabrits, the boa constrictor among them. At least two of the three species of marine turtles that nest on Dominica's sandy beaches—the green and the hawksbill—nest on the southeast and northeast beaches of the peninsula from April to September.

The north side of the Cabrits plunges to the sea along a rocky shoreline where rock and coral formations are interesting for snorkelers and divers. The beach curving north along Douglas Bay is shaded by West Indian almond trees and edged with coconut palms and seagrape. The marine park is a popular snorkeling area. Beyond Douglas Bay the road passes through teak plantations to Toucari Bay and continues on secondary roads to Capucin Point at the island's northern tip, where there are white sand beaches and views of Guadeloupe's Iles des Saintes.

MORNE AUX DIABLES

The entire area north of Portsmouth and the Cabrits forms a large peninsula dominated by Morne aux Diables, 2,828 ft/1,144 m. Its north coast faces the Guadeloupe Channel, a treacherous passage for sailing ships of old and an area of great interest to treasure hunters. In 1567 the entire Spanish treasure fleet loaded with gold and silver went down here—and that was only one incident. The conservative estimate is that 200 ships lie off Dominica's shores.

SOUFRIÈRE BAY AND THE SOUTHERN AREA

Five mi/8 km south of the capital, the fishing village of Soufrière sits on a wide scenic bay bounded on the south by a rocky peninsula that ends at Scotts Head, a promontory overlooking the Martinique Channel, where the Caribbean meets the Atlantic. From the summit of Scotts Head there are great views of Martinique to the south and Soufrière Bay to the north.

Along the short stretch of road between the town and the promontory, one can see weathered fishermen mending their nets and repairing their boats. On Friday nights the area is transformed into an outdoor disco and street fair where Dominicans from the capital and all over the area come for a rowdy good time.

En route to Soufrière from Roseau, the villagers of Pointe Michel grow khous khous, the grass used to make Dominica's distinctive rugs. The tough grass is put on the road for cars to run over it to make it more pliant for weaving. The roots of the plant are used to make a perfume.

At Loubière a road runs 10 mi/16 km to Berekua at Grand Bay, a wide bay on the south coast with a good beach and a view of Martinique. From here it is possible to continue east to Fond St. Jean and north to Petite Savane from where a footpath tracks north to Délices, the starting point for hikes into a mountainous area, the least accessible part of Dominica, where there are many beautiful waterfalls.

A secondary road in the center of Soufrière turns east to a hillside of sulphur springs with water almost too hot to touch. A branch of this road leads past the ruins of a sugar estate that once belonged to the Empress Josephine, who apparently spent a year in Dominica when having a baby. The Empress was supposedly given the southern half of the island by the then-French governor. In the southeastern corner of the island, the old sugar plantation of Petit Coulibri Estate has been turned into an aloe farm by an American couple. In addition to showing visitors the method of growing and processing aloe, the couple is knowledgeable about the flora and fauna of the area. There is no organized hiking in this region but one could follow old farm tracks and secondary roads to the rocky cliffs along the south coast, which is a good bird-watching area. The black-capped petrel, one of whose names is the same as Dominica's highest peak, Diablotin, and once thought no longer to exist in Dominica, has been seen at Petit Coulibri.

Outdoor Activities

HIKING: Trails to the main sites in the National Park range in their ease of access from a comfortable thirty-minute walk to the Emerald Pool to a tortuous four-hour trek to the Boiling Lake. To reach a destination, one usually drives several miles by car or Land Rover from the capital to the edge of the park, where footpaths begin. Park Service brochures with rough sketches of trails and information on trail conditions are available from the Dominica Tourist Office in Roseau. There are other hiking opportunities all over the island.

SWIMMING: Most of Dominica's beaches are steel-gray volcanic sand, except on the northeast coasts where there is a series of palm-fringed golden sand beaches and bays—Hampstead, Pointe Baptiste, Anse Noire, Woodford Hill Bay. But some of the most pleasant swimming is in the interior, especially at a waterfall such as the Emerald Falls. At Layou on the west coast where the Layou River, the island's widest river, empties into the sea, a ten-minute walk above town along the river valley leads to a pool popular for swimming.

Two endangered parrots found only in the Northern Forest Reserve. Left: Red-necked parrot. Right: Imperial parrot. Facing page: The widest of 350 rivers and streams that traverse the forested terrain is the Layou River, which originates in the northern reaches of Dominica National Park.

SNORKELING AND DIVING: Water sports, generally, are not developed here. Dominica does have reefs in several places on the north and west coasts, and there is great potential for wreck diving. Hodge's Beach, a white sand beach on the northeast coast, faces three small offshore islands and is popular with snorkelers and divers. The best underwater features of the north coast are the banks of brain corals and sea fans and an abundance of tropical fish.

Douglas Bay, the island's best snorkeling location, has a large reef about 180 ft/55 m from shore in 20 to 50 ft/6 to 15 m of water with good corals and varieties of small, colorful tropical fish and sponges. Historic Rodney's Rock, easily accessible by land and sea, is the island's most popular dive site. It was once lighted up like a warship to scare off the French, who were planning to attack Dominica. The rock has a canyon-like feature between the main part at the shoreline and another almost totally submerged section. There are many varieties of fish and coral, including rare purple coral.

At Canefield, there are two wrecks: a large one lying at approximately 30 ft/9 m and a sunken tug at approximately 90 ft/27 m that harbors a few barracudas and is accessible by land or boat.

South of Roseau and about 300 ft/91 m north of the Anchorage Hotel, a reef approximately 180 ft/55 m from shore starts at about 45 ft/14 m depth and drops southward to approximately 140 ft/43 m. It is accessible from the hotel. At Pointe Guignard, less than a mile north of Soufrière, there are walls, caves, black and brown coral, reef formations, plants, sponges, lobsters, and many other forms of marine life. Just north of the Point, around a smaller protrusion, there is good snorkeling with underwater springs on the ocean floor; the south side has shallow-water snorkeling too.

Scotts Head at the south of the island has a variety of diving locations, from the Caribbean side around to the Atlantic side of the promontory. These are mainly drop-offs and reef dives with characteristics similar to Pointe Guignard. The area is accessible by land. The beach on the north side of Scotts Head is rocky but it is popular for snorkeling since the coral is within swimming distance. The area is small and features mostly finger corals, but it also has a large variety of small, colorful reef fish. The coral directly off the north side does not appear to be in good condition; however, divers should not be deterred. Diving around the southwest-side wall of the Point and along the south coast of Scotts Head is excellent. Generally, heavy winter seas limit diving on the south coast to summer months, when the seas are calm. A plan to make Scotts Head into a marine park is being considered—and none too soon.

The island has a qualified dive operation that offers a full range of services, including PADI instruction and a ten-passenger dive boat. Deep-sea fishing also can be arranged.

WINDSURFING: The best areas for windsurfing are the north coast at Hodge's Beach, the northwest coast at Douglas Bay, the west coast south of Roseau, and Soufrière Bay.

EXPLORING THE ISLAND

Dominica now has more than 300 miles of excellent new roads connecting the major centers of the country within a few hours' drive from Roseau. But the network of secondary roads and tracks in the interior varies from good to terrible; and none of the roads, even the new ones, is well marked. A map is a must, but even the best maps take a certain amount of guesswork since many important places are not marked. Some places have local names that differ from those used in government and other literature.

Three trans-island highways connect Roseau via Pont Casse, a junction in the center of the island. One leads north and east to Rosalie; another leads north and northeast to Castle Bruce; and the third, known as the Imperial Road, heads in an almost straight line northeast to Marigot. No highway makes a complete circle around the island. Also at Pont Casse, a road west descends for 12 mi/19 km through banana, citrus, and cacao plantations of the fertile Layou River Valley to the town of Layou on the Caribbean coast. It is often used as an alternative route from Roseau to Pont Casse.

While it is possible to motor through the countryside on the good highways, to see the best of Dominica one must leave one's car or van and hike to the mountains, lakes, and waterfalls. For the forested mountain interiors, one must have a guide. They can be obtained through the Dominica Tourist Office, Forest Department, and local companies specializing in safari-type excursions (names available from the Tourist Office). It is foolhardy—even dangerous— to hike in the deep interior without a guide because it is very easy to get lost. Due to the heavy rains (which fall mainly from June to December) and the warm climate (from 60° to 90°F/15.5° to 32°C) that spur the rapid growth of vegetation, trails deteriorate quickly and can be obliterated in a very short time.

Camping in the forests is neither encouraged nor advised, and no provisions are available. However, there are unpretentious hotels near scenic areas which make suitable bases for exploring the immediate area around them. These hotels also organize guided excursions for guests.

There is little public transportation, but there are private taxis and minivans in Roseau and minivans between towns and villages. Cars are available for rent; one needs a visitor's driving permit which can be obtained upon arrival at either airport upon presentation of a valid license and payment of a fee. Driving in this former British Colony is on the LEFT, but visitors should be aware that driving is hazardous since Dominicans tend to race up and down hills, and along narrow mountain roads and highways, taking blind curves on any side of the road.

INFORMATION: In North America: Dominica Tourist Office, % Caribbean Tourism Organization, 20 East 46th St., New York, NY 10017; 212-682-0435. In the U.K.: 1 Collingham Garden, Earl's Court, London SW5 OHW; 71-370-5194. In Dominica: Cork St., Box 73, Roseau, Commonwealth of Dominica, WI; 809-44-82351 and 44-82186. Dominica Hotel Association, P.O. Box 384, Roseau; 809-448-6565. Forestry and National Parks, Botanic Gardens, Roseau; 809-449-2733/445-2731.

Published sources include: *The Dominica Story* by Lennox Honychurch (The Dominica Institute, 1984) and *Vegetation* by P. N. Honychurch (Dominica National Park Service, 1978). The Forestry and Wildlife Division, Ministry of Agriculture, has published *Cabrits Plants and Their Uses* (1986) and *Flora and Fauna of the Cabrits Peninsula* (1985). Topographical maps can be purchased at the Tourist Office in Roseau.

MARTINIQUE

ST. LUCIA

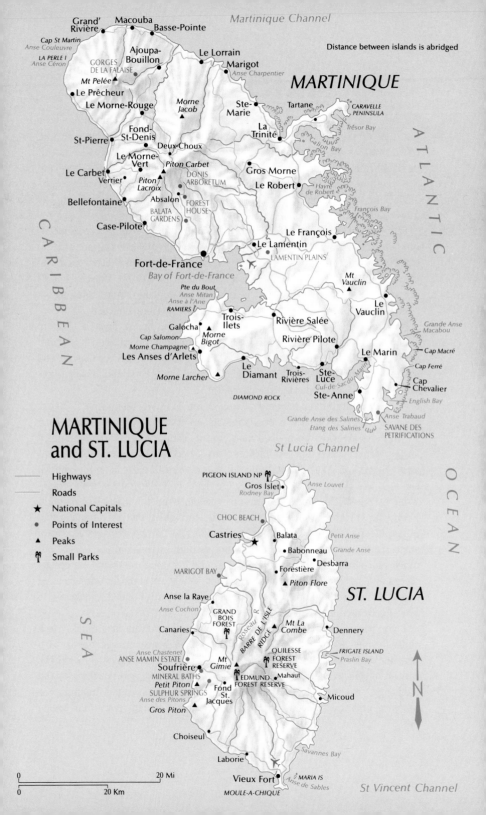

Grand'
Rivière
Macouba
Basse-Pointe
Cap St Martin
Anse Couleuvre
LA PERLE I
Anse Céron
GORGES
DE LA FALAISE
Ajoupa-
Bouillon
Le Lorrain
Marigot
Anse Charpentier
Mt Pelée▲
Le Prêcheur
Le Morne-Rouge
Morne
Jacob ▲
Ste-
Marie
Tartane
CARAVELLE
PENINSULA
Trésor Bay
Fond-
St-Denis
St-Pierre
Deux-Choux
La
Trinité
Galion Bay
Le Morne-
Vert
Piton Carbet
DONIS
ARBORETUM
Gros Morne
Le Carbet
Verrier
Piton
Lacroix
▲
Absalon
FOREST
HOUSE
Le Robert
Havre
de Robert
Bellefontaine
BALATA
GARDENS
François Bay
Case-Pilote
Le François
Le Lamentin
LAMENTIN PLAINS

Fort-de-France
Bay of Fort-de-France
Pte du Bout
Anse Mitan
Anse à l'Ane
RAMIERS I
Galocha
Trois-
Ilets
Rivière Salée
Mt
Vauclin ▲
Le
Vauclin
Cap Salomon
Morne
Bigot ▲
Rivière Pilote
Grande Anse
Macabou
Morne Champagne ▲
Les Anses d'Arlets
Le
Diamant
Trois-
Rivières
Ste-
Luce
Le Marin
Cap Macré
Cap Ferré
Morne Larcher ▲
Ste-Anne
Cap
Chevalier
DIAMOND ROCK
Cul-de-Sac Marin
English Bay
Grande Anse des Salines
Etang des Salines
Anse Trabaud
SAVANE DES
PETRIFICATIONS

MARTINIQUE Channel

MARTINIQUE

Distance between islands is abridged

A T L A N T I C

C A R I B B E A N

O C E A N

S E A

MARTINIQUE
and ST. LUCIA

⎯⎯⎯	Highways
⎯⎯⎯	Roads
★	National Capitals
●	Points of Interest
▲	Peaks
⛺	Small Parks

St Lucia Channel

PIGEON ISLAND NP ⛺
Gros Islet ●
Anse Louvet
Rodney Bay
CHOC BEACH ●
Castries ★
Balata
● Babonneau
Petit Anse
Grande Anse
● Forestière
Desbarra
MARIGOT BAY
▲ Piton Flore
ST. LUCIA
Anse la Raye ●
Anse Cochon
GRAND
BOIS
FOREST ⛺
Mt La
Combe ▲
Canaries ●
QUILESSE
FOREST
RESERVE
Dennery
Anse Chastenet
ANSE MAMIN ESTATE ●
Soufrière ●
Mt
Gimie ▲
⛺ EDMUND
FOREST RESERVE
Mahaut
FRIGATE ISLAND
Praslin Bay
MINERAL BATHS
Petit Piton ▲
SULPHUR SPRINGS
Anse des Pitons
Fond
St.
Jacques
● Micoud
Gros Piton ▲

Choiseul

Laborie
Savannes Bay

Vieux Fort
▲ MARIA IS
Anse de Sables
St Vincent Channel
MOULE-A-CHIQUE

ROSEAU R.
BARRE DE L'ISLE RIDGE

N

0		20 Mi
0		20 Km

MARTINIQUE

As DISTINCTIVE IN ITS LANDSCAPE as in its character, Martinique is a paradox of jagged peaks and gentle hills, razorback ridges and flowing meadows. Its ever-surprising scenery ranges from cloud-capped volcanic peaks to rain forests, pastureland, canefields, and bone-dry desert. Around the coastline long stretches of white sand beaches give way to vertical cliffs sheltering volcanic black sand beaches. And everywhere masses of tropical flowers color the landscape.

Indeed, the name of Martinique is said to derive from a Carib word, *madinina* or *madinia*, meaning "island of flowers." Some dispute the romantic connection, saying instead that Columbus, who discovered the island in 1493, named it for a saint, as was his usual custom. But there is no dispute that "Island of Flowers" is an appropriate name. Martinique sometimes seems like one large garden floating on a peacock-blue sea.

Martinique, Guadeloupe, Iles des Saintes, St. Barts, and St. Martin comprise the French West Indies. Like Guadeloupe, Martinique is a *région* of France whose people have all the privileges of French citizenship and culture. Its unusual blend of French, African, and East Indian heritages further enhances its distinctive character.

Although the island is only 50 mi/80 km long, it seems much larger because there is hardly a straight line on its coast or a straight road through its interior. Composed mostly of volcanic rocks, Martinique has a series of distinctive topographical features, each with its own environment and vegetation. At the northern end where volcanic cliffs hang high above the sea, the land rises along deeply creviced mountain slopes to the somewhat symmetrical cone of an active volcano over 4,500 ft/1,372 m high. From the volcano's southern base, fertile terrain, green with banana and pineapple plantations, rises again through the north-central region in a series of rugged peaks and ridges—not as high as those of the north, but much more spiked and irregular—covered with rain forests and carved by rivers and streams. The Pitons du Carbet, where six conical cloud-crowned peaks rise over 3,500 ft/1,067 m, form the highest ridge and the backdrop to Fort-de-France, the capital.

From these jagged, rain-drenched heights, the terrain falls quickly to a central plain created by alluvial deposits. The gentle meadowlands with grazing cattle stretch south from the Bay of Fort-de-France through the center of the island. Around the edges on the east and southwest, the landscape becomes hilly again, rising in irregular round mounds, or *mornes,* and toward the south there are areas of mangroves and saline flats.

The east or windward coast (Côte au Vent) is more exposed to the wind and rain brought by the northeast trade winds than the west or leeward coast (Côte sous le Vent) and this affects the vegetation. On the volcanic slopes of the northeast coast where rainfall is heaviest, the rain forest begins at a low altitude. In the central and south regions, there are pockets of seasonal evergreen and dry forests, depending on the altitude, and along the coast there are large areas of mangrove swamp. The driest areas, particularly in the southeast, are mostly covered with scrub and cactus.

FORT-DE-FRANCE

The main town of Martinique, Fort-de-France, is a sugar-white city that has retained much of its colonial character. Its central location and deep harbor have long made it a natural center of the island's commercial activity, but it did not become the capital until the old capital, St.-Pierre, was devastated by volcanic eruption in 1902.

At the heart of Fort-de-France—near the waterfront where ferryboats depart for Point du Bout across the bay—is La Savane, a large public park with a statue of the Empress Josephine. The spacious, manicured lawns brightened with beds of calla lilies and hedges of bougainvillea are shaded by the spreading arms of flamboyant and other tropical trees and two species of royal palm: *Roystonea regia*, a Cuban native that grows to a height of 50 to 66 ft/15 to 20 m, and Caribbean royal palm, an eastern Caribbean variety that reaches 132 ft/40 m. The two species, distinguishable also by their leaves, can be seen along the Route de Didier, a scenic road through an affluent hillside suburb of luxurious colonial and Creole-style villas set in splendid private gardens. The road ends at the Fontaine Didier, a mineral spring whose much-esteemed water is bottled for drinking. One is warned not to leave the roads or hiking trails in this area and the adjacent Case-Navire Valley because a poisonous snake, the fer-de-lance, a relative of the rattlesnake, is rather common here. During colonial times, mongooses were introduced to combat the snakes; instead they were destructive of birds and other wildlife.

On the west side of La Savane, the Martinique Departmental Museum contains a collection of Arawak and Carib artifacts and old maps of the sixteenth and seventeenth centuries. Several blocks west of La Savane at Place Clémenceau is a small tree-shaded park, Parc Floral, with geological and botanical exhibitions. Almost 2,800 species of plants have been identified in Martinique.

Pages 334 and 335: The lush rain-forest vegetation on Martinique's mid-island hillsides includes elephant ear, anthurium, castor bean, and oleander.

Regional Natural Park of Martinique

The Regional Natural Park of Martinique (Parc Naturel Régional de la Martinique, or PNRM) is a comprehensive term covering a number of separate protected areas and the bodies responsible for them. Its mandate involves the development of rural areas as well as the preservation of the natural and cultural heritage. The main areas under the park's umbrella are, from north to south: the volcanic region of Mt. Pelée; the Botanic Garden at Fond-St.-Denis, a mountain village of the northwest; an arboretum on the Route de la Trace north of Fort-de-France; the Caravelle Peninsula together with a recreation center on Trésor Bay on the east coast; and almost the whole of the southern highlands with the Montravail Forest north of Ste.-Luce.

Route de la Trace

From Fort-de-France, a narrow road known as the Route de la Trace, or simply the Trace, winds its way north through the dense rain forests of the Regional Natural Park to Deux-Choux, a tunnel on the north side of the Pitons du Carbet. Each hairpin turn in the road looks back over sweeping views of Fort-de-France and the bay. As soon as the road begins to climb out of the city, Sacré-Coeur de Balata, a miniature of the church of Montmartre in Paris, comes into view. To those familiar with the Parisian landmark, the Caribbean copy set in the tropical splendor of the Pitons may seem incongruous. The Route de la Trace ultimately leads to Mt. Pelée, an active volcano that is the highest peak on the island.

Balata Gardens

Higher up the Trace on a hillside overlooking Fort-de-France is Le Jardin de Balata (Balata Gardens), a private botanical park at 1,476 ft/450 m with more than a thousand varieties of tropical plants. Created by the owner, Jean-Philippe Thoze, who is an artist and landscape designer, the park has as its centerpiece a restored Creole house furnished with antiques. Walkways bordered by a great variety of ferns and palms lead past flowering shrubs and trees and a lily pond framed by the majestic Pitons du Carbet. One sees herbs and gingers, mosses, heliconias, anthuriums, hibiscus, and other tropical plants. There are hedges of brilliant magenta bougainvillea, a flower found in Martinique in many colors—white, pink, coral, orange, red, mauve—and named for Louis de Bougainville, who imported the plant from Brazil in 1768. Balisier, abundant in the wild and widely cultivated, can be recognized by its leaves similar to the banana tree and its bright red flower trimmed with pale or mustard-yellow. Known as the lobster claw, or hanging bicolored heliconia, it has 600 species. Angel's trumpet, or datura, is recognized by its pretty flower which looks like a trumpet: it also has hallucinogenic properties. As impressive as the flora are the magnificent views overlooking Fort-de-France as far south as Cap Salomon. The gardens are open daily from 9 A.M. to 6 P.M.; signs and literature are in French. The entrance from the Balata Road—another name for the first section of the Trace—is marked by large signs.

MAISON DE LA FORÊT AND ARBORÉTUM DE LA DONIS

La Maison de la Forêt (Forest House), maintained by the Office National des Forêts (ONF), is located on the side of the Arborétum de la Donis (Donis Arboretum), where trees, shrubs, and herbaceous plants are cultivated for scientific and educational purposes. The rain forest is thick with immense hardwood trees such as gommier and mahogany on which epiphytes and bromeliads grow and from which curtains of elephant ears and creepers dangle above the carpets of ferns. The most beautiful species is the tree fern, which grows profusely in Martinique. Its slender fibrous trunk supports orchids and other epiphytes under an umbrella of light green fronds. From the picnic area a trail leads through the arboretum where signs in French identify the trees and other vegetation.

The African tulip, called *tulipier du Gabon*, can be seen here and throughout the island, particularly from December to May when its orange red blossoms are displayed. The trail continues on its serpentine climb across private property planted with fruit trees and anthuriums to an abandoned mahogany plantation, and ends at the summit of Morne Césaire from where there are panoramic views of the Pitons and the south coast.

ABSALON THERMAL SPRING AND FOREST TRAILS

West of the Trace is the iron-rich Absalon Mineral Spring and the start of the Absalon-Verrier Trail, one of the main footpaths through the central mountains. The trail begins on a steep slope through a dense rain forest under a canopy that includes gommier, or white gum, and bois canot, or trumpet tree. After about twenty minutes the trail comes to a fork, where the path on the left descends to and across the Rivière Duclos (Duclos River), which flows from the Pitons along the north side of the Morne Chapeau Nègre Ridge. The trail continues west for about an hour to the Concorde Plateau, 2,172 ft/662 m, passing through forests of gommier and a reserve of mahogany planted for harvesting by the ONF. From the Concorde Plateau, a trail on the left cuts away to the Morne Bois d'Inde (1,818 ft/ 554 m), a ridge immediately north of Fort-de-France, and descends through a forest of chataignier to fields cultivated with thyme and vegetables. Views of Fort-de-France and the Caribbean coast can be enjoyed along the

way. A hike on this trail also can start from the west coast north of Fond-Lahaye, going inland via La Démarche.

Continuing west on the Absalon-Verrier Trail, the walk in the woods is relatively easy as far as Savane St.-Cyr, where another cutaway on the left to Morne Rose descends southwesterly through plantations of Caribbean pine and mahogany to Case-Pilote on the coast. Beyond Savane St.-Cyr, the Absalon-Verrier Trail ascends the Morne Chapeau Nègre ridge, which peaks at 2,992 ft/912 m. The first hour of the trail passes through a rain forest; then the track gets much steeper as it reaches the elfin woodland that covers the cloud-swathed summit. At these higher altitudes, where the wind and moisture are greater, the trees are dwarfed and the vegetation is thick with mosses and ferns. The last part of the climb across a small crest has sweeping views overlooking the lushly forested slopes of Morne Rose and Morne Bois d'Inde to Fort-de-France on the Caribbean coast and east across cultivated plains to the Atlantic coast. The hike from Absalon to Morne Chapeau Nègre takes three hours, one way. The long hike is steep and strenuous in some parts, and suitable only for those in good condition.

From the crest there are two options: an hour's descent westerly along the ridgeline to Verrier where the trail meets a road to Bellefontaine on the coast; or a much more difficult trail north across the ridgeline to Piton Lacroix, the highest peak. From there, one has further choices: west to Source Chaude or to Le Morne-Vert; north to Piton Boucher; or east to Piton Dumauze and the Route de la Trace. These are extremely arduous journeys of at least three hours from the summit to be undertaken only by the most experienced climbers accompanied by guides.

ABSALON CIRCUIT TRAIL

An easier walk of about three hours on a loop trail also begins at the Absalon Thermal Spring on the same steep ascent through the rain forest to the fork where it bends right, leaving the Absalon-Verrier Trail on the left. The loop follows a lightly wooded crest along a branch of the Duclos River and descends the ridge. On the return leg, it fords a small stream and comes to a junction where the eastern branch zigzags for about an hour to the Colson Hospital and the Trace. The looping trail continues straight (south), fords another stream, descends through dense rain forest, and emerges on the Trace immediately north of the Absalon parking area. A mile north of the Absalon Thermal Spring, the Trace reaches its highest altitude, 2,133 ft/650 m.

Bromeliads are among the 2,800 plant species found on Martinique, whose name may come from a Carib word meaning "island of flowers."

PITONS DU CARBET

The spiked and scarped mountains dominating the north-central region are the Pitons du Carbet. The main ridge, which runs northeast–southwest, has Piton Boucher (3,511 ft/1,070 m) and Piton Carbet (3,675 ft/1,120 m) on the north; Mt. Piquet (3,806 ft/1,160 m) and Piton Lacroix (3,924 ft/1,196 m) to the west; and Piton de l'Alma (3,626 ft/1,105 m) and Piton Daumaze (3,639 ft/1,109 m) to the east. Each of these peaks has very steep, difficult trails suitable only for experienced mountain hikers. Some trails lead from one peak to another along slippery paths over narrow, razorback ridges that are less than a foot wide in some places. The hikes take between six and eight hours and should be done in a group or with a guide. Hikers must watch for poisonous snakes.

FOND-ST.-DENIS AND BEAUREGARD CANAL

Immediately before the underpass of Deux-Choux, the Trace is intersected by another artery (D. 1) which runs through the luxuriant tropical forest east to Gros-Morne and west through a deep gorge known as the Porte d'Enfer, or Gate of Hell, to the village of Fond-St.-Denis and on to St.-Pierre on the coast. At Fond-St.-Denis, gardens cover the slopes on both sides of the road for a mile or more; the town is a perennial winner of Martinique's coveted annual flower award.

Immediately after Fond-St.-Denis at Fonds Mascré a road on the left descends to the Canal de Beauregard, a two-hundred-year-old canal built to bring water to Beauregard and four other sugar mills in the Carbet River Valley. There is a path on the hillside above the canal that is an easy walk, though it narrows to only about 16 in/41 cm in some places and in others it hangs about 450 ft/137 m above the Carbet River; thus it is not recommended for anyone subject to vertigo. Views of the river valley and the Pitons are spectacular. Along the way one will see holes dug in the ground by the *ciriques d'eau douce*, one of several species of crab that abound in Martinique. The trail takes four hours round trip and passes through private property; hikers are advised to go with a group such as one organized by the PNRM, and not to stray from the path. Do not go into the water: it contains the worm parasite bilharzia.

TRACE DES JÉSUITES

Less than a mile north of Deux-Choux on the Trace is the starting point for La Trace des Jésuites (Jesuits' Trail), one of the most popular hikes in Martinique. The signposted trail passes under a high canopy of immense gommiers, the dominant tree of eastern Caribbean tropical rain forests. Known also as the white gum, its tall, straight trunk exudes a resin that early Jesuit missionaries extracted to use in making incense—hence, the name of the trail. Here and in neighboring Dominica and St. Lucia, fishermen hollow out the trunks to make fishing boats called gommiers, which are derived from the traditional dugout canoes of the Amerindians.

The vegetation along the trail is immensely diverse: there are bromeliads with red torch blossoms, bird-of-paradise, lobster claw and other heliconias, ferns, and hundreds of mosses. Occasionally, the mountain whistler, as the rufous-throated solitaire is known here, can be heard singing; Lesser Antillean and black swifts and perhaps a broad-winged hawk, known as *malfini* in Creole, can be seen overhead.

From the Trace, the trail descends into the valley for about an hour's walk to the Rivière du Lorrain (Lorrain River), a cool and pleasant place for a rest stop and picnic. After fording the river, the trail ascends gradually to highway D. 1, emerging 1.5 mi/2.4 km east of the Trace. Hiking time is about three hours. For those whose time is limited or who want a relatively easy hike through a typical tropical rain forest, Trace des Jésuites is ideal. Organized hikes led by PNRM guides are scheduled regularly.

MORNE JACOB

One of the oldest volcanoes on Martinique, steep-sloped Morne Jacob (2,900 ft/884 m), lies east of the Route de la Trace. A large anthurium plantation is situated in the rain forest on its western flank. Several trails lead to the summit from where one has panoramic views of the entire north from Mt. Pelée and the Atlantic coast to the Pitons du Carbet. The more difficult of two marked trails is a loop from Ste. Cécile, an inland hamlet about a mile north of the Jesuits' Trail. A long, strenuous, but less difficult ascent to Morne Jacob leaves from the hamlet of Carabin, inland from Le Lorrain on the east coast.

LE MORNE-ROUGE

On its final leg to Mt. Pelée, the Route de la Trace descends gradually through an area of large pineapple plantations with the Champ Flore plains on the west and the Petite Savane on the east. At Le Morne-Rouge, the Trace meets the north cross-island highway between the Caribbean and Atlantic coasts. Immediately south of the intersection, at Morne Balisier on the west side of the Trace, a "park" of orchids was recently discovered; a plan is being formulated to open the area to the public.

Le Morne-Rouge (1,476 ft/450 m), the gateway to Mt. Pelée, is a small resort town on the southern slopes of the mountain. It was rebuilt after being destroyed by a second eruption in 1902, four months after the one that devastated St.-Pierre.

MT. PELÉE

Dominating the northern profile of Martinique from almost any location on the island is its highest peak, Mt. Pelée (4,584 ft/1,397 m), usually crowned with swirling mists. The volcano's eruption in 1902, in which 30,000 people died within minutes, was one of the most devastating ever recorded in the Caribbean, all the more so because weeks of advance warnings had gone unheeded. Although the bubbling mud, steaming fumaroles, and other outward signs of volcanic activity have subsided, the volcano is by no means extinct. Now, her every sigh is monitored.

At Petite Savane a side road marked in the direction of l'Aileron le Chinois winds 2 mi/3.2 km up the side of Mt. Pelée to a television transmitter, a large car park, and the *south trail* to the summit of the volcano. The trail, the steepest ascent, leaves from above the first of three mountain shelters at 2,690 ft/820 m, near the transmitter, and takes the hardest part of the trek first. The first leg, a climb of about forty-five minutes, goes up a steep slope overgrown with vegetation and along slippery ravines that cut up the mountainside. In some places hikers must climb and scramble over large boulders en route to the Aileron, a plateau at 3,635 ft/1,108 m. From here wonderful views stretch from St.-Pierre and the west coast to the Pitons du Carbet and east to the Atlantic. The footpath narrows and follows the ridgeline on a more gentle slope for about thirty minutes and then makes a short, steep ascent to the rim of the crater. It continues along the rim to the Calvaire (4,003 ft/1,220 m) and the second shelter, from where one can see the crater's interior, covered with mosses, ferns, and bromeliads. The trail goes downhill, bearing left, and up again to the volcanic cone at 4,462 ft/1,360 m where the lava formations left by the eruption of 1902 are in evidence. Nearby is a third shelter. Hikers must be cautious as there are fumaroles and breaks in the ground hidden by the vegetation; it is not unusual for people to fall into these cracks and need rescue.

Most of the time the summit of Mt. Pelée is pelted with strong winds and hidden in a swirl of clouds and mist. The final ascent to Le Chinois (4,584 ft/ 1,397 m), as the main peak is known, goes around to the north side. The trail is slippery and often obscured by fast-growing vegetation. On a clear day, there are superb distant views extending to Dominica on the north and St. Lucia on the south. The return to the car park is made on the same route. The hike takes five hours round trip, and requires stamina.

Another trail to the summit, the *west trail*, a less verdant and less strenuous route, leads up from the coast south of Le Prêcheur via the gentle slopes of the Grande Savane to the second refuge at Mt. Pelée; it takes four and a half hours round trip. Although this trail is shorter than the others, most of it is in open savanna under hot sun. The trail starts on a dirt road through cultivated fields and orchards and after forty-five minutes gives way to a footpath. As the trail gains altitude the open savanna changes to rain forest and then to elfin woodland near the summit. After an hour's walk, there are views of the Caribbean coast and St.-Pierre and the deep gorges on the volcano's sides. In another thirty minutes of steep climbing, the path reaches the crater rim and the second shelter.

The *north trail* is the most dramatic and longest route. It goes via Grand' Rivière and treks up the north face to the second refuge. The trip takes six hours and is seldom traveled due to the difficulty of the terrain.

GORGES DE LA FALAISE

Beyond the turn-off to Mt. Pelée, the main highway makes its hairpin way northeast through a beautiful part of the highlands with tall bamboos, tree ferns, and palms arching in a canopy over the road to Ajoupa-Bouillon, a pretty seventeenth-century village. Both sides of the highway here are planted with magnificent tropical flowers; the town is another leading contender for flower honors. On the north side of the village, a narrow dirt road marked with a hard-to-read sign "Gorges de la Falaise–Narrow Passes" leads inland to a footpath through lush rain-forest vegetation. The path brings one to a narrow river canyon with a beautiful cascade that falls about 40 ft/12 m into a natural pool. Although the Gorges de la Falaise is not marked on many tourist maps, it is one of Martinique's most beautiful spots.

In the northern mountains, a footpath leads through a rain forest to the Gorges de la Falaise, where a narrow river cascades into a natural pool.

The marked trail begins on the edge of a cultivated field and zigzags down to the riverbed where it turns upstream for a short walk to the start of the gorge. In some places one must wade—or swim—through the rock-strewn river. The gorge narrows to less than 6 ft/2 m in width. Usually there are self-appointed guides who ask to show you the way; since some of the track runs through their property, it may be hard to refuse. The hike takes about one and a half hours round trip. Often after heavy rains, when water thunders through the gorge, the trail is closed. Inquire in Ajoupa-Bouillon.

LE MORNE-VERT

North of Fort-de-France the coastal road passes through Schoelcher, a former fishing village that is now a residential suburb, to Case-Pilote, one of the oldest settlements on the island. Le Carbet, the site where Columbus is believed to have landed, has the Amazona Zoo, a small private zoo. Anse Turin, where the painter Paul Gauguin lived in 1887, has a small museum in a rustic setting. From all these coastal villages side roads climb inland to pretty mountain villages and the trails on the Pitons du Carbet.

A road inland from Bellefontaine leads to Le Morne-Vert (1,312 ft/400 m) at the foot of Piton Lacroix. The cool climate and the beauty of the landscape have earned the area the name of Little Switzerland. A new road connecting the Bernadette and Urion districts is particularly beautiful but very steep; it provides access to Caplet, a hamlet in the wooded landscape of the Café Bois, a popular picnic spot maintained by the ONF. It is the departure point for the difficult climb to Piton Lacroix.

ST.-PIERRE

Once called the Paris of the Antilles, St.-Pierre was devastated by the eruption of Mt. Pelée on May 8, 1902, when ash and stones rained down on the town and a cloud of burning gas, with temperatures over 3,600°F/ 2,000°C, snuffed out all life. Today, St.-Pierre is only a small village overlooking a black sand beach. The eruption was not a complete surprise, for an increase in Mt. Pelée's volcanic activity had been observed for several years prior to that fatal day. The St.-Pierre Town Museum (Musée Volcanologique) is dedicated to the 1902 eruption of Mt. Pelée, and contains photographs of the old town and exhibits of molten glass, twisted metal, and stopped clocks, revealing the ferocity of the deluge. Today, the Observatoire du Morne des Cadets on the road between St.-Pierre and Fond-St.-Denis monitors Mt. Pelée's volcanic activity.

Twelve of the ships that were in the harbor when Mt. Pelée erupted have been located. Because bones of survivors also were found, the site is considered a memorial grave to be kept intact. The team that researched the site was headed by Jacques Yves Cousteau, who filmed the exploration.

North of St.-Pierre, the Coulée Rivière Blanche is a trail on the southwest side of Mt. Pelée leading to the Sources Chaudes et Cascades (Hot Springs and Waterfalls). The signposted trail begins on a gravel road in an area used by the army for firing practice and closed to the public on Tuesdays, Wednesdays, and Fridays. The trail passes over terrain that bears evidence of volcanic activity. The great gorges on the west and north faces of Mt. Pelée offer some of the most spectacular scenery in Martinique.

Le Prêcheur and Grand' Rivière Trail

On the coastal road beyond the turn-off to the Hot Springs is a group of limestone hills, Tombeau des Caraïbes ("tomb of the Caribs"), from which the last Caribs are said to have thrown themselves to their deaths rather than surrender to pursuing Europeans. The road north skirts the coast below the spectacular scenery of Mt. Pelée's ridges and gorges. The turn-off for the western trail up Mt. Pelée is at Le Prêcheur, one of the island's oldest villages. Beyond Le Prêcheur, a secondary road twists its way along the coast to Anse Céron, a beautiful beach with heavy surf and a tiny offshore island, La Perle, a dive site.

An 11-mi/18-km trail around the northwestern corner of Martinique to Grand' Rivière, an old fishing village set among graceful palms and leafy breadfruit trees, starts at Anse Couleuvre. The popular long hike follows the remnants of an old road and passes orchards, cultivated fields, old plantations, virgin forest, savannas, and rain forests. Trees are labeled, and the variety of microclimates and soil variants is reflected in the diversity of vegetation. Of particular interest is that the humid forest is the home of the rare whistling warbler, found here and on St. Vincent. This is the only trail on the island—and one of the few in the Caribbean—that passes through virgin forests and vegetation at a low altitude where growth reborn after a volcanic explosion lives beside the remnants of once-thriving mango, coffee, and cocoa plantations. The ruins of old distilleries and plantations can also be seen.

Several small beaches are accessible near Anse à Voile but for the most part, the coast is characterized by high volcanic cliffs that drop directly into the sea. Hikers should be on the lookout for the *matoutou falaise*, a fat, hairy spider that is poisonous; it is seen mostly on tree trunks. The hike takes about five to six hours and involves a series of ascents and descents. Other than length, the trail is not considered difficult. However, hikers are advised to go in a group with a guide and are warned not to leave the trail. One can also begin this hike in Grand' Rivière.

LAMENTIN PLAINS

Across the waist of Martinique south of Fort-de-France, the various areas to the west, south, and east are separated by a wide savanna edged by a landscape of tumbling hills, or mornes, covered with dry evergreen forests and, in the driest areas, dense thorny woods of campêche, or logwood, acacia, and cactus. The Caribbean coast bulges with a peninsula that stretches west to Cap Salomon and is scalloped by white sand beaches and coves. This is where the island's main resorts and marinas are located. It is bordered by a coast road. The Atlantic bays and beaches are not developed for tourists, although they do have camping sites. They are accessible on feeder roads, tracks, and footpaths from the main road, but the most popular way to discover them is by boat. The central savannas, or plains, cleared long ago for sugar plantations and other cultivation, are now grazed by large herds of cattle and oxen. The region is watered by the Blanche River and other streams that flow into the Lézarde River, which empties into the Bay of Fort-de-France at Le Lamentin where there are marshes with some bird and marine life. The name Lamentin comes from the French, la mantin meaning "manatee," though this gentle marine mammal is no longer found in these waters.

LES TROIS-ILETS

Overlooking the south coast of Fort-de-France Bay, about halfway between Pointe du Bout and Rivière Salée, is the historic town of Les Trois-Ilets, which takes its name from three rocky offshore islets. Despite the tourist development surrounding it, things here remain small-scale. A recreational park at Pointe de la Vatable has walking and jogging paths that go through mahogany and pine forest to the waterfront and picnicking areas. Parc des Floralies, a pretty landscaped park with gardens, ponds, and walkways and surrounded by wooded hills, is located immediately before La Pagerie, the birthplace of Napoleon's Empress Josephine, where her family's manor house is a museum. The gardens, which are the setting for a quinquennial International Flower Exhibition, have beds of bright red ginger and other exotic plants, many kinds of palms and ferns, and stately Norfolk Island pines.

MORNE BIGOT

Southwest of Trois-Ilets a horseshoe trail ascends Morne Bigot (1,509 ft/460 m) and descends to Galocha on the west coast. On the ascent the evergreen forest has bamboo, breadfruit, and tamarind; on the descent, there are dry

On Martinique's rocky northwest coast, volcanic cliffs rise to Mt. Pelée, an active volcano that erupted in 1902 and buried the town of St.-Pierre.

secondary forests of bayleaf, *mahot piment,* logwood, and *ti-baume.* From the summit, where there is a television transmitter, the splendid panorama extends north to Fort-de-France with the Pitons du Carbet in the background, and south to Morne Larcher, Diamond Rock, and the island of St. Lucia. The hike takes about two hours.

LES ANSES D'ARLETS AND MORNE CHAMPAGNE

Pointe de Bout, a small finger poking into the Bay of Fort-de-France, is the heart of the tourist center, with several luxury hotels and a marina where one can arrange day-sailing excursions down the coast for swimming and snorkeling. South from Pointe du Bout to Ste.-Anne, the Caribbean coast has one pretty cove and beach after another. Anse Mitan (Mitan Cove) is one of the island's main water-sports centers. Anse à l'Ane has a large campsite, a riding stable, and a small shell museum, the Musée d'Art en Coquillage. Off the coast is Ramiers Islet, a tiny, heavily wooded island crowned with the ruins of an eighteenth-century fort.

South of Anse à l'Ane, the road winds over hilly terrain down to Les Anses d'Arlets, a large bay with two palm-shaded coves—Grande Anse and Petite Anse—and beautiful mile-long white sand beaches separated by a hill, Morne Champagne, which is the crater of an ancient volcano. These are some of the idyllic coves that inspired the painter Paul Gauguin, who lived here in 1887. The north end of the bay is cupped by Cap Salomon, the westernmost point of Martinique's southern Caribbean coast. Grande Anse has a small fishing village with colorful gommiers—traditional dugout canoes—at the north end; a footpath at the south end of the beach leads to Morne Champagne. Petite Anse also has a fishing village and a pretty beach with crystal-clear Caribbean waters. Both coves are popular weekend yacht havens.

MORNE LARCHER AND DIAMOND ROCK

A narrow road twists south to a pretty beach at Petite Anse du Diamant and continues to Point Maurice and around Morne Larcher to Diamond Bay, another resort center. Alternatively, a trail over Morne Larcher (1,565 ft/477 m) connects Petite Anse du Diamant and the western end of the bay at Anse Caffard. Tall trees with an abundance of lianas and epiphytes appear as the path gains altitude. From the summit there is a good view of the Diamond Rock off the south coast. On the descent to Anse Caffard, the vegetation changes from the humid forest to mango and guava trees to dry woodland with *ti-baume,* whose pale green and orange leaves give off a peppery odor when crushed. The moderate hike takes about two and a half hours.

About 2 mi/3.2 km off the south shore a steep-sided volcanic rock called Diamond Rock (Rocher du Diamant) juts out of the sea to a height of 590 ft/ 180 m. Diamond Rock is probably the only piece of land ever commissioned as a "sloop of war." As the story goes, the British in 1804 succeeded in landing a party of 200 armed sailors on the rock and declared it *HMS Diamond Rock*, from where they bombarded any French vessel within range. For eighteen months the British were able to repel all French attacks, but finally the French loaded a boat with rum and caused it to run aground on the Rock. As expected, the British garrison made short work of the rum, and the French took the rock without difficulty.

There is a 2-mi/3.2-km stretch of beach along the bay overlooking Diamond Rock, with Le Diamant, one of the oldest villages on the island, at its eastern end. The beach, abundantly shaded by coconut palms and big almond trees, is popular for camping, and the bay is one of the island's main windsurfing locations. A boat can be rented to go to the rock, but its stunted vegetation and poisonous snakes make it a questionable destination, and the crossing is sometimes rough. From Le Diamant, one can return on the expressway to Fort-de-France or continue south to the pretty beaches at Trois Rivières and Ste.-Luce.

STE.-ANNE AND GRANDE ANSE DES SALINES

Ste.-Anne is a popular resort with an excellent beach, water-sports facilities, and a campsite. A semisubmersible Aquascope parks at the town dock to take passengers on excursions to nearby reefs. Grande Anse des Salines at the tip of the island is a mile-long crescent of sugar-white sand shaded by coconut palms that bow to the sea. The beach is trimmed with almond and white pear trees and huge *raisinier bord la mer*, or seagrape, with large dark green leaves and bent, knotted trunks.

There is an abundance of manchineel trees, *mancenillier* in French, which grow up to 40 ft/12 m. Be sure not to eat its small, green fruit; the sap is poisonous and was used by the Caribs to coat their arrowheads. Rainwater can wash sap from the leaves and bark and cause severe blisters. At Salines and elsewhere around the island the trees are marked with bands of red paint as a warning. Growing in the same area is the seaside olive, with small, oily leaves and inedible fruit whose extract provides an antidote for manchineel blisters.

A dirt road at the eastern end of Grande Anse des Salines passes a camping area and skirts the south end of Etang de Saline (Salt Pond), which is a dry lake most of the year. An extremely arid region to the southeast has very little vegetation and is known as Savane des Pétrifications. Here, within living memory, was the remnant of a petrified forest, but souvenir

Bordered by coconut palms and almond and pear trees, Grande Anse des Salines is regarded as the best of many fine beaches along the southern coast.

hunters and others have picked the site clean. A series of PNRM trails follows the east coast from the Savane to Le François. They are designed in two-hour segments and provide access to seldom-visited coves and beaches. The region is dry and hot; carry water and wear protective head covering.

LE VAUCLIN

Le Vauclin, known as the capital of the South, is an old fishing port dating from pre-Columbian times. It has a beach and facilities for water sports. West of the town is Mt. Vauclin (1,654 ft/504 m), an extinct volcano and the highest point in the south. A trail to the summit takes one and a half hours.

Farther north, Le François, another fishing village, is one of the prettiest spots on the east coast, with water so shallow and calm it is like a wading pool. Ste.-Anne, one of the islets, is a bird refugee for sooty terns, known locally as *touaous*, roseate terns, and other seabirds that can be seen flying about in great numbers. Boat excursions from Le François to the islets are available. Between François Bay and Havre de Robert is a 3-mi/5-km stretch of coastal parkland dominated by Morne Courbaril (611 ft/185 m) on which there are tracks and footpaths but no marked trails. The town of Le Robert on the north side of the bay is connected to Fort-de-France by an expressway (a twenty-minute drive).

CARAVELLE PENINSULA AND NATURE RESERVE

Jutting into the Atlantic directly east of Fort-de-France at La Trinité is Presqu'île de la Caravelle, a peninsula with a nature reserve of 1,277 acres/ 517 hectares on the eastern half. A road of about 5 mi/8 km crosses the peninsula to the ruins of Château Dubuc, a seventeenth-century plantation house, from which point a well marked trail winds down to Trésor Bay. It passes through diverse coastal scenery from dry evergreen forests to mangroves fringing the bay, the most accessible mangroves on Martinique. At the edge of the dense tropical thickets are the huge buttress roots of red mangrove forming new land as they "walk" into the sea. One is likely to see *cé ma faute*, the local name, meaning "it's my fault," for a kind of fiddler crab that has a single giant pincer. The birdlife is rich with common moorhens, yellow-crowned night-herons, green-backed herons, and great blue herons. In the area of the white mangrove, there are land crabs and a variety of birds including mangrove cuckoos, yellow warblers, and the endemic Martinique oriole, known locally as *carouge*. From July to December, one can spot ruddy turnstones, semipalmated plovers, *grives des savanes*, or tropical mockingbirds, and greater and lesser yellowlegs.

The trail continues along small bays overlooking rocky shores and the Islet du Trésor, and leads on to the easternmost point of the peninsula marked by a nineteenth-century lighthouse. From here there are sweeping views. Frigatebirds, sooty terns, and brown noddies can be seen along the coast. The trail returns to the Château through dry forests of local white pear, gommier rouge, silk-cotton, and small shrubs. The easy trail is a pleasant three-hour hike over a wide variety of terrain and vegetation. On the peninsula's north coast are Raisiniers and Tartane, beach enclaves with safe swimming, snorkeling, and water-sports facilities.

OUTDOOR ACTIVITIES

HIKING: The Regional Natural Park of Martinique (PNRM) and the National Forestry Office (ONF), with Le Club des Randonneurs (Hiking Club), have laid out thirty-three marked trails and prepared a detailed guidebook in French available from the government tourist office in Fort-de-France. The trails, except those for which guides are recommended, are designed to enable hikers to go on their own without danger so long as they stay on the trail. Hikers may phone the PNRM (tel: 73-19-30) in advance to ask about trail conditions. PNRM trains guides who complete a year of specialized courses and serve five years as apprentices. Inexpensive Sunday hiking excursions with PNRM guides to various areas of the island are organized year-round on a published agenda. Their primary purpose is to acquaint local people with the natural environment, but visitors are welcome; commentary is in French. PNRM will organize group trips and seminars for botanists upon several weeks' advance notice.

CAMPING: Camping is permitted almost everywhere, including the mountains, forests, and many beaches, but one should check with the local mayor's office (Hôtel de Ville) or property owner before setting up camp. Campsites are very basic. Camps with cold showers and toilets are found in the south at Macabou, Ste.-Luce, Le Marin, Ste.-Anne, and Anse à l'Ane. Tents and fully equipped camping cars for five persons are available for rent in Fort-de-France and Anse Mitan. Inquire at the tourist office.

HORSEBACK RIDING: Martinique has three riding stables offering cross-country riding and excursions: Black Horse at La Pagerie–Trois-Ilets (tel: 66-03-46); La Cavale (tel: 76-22-94) in the Diamond Rock area; and Ranch Jack at Anses d'Arlets–Galocha (tel: 68-63-97).

SWIMMING: The beaches south of Fort-de-France are white sand while those of the north are mostly gray and black sand. The nicest beaches are found on the south Caribbean coast with the mile-long crescent at Grand Anse des Salines, near Ste.-Anne, the standout. Swimming on the Atlantic coast is generally not recommended except at coves protected by coral reef or along peninsulas such as Cap Ferré and Caravelle Nature Reserve. Public beaches do not have changing cabins or showers; hotels normally charge nonguests for use of facilities. There are no nudist beaches but large hotels generally permit topless bathing.

SNORKELING AND DIVING: Martinique is all but surrounded by reefs, but there are rough seas and tricky waters: seek advice of local specialists. There are walls and caves, and reefs with a splendid assortment of colorful sponges, corals, and sea fans and a great variety of marine life from brightly colored angelfishes and parrotfishes to barracudas.

The main dive locations in the south are Diamond Rock for more advanced divers and Anses d'Arlets, suitable for novices. The latter is super for snorkeling too. On the west coast north of Fort-de-France, Cap Enragé, immediately north of Case-Pilote, is popular for walls and caves that are home to lobster and large schools of soldierfishes and triggerfishes. The most interesting dive is the harbor of St.-Pierre on the northwest coast where twelve ships sunk in the 1902 eruption of Mt. Pelée lie in a grave-memorial. Le Perle Island north of Le Prêcheur, a site for experienced divers, has moray eels, lobster, groupers, snappers, and other fishes.

Dive operators are located in the main tourist centers and serve the hotels of a particular area. In the Pointe du Bout area, the operators have American and French licensed instructors and provide instruction for beginners, starting in hotel pools; diving trips usually go to areas off Anses d'Arlets and Ilet à Ramiers, both areas that are rich in fish and coral. Marinas have glass-bottom boats, and two Aquascopes (semisubmersibles) leave from the Pointe du Bout Marina and Ste.-Anne on forty-five-minute tours.

DEEP-SEA FISHING: Most hotels can make arrangements for deep-sea fishing, when given a day or two advance notice. The most popular catches are tuna, barracuda, dolphin, and kingfish. Cap Macré, Cap Ferré, and Cap Chevalier on the southeast are the best spots for surf casting.

SAILING: Martinique, with its irregular coastline and many coves, is a sailor's paradise. Boats with all amenities are available for day picnic sails or excursions of a week or longer. Fort-de-France is one of the safest and most beautiful bays in the Caribbean and a popular departure point for yacht charters sailing to St. Vincent and the Grenadines. Members of yacht clubs (with membership cards) may use the facilities of the local yacht clubs: Club de la Voile, Pointe Simon (tel: 70-26-63), and Yacht Club de la Martinique, Blvd. Chevalier, Ste.-Marthe (tel: 70-26-63). The keelless yawl with a square sail, a local fishing vessel, has recently become popular for competition.

WINDSURFING: All beachfront hotels have windsurfing equipment and many offer lessons. Beginners are likely to start in the calm coves of the Caribbean southwest coast; more-advanced windsurfers will find Diamond Bay challenging.

EXPLORING THE ISLAND

Martinique has some of the best roads in the Caribbean, including two expressways connecting the capital with the southern and eastern districts. All areas except the most northerly and southerly tips are served by good roads, but since they follow the contour of the hilly and mountainous land, the roads are winding. Essentially, the road system fans out from the capital and intersects with cross-island highways.

Martinique has a series of seven "Circuits Touristiques" developed by the tourist office for self-drive tours of the island. All depart from Fort-de-France and vary in driving time from a half-day to a full day. They use one road on the outbound and a different one for the return, and cover the north in three circuits, the central in one, and the south in three. Each is named and marked in a different color on a tourist map, "Information and Guided Tours" (widely available in Fort-de-France), to correspond with color-coded road signs en route.

Car rentals are available at the airport, in town, and at major hotels. Drivers need a valid license to rent a car for up to twenty days. Bicycles and motorbikes can be rented in Fort-de-France. Driving is on the RIGHT.

Taxis are plentiful but tend to be expensive; a surcharge of 40 percent is added between 8 P.M. and 6 A.M. Taxi stands are found at the airport, in downtown Fort-de-France, and at major hotels. Less costly are collective taxis, eight-seat limousines bearing the sign TC, widely used by the local population as well as by tourists. They depart frequently from early morning to 8 P.M. from the main terminal at Pointe Simon on the Fort-de-France waterfront to outlying areas, discharging passengers en route. Inexpensive public buses serve all parts of the island but they are less likely to be used by tourists.

Fort-de-France is linked with the southwest-peninsula tourist centers by frequent daily ferry service to Pointe du Bout from early morning until after midnight, and to Anse Mitan and Anse à l'Ane from early morning until late afternoon. Sightseeing tours by car, motorcoach, and helicopter are available through hotels and local agencies.

INFORMATION: In the U.S.: Martinique Development and Promotion Bureau, 610 Fifth Ave., Suite 516, New York, NY 10020; 212-757-1125. In Canada: Office de Tourisme de la Martinique, 1981 Avenue McGill College, Suite 490, Montreal H3A 2W9; 514-844-8566. In the U.K.: 178 Piccadilly, London W1V OAL; 71-491-7622. In Martinique: B.P. 520, Blvd. Alfassa (Bord de Mer), 97206 Fort-de-France; 596-63-79-60. Parc Naturel Régional de la Martinique, Caserne Bouille, Rue Redoute du Matouba, F-97200 Fort-de-France; 596-73-19-30 or 596-64-42-59.

ST. LUCIA

St. Lucia's scenery is so grand that it belies the island's small size. Almost every turn in the road reveals spectacular verdant landscapes alive with birds and colored by flamboyant and frangipani and trees laden with exotic fruit. It counts among its wonders a drive-in volcano gurgling with hot sulphur springs, the world's rarest snake, a highly endangered parrot, and the ultimate postcard image of the tropics—the magnificent Pitons, twin volcanic peaks that rise dramatically at the water's edge.

The second largest of the Windward Islands, St. Lucia is 27 mi/43 km in length. Like her neighbors in the Lesser Antilles, St. Lucia consists mostly of volcanic rock with contours that reflect the island's age. The northern part is the oldest region geologically and reaches a height of about 1,640 ft/ 500 m. The terrain climbs to a younger, central mountain range where peaks exceed 3,000 ft/914 m and where continuing volcanic activity is evident. On the south side of the central mountains, the heights give way to rolling hills and a coastal plain built up from soil deposited by mountain rivers and streams as they flow toward the sea. Along the central and southwest coasts tiny coves hide between dramatic mountain peaks that drop precipitously to the sea; on the north and south coasts, rocky fingers of land jut into the water, sheltering long stretches of white sand beach.

Long before Europeans arrived, St. Lucia was inhabited first by the Arawaks, then later by the Caribs. Which of the early explorers—Columbus or Juan de la Cosa, Columbus's navigator—discovered the island and the exact date are matters of dispute. But sixty-seven English settlers arrived here in 1605; they were on their way to Guyana and had been blown off course. Within a few weeks the Caribs had massacred most of them, but they allowed the nineteen survivors to leave the island in a canoe. Over the next two centuries England and France battled over possession of St. Lucia; England finally secured its domination in 1815. The result has been a blend of English, French, and African cultures. English is the official language but the patois is a French Creole sprinkled with English; the island's festivals and cuisine also reflect a mingling of cultures. In 1979, St. Lucia became an independent member of the British Commonwealth.

CASTRIES

Castries, a busy port since the nineteenth century and the country's capital, is situated on the northwest coast along a deep natural harbor sheltered by an amphitheater of green hills. One reason Britain and France

In a remnant of a volcanic crater known as "the drive-in volcano," mineral residues discolor rock and hot sulphur pools belch clouds of steam into the air.

fought so hard for its possession was the port's strategic value. Most of the town postdates 1948, when fire destroyed many of its historic buildings and old wooden houses. At its heart is Columbus Square, a plaza shaded by the spreading arms of a huge saman tree, particularly pretty in April when it is pink with blossoms.

A hill on the southeast side of town, Morne Fortune, or "hill of good fortune," earns its name for all who visit there in the late afternoon to watch one of St. Lucia's spectacular sunsets. The panorama stretches from Pigeon Island on the north to the Pitons on the south. Fort Charlotte, which crowns the Morne's summit at 853 ft/260 m, was built in 1794. Many of the original fortifications of this strategic hill are still in place, having been restored by the St. Lucia National Trust; a museum is being established.

MARIGOT BAY

South of Castries along the lower reaches of the Cul-de-Sac Valley, the main west-coast road twists through seemingly endless banana plantations and bumps along to Marigot, where a very steep feeder road winds down to Marigot Bay, one of the most beautiful and romantic settings in the Caribbean. The teardrop-shaped lagoon, almost completely encircled by steep, densely forested hills, is a natural harbor that made a superb hideaway for ships in the old days of pirates and colonial wars. Today the bay is the location of a resort, well hidden in the foliage, and a popular anchorage for yachts from around the world. The scene at sunset is breathtaking. Marigot Bay is private land but encompasses a protected area with mangroves which are readily accessible by boat from the marina.

After passing the Roseau River the main road follows a tortuous route through hills and across riverbeds near the fishing villages of Anse La Raye and Canaries and skirts deserted beaches framed by high rocky cliffs, usually accessible only by boat. The most impressive part of the drive begins when the road turns inland along the lush and picturesque Duval Ravine toward the mountains at the southern edge of the Central Forest Reserve, along an area more commonly called the St. Lucia Rain Forest.

SOUFRIÈRE

The final leg of the road snakes through the hills to the last ridge before Soufrière, where travelers come upon a stunning view of the Pitons—a rich reward for enduring the bumpy road. In addition to the Pitons, the picturesque little port of Soufrière is the gateway to many of St. Lucia's natural wonders. Although it is the oldest settlement on St. Lucia, Soufrière was never the island's capital. It flourished under the French in the late eighteenth century when it was a major center of trade for the produce of as many as one hundred sugar and coffee plantations. A major restoration of the historic town is under way. Saturday is the town's market day; be sure to go early to get the full flavor of life in a small West Indian village.

On the east side of Soufrière, the Soufrière Estate, a coconut and banana plantation that has been in the same family since 1713, offers a tour demonstrating coconut production from planting to processing and a small zoo of indigenous animals including agoutis, opossums (known here as manicous), and iguanas. Small zoos such as this, established with the help of the Forestry Department, are more than mere tourist attractions; their programs of local education also promote wildlife conservation.

THE PITONS

These ancient volcanic spikes—Petit Piton, 2,438 ft/743 m, the more northerly of the two, and Gros Piton, 2,619 ft/798 m—are among the most remarkable natural features in the Caribbean. The Pitons are strikingly beautiful from several viewpoints, whether one approaches them from the north or south. And no place offers a better vantage point than Dasheene, a hotel south of Soufrière perched on a cliff almost directly behind the Pitons. The hotel, closed for several years, is rumored to be reopening soon. It is worth inquiring; on rare occasions the watchman has permitted visitors to enter the grounds to admire the panorama.

The Pitons bracket a steep, thickly forested hillside that drops to a beautiful deep-water bay, Anse des Pitons, with a small palm-fringed beach at its north end, directly south of Petit Piton. A footpath from the tiny village of Plaisance about 1 mi/1.6 km south of Soufrière leads to the beach at Jalousie, but the best way to reach the bay is by boat from Soufrière or Castries. Sailing into the bay and up to the base of the Pitons towering a half-mile overhead is one of the great travel experiences of a lifetime. At sunset, the setting is particularly dramatic as the reflected light gives the peaks an almost ethereal quality.

The geological formation of the Pitons is obscure. According to one theory, they are the remains of a volcanic crater ridge, most of which has fallen into the sea; another holds that they are extruded volcanic plugs. The Pitons are exceedingly steep and unstable, with frequent landslides, and their vegetation must survive in very shallow soil. Species change with increasing elevation: xerophytic vegetation and seasonal deciduous forests at the lower elevations, seasonal montane forest higher up, and elfin wood-

Pages 358 and 359: Just south of Soufrière, the twin volcanic Pitons tower above the Caribbean and extend deep underwater.

land on the peaks. The lowland is dominated by coconut palms remaining from abandoned cocoa estates. In the seasonal deciduous forest are Spanish ash, with a purple-mauve flower that blooms in late spring; birch gum, or gommier rouge, distinguished by a shiny reddish brown bark that peels off in thin layers; and white wood, with pinkish white flowers that bloom in early spring. Both Pitons have trails, but climbing should be limited to times of dry weather. For the time being, Petit Piton is closed; rockfalls have been frequent since a fire in 1987 damaged much of its vegetation. The ascent of Gros Piton takes about three hours; it is difficult and challenging, since the sides of the peak are almost perpendicular. Climbers do not need ropes, but they do need experience and must have a guide, because it is easy to become disoriented and lost.

The Pitons, which reach as far below sea level as they do above, provide a thrilling setting for divers. Along their walls grow many species of sponges, particularly huge barrel sponges. There are underwater caves and myriad fish, and the currents along their faces make for good drift diving.

THE DRIVE-IN VOLCANO AND SULPHUR SPRINGS

On the southeast side of Soufrière is a natural wonder which St. Lucians call the world's only drive-in volcano. That's a bit of hyperbole, but a road does, indeed, lead into the remnant of a volcanic crater—a moonscape of barren earth and gravel where pools of muddy water bubble and belch out clouds of steam that shoot 50 ft/15 m into the air. Evidence of five minerals—iron, copper, sulphur, magnesium, and zinc—can be seen from the streaks of bright orange, green, yellow, purple, and brown deposited by the water on the grayish earth. The smell of sulphur is present but not offensive; one is advised to avoid wearing silver jewelry as the sulphur fumes may discolor it.

A tour guide from the Government Tourist Office kiosk at the entrance, must accompany visitors to the active area. There is a small admission fee. Here, one can watch—and touch—the hot mud and steaming water. The springs are not beautiful, but they are fascinating. Other Caribbean islands have sulphuric fields in crater remnants but none is as accessible. A method of harnessing the geothermal energy of the volcanic gases to produce electricity has been under development for several years.

DIAMOND FALLS AND MINERAL BATHS

Diamond Falls starts as clean, fresh water that runs into the sulphur springs. The water then becomes heated to about 180°F/82°C and saturated with minerals before it cascades from the center of the volcano about 1,800 ft/550 m down the mountainside in six falls of varying height. It is possible to hike along the course of the water after it leaves the volcanic highland, but the most accessible and one of the prettiest cascades is the lowest one, Lower Diamond Falls, less than 1 mi/1.6 km east of Soufrière.

From the entrance under an umbrella of palms and gigantic tree ferns a narrow walkway bordered by red ginger, heliconias, and other tropical flowers leads to the Diamond Falls and Mineral Baths. At the head of the gardens one sees the falls tumbling down a hill through mineral-streaked rock walls and jungle-thick ferns into a stream that flows through underground pipes to a series of baths of different temperatures. The baths were built in 1784 by Louis XVI for his soldiers after analysis of the waters found their curative properties to be similar to those of Aix-les-Bains in France. They were almost totally destroyed at the time of the French Revolution, and only in recent times have they been made to function again. A part of the original eighteenth-century baths is now in use. There is a small fee for visiting the falls and gardens, and another for the baths.

Anse Chastanet and Anse Mamin

Some of St. Lucia's best reefs are concentrated within a few miles of the leeward coast between the Pitons and Anse Chastanet Beach north of Soufrière, with at least twenty dive sites in calm, protected waters near the shore. At Anse Chastanet snorkelers can swim directly from the beach to the reef only 60 ft/18 m away in water about 20 ft/6 m deep. Divers can enjoy a sloping wall that drops more than 150 ft/46 m. The Anse Chastanet Hotel has a dive shop and an instruction program. The facilities are open to nonguests for a fee.

A ten-minute walk north by the sea leads to a pretty beach and the old French colonial plantation of Anse Mamin, part of the Anse Chastanet resort and interesting for its tropical flowering and fruit trees. Anse Mamin was one of the earliest estates on St. Lucia; its colorful history is recounted by the property manager, who also acts as a guide.

St. Lucia Rain Forest

About 13 percent of the woodlands that cover St. Lucia is rain forest protected in a nature reserve of 19,044 acres/7,707 hectares in the interior highlands. To the south of this area, in the region of the Edmund Forest Reserve and the Quilesse Forest Reserve, the Forestry Department has established a Rain Forest Walk, about 7 mi/11 km in length, between the villages of Mahaut in the east and Fond St. Jacques in the west. On the west side of the trail, the Pitons are in view as is Mt. Gimie, 3,117 ft/950 m, a peak of another ridge on the north and the highest point on the island.

The walk traverses the main north–south ridge from which water runoff forms four of the island's major rivers—Canelles, Roseau, Vieux Fort, and Troumasseé. The rain forest gets 100 to 150 in/250 to 380 cm of rain per year (as compared with the northern part of St. Lucia, which averages 40 to 50 in/100 to 127 cm). Showers are frequent and from time to time clouds or heavy mists roll in. When the air is clear, hikers can enjoy superb panoramic views across the mountains from various lookouts. The walk takes in plantation as well as rain-forest land (even the high mountains of St. Lucia have been lumbered and cultivated since colonial days). Hikers are likely to encounter local farmers carrying sacks of the produce they grow deep in the valley and on the mountainsides. The drive up to and along the ridge affords a panoramic view of the mountains and valleys, passing villages and country roads bordered with pretty wild ginger, called wild orchid or *jejam doule* locally, which grows profusely and perfumes the air. Along the trail one sees ferns, bromeliads, wild orchids, and anthuriums. At times the tree canopy is so dense that little grows below except large leafy philodendrons and epiphytes, or air plants, that anchor on the tree trunks.

Birdlife is abundant and includes three hummingbird species. The Antillean crested, known locally as *fou-fou*, has a brilliant metallic-green crest; the smallest of the three species, it is common in the Edmund and Quilesse forests. The purple-throated carib, the largest, is a dark bird with a purplish red throat and blue-green wings and tail. It and the slightly smaller green-throated carib are found at lower elevations of the forest and in the banana fields.

For many people the bird of greatest interest is the rare and highly endangered St. Lucia parrot which makes its home in the rain forest high at the tops of the gommier trees. Known locally as *jacquot*, only about 250 parrots are alive today, compared to an estimated million at the time of Columbus. St. Lucia has had an intensive conservation program under way since 1979 to save the parrot, its national bird, from extinction. As a result, there has been a 100 percent increase in the bird's numbers in ten years. Once hunted for their meat, the parrots' most serious threats today are poaching for the lucrative international pet market and loss of habitat due to destruction of the forest. Parrots mate for life, and the female lays just two eggs a year; reproduction in captivity has only recently been successful. Parrots are most active in the early morning and late afternoon, and usually are seen flying in pairs or small groups between trees that are in fruit or flower. They tend to feed at the edge of the forest, returning to the central areas during the late afternoon.

The flame of the forest tree grows on the Pitons, which also support seasonal deciduous forests, seasonal montane forests, and elfin woodland.

St. Lucia has about 119 species of resident and migrant birds, of which four are endemic. In addition to the parrot, the endemics are Semper's warbler, which may be extinct as it has not been seen since 1970; the St. Lucia black finch, probably the most common bird on the island; and the St. Lucia oriole. The white-breasted thrasher is very rare, being found only in the Grande Anse region of St. Lucia and on Martinique. The trembler and the rare forest thrush are endemic to the eastern Caribbean. No hunting is allowed in St. Lucia, and its wild-bird protection laws cover eighty-seven species, including some migrants.

The St. Lucia Rain Forest Walk can be approached from either the east or west coast; permission must be obtained from the Forestry Department. Hikers must also arrange in advance to be picked up at the far end, since no local transportation is available until one reaches the coast. The hike between the entrance of the Edmund Forest Reserve on the west to the eastern entrance of Quilesse Forest takes about three and a half hours.

If one is based in Castries, it is practical to join a guided hiking expedition, available through the Forestry Department, hotels, and local travel agencies. Hikers are driven by mini-van to Mahaut on the east side of the Quilesse Forest Reserve and walk across the mountains to the village of Fond St. Jacques, or loop through the forest to return to their starting point. Those starting from Soufrière should inquire at the Government Tourist Office in Soufrière or from Anse Chastanet Hotel, which organizes hiking excursions with a local naturalist. To get to the Rain Forest Walk from Soufrière, one drives for about thirty minutes through a lush river valley, where the waters of several streams converge, to Fond St. Jacques. From here, a small country road via Migny climbs up the mountainside to the top of the ridge known as Morne Fond St. Jacques. The road must be taken on foot. As soon as the ascending road reaches the top of the ridge, it meets another badly deteriorated road that runs east along Morne Fond St. Jacques for 2 mi/3.2 km to the entrance of the Edmund Forest Reserve, marked by a sign. The condition of the roads on the western approach adds another hour or more of steep hiking to the excursion, making the eastern approach easier for most people.

VIEUX FORT AND THE MOULE-À-CHIQUE PENINSULA

From Soufrière to Vieux Fort at the southern end of the island the drive passes through the fishing village of Choiseul, the arts-and-crafts center of St. Lucia. By the side of the road one can see a rock with a clearly visible Amerindian petroglyph, often pictured in St. Lucia brochures and publications. After the fishing village of Laborie, the terrain stretching south to the coast is almost flat, in marked contrast to the rest of the island. Two common birds of the grassland here are the black-faced grassquit and yellow grass finch. In recent years Vieux Fort, the main town of the south, has been developed as a tourist resort.

At the south end of town, Moule-à-Chique Peninsula, a promontory over 800 ft/244 m high, reaches out about a mile into the sea where the Atlantic Ocean and the Caribbean Sea meet. A road runs almost to the end of the peninsula but one must walk the last stretch to the lighthouse from where the panoramic view takes in St. Lucia's south shore with the Maria Islands to the east and St. Vincent to the south.

Offshore at Vieux Fort two aircraft were sunk in the 1970s to create an artificial reef, and in 1983 the freighter *Wauwinet* was added to create a marine park, although the plan has yet to be fully implemented. The ship rests in only 50 ft/15 m of water and receives plenty of natural illumination. Large schools of sprats, stingrays, jacks, and tarpon, as well as moray eels and lobsters, can be seen, along with groupers, angelfish, and other fish.

BARRE DE L'ISLE VIEWPOINT AND MT. LA COMBE

From Castries on the west coast to Dennery on the east the road passes over a spine of forested mountains known as the Barre de l'Isle, a ridge in the center of the island. It is the major divide between the eastern and western halves of St. Lucia.

The signposted entrance to a hiking trail is located on the south side of the main highway about midway between the two coasts. The trail, a short loop of 0.25 mi/0.4 km, leads to a picnic hut and viewpoint that presents a pretty panorama of the interior highlands, with the large Cul-de-Sac Valley directly to the west and Mt. Parasol, Grand Bois Forest, and the Caribbean Sea to the southwest. On the northeast, across the Barre de l'Isle Forest Reserve, one can see La Sorcière Mountain and the upper reaches of the Grande Rivière du Mabouya Valley on the east. Several of the plants along the trail are numbered, and a brochure available from the Forestry Department identifies them. Advance arrangements with the Forestry Department are not required. From the viewpoint one could continue to Mt. La Combe, the highest peak of the ridge, but the old trails are overgrown and too difficult to follow. The Forestry Department is planning improvements.

PRASLIN BAY

The region around Dennery, a village on the east coast, is green with huge banana plantations. Many parts of the east coast have dramatic rock formations created by the pounding of the Atlantic Ocean, while other parts of the coast feature deep bays where the waters are placid. One such cove is Praslin Bay south of Dennery. On the beach here one can usually see men making dugout canoes from the gommier tree in the same manner used 500 years ago by the Arawaks and Caribs. The gommier, a rain-forest species, is one of the principal nesting trees of the St. Lucia parrot.

FRIGATE ISLAND

Off the northern tip of Praslin Bay, Frigate Island, as the name implies, is a refuge for the magnificent frigatebird and other birds. The frigatebird, known locally as *sizo* (scissors) for its distinctive forked tail, nests in colonies in low bushes in isolated areas. It can also be seen on other small islands along the coast. The National Trust's plan to make all the tiny islands of St. Lucia's east coast into bird sanctuaries should be in place by 1990.

SAVANNES BAY

Farther south, Savannes Bay is a protected area with the island's best-preserved mangroves along its north and south shores fronted by a coral reef. Four species of the mangrove are found here: fringing the shore is red

The highly endangered St. Lucia parrot lives at the tops of gommier trees in the central rain forest, which teems with other birdlife.

mangrove, or *mangle rouge* (called *mang wouj* in patois); it stabilizes itself on the sandy bottom with prop roots that trap silt, sand, leaves, and flowers which decompose and form new land. The seeds of the red mangrove germinate on the tree; when they are about 6 in/15 cm long, they drop off the parent plant. The heavy seed penetrates the mud and sand when the tide is out and begins to grow. The muddy swamps that form behind the red mangrove catch rainwater runoff from the hills and provide a habitat for the black mangrove (*mang sale* in patois). It can be recognized by its thin shoots sticking up from the mud and by the salt deposits on its leaves. These shoots or roots, called pneumatophores, allow the trees to excrete salt, thus enabling them to survive in a salty environment. Behind the black mangrove is the yellow mangrove, or *mangle blanc* (*mang blan* in patois), and buttonwood (*paltivve*).

In the murky waters around the mangrove, the decomposing leaves from the trees provide food for a variety of crustaceans and other forms of marine life that are a primary link in the food chain. The mangrove could be called a nursery for small fish, which spend their early life hiding among the prop roots before moving out into the more dangerous open sea. The mangrove is also valuable as a protection against coastal erosion.

MARIA ISLANDS NATURE RESERVE

At the edge of the sea on Sables Bay is the Nature Centre of the Maria Islands Nature Reserve, located about 0.5 mi/0.8 km offshore. Created in 1982 and operated by the St. Lucia National Trust and the Eastern Caribbean National Area Management Program, the reserve comprises two small never-inhabited islands. In addition to their birds and plants, they are home to several species of lizards, including a unique species of blue lizard, known as the Maria Islands ground lizard (locally called *zandoli te*), and a small, harmless nocturnal snake, the kouwes or couresse, which is said to be the rarest snake in the world. Found only on Maria Major, it was thought to be extinct until one was identified in 1973. The kouwes is less than 3 ft/0.9 m long and of a dull olive-brown color with some darker markings. Scientists estimate the total population of this very shy species to be no more than one hundred.

The Maria Islands are a bird refuge as well. Among the most numerous birds are the bridled and sooty terns and the brown noddy, which builds its nest on the ground at the base of prickly pear cactus or in nooks in the cliff face. The Caribbean martin, magnificent frigatebird, and red-billed tropicbird are seen here, too.

The waters around the Maria Islands are rich in marine life. Seagrass beds and mangroves occur near the islands, while four small patch reefs with elkhorn, star, and starlet corals are within the reserve. The most accessible snorkeling in calm water is on the southwest side of Maria Major.

Despite their small size and harsh climate of constant wind, salt spray, and less than 40 in/100 cm of annual rainfall, the Maria Islands have about 120 different types of trees and plants that grow in two distinct areas. A miniature forest of larger trees found on the protected leeward side of Maria Major is made up mostly of white cedar and birch gum, or turpentine tree, known locally as gommier.

A visit to the islands must be arranged with the National Trust office in Castries. The Centre can be visited in the morning hours daily except Tuesday by prior arrangement with the National Trust office. To reach the islands a small boat can be hired on the beach near the Centre.

UNION NATURE TRAIL

The stretch of coast north of Castries has some of St. Lucia's best beaches and several of its main resort areas. Immediately beyond the Halcyon Beach Hotel on Choc Beach, a road leads east into the mountains to Balata and Babonneau, giving access to the forested regions of the north-central highlands. These mountains are not as high or as wet as those in the rain forest. The Babonneau road gives access to a new (1987), easy-to-walk trail through a dry woodland forest, good for schoolchildren and visitors who want to acquaint themselves with some of St. Lucia's natural attractions. The nature center has a small zoo of animals such as the agouti, iguana, and boa constrictor, as well as a medicinal garden featuring herbal remedies used in the Caribbean. The small entrance fee is used for trail maintenance and local environmental education.

The Union Nature Trail, which takes about forty-five minutes to complete, is marked and labeled for self-guidance; it can also be taken with a guide. There is an excellent brochure that identifies the species found along the trail. Among them are white cedar, or *poye*; Caribbean pine, used extensively for cabinetmaking and boatbuilding; sandbox, with its prickly skin; gliricidia, which is used to make fence posts; logwood; cashew; silk-cotton, or kapok; cinnamon; saman; and calabash, St. Lucia's national tree. Blue mahoe and mahogany are introduced species that the Forestry Department uses for plantations.

The woodlands attract a variety of birds common to the island such as the green-throated carib hummingbird, mangrove cuckoo, pearly-eyed and scaly-breasted thrashers, black-whiskered vireo, Adelaide's warbler, yellow warbler, tropical mockingbird, gray kingbird, and Lesser Antillean bullfinch. A longer hike on a steep trail of about two hours' duration leads up the mountainside to a secondary woodland with a variety of trees that are associated with the drier parts of the island.

Piton Flore

Determined hikers might consider Piton Flore (1,871 ft/570 m), a peak with true rain forest located at the extreme northern end of the Barre de l'Isle, from where there are splendid views of the entire chain of mountains and the Caribbean and Atlantic. It is the last recorded site of the endemic Semper's warbler. The peak is situated almost midway between Castries and Dennery as the crow flies; however, it cannot be approached from the cross-island highway. Rather, access is obtained on secondary roads from the west coast via Forestière. Prior to the hurricane of 1980, the Forestry Department organized half-day tours to Piton Flore, but the storm damaged the trail and it was never officially reopened, although people do walk it.

To find the trail, hikers proceed through the village of Forestière to the end of the road. From the Forestry Department house on the left, they should walk up through Forestry plantations from where they will have fine views of the Cul-de-Sac Valley. After about 0.75 mi/1.2 km they will come to a concrete blockhouse, where they must turn right onto a small path. Follow the right-hand path to the top of the ridge and proceed carefully. The route is muddy and very steep; some of the old steps have rotted. A guide is not necessary, but hikers should obtain permission from the Forestry Department, which will supply a naturalist guide if required. The opening of a trail from the north side is under study.

Pigeon Island National Park

Inhabited since the time of the Arawaks, Pigeon Island on the northwest coast was a pirates' lair in the early days of exploration, a strategic fort of the British in the eighteenth century, a quarantine station, a whaling station, and a U.S. naval station. Today, it is a park. In 1971, as part of a plan for resort development of the north end of St. Lucia, Pigeon Island was connected to the mainland by a causeway that closed the north end of Rodney Bay and created a long sandy beach. The closing of the sea between the island and the mainland was not without environmental cost, however. The redirected coastal currents eroded beaches and killed the lobster fisheries of a nearby village.

Pigeon Island National Park has caves in its southwest corner and several trails leading to the promontory at the western tip where there are ruins of the eighteenth-century Fort Rodney. From here there is a wonderful panoramic view of Rodney Bay and St. Lucia's north coast. The island, cleared of its natural growth centuries ago, has been replanted in a garden setting with a variety of trees including palms, frangipani, oleander, bougainvillea, and other tropical trees and shrubs typical of St. Lucia.

GRANDE ANSE

Almost all of the northeast coast—the least accessible part of St. Lucia—has rockbound shores interspersed with sandy coves; the terrain is arid and unwelcoming. A winding secondary road across the island connects the capital with the town of Desbarra. The road after Babonneau is a bit bumpy, but it can be driven by car, although a four-wheel-drive vehicle is preferable; from Desbarra to Grande Anse, four-wheel-drive is essential. The remote area of Grande Anse is home to several rare bird species including the white-breasted thrasher. It is also one of the areas where the fer-de-lance, the only poisonous snake on the island, is common. One should exercise great caution in the Grande Anse area; the fer-de-lance is found in dry scrub and under piles of coconut husks.

Several beaches on the northeast coast—Anse Louvet, Grande Anse, Petite Anse—are nesting grounds for four sea turtle species: leatherback, loggerhead, hawksbill, and green. The nesting season runs from February to October, which is also a closed season for hunting. St. Lucian laws prohibit the hunting of any sea turtles within 1,500 ft/457 m of the shore as well as the harvesting of turtle eggs at any time of the year. The Grande Anse region has been proposed as a nature reserve.

OUTDOOR ACTIVITIES

HIKING: The most popular area for hiking is the central mountains. All government forest reserves have restricted access; permission to enter for recreation must be obtained from the Forestry Department, a measure designed to prevent illegal felling of trees, hunting, and disturbance of wildlife habitat—by locals as well as by tourists.

A topographical map is essential; "trails" marked on maps may prove to be overgrown and inaccessible; often, they cross private land. Individual guides for hiking can be obtained through the National Trust, Forestry Department, or Government Tourist Office. Be sure to settle the price, scope of service, and drop-off and pick-up points in advance. The Forestry Department and travel companies approved by it also organize trips to the rain forest several times

weekly during the winter season. Participants should be in fit condition and wear proper walking shoes or light tropical boots. Tours usually include lunch, and part of the tour fee goes toward a fund for conserving the forest. In the rain forest, keep cameras in waterproof cases.

HORSEBACK RIDING: St. Lucia can be explored on horseback on trips organized by Trim's Riding Stable (tel. 450-8273) at Cap Estate at the northern end of the island. Trim's offers picnic rides along the Atlantic coast and trail rides overlooking the Caribbean. There are six trails, ranging from 2 mi/3.2 km to 7 mi/11 km, taking one and a half hours to four hours to cover.

SWIMMING: St. Lucia has more than 120 beaches but many can be reached

In dry weather, experienced climbers can ascend the almost perpendicular trails of Gros Piton, the southerly and slightly taller of the two volcanic peaks.

only by boat. The most accessible beaches are on the calm west coast north of Castries and on the south coast east of Vieux Fort. Some of the prettiest, most secluded beaches are in coves south of the capital, a half-hour away by boat. Boat trips for swimming and snorkeling along the coast are readily available from Castries and major resort centers. One should inquire locally before swimming in east-coast waters and avoid places where there are strong waves and dangerous currents.

SNORKELING AND DIVING: St. Lucia offers uncrowded diving along 24 mi/ 38 km of reef, accessible from land or by boat, with visibility up to 100 ft/30 m. The quality and variety of sites on both the Atlantic and Caribbean coasts are excellent, but the rough Atlantic attracts far fewer divers. Much of the coastline has yet to be explored. The west coast can be described as a wall with patch reefs—coral gardens sprinkled on the sandy ocean floor in fairly shallow water near the shore. The reefs have an abundance of colorful squirrelfishes, fairy basslet, French grunts, assorted butterflyfishes, damselfishes, and gobies, as well as others from the open sea. The proximity of the shallow-water reefs to shore makes St. Lucia a good place for snorkelers as well as novice divers.

In addition to the special experience of the Pitons, experienced divers can explore deeper reefs, caves, walls, and canyons that are home to groupers, wrasses, and barracudas. Large coral arches and basket sponges are outstanding features. There are also numerous wrecks; those off the coast at Vieux Fort have been made into an artificial reef but this is a difficult dive, for experienced divers only. Due to strong currents in the channel, dive operators are sometimes reluctant to take divers there.

Dive operators rent custom dive boats and underwater camera equipment; instruction is available. Anse Chastanet Hotel and Marigot Bay Resort have comprehensive diving packages.

FISHING: Half-day and full-day charters are available and are best arranged through one's hotel and the marinas at Rodney Bay and Castries. There are two main fishing seasons: January to June, the best time for open-sea species such as tuna, kingfish, and dolphin (the fish, not the mammal); and July to December, when the catch is better closer to shore. Fishing is a tradition, providing St. Lucians with a major source of food. Lines and pots are used to catch snappers, lobsters, and numerous types of reef fishes. The making of the fish pot, with its specific type of woven design, is a technique inherited from the Caribs.

SAILING: Soufrière Bay, with the Pitons towering over it, is understandably a favorite rendezvous for yachtsmen and day-trippers from Castries. Marigot Bay is the Eastern Caribbean home of The Moorings (tel. 809-45-34357), one of the region's major boat charterers with yachts for four or six passengers available bareboat or with crew. It also offers day-sails with lunch and drinks. Similar sailing trips are available from the marina at Rodney Bay, home of Stevens Yachts, one of the Caribbean's oldest charterers.

Aspiring sailors and true salts like to be in St. Lucia in late May or early June for Aqua Action, which is something of a Soap Box Derby of the sea with some marathoning and lots of partying. On the serious side, the St. Lucia Yacht Club oversees the three-day annual Southern Caribbean Match Racing Championship, an international competition involving several islands.

WINDSURFING: Anse de Sables, the bay on the southeastern tip of the island between Moule-à-Chique and the Maria Islands, is the best place in St. Lucia for windsurfing. The entire south coast, on both its Atlantic and Caribbean sides, has ideal conditions for competition. The Atlantic side presents the challenge of strong tradewinds and choppy waves for experts, while the Caribbean offers gentle winds for easy cruising.

EXPLORING THE ISLAND

St. Lucia is a densely populated and intensively cultivated island with some of the best and worst roads in the Caribbean. One could easily stay on the good ones for a tour of the island, but to see the best scenery and to visit rain forests, it will be necessary to negotiate the bad roads too.

Cars are available for rent, but visitors might enjoy their sightseeing more if they do not drive themselves over the winding roads, considering their state of disrepair. Taxi drivers can act as guides, but be sure to agree on the length of the tour and the price in advance. Well organized tours for small groups to the main attractions are available through tour companies and hotels. For visitors who prefer to drive themselves, a temporary driving license is required, which is usually arranged through the car rental company. Driving is on the LEFT.

The road network on St. Lucia divides conveniently into south and north circuits. No road circles the island completely, but the main highway that loops around the southern half of the island provides access to the important natural attractions. The eastern portion is St. Lucia's best highway, and crosses the center of the island from Castries to Dennery and turns south to the international airport.

The construction of a new road from Castries south along the west coast to Soufrière was begun in 1988, but it will take several years to complete. Meanwhile, the route is a bone-shaking ride of about ninety minutes, but it offers some of the most spectacular scenery in the Caribbean and is worth every bump—if the road is open. It is frequently closed after heavy rains due to landslides and flooding.

An acceptable compromise is to use the west-coast road southbound from Castries to Soufrière and the east-coast road for the return trip. Alternatively, a forty-five-minute motorboat trip from Castries to Soufrière also provides a wonderful view of the coast. The coastal road from Soufrière south to Vieux Fort is good and takes about forty-five minutes.

INFORMATION: In the U.S.: St. Lucia Tourist Board, 820 Second Ave., Suite 900 E, New York, NY 10017; 212-867-2950. In Canada: 4975 Dundas St. West, Suite 457, Etobicoke D Islington, Ontario M9A 4X4; 416-236-0936. In the U.K.: 421A Finchley Rd., London NW3 6HJ; 71-431-4045. In St. Lucia: P.O. Box 221, Castries; 809-45-24094. Government Tourist Office, Ministry of Trade, Industry and Tourism, Government Bldg., Castries, St. Lucia, WI; 809-45-21706.

St. Lucia National Trust, P.O. Box 525, Castries, St. Lucia, WI (809-45-21654 and 809-45-25005), publishes studies and pamphlets on the island's nature and wildlife. Publications of the St. Lucia Naturalists' Society, c/o St. Lucia National Trust (or tel: 47254), include a St. Lucia bird list compiled by Robert J. Devaux (1978), *A–Z of St. Lucia's Protected Wildlife* (1981), and field guides on St. Lucia's butterflies and other species. The Society holds monthly meetings on the first Wednesday of each month at 6:00 P.M. in the Castries Public Library. It also conducts regularly scheduled field trips to La Soufrière volcano, St. Lucia Rain Forest, Grande Anse, and other locations. Inquire at the National Trust office. Interested parties might also assist the Naturalists' Society in nighttime turtle watches during the nesting season.

Forestry Dept., Ministry of Agriculture, Lands and Fisheries (809-45-23231), supplies qualified naturalist guides for the Union and Rain Forest trails.

ST. VINCENT AND THE GRENADINES

GRENADA

BARBADOS

but the rebellion was harshly suppressed by the British, who sent hundreds of the Caribs into exile on Roatan, an island off the coast of Honduras. St. Vincent and the Grenadines became independent in 1979.

Kingstown, the capital, is situated on St. Vincent's only deep-water harbor and is a historic town dating from the late eighteenth century. A sightseeing circuit from the docks, to the market (a colorful scene on Saturday mornings), to a complex of shops, restaurants, and an inn housed in a renovated warehouse, to the nineteenth-century churches on the north side of the town, is an easy hour's walk. The best view of Kingstown is had from Fort Charlotte, an eighteenth-century fortification perched on a 600-ft/183-m hill west of the town.

THE BOTANIC GARDENS

North of Kingstown on 20 acres/8 hectares east of the Leeward Highway are the oldest continuous botanic gardens in the Western Hemisphere, established in 1765. The Gardens are among the most ornate in the Caribbean, providing a peaceful, park-like haven where an enormous variety of tropical trees and flowering plants flourish. Flamboyants, yellow pouis, frangipanis, jacarandas, and African tulips are among the showiest flowering trees. There are indigenous hardwoods such as mahogany, teak, and red cedar and imports such as banyan and rubber trees. Ixora, the national flower, is well represented. There is also a great variety of spices and fruit trees. Two prizes are mangosteen, a tree from India whose fruit has a flavor suggesting both peach and pineapple, and *Spachea elegans*, an exceptionally tall, leafy, and hardy tree, known locally as the Soufriere tree.

The Gardens have a small aviary which includes a breeding group of St. Vincent parrots. Near the entrance to the Botanic Gardens is the Archaeological Museum, built in 1891, which houses pre-Columbian artifacts found in St. Vincent and the Grenadines.

BUCCAMENT FOREST NATURE TRAIL

Directly behind Kingstown, a series of irregular mountain ranges extend up the center of the island from Mt. St. Andrew to Richmond Peak immediately south of the Soufriere Mountains. The southern range is dominated by Grand Bonhomme and Petit Bonhomme, the highest peaks (over 3,000 ft/ 900 m), which form the heads of two large, intensively cultivated valleys: Buccament Valley on the leeward or west side of the island and the Marriaqua Valley, better known as the Mesopotamia Valley, on the east. The road to the Buccament Valley, about 5 mi/8 km west of Kingstown, winds through the former Pembroke Estate, a 1,000-acre/405-hectare plantation whose old sugar mill and aqueduct are a backdrop to the Aqueduct Golf Course.

Beyond the golf course, the road inland along the Buccament River continues to the head of the valley and the Buccament Forest Nature Trail on the slopes of Grand Bonhomme. It is an excellent, sign posted loop trail of about 1.5 mi/2.4 km. Upgraded and improved by the Forestry Department with the aid of Peace Corps foresters, the trail ascends Grand Bonhomme between the levels of 1,000 and 2,000 ft/300 and 600 m, passing through evergreen forest to a tropical rain forest. Here gigantic gommier and other hardwoods make up the thick canopy which towers 100 ft/30 m overhead. The buttress roots of the older trees here are among the largest to be seen in any Caribbean rain forest, their trunks and limbs entangled with vines and epiphytes. The floor of the forest, carpeted with enormous ferns, has splashes of colorful heliconias and bromeliads. Throughout the steep hillsides new plantations of galba, blue mahoe, gmelina, eucalyptus, and other hardwoods have been added as part of the Forestry Department's soil and water conservation program. At the outer edges of the forest along the ravines are huge bamboos, tree ferns, and Caribbean pine, whose branches are densely covered with extraordinarily long needles.

Along the trail hikers might hear—if not see—the ruddy quail-dove and trembler. Other birds of the mountain forest are the common black-hawk, Lesser Antillean and black swifts, purple-throated carib hummingbird, scaly-breasted and pearly-eyed thrashers, and cocoa thrush. Endemic to St. Vincent (and Martinique) is the shy and elusive whistling warbler, a species of the high forest. The short-tailed swifts, most likely seen around Kingstown, and black and Lesser Antillean swifts are all known by the name of "rain bird" in St. Vincent. The Antillean euphonia is found in the low mountains, particularly around mistletoe, by which name the bird is known locally.

About halfway along the trail, there is a parrot-viewing area where in the late afternoon one's patience is likely to be rewarded with the sight of the handsome St. Vincent parrot, the national bird of St. Vincent and the Grenadines. This species, one of the largest Caribbean parrots, has a white head and brownish green body with deep lavender and yellow on the wings, tail, and neck. Destruction of habitat and capture to supply the lucrative international market for exotic birds have reduced this parrot's numbers to an alarming 500 or so. A major effort is under way to save the parrot and reverse this trend. A parrot sanctuary has been established in the upper Buccament Valley rain forest and in the Cumberland, Hermitage, and Colonarie valleys. Legislation dealing with wildlife has been strengthened to protect the parrot more effectively from poaching.

Hikers on the Buccament Forest Nature Trail pass through an evergreen forest on their way to the rain forest.

Parrots are best spotted at daybreak, or from 4:00 P.M. to dusk, when they return to their roosts high in the trees above the canopy. Hermitage, in the mountains above Cumberland, is another parrot-viewing area; it can be reached by a road along the Cumberland River to Grove from where a track leads about another mile or so higher up into the mountains. One can have a close-up look at the St. Vincent parrot at an aviary in the Botanic Gardens.

TABLE ROCK

En route to the Nature Trail, about a mile after the town of Vermont, a footpath of 600 ft/180 m on the right of the road, marked by a sign, leads to Table Rock. It is a long, enormous sheet of lava rock in the bed of the river where the cascading waters have carved channels and basins convenient for swimming—except after heavy rains when the rushing water is too strong. It is a pleasant picnic site, too.

At several places in the vicinity of the golf course and Layou one can see Arawak and Carib petroglyphs on huge boulders and cliffs. Ask locally for directions, since many of the petroglyphs are off the beaten path.

MONTREAL GARDENS VIA MESOPOTAMIA VALLEY AND YAMBOU GORGE

High on the windward slopes of Grand Bonhomme, 12 winding miles/19 km from Kingstown, are the Montreal Gardens, a botanic garden and nursery with beds of anthuriums, orchids, heliconias, and wild ginger surrounded by citrus trees and tree ferns and other rain-forest vegetation. The Gardens have paved walkways, a swimming pool, and mineral springs.

Even more interesting than the Gardens is the drive to them. From the south coast at Arnos Vale near the international airport, the road ascends from the intensively cultivated Mesopotamia Valley to Richland Park along high slopes planted with banana, nutmeg, cocoa, and coconut. The cultivated mountainsides are the favorite feeding grounds of the yellow-bellied and Caribbean elaenias and the purple-throated carib, one of three hummingbird species to be seen on St. Vincent, along with the green-throated carib and Antillean crested. All along the way there are magnificent views to the sea. A return from the Gardens can be made via Yambou Vale at Argyle.

Rivers and streams that drain from Grand Bonhomme and Petit Bonhomme through the Mesopotamia Valley tumble over the rocks of the Yambou Gorge on their way to the sea at Argyle. The south side of the gorge has a high lava cliff that is a relatively new formation, while the north side is composed of weathered lava and boulders. Petroglyphs can be seen in five separate areas; one series is found on the lava cliff and the others are on large boulders higher up the gorge. The lower reaches of Mesopotamia Valley are the country's breadbasket, cultivated with bananas and plantains and such root crops as eddo and dasheen—all staples of West Indian cuisine. These huge, leafy plants help to give the valley its magnificently lush appearance. Many kinds of birds live here, including the tropical mockingbird, gray kingbird, and smooth-billed ani.

BLUE LAGOON AND YOUNG ISLAND

East of the airport at Arnos Vale, on the hilly south coast, is St. Vincent's main hotel and resort area with white sand beaches and calm waters, cupped by Greathead Bay on the west and Calliaqua Bay and the Blue Lagoon on the east. Blue Lagoon, also known as the Careenage, is a yacht basin sheltered by wooded hillsides and edged by palm-shaded beaches. There are reefs and mangroves in a few places. Yachtsmen are warned to avoid the shallow south entrance to the Blue Lagoon and to use the west entrance, marked by buoys and stakes, instead.

Only 200 yd/180 m off the coast is Young Island, a thickly wooded islet of 36 acres/14 hectares devoted to one resort. Except for a few small thatched-roof pavilions by the beach, it is difficult to see any of the villas nestled on the hillside obscured by the profuse tropical foliage and masses of flowering trees. A two-minute boat ride dock-to-dock crosses the Young Island Cut, a narrow, protected channel that is the center of St. Vincent's water-sports activity. Birds of the south coast include magnificent frigatebirds and red-billed tropicbirds.

KING'S HILL FOREST RESERVE

Located on the remains of a volcanic feature known as a spatter cone, the King's Hill Forest Reserve was one of the first protected areas in the Caribbean, established in 1791. The 55-acre/22-hectare area includes shoemaker bark, white wood, penny piece, and birch gum (known on St. Vincent as gumbo limbo or as *gommier rouge* in Creole); it is one of the last remaining examples of this type of forest community in the Caribbean.

LA SOUFRIERE

The Soufriere Mountains covering the northern third of St. Vincent are dominated by a huge active volcano, La Soufriere. This volcano and Mt. Pelée in Martinique are two of the most active in the eastern Caribbean. Four eruptions—in 1718, 1812, 1902, and 1979—plus minor disruptions in 1971, are documented, but archaeological evidence found in the region in the form of offerings to the god of the volcano suggests it exploded as early as the second century A.D.

Following the eruption of 1812, in which 2,000 people were killed, clouds of gas and ash rose over 6 mi/10 km in the air and settled as far away as Barbados, more than 100 mi/160 km to the east. A second crater formed within the cone and was filled with what at the time was a small lake, 1,200 ft/366 m below the crater rim. As a result of the minor eruptions in 1971, an island of lava formed in the center of the lake, rising 300 ft/90 m above the water.

During the most recent eruption, in 1979, ash and cinder pushed high into the sky by hot gases fell over the mountains, searing the vegetation and destroying the thick forests. More than 20,000 people were evacuated

from the northern half of the island and miraculously no one was killed, but damage to homes, crops, and roads was extensive. The forest is thick with new growth, but along the outlines of the devastation, particularly in the region between Larikai and Trois Loups on the west side of the volcano, and the paths of ash flow are still visible. It is a fascinating and spectacular primordial sight; indeed, there is nothing in the Caribbean to rival the intensity of color of the new growth here.

The name of La Soufriere, an active volcano that last erupted in 1979, may come from the French word soufre, meaning sulphur, or from souffrir, to suffer.

The volcano is once again safe to climb and may be approached from either side of the island on a trail that runs along the southern rim of the crater. The ascent is a beautiful hike of 3 mi/4.8 km through rain forest and on up to the final stretch of barren slope and gravel track that brings you to the rim and a breathtaking view down into the crater.

A primitive plant, known locally as Soufriere grass, is common to these mountains. Along the trail one can hear the rare and elusive rufous-throated solitaire, known here as the Soufriere bird. Other birds of the Soufriere rain forest are the house wren, scaly-breasted thrasher, and whistling warbler.

The more frequently used *eastern trail* starts on the east side of La Soufriere, 1 mi/1.6 km north of Georgetown at Rabacca, where one first sees the peak. On the north side of the Rabacca Dry River is a rough and rutted plantation road of about 2 mi/3.2 km to be traversed only by foot or four-wheel-drive. It runs through the extensive banana and coconut groves of Rabacca Farms to the base of the crater. Here, at about 1,200 ft/366 m elevation, in an area known as Bamboo Range, a well-defined 3-mi/4.8-km trail to the summit begins. Experienced hikers can use this trail on their own.

For the first 2 mi/3.2 km the trail ascends gradually on a winding route up the mountainside, passing giant tree ferns and bamboo before reaching the more heavily wooded area of the rain forest at about 1,600 ft/488 m. The trail then comes to an open space called River Bed, the upper surface of a lava flow; it is convenient to rest beside the small stream there. The next mile is the hardest, steepest part of the trail, rising from 1,600 to 3,000 ft/488 to 914 m in a series of switchbacks up to the crater rim. All along the trail there are wonderful vistas, sometimes looking down the Atlantic coast to Georgetown. The eastern trail is a 29-mi/46-km drive from Kingstown.

The *western trail* begins at Chateaubelair where the coastal road from Kingstown ends. It is followed by a three-hour hike, more scenic but more demanding than the eastern trek; a guide is necessary. The trail is over-grown and bushwhacking with a machete, or cutlass as it is called on St. Vincent, may be required. North of Chateaubelair, one must walk along Richmond Beach (the road is washed away) to the Wallibou Dry River and turn inland along a trail that follows the dry riverbed to about 300 ft/90 m elevation; from here a narrow path zigzags north for about 2 mi/3.6 km to the rim of the crater. The descent takes about one and a half hours. The drive from Kingstown to Chateaubelair takes about two hours on a very tortuous but scenic 26-mi/42-km route via the coastal town of Layou and the

Black Point Beach, where Atlantic waves pound St. Vincent's east coast, is an excellent place for beach combing and shelling.

fishing village of Barrouallie. Those who have hiked this trail say that because the peak is always in sight and never seems to get closer, the climb seems longer and more tiring than the eastern trail.

Soufriere expeditions need a full day. One is advised to bring water and a picnic lunch and to start early to avoid the heat of the sun on the ascent. Conceivably, one could start on one coast and hike across to the other, but this cannot be done without a local guide and adequate provisions.

RABACCA DRY RIVER

A remarkable legacy of the volcanic eruptions are the island's "dry rivers." After the eruptions of 1812 and 1902, river channels were filled with cinders (scoriae) and gravel. The water that flows into one of these river-beds seeps through the porous material and disappears, becoming a subterranean river as it nears the coast. At its mouth, where it empties into the sea, the riverbed is covered with several feet (about a meter) of loose ash and is bone dry on the surface. Sometimes, however, unusually heavy rains have a flash-flood effect: water flows on the surface of the channel, making the expanse too dangerous to ford; cars can get mired in the wet ash and be completely or partially buried.

The two most vivid examples of nature's strange work are Wallibou Dry River on the Caribbean coast and the Rabacca Dry River on the Atlantic coast. The latter enters the sea at Rabacca, about 24 mi/38 km north of Kingstown, having drained from Mt. Brisbane and the southeastern side of La Soufriere through two separate courses that meet about 2 mi/3.2 km inland from the coast. No water is visible on the surface at the mouth, but where the terrain starts to gain altitude, water can be seen and, depending on the time of the year, it will be either a modest stream or a torrent.

On the north coast at the base of La Soufriere are the villages of Sandy Bay, Owia, and Fancy. Sandy Bay has the largest concentration of Vincentians of Carib descent, although, unlike their counterparts in Dominica, they are not culturally distinct by reason of their lifestyle or crafts. The road north of Sandy Bay to Fancy is rough and mostly unpaved; a jeep or four-wheel-drive vehicle is recommended. Beyond Fancy, there is a trail which skirts the north coast to the Falls of Baleine, but it is an extremely rugged hike even for well-conditioned hikers who are accustomed to mountainous tropical terrain. The falls are best reached by boat from Kingstown.

THE FALLS OF BALEINE

Situated at the head of a steep-sided gorge at the northwest foot of the Soufriere Mountains, St. Vincent's prettiest cascade tumbles more than 70 ft/21 m over the lava rocks through dense tropical foliage into a large, deep, rockbound pool near the sea. The mountain slopes above Baleine are covered by the Windsor Forest, the only part of the Soufriere woodland not damaged by the eruption in 1979.

The Falls of Baleine are about 7 mi/11 km north of Richmond Beach and 18 mi/29 km from Kingstown, as the crow flies. Access from Kingstown is by sea and takes about an hour by fast motorboat and two to three hours by sailboat, one way. One must make a wet landing and, except at low tide, it may be necessary to swim from the boat to shore. It takes about fifteen minutes to reach the falls over a new paved trail from the beach that bridges the rocks and riverbed. Hotels and water-sports operators in Kingston have excursions to Baleine Falls almost daily and include stops for swimming and snorkeling at tiny coves about midway on the coast.

A boat ride along the coast is the best way to appreciate the island's restless volcanic origins and history. Where the rivers of lava flowed there are deep cuts in the terrain. Equally impressive is the sight of nature recreating itself as new growth rises out of the ashes and devastation of the past.

THE GRENADINES

The Grenadines comprise three dozen islands and cays that stretch from St. Vincent to Grenada over a distance of 65 mi/104 km. All but Carriacou and Petit Martinique, the two islands closest to Grenada, are Vincentian territory; they cover 45 mi/72 km of the distance. Only eight islands are populated; the others are sanctuaries for birds and hideaways for sailors, swimmers, and snorkelers. Most are dry, low-lying, volcanic islands surrounded by white sand beaches and rich coral gardens close to shore. But the water around them is perhaps their most attractive feature. Not only do its colors range across the spectrum of blues and greens, but the water between the islands is deep, without the unmarked shoals that often make Bahamian sailing difficult. At the same time, the islands are so close together that sailors are never out of sight of land. This combination of superb weather, beauty, safety, and convenience has earned the Grenadines the admiration of yachtsmen from around the world.

Bequia. Across the Bequia Channel 9 mi/14.4 km south of St. Vincent is the 10-sq-mi/26-sq-km island of Bequia (pronounced BECK-way), the largest of the Grenadines. It is a low-lying island of rolling green hills, cultivated in parts, covered with thick dry woodlands elsewhere, and colored with oleander, bougainvillea, and hibiscus; the white sand beaches are shaded by palm trees and seagrapes. From Admiralty Bay, hiking on unpaved roads and footpaths is easy and takes one to such places as Mt. Pleasant where the reward is a view of Bequia and its neighbors, or to Hope Bay where a pretty beach with breakers is popular for body surfing.

Untouristed Bequia, the largest of the thirty-six Grenadine islands and cays, attracts divers, body surfers, snorkelers, and birders.

On their walkabouts, birders might see a common barn-owl, smooth-billed ani, Grenada flycatcher, yellow-bellied elaenia, green-throated carib, Antillean crested hummingbirds, even a rare rufous-vented chachalaca, locally called cocorico. The Carib grackle, called the "Bequia sweet," and bananaquit, known here as the yellow see-see, may steal the food from one's table or picnic basket at the first opportunity. The bananaquit of the Grenadines is the yellow form typical of the eastern Caribbean, but on St. Vincent it is mostly black and is called the black see-see.

Some of the best reefs for snorkeling are found north of Spring Bay on the east coast and at Friendship Bay on the south coast where the reefs protect a half-mile crescent of white sand beach. Windsurfing is available at Princess Margaret Beach on the leeward side for novices and at the Spring Bay area on the rougher Atlantic coast for competitors. The island has two dive operators. Sport-fishing is not organized, but one can go with a local fisherman, who needs only the most rudimentary equipment to hook wahoo, kingfish, tuna, marlin, or other big ones.

Bequia has not been developed for tourists, which has endeared it to artists, writers, and assorted city dwellers who have never found their way back home. Most hotels are small guesthouses; some are in former plantation houses. There is twice-daily ferry service between Bequia's main town of Port Elizabeth and Kingstown; the trip takes about an hour. Plans have been approved to construct an airstrip but not everyone on Bequia is pleased. Occasionally, Bequia is a stop for cruise ships.

Mustique. Developed in the early 1970s by British and international investors, Mustique was put on the map by the British royal family and by the international celebrities like Mick Jagger and David Bowie who vacation here. Primarily a dry island, 4-sq-mi/10-sq-km Mustique has a more manicured appearance than her sister islands and is one of the few with paved roads. At one time it had several sugar plantations, one of whose estate houses is now the only hotel on the island. It is located on the northwest side of the island. The woodlands adjacent to the hotel are a bird sanctuary.

The northern part of the island has gentle hills, while the central and southern areas have a range of steeper mountains that reward hikers with wonderful vistas. Sandy Bay at the north end of Mustique has a spectacular mile-long curve of white sand beach, the best on the island, where the color of the water is even more fabulous than that of the sand. One can hike to Rosemary Point on the west side for a fine view of the bay and the wreck of the French liner *Antilles* offshore. Other good beaches are found at Pastor Bay on the east side and Landing Cove on the west.

Good snorkeling can be found in many places but particularly on the south end of Britannia Bay (also called Grand Bay) and at Lagoon Bay in

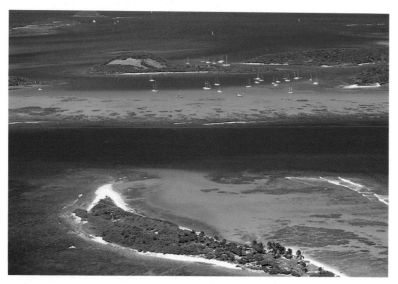

From any of the serene uninhabited islets called Tobago Cays, one can walk or swim to reefs and watch fish swimming through coral gardens.

the southwest corner of the island. Petit Mustique and Savan Island on the south are good locations for fishing. One is likely to spot magnificent frigatebirds soaring overhead. Mustique has an airstrip connecting it to St. Vincent and Barbados. Boats tie up on the west coast at Britannia Bay where they are likely to line up with yachts as luxurious as the homes of the celebrity residents.

Canouan. This is the driest of the Grenadines, covered with scrub, acacias, and cacti but encircled by beautiful beaches. From Charlestown Bay, the main anchorage and a popular stop for yachts and the occasional cruise ship, one can walk about 0.5 mi/0.8 km over the hill to the east side where there are more pretty beaches and good snorkeling, particularly north of an area known as The Pool where the colors of the water are spectacular. Also from Charlestown Bay, a dirt road leads north to Carenage Bay, another beautiful white sand beach on the east side. Maho Bay on the north end has a mile-long beach with surf. On the south side of the island there are reefs and a shipwreck. Canouan Beach Hotel offers sailing excursions and water-sports facilities. Petit Canouan, north of Canouan, has large colonies of terns, known locally as eggbirds, whose eggs the islanders gather to eat.

Mayreau. The newest of the Grenadines to be developed, Mayreau, or Mayero, had no facilities until a new resort opened on the north coast at Salt Whistle Bay, a pretty horseshoe bay with a crescent of beach framed by palms and seagrape trees that all but hide the rustic resort. At the north end of the beach, a trail of a few yards crosses over to the east side where there is a long stretch of white sand beach, only one of the several superb beaches surrounding the island. There are no roads or cars here, but from the bay a track leads to the tiny hilltop village in the center of the island where one can look out over Tobago Cays, one of the spectacularly beautiful spots that have made the Grenadines famous. Saline Bay on the southwest coast has a half-moon band of sand that stretches almost a mile. At the north end off Grand Col Point, the wreck of a British gunboat in only 36 ft/11 m of water makes a very popular, aquarium-like dive site. The southeast coast has a large reef that starts at a depth of about 30 ft/9 m and drops to 100 ft/30 m; there is a cave off the east side of the reef that starts at about 20 ft/6 m.

Tobago Cays. The highlight of cruising the Grenadines is Tobago Cays, four uninhabited, green, and palm-fringed islets ringed by pristine white sand and clear aquamarine waters. This is for many people the most beautiful spot in the Caribbean, so serene it seems unreal. From a beach on any of the islets, one can walk or swim to clusters of reef to see large schools of angelfish, parrotfish, trumpetfish, and sergeant majors swimming through the coral gardens. The northernmost cay, Petit Rameau, has a short trail through heavy mangrove foliage along sandy beach on its south side; Petit Bateau, the second largest, has a long palm-shaded beach on the north and another beach on the east. Barabel, the easternmost of the four, is completely surrounded by reef and has a beach on its south side. Jamesby, the southernmost cay, has the best beach of the group on the east side, where there are large boulders, too. Wrapping the four islets on their east side is Horseshoe Reef where some parts are shallow enough for wading. The northern half of the reef, with its huge sea fans, is considered the most spectacular.

Tobago Cays was declared a wildlife reserve by the St. Vincent government in the 1970s but it has not yet laid out a marine park to protect it. Meanwhile, the reefs are being seriously damaged by visitors: a multitude of boats—sometimes as many as forty—with their anchors and debris, and cruise ship passengers who come ashore via the tenders of their large ships and leave litter behind them. Environmentalists also point out that the surrounding waters are being overfished by international companies. Without concerted effort, the reefs are bound to deteriorate further.

Palm Island. A private island of 110 acres/44.5 hectares with one resort, Palm Island was known as Prune Island until John Caldwell planted 2,000 palm trees and created a fabulous resort. The island has pretty beaches on each of its five sides and an encircling reef a short wade or swim away. A host of seabirds—red-billed tropicbirds, royal terns, brown pelicans, boobies, frigatebirds, and laughing gulls, to name a few—find it a convenient stop; and the gardens of fruit and flowering trees do their share to feed bananaquits and tropical mockingbirds.

Palm Island Beach Club has full water-sports facilities which are available to day visitors upon payment of appropriate fees. Those planning to dive should telephone the resort in advance for arrangements (809-458-4804).

Petit St. Vincent. Another private island with a deluxe resort, Petit St. Vincent, appears frequently on the lists of the "ten best" Caribbean resorts. Half of its 113 acres/46 hectares were turned into a park setting, more manicured than the neighboring resorts; the other half of the property was left in its natural state. As outstanding as the beaches that almost encircle Petit St. Vincent are two sandbars on the north—Punaise and Mopion—with blinding white sand and a few palm trees surrounded by incredibly beautiful water and reefs. The water is shallow and offers some of the best snorkeling in the area.

Union Island. Situated about halfway between St. Vincent and Grenada, Union Island is the entry port at the southern end of the Grenadines. It offers a challenge to hikers in a spine of jagged, slab-faced mountains that run north–south; here stands Mt. Tabor, at 999 ft/304 m, the Grenadines' highest peak. Richmond Bay, on the north, is the best snorkeling spot. Bloody Bay on the northwest coast and Chatham Bay on the west coast are popular anchorages for sailors. A footpath inland from Ashton around "Rock Fall" leads down into Chatham Bay, where a resort is planned.

The island is covered with dry deciduous woodland with many varieties of cacti around rock outcroppings and beaches fringed with seagrape and poisonous manchineel trees. White cedar, coconut palm, mango, plum, and soursop are remnants of the past when this island was extensively cultivated. Tamarind, calabash, almond, frangipani, and flamboyant grow wild.

Union Island, the second most populated of the Grenadines, has several small hotels and an airstrip served by scheduled flights from Kingstown as well as Grenada, St. Lucia, and Martinique. Boat service also is available. The island is one of the main locations for independent boat charterers who offer day excursions to Tobago Cays and other nearby islands for picnicking, swimming, and snorkeling; they offer longer cruises as well. There are several dive operators, and glass-bottom boats are available for trips over the reefs.

OUTDOOR ACTIVITIES

HIKING: Almost all of St. Vincent's terrain is steep mountains, while most of the Grenadines are rolling hills. Hiking is a necessity for people here as much as it is a pastime for visitors. Ask locally for information; someone is likely to offer to show you the way, particularly in the Grenadines. In St. Vincent, guides for hiking are available through the Forestry Division and the Government Tourist Board; those planning to hike without a guide should consult these two departments about trail conditions. Hotels and local travel companies organize hiking to La Soufriere. Bird lists are sometimes available from hotels, especially in the Grenadines.

HORSEBACK RIDING: Only the Cotton House Hotel on Mustique has horseback riding.

SWIMMING: All beaches are public. The south and east coasts of St. Vincent are the safest for swimming. Those along the south coast have white sand while on the west the sands are slate-

Pages 392 and 393: Petroglyphs in Yambou Gorge, St. Vincent.

colored. Swimming on the windward coast is not advised due to the rough seas and rocky coast, but the beaches are suitable for beachcombing and shelling.

SNORKELING AND DIVING: Dive aficionados call St. Vincent the sleeper of Caribbean diving. Reef life normally found at 80 ft/24 m in other locations grows here at depths of only 25 ft/8 m, and there is an extraordinary variety of tropical reef fish, such as angelfish, parrotfish, trumpetfish, sergeant majors, and peacock flounder. St. Vincent offers walls with black coral and gigantic samples of brain and pillar corals; in some places the strong current is suitable for advanced drift diving only.

While there is snorkeling along the beaches bordering Young Island Cut and the leeward coast, the best snorkeling is in the Grenadines where shallow-water reefs surround almost every island and huge schools of fish travel through the archipelago. Divers seeking less crowded waters have begun to explore the Grenadines' fringing reefs.

The variety of sea shells is outstanding, including some species that are found only in St. Vincent; rooster-tail conch, hawkwing conch, cones, cowries, and music volutes are some to be collected. Shelling is permitted.

There are dive operators on the south coast in St. Vincent and on Bequia, Union, and private resort islands. Generally, prices are lower than in other Caribbean locations.

FISHING: The seas around St. Vincent and the Grenadines have abundant fish, but sport-fishing is not a developed sport. However, water-sports operators can arrange deep-sea fishing upon request, and one might be able to go out to sea with a local fisherman, particularly in the Grenadines.

SAILING: Renowned throughout the world for their magnificent waters, the Grenadines offer the Caribbean's most fantastic sailing experience. Yachts for four to eight people can be chartered from Caribbean Sailing Yachts, Box 133, Blue Lagoon (809-84308); or CSY, PO Box 491Y, Tenafly, NJ 07670 (800-631-1593). The St. Vincent Tourist Board can provide information on charterers based in the Grenadines. The yachts are fully provisioned. Chartering a boat with crew opens the opportunity for those who do not sail or sail well. Before start-

ing from St. Vincent, passengers meet their skipper and are briefed by a staff member who answers questions and suggests sailing routes. The week is spent at sea, stopping at the islands and reefs of one's choice. The skipper, an experienced helmsman from the islands, sails the boat, prepares meals, and tidies the galley. Passengers are free to do any of these tasks, including sailing the yacht.

WINDSURFING: Equipment on St. Vincent is available for rent at the windsurfing center on the south coast, where there also is a windsurfing school. Inquire from water-sports operators. All islands in the Grenadines with hotels have windsurfing equipment as well.

EXPLORING THE ISLANDS

St. Vincent and the Grenadines have very limited road systems. The best roads on St. Vincent are in the southern third of the island; the rest are narrow and winding, but, with a few exceptions, they are adequate. There are far fewer roads in the central area and almost none in the northern third of the island. No road completely rings the island.

There is no road on the east coast beyond Fancy, only a narrow, difficult trail that leads to the northwest coast. Public bus transportation is available to Fancy; however, taxis and private vehicles do not like to go beyond Orange Hill, and indeed, some will not go beyond Georgetown.

On the west coast, the Leeward Highway from Kingstown winds north to Chateaubelair where the road ends. Although maps show the road continuing as far as Richmond Beach, this leg can be traversed only by jeep or truck. Buses run between Kingstown and Chateaubelair.

On the west side beyond Richmond Beach there is no road, only a track that becomes a narrow and sometimes nonexistent trail. This region is the most inaccessible part of St. Vincent, with jagged peaks covered with impenetrable jungle and precipitous bluffs.

Cars and jeeps are available for rent in Kingstown, but visitors might enjoy their sightseeing more if they let someone else do the driving. Taxis can be hired for the day; be sure to agree on the itinerary and price in advance. Those who prefer to drive will need a temporary licence. Driving is on the LEFT.

Characteristically, each of the populated Grenadines has one unpaved road and many dirt paths. Bequia, Mustique, and Union have taxis.

St. Vincent and the Grenadines suffer from inadequate air service. St. Vincent is connected by air and regular boat service to two of the Grenadines—Mustique and Union; a frequently used alternative is to hire an air taxi. The best way to visit the Grenadines is by private yacht, which is more reasonable than most people imagine. Yachts can be chartered, with or without crew, from operators headquartered in Kingstown for a week's cruise of the Grenadines.

INFORMATION: In the U.S.: St. Vincent and the Grenadines Tourist Board, 801 Second Avenue, New York, NY 10017; 212-687-4981. In Canada: 32 Park Rd., Toronto, Ontario M4W 2N4; 416-294-5796. In the U.K.: 10 Kensington Ct., London W8 5DL; 71-937-6570. In St. Vincent: PO Box 834, Egmont St., Kingstown, St. Vincent, WI; 809-457-1502.

Forestry Division, Ministry of Trade and Agriculture, Kingstown, St. Vincent (809-456-1111, ext. 321) has foresters and trainees who act as guides for naturalists and others with a keen interest in wildlife. There are no comprehensive books on the natural history of St. Vincent. *Birds of Grenada, St. Vincent and the Grenadines*, by Fr. Raymond P. Devas (1970), is an elementary list. For cultural background, *The Rise and Fall of the Black Caribs*, by I. E. Kirby and C. I. Martin, Ministry of Foreign Affairs, Caracas, Venezuela (1985).

GRENADA

IN THE SPECTACULARLY BEAUTIFUL country of Grenada, the banana trees by the side of the road grow as tall as the palm trees fringing the powdery beaches. The scent of almond and nutmeg fills the air that rises up the thickly forested mountainsides. Known as the Spice Island, Grenada is one of the world's largest producers of nutmeg. Cloves, cocoa, cinnamon, ginger, vanilla, and about every fruit known in the tropics grow in profusion. Over 160 in/406 cm of rain fall from the moisture-laden tradewinds that blow across the interior of the island. The abundant rain helps to create lush forests with a diversity of plants and wildlife and rivers and streams that rush down the mountains to the sea.

Like the other islands of the Lesser Antilles, Grenada was born millions of years ago from volcanoes that poured lava in great fiery rivers or exploded in catastrophic blasts, creating large craters. Indeed, volcanic activity continues near its shores beneath the sea. A submerged volcano, Kick 'em Jenny, lies only 500 ft/152 m under the sea off the island's north coast. From the shoreline of coral reefs, bays, coves, lagoons, mangroves, and rugged cliffs, the deeply creviced terrain climbs through lowland dry forests to rain and montane forests, to elfin woodland at the mountain peaks—comprising virtually every ecosystem found in the Caribbean. The landscape is adorned with more than 450 species of flowering plants and more than 150 species of birds.

First sighted by Columbus on his third voyage in 1498, Grenada is the southernmost member of the Windward Islands, 100 mi/160 km north of Venezuela. Carriacou and Petit Martinique, which belong to the Grenadine Islands chain that stretches north to St. Vincent, are two dependencies of Grenada and lie off her north coast. Despite Grenada's small size, the 133-sq-mi/344-sq-km island has always been important in Caribbean history because of its strategic location. It changed hands many times between Britain and France until 1783, when it became a British Colony, and it remained British until its independence in 1974. Yet even today, remnants of the French influence remain in the names of the people and places, in the patois, and in the cuisine, which is one of the best in the Caribbean.

ST. GEORGE'S

St. George's, the capital, is set on a horseshoe bay with a medley of yellow, blue, and pink houses clinging to green mountains in the background. The inner harbor, called the Carenage, has one of the best anchorages in the

West Indies and is always busy with boats of all sizes and descriptions, besides being the center of life in the town. A weekly highlight is the loading of schooners—usually on Tuesday afternoons—with Grenada's rich harvest of fruits and vegetables bound for markets in Barbados and Trinidad.

The Grenada National Museum, set in an eighteenth-century building that was once part of a prison and barracks, is maintained by the Grenada Historical Society. Its exhibits trace the island's history from the Ciboneys and Caribs to colonial times. Indian petroglyphs have been found on Grenada as recently as 1980, and throughout the island ancient sites are discovered often. Unfortunately, as the museum's condition shows, Grenada lacks the financial resources to preserve its cultural heritage. Much is being eroded by neglect, new building, and treasure seeking; unaware of their significance, local kids have found quick buyers for artifacts among the tourists, who are equally unaware of their importance.

The lower town along the Carenage and the new town "over the hill" on the Esplanade are connected by a vehicular tunnel under the hill. Both parts are best seen on foot. On the south side of the Carenage, a second harbor known as the Lagoon is the yacht basin, marina, and commercial port. The Lagoon is actually the crater of an ancient volcano. On the east side of the Lagoon road are the Botanical Gardens, begun in 1887; buildings on the grounds house government offices.

BAY GARDENS

About a half-mile from Fort Frederick, the 3-acre/1.2-hectare botanical oasis of Bay Gardens occupies the site of an old sugar mill. Good trails covered with nutmeg shells wind through exotic vegetation; there are an estimated 3,000 species representing virtually every kind of flora found in Grenada and the Caribbean. In addition to spice and fruit trees—all labeled—there are sections for flowers and various kinds of orchids, ponds stocked with different species of fish, and a turtle aquarium. There is a small entrance fee, and a guide is available.

On the St. Paul Road east of Bay Gardens is Tower House, the estate house of a working fruit and spice plantation and one of the few that are open to the public. The house, one of the island's last remaining old houses constructed of volcanic rock, is surrounded by gardens of exotic plants. The owner's private collection of Carib artifacts and other antiques is on display. Tours are available by appointment.

Atlantic breakers roll in on Antoine Beach on the northeast coast of Grenada near Lake Antoine, a crater lake.

ANNANDALE FALLS

En route from St. George's to the Grand Etang Forest Reserve in the center of the island, a 0.5-mi/0.8-km detour might be made at Constantine to visit Annandale Falls, the most accessible of the many streams that cascade through the mountains from the Grand Etang catchment. The falls are only a few yards from the road in what was until recently a completely natural setting. The addition of cement steps is something of an intrusion, but the rest of the area remains thick with lush vegetation. A hillside next to the falls is being developed as a spice and herb garden to enable visitors to learn about Grenada's main crops firsthand.

GRAND ETANG FOREST RESERVE

The Grand Etang Forest Reserve encompasses the spine of mountains that dominate most of the interior of Grenada and reach their highest peaks at Mt. St. Catherine (2,757 ft/840 m) on the north, Mt. Qua Qua (2,373 ft/723 m) near the center, and Mt. Sinai (2,305 ft/702 m) on the south. The highway cuts across the reserve at 1,910 ft/582 m, almost at its center and within a few hundred yards of Grand Etang, an extinct volcano whose crater is filled with water and for which the reserve is named. (Grand Etang means "large pond" in French.)

The Grand Etang Lake, clearly visible from the visitors' center, is only about 1,500 ft/457 m away. Visible too is the summit of Mt. Qua Qua on the north side of the lake. Its slopes are covered with dwarf or elfin woodland whose gnarled miniature appearance is the result of adaptation by trees and plants for survival at high altitudes where they catch the brunt of the winds and water sweeping across the mountains. On a clear day Mt. St. Catherine's flattened cone is also in view.

Grenada is in the process of establishing a system of national parks and protected areas that will incorporate its most outstanding natural and cultural features; already there are good hiking trails in the Forest Reserve.

The rain-forest flora includes wild orchids and heliconias and a great variety of ferns, including an endemic species, the Grand Etang fern. Mahogany and giant gommiers are among the tallest trees, their thick foliated canopy providing habitat for many species of birds, frogs, and lizards. Their large buttress roots bridge out across the forest floor, giving support to the tall trees and helping to hold the soil in place. Indeed, soil and water conservation were primary objectives in establishing the park.

Some of the animals to be seen are the mongoose, mona monkey, opossum (known also as manicou), and nine-banded armadillo (known locally as tatou). The opossum and armadillo are hunted by Grenadians for their meat, which is considered a delicacy. Despite clearly established hunting seasons, there is poaching and the numbers of these animals are rapidly decreasing. Grenada's forests have no dangerous animals or poisonous snakes. Among the many birds seen here are the broad-winged hawk with its black-and-white-banded tail feathers (known here as gree-gree), Lesser Antillean, or mountain, swift, gray kingbird, bat falcon, Antillean euphonia, blue ground-dove, purple-throated carib, Antillean crested hummingbird (known locally as little doctor bird), and Lesser Antillean tanager (locally called soursop). The highland piping frog and an occasional yellow-billed cuckoo might be heard as well.

The Grand Etang Forest Center has displays, brochures, and information on the nature trails for self-guided hiking around the lake and environs. Hikes from the Forest Center range from fifteen minutes to three hours.

Morne LaBaye Trail, an interpretive trail beginning behind the visitor's center, features twelve points of interest explained in a self-guided brochure and leads to a lookout for viewing the east coast and the summit of Mt. Sinai to the south. This is a fifteen-minute walk.

Ridge and *Lake Circle Trail* is a thirty-minute walk to and along Grand Etang Lake. It starts on the south side of the Forest Center and for about the first half, is the same trail as the one to Mt. Qua Qua. Along the way one sees many orchids growing on the trees. Orchids are epiphytes, or air plants; they use the trees for support only and are not parasitic. There are also lianas, climbing vines that send their shoots down from the treetops to root in the soil below.

Mt. Qua Qua Trail is a hike of about one and a half hours on well-defined, marked paths with little gradient as far as the Grand Etang Lake trail junction. From there the trail becomes steeper, and the red clay soil is often slippery along the crater rim. The trail follows the contours of the ridge, winding up and down, sometimes narrowing to a width that requires caution. Along the way, hikers can enjoy a grand display of the area's plant life and panoramic views from clearings.

Seven Sisters Trail, one of the most interesting trails in the central mountains, begins southwest of Grand Etang Lake and leads to an area with seven waterfalls and pools and an abundance of birds and wildlife, including mona monkeys. The trail (three hours round trip for experienced hikers) starts in an area of nutmeg and banana cultivation but continues into virgin forest; parts of the trail are difficult as the track crosses dense bush and proceeds along steep ridges that require a good sense of balance to negotiate. Also, the trails can be very slippery during the rainy season from May to November. A guide is recommended.

The summit of Mt. Sinai can be approached from the south side of the mountain by taking the Petit Etang Road to the tiny village of the Petit Etang where a track leads north; the hike takes about two hours. Other hikes can be made in the southwestern part of Mt. Sinai and on Mt. Lebanon, but hikers would need a local person to show the way; these trails have not been maintained.

Hikers should wear sneakers or jogging shoes, since the trails are often wet. An early start allows you to return in daylight without having to hurry. Carry drinking water and always have a hiking companion.

CONCORD VALLEY

From St. George's along the Esplanade on the leeward side of the island, the road hugs the coast as it passes through small fishing villages and magnificent scenery of lush, thickly carpeted mountainsides that drop almost straight down to the sea. Almost hidden from view are little coves with small black sand beaches. At Halifax Harbor, by the Woodford Estate House, a road turns inland to the Concord Valley along the Black Bay River whose waters are formed by Concord Falls, a triple-stage cascade deep in the central mountains. Above Concord village the road stops directly in front of the falls' first stage where there is a bathhouse and concrete steps

Hiking trails of varying lengths and difficulty explore the Grand Etang Forest Reserve that encompasses Grenada's central mountains. Facing page: Annandale Falls, in the Grand Etang catchment.

down to a swimming area. This section of the falls is popular with local children and scout troops for outings. The modern facilities distract from the setting, but hikers can proceed to the second falls, where nature still rules the day.

There is a footpath along the river, and large rocks have been placed in the riverbed at strategic points to make crossing the river easier and the second cascade more accessible. Hiking to these falls is not easy: the rocks are very slippery, particularly during the wet season, and the rushing river must be crossed several times. The reward is a cascade dropping 40 ft/12 m through jungle-thick vegetation to a pool where one can have a refreshing swim. The hike up to the second stage takes about forty-five minutes going, twenty-five minutes returning. The climb to the third cascade, Fontainbleu Falls, is much tougher and takes three hours, round trip, from the second cascade.

FEDON'S CAMP

On Mount Fedon northeast of the Concord Valley is Fedon's Camp, once the strategic outpost of Julian Fedon, a Grenadian of French origin who led a rebellion against the British in 1795. An arduous, five-hour walk to camp takes hikers into the heart of the rain forest of the Grand Etang National Forest Reserve where they can see a great variety of vegetation, birdlife (particularly the green-throated carib and yellow-billed cuckoo), and perhaps monkeys. Starting at the Concord Valley, upwards from the falls, the trek follows the course of the river along very steep mountainsides. This is the most difficult part of the trail, which gets easier when it reaches the forest reserve area. The trail is an ancient Indian path, used over the centuries by local people and well maintained today. Along the way hikers will see giant mahogany trees, teak, and enormous ferns. Near the site of the camp in elfin woodland is a deep recess in the mountain—not truly a cave, although it looks like one—where Fedon used to hide out. From the "cave" hikers can continue on the less strenuous Mt. Qua Qua trail to Grand Etang Lake and the visitors' center. Or they can proceed over the summit of Mt. Qua Qua to the village of Beaureguard near Birch Grove and a main north–south interior island road.

FROM GOUYAVE TO SAUTEURS

From the west-coast road just before Gouyave, a turn-off east leads about a half-mile to Dougaldston Estate, a nutmeg plantation where staff members explain the cultivation of Grenada's most important spices. In Gouyave, one can visit the country's major nutmeg processing station, a growers' cooperative.

The fishing town of Gouyave was the site of the first British landing in 1609, when the Caribs so fiercely defended their island that the British were forced to leave. Today this town of robust fishermen has a reputation among local people for being a bit raucous. In contrast, the next town up the road, Victoria, is quiet and sedate. From Victoria a climb to the summit of Mt. St. Catherine, Grenada's highest peak, can be made via secondary roads, tracks, and footpaths; a guide is necessary since the trails are not well defined. This hike, which takes about two and a half hours, is steeper but more interesting than the shorter, one-hour hike that can be made on an inland road via Mt. Hope.

At the town of Sauteurs on the north coast, a promontory alongside St. Patrick's Roman Catholic Church and Cemetery is a cultural landmark. The north side of the promontory, known as Carib's Leap or Leapers Hill, has a steep face that drops vertically into the sea for more than 100 ft/30 m. Here, the last of the Caribs, the inhabitants of the island at the time of Columbus, leaped to their death rather than surrender to the French, whose policy had been to exterminate them.

South of Sauteurs, Morne Fendue is a plantation house built at the turn of the century in the traditional method with hand-cut local stones and mortar made with lime and molasses. The owner, Betty Mascoll, opens her house to guests for a Grenadian lunch—provided they call in advance. It is not a restaurant; one dines in Mrs. Mascoll's drawing rooms. This is the only place in this vicinity to eat; otherwise one would need to bring a picnic lunch.

LEVERA NATIONAL PARK

East of Sauteurs, the Levera National Park is one of the most scenic coastal areas in Grenada. Levera Beach is a beautiful, rustic area with white sand beaches fringed by seagrapes and palm trees. It is a favorite swimming spot for Grenadians but is usually deserted on weekdays. The beaches, bordered by coral reefs abundant with lobsters and colorful fish, are an important hatching ground for sea turtles, which are protected from May to September. The vegetation provides a habitat for iguana, land crabs, and similar wildlife.

The park also has a lagoon which is one of the largest, most productive areas of mangrove swamp in the country and an important wildlife habitat, where birdlife includes black-necked stilts, common snipes, herons, water-fowl, and migratory warblers. The drier areas above the mangroves are covered with cactus, coconut palm, and woody scrub. The park and the offshore islands—Sugar Loaf, Green, and Sandy—are nesting grounds for gulls, boobies, terns, and other seabirds. Audubon's shearwater, known here as jablotin, breeds on Green and Sandy islands from April to May. Adventurous travelers who are willing to cross the rough sea of the channel where the Atlantic and Caribbean meet can arrange for a private fishing boat to take them to the islands. For hiking in the Levera Lagoon area, there is a trail that circles the lagoon. The trail is slated for improvement, but until this is accomplished, one may need to be accompanied by a guide who can cut a path with a machete—or cutlass, as the instrument is known here—through the thick growth.

LAKE ANTOINE NATIONAL LANDMARK

South of Levera Park is the Lake Antoine National Landmark, a crater lake formed by volcanic eruption. The depth of the water in the lake is normally not more than 20 ft/6 m. While the crater's lower slopes have been used for agricultural purposes, the crest is still partially covered with forest. There is a circular trail around the lake that is well worth the hike. A road, negotiable by four-wheel-drive, also circles the lake. Birdlife includes the snail kite, fulvous whistling-duck, gray kingbird, large-billed seed-finch, and limpkin.

SOUTH COAST PENINSULAS AND BAYS

From St. George's along the Lagoon Road the highway leads south to Grand Anse Beach, one of the most beautiful beaches in the Caribbean, and to the southern part of the island. On the north side of the road behind the beach, Blue Horizons Cottage Hotel's gardens are a natural aviary with a large variety of flowers and fruit trees. The hotel has a descriptive list of twenty-one birds seen here regularly. Among them are the Antillean crested hummingbird, eared dove, yellow-bellied seedeater, tropical mockingbird, black-faced grassquit, gray kingbird, Lesser Antillean bullfinch, brown-crested flycatcher, and smooth-billed ani.

Grenada's entire south coast, from Point Salines on the west where the international airport is located to Great Bacolet Bay on the east, is made up of a series of hilly peninsulas and very deep bays. Some fingers have hotels and other tourist facilities; others are elegant residential areas such as Westerhall, where hilltop homes have pretty views of the sea and the countryside. The fingers and bluffs farthest east from the city have coves and beaches that are usually deserted. Fort Jeudy, the southernmost point of the island, has a spectacular seascape where the Atlantic crashes against cliffs several hundred feet high. A road ends in a cul-de-sac about 200 ft/61 m from the windy edge and from there one walks to the cliffside. Offshore, Hog Island is a nesting area for the royal tern and other seabirds.

LA SAGESSE ESTUARY

At La Sagesse on the southeastern coast, an estuary is being developed as a nature center under the national parks scheme. It comprises a mangrove estuary, salt pond, three pretty beaches, interesting geological formations, coral reefs, and good examples of Caribbean littoral dominated by dry thorn scrub and cactus woodlands. The tree varieties include seagrape, seaside mahoe, Indian almond, coconut palms, and manchineel, whose apple-like fruit has a poisonous milky juice that can cause a skin rash.

The quiet, isolated pond is populated by a variety of birds, making it one of the best bird-watching areas in Grenada. The brown-crested flycatcher, common moorhen, Caribbean coot, green-backed heron, northern jacana, and little blue heron are among the most common species. Walks can also be made in the adjacent wilderness. Near the estuary is a small guesthouse with an outdoor restaurant and equipment for water sports.

A nature center is developing around La Sagesse Bay, which has three swimming beaches, a salt pond, a mangrove estuary, coral reefs, and fine birding.

La Baye Rock and Marquis Island

Two scenic, uninhabited islands—La Baye Rock and Marquis Island, directly off the Atlantic coast at Marquis—are a naturalist's delight. La Baye Rock, which is surrounded by reefs, represents one of the few undisturbed environments in Grenada. Large iguanas may be seen here, as well as nesting brown boobies, red-billed tropicbirds, and brown noddies. The island also has a pristine, dry thorn scrub forest, and its reefs offer good snorkeling.

Marquis Island and its surrounding coral reef have particular geological interest since they were part of the mainland at one time. Ash layers formed by volcanic eruptions as far away as Grand Etang and Mt. St. Catherine are visible. Vegetation consists of dry thorn scrub cactus. Farming has been practiced on the island intermittently, but now the natural vegetation is growing back. Both islands are home to the magnificent frigatebird.

The islands can be visited by boat, which must be arranged with a local fisherman or a nature guide. The people along this coast are famous for boatbuilding; a boat trip to the offshore island will most likely be taken in one of their handmade boats.

Carriacou

One of the two islands that make up the country of Grenada is Carriacou, 23 mi/37 km away to the northeast. It is a 13-sq-mi/34-sq-km island with a diverse and interesting cultural and natural heritage. A national parks program is under way to put the important areas under protection.

Two-thirds of Carriacou is volcanic in origin; the balance is limestone containing fossils of great interest to scientists. At the time Carriacou was settled it was covered by deep fertile soil ideal for sugar plantation. Intense sugarcane and later cotton cultivation caused soil erosion and loss of fertility and water retention. Today, the vegetation is made up of species that can survive long dry seasons, known to scientists as dry deciduous seasonal forest, where trees such as acacia and cactus are common.

Water, however, was always critical on Carriacou. Although the island is mountainous on its windward side, the mountains are not high enough to cause condensation; hence Carriacou gets about a third as much rainfall annually as Grenada. To overcome the problem of droughts, earlier settlers created an elaborate collection system of cisterns and catchments.

Hillsborough, the harbor and main town, is worth a brief walk, particularly to visit the new museum, which has a good collection of Amerindian and other artifacts. Sandy Island, facing the harbor, is surrounded by a shallow-water reef only a few feet from shore and is therefore a popular location for snorkeling. A boat can be rented for the five-minute ride to the island, but snorkelers must bring their own gear.

From the Hospital Scenic Overlook at the north end of the island there is a view that helps one get oriented to the island quickly. High North Peak, 955 ft/291 m, is the highest point and least disturbed area in Carriacou and encompasses the full spectrum of ecosystems on the island. The peak's northwest slope is covered with dry thorn scrub that changes to seasonal evergreen forests at the lower elevations. At the foot of the slope is l'Anse La Roche, a beautiful beach fronted by coral reefs and fringed with sea-grape, manchineel, and coconut trees. Overlooking l'Anse La Roche are stone ruins of an eighteenth-century plantation that once comprised about 266 acres/108 hectares of forest and grazing lands. At the foot of the peak's northeast slope, Petit Carenage Bay has mangroves that ecologists consider to be the finest mangrove and mud flat ecosystem in Grenada. The area is also one of the island's best bird-watching spots, attracting numerous migratory and shorebird species. The area directly south of Watering Bay, Limlair-Thibaud, is particularly significant for its fossil beds. The only known beds that are plainly visible in Grenada, they provide an excellent opportunity for studying prehistoric shellfish, some of which are extinct.

Dumfries on the south side of the island is the home of rare birds, such as the mangrove cuckoo. Off the southern coast at Manchineel Bay, tiny Saline and White islands are interesting for their geological formations that indicate major volcanic activity. Saline has a brackish lagoon and salt pond surrounded by a mangrove that attracts shorebirds; the adjacent coral reefs are considered to be Grenada's most diverse and extensive, with a great number of species. The red-billed tropicbird, which may grow a tail 20 in/50 cm in length, breeds here from April to May. White Island is surrounded on three sides by sandy white beaches with pristine littoral vegetation. Birdlife on both islands includes the Audubon's shearwater, black skimmer, brown booby, brown pelican, Grenada flycatcher, Lesser Antillean tanager, roseate tern, and scaly-breasted thrasher. At Harvey Vale on the southwest leeward coast, Tyrrel Bay is an excellent anchorage for yachts and has a pretty beach for swimming. The quiet, secluded bay, bordered by palm trees and a more lush vegetation than on the windward coast, is host to a variety of shorebirds.

The 486-acre/197-hectare island of Petit Martinique is the largest of Carriacou's offshore islands and the only one that is inhabited. Lying 2.5 mi/4 km off the east coast, it is dominated by a 745-ft/227-m volcanic cone. The chief occupation of its 600 residents is boatbuilding and fishing.

Carriacou is a twenty-minute flight from Grenada's Point Salines Airport. Boats depart Grenada twice weekly. In Hillsborough one can hire a taxi or rent a car to tour the island. Boats can be rented for day trips to nearby islands.

OUTDOOR ACTIVITIES

HIKING: The Grand Etang Forest Center has displays, brochures, and information on the nature trails for self-guided walks. Hikes from the Forest Center range from fifteen minutes to three hours. Those who intend to climb volcanic peaks or do serious hiking in remote areas need a guide. Henry's Tours (809-443-5313) designs hiking programs specifically to Grenada's natural attractions at close range. Telford Bedoux, Soubise, St. Andrews (809-440-7458), is one of the most knowledgeable nature guides in the country, and can arrange trips to La Baye Rock and Marquis Island.

Soursop on pomarock flowers.

SWIMMING: The 2-mile crescent of white sand beach fringed by tropical trees and fronting the calm waters of the Caribbean makes Grand Anse Beach one of the loveliest beaches in the Caribbean. Levera Beach on the northeast coast is empty on weekdays. Beaches on the west coast have steel-gray, volcanic sand. Carriacou and its offshore islands have wonderful beaches that visitors can have to themselves.

SNORKELING AND DIVING: Grenada is said to have an estimated forty species of coral in water with visibility to 200 ft/ 61 m. Offshore reefs within swimming distance south of Grand Anse Beach and neighboring Morne Rouge Bay are well suited for snorkeling. These reefs attract a variety of small fish, but the coral is not in good condition. The reefs' best feature is the profusion of huge sea fans, some of the largest in the Caribbean.

Grande Anse Bay is the center for water sports; facilities for snorkeling, sailing, windsurfing, and scuba diving are available from vendors at the beachfront resorts here. The best area for scuba diving is the Molinière Reef off the west coast at Grand Mal Bay about 3 mi/ 4.8 km north of St. George's. It begins in about 30 ft/9 m of water, slopes to 60 ft/ 18 m, and drops off to 120 ft/36 m. The reef is best and the fish more abundant below 40 ft/12 m. Another popular area is Martin's Bay, about 1 mi/1.6 km north of Grand Anse Beach, where patch reef rests in 30 to 50 ft/9 to 15 m of water. The favorite wreck dive is the *Bianca C.*, a cruise ship that caught fire and sank in 1961, and is now home to giant turtles, rays, and a variety of other fish.

The island's dive operators offer regularly scheduled dive excursions and certified diving courses at all levels. Both snorkeling and diving are less expensive here than in the more northerly islands.

Ripening nutmeg.

FISHING: While the fishing in Grenadian waters is good, it is not well organized. There is offshore fishing for barracuda, kingfish, red snapper, dolphin, and groupers, and deep-sea fishing for sailfish, blackfin tuna, blue marlin, and yellowtail tuna, among others. Those up to the task can sometimes go out with local fishermen for whom fishing is a livelihood, not a sport. The best places to locate someone willing to take an outsider would be on the waterfront in St. George's, Gouyave, or Grenville.

SAILING: Grenada has some of the best anchorages in the Caribbean along her south and leeward coasts. Yacht services at the Lagoon in St. George's and in Anse aux Epines on the south coast have full charter facilities as well as daysails and short excursions for snorkeling and beach picnics.

EXPLORING THE ISLAND

Grenada is easy to explore. Half-day and full-day tours to different parts of the island are readily available. Or, one can get a good map and can rent a car or hire a taxi. Car rental prices are comparable to those in the U.S. A valid driver's license and a small fee are required for a local permit from the traffic department. Driving in this former British Colony is on the LEFT.

Taxis are expensive unless one can share costs with others. Public transportation is not well developed. Local and longer-distance bus services are privately operated. Minibuses leave frequently throughout the day from the Esplanade in St. George's. For touring the hilltops overlooking the capital, a car is recommended because the hillsides are very steep and the sun is very hot. As an alternative, one might ride a local bus to the top of a hill and walk down.

New roads have improved access to the interior. The best road in the country is the cross-island highway between St. George's and Grenville. The drive from St. George's to the Grand Etang Forest Center in the middle of the island takes about twenty-five minutes. Major roads around the perimeter of the island are good near St. George's but deteriorate farther north along the west and east coasts. Beyond these vital arteries, secondary roads and dirt tracks reach most villages.

Cocoa pods.

INFORMATION: In the U.S.: Grenada Tourist Office, 820 Second Ave., Suite 900 D, New York, NY 10017; 212-687-9554 or 800-927-9554. In Canada: 439 University Ave., Suite 820, Toronto, Ontario M5G 1Y8; 416-595-1339. In the U.K.: 1 Collingham Gardens, Earl's Court, London, SW5 OHW; 71-370-5164 (or 5165). In Grenada: P.O. Box 293, The Carenage, St. George's, Grenada, WI; 809-440-2001 or 2279. Ministry of Agriculture and Tourism, St. George's; 809-442-7425 (or 440-2934).

Books on the flora and fauna of Grenada are available in local bookstores. They include *Birds of Grenada, St. Vincent and the Grenadines* by Raymund P. Devas (Grenada: Carenage Press, 1941); *Grenada, Isle of Spice* by Norma Sinclair (London: Macmillan, 1987); *A Natural History of the Island of Grenada* by J. R. Groome (Trinidad: Caribbean Printers, 1970); and *This is Grenada* by F. Kay (1971). A topographic map of the island can be purchased at the Grenada National Museum.

BARBADOS

SOFT, ROLLING GREEN hills fringed with white sand beaches and calm blue Caribbean waters on the west side of Barbados provide a sharp contrast to the white-topped Atlantic rollers that wash the rocky shores of the island's east coast. Surrounded by coral reefs that are often within swimming distance from shore, Barbados is the easternmost land in the Caribbean, situated 100 mi/160 km east of the Lesser Antilles. Its name, Isla de los Barbados, is said to derive from the bearded fig tree, which still grows here.

From its highest point at Mount Hillaby near the center, the slightly pear-shaped island slopes gently north, west, and south to the sea in a series of coral limestone terraces that indicate the various levels of the land's early formation. In the northeast is the Scotland District, an amphitheater-shaped region that extends over 20 percent of the island. Erosion in this area has stripped away the coral cap and exposed the underlying rock, part of an uplifted inner core of Tertiary age and the oldest rock visible on the island. Elsewhere on the east, the land falls abruptly to the sea from a plateau and a 2-mi-/3.2-km-long limestone massif. Parts of the north, east, and southeast coasts have unusual rock formations carved by the relentless crash of the Atlantic against the shore.

Once covered with forest, the land was cleared for sugar cultivation more than 300 years ago and has been intensively cultivated since then. The island has few permanent rivers, but over the eons watercourses have cut many deep gullies that are now thick with vegetation. Throughout the land, caves and sinkholes also have been carved in the porous limestone terrain.

Discovered by the Portuguese in 1536, Barbados was neither claimed nor colonized until almost a century later when British settlers arrived in 1625. Unlike most other Caribbean islands, which seesawed between rivaling European powers, Barbados remained a British Colony for over 300 years. Now, after almost three decades of independence, Barbados still seems as British as the Queen; the island even resembles the English countryside.

As a consequence of Barbados's intense cultivation and dense population, the island's natural attractions are fewer and more developed but usually more accessible than on some of her less-developed neighbors. The island appeals most to those who enjoy wandering about on short walking or driving jaunts and those with a strong sense of history, since Barbados's past is as much a part of the landscape as its scenery.

Bridgetown, the capital, dates from 1628 and has retained enough of its historic character to make for an interesting walk, particularly in the vicinity of the Careenage, the picturesque old harbor. On the east side of town, Queen's Park, once the residence of the commander of the British troops of the West Indies, is a public park with flowering gardens. The Barbados Museum, situated in a former military prison southeast of town, houses a magnificently displayed collection illustrating the natural history and culture of Barbados and the Caribbean.

In the center of the island, less than a thirty-minute drive from town, are three attractions within a mile of one another. They can be reached directly or via the coastal route, a delightful introduction to Barbados's tropical beauty, where seaside resorts and homes are set in gardens of brilliant bougainvillea, flamboyant, Pride of Barbados, and other flowering trees.

HARRISON'S CAVE

Among Barbados's many limestone caverns, the most accessible and impressive is Harrison's Cave, which belongs to the highly ramified underground river system of this area. The cave, first explored in 1781, was developed about a decade ago as a tourist attraction by the government with the aid of Danish speleologists. A battery-powered tram with a driver and guide takes visitors down into the lighted cavern. The most spectacular space is the Great Hall, a cavernous expanse with stalagmites and stalactites sparkling under artificial lighting. The vehicle continues to a lower level and a twin cascade that disappears under a passageway below. Near the lowest point in the cave, the tram rounds a curve to reveal the waterfall plunging into a blue-green pool. The return route winds back up through several chambers to the surface.

WELCHMAN HALL GULLY

The south entrance to Welchman Hall Gully, a rocky ravine formed by a split in the limestone cap that covers most of Barbados, is just 0.75 mi/ 1.2 km west of Harrison's Cave. Once part of a cave whose roof collapsed, the gully, humid and protected from high winds, was converted into a tropical garden of fruit and spice trees in the mid-nineteenth century. By the turn of the century, however, nature had taken over again. Today, it is a luxuriant nature reserve developed by the National Trust as a tourist attraction. A path meanders through the gully along limestone walls so thick with vegetation that the greenery appears to be growing out of the rocks. It passes a massive pillar more than 4 ft/1.2 m in diameter formed over eons by the joining of the stalactite and stalagmite and said to be one of the largest in the world. Another section features palms, including the endemic macaw palm, whose slim stems are covered with sharp, 3-in/ 7.6-cm spines. Splashes of color come from red ginger and white begonia. The gully has green, or vervet, monkeys and various birds including bananaquit, American redstart, and elaenias and other flycatchers. Al-

From the top of Mt. Hillaby near Farley Hill National Park, the panorama encompasses St. Andrew's Parish in northeast Barbados.

though Barbados does not have large numbers of resident species, it is a station for migrating North American birds where 160 species have been recorded. Both the south entrance and the north entrance (where the carpark is) of Welchman Hall Gully can be reached by public bus.

THE FLOWER FOREST

North of Welchman Hall Gully and Harrison's Cave is a 50-acre/20-hectare tropical garden created by a private group of Bajans and foreigners. Situated on Richmond Plantation, an old sugar estate in a scenic location at 850 ft/ 260 m elevation, the Flower Forest has a great variety of tropical fruit trees such as breadfruit, nutmeg, Barbados cherry, soursop, guava, and golden apple, as well as herbs and flowering shrubs. Red ginger, petrea, and coral lilies are some of the tropical flowers. Footpaths through the gardens follow the contours of the steep hillside; plants are labeled and there are benches for resting and lookouts from which to enjoy views of distant hills and the coast along the way. Visitors can taste some of the exotic fruit drinks such as tamarind, golden apple, and soursop at a small bar near the entrance.

The gardens here as well as those around homes and hotels are populated with Barbados's three species of hummingbirds—the Antillean crested, green-throated carib, and purple-throated carib. Almost any mango tree—and the island has many—might host the protected ramier, or scaly-naped pigeon, and in April or May there are scarlet tanagers.

FOLKSTONE PARK AND BARBADOS MARINE RESERVE

On the west coast north of Holetown is the Folkstone Park, a picnic and swimming location popular with Bajans. It includes the Barbados Marine Reserve, which consists of a small marine museum, research laboratory, and a marine park with an artificial reef offshore. The marine park is divided into four zones according to usage. There is a marked underwater trail for snorkelers along the protected inner reef; a segment of outer reef can be used by divers. The latter, known as Dottin's Reef, is a 7-mi/11.2-km stretch of intermittent banking reef lying between 0.25 to 0.5 mi/0.4 to 0.8 km offshore. The park's other zones are designated for water skiing, sailing, other water sports, and scientific research. The artificial reef was created by sinking the Greek freighter *Stavronikita*, destroyed by fire in 1976. It lies about 0.5 mi/0.8 km offshore at Prospect at depths ranging from 40 to 90 ft/12 to 27 m, with the main mast reaching within 15 ft/4.5 m of the surface of the sea where it is marked by a buoy. The site is recommended for experienced divers.

FARLEY HILL NATIONAL PARK

At Speightstown, the second largest town, the coastal road turns east to Farley Hill National Park and the Barbados Wildlife Reserve. The park, approached by an avenue of royal palms and casuarina trees, is named after a mansion built in 1861 for the visit of Prince Alfred and later used to house other members of the British royal family. After a fire in 1965, the house was taken over by the government but not rebuilt, and the grounds were made into a park that covers 30 wooded acres/12 hectares and gardens with labeled plants. The views south and eastward of the Scotland District and the rugged coast are spectacular.

Barbados Wildlife Reserve

Opposite the park entrance a track leads through a canefield to the 3-acre/ 1.2-hectare Barbados Wildlife Reserve, primarily a sanctuary for the green, or vervet, monkey. Created in 1985, it is the only one of its kind in the Caribbean. The monkeys, although called green, are brownish gray with yellow and olive-green flecks. They are naturally shy and difficult to observe in the wild, but here they are uncaged in a well-developed mahogany grove and can be seen along with agoutis, caimans, deer, peacocks, opossums, rabbits, raccoons, tortoises, and wallabies. The reserve has a stream with otters, swans, and ducks and a walk-in aviary of tropical birds. Visitors walk through the reserve on well-defined, tree-shaded paths.

Monkeys, brought to Barbados from West Africa, were considered agricultural pests as early as 1680, and a bounty was offered for them. In the last decade, they again became so numerous and caused so much damage to crops that the government reactivated the bounty practice. The solution to the problem was the formation of the Wildlife Reserve with a policy of humane trapping and wildlife management, and, at the same time, the development of a program for using the animals in research, particularly in the production of the polio vaccine.

Cherry Tree Hill

East of Farley Hill Park en route to Cherry Tree Hill is St. Nicholas Abbey, a well-preserved plantation house of Jacobean architecture built in 1650 and one of only three such houses still standing in the Western Hemisphere. The private owners of the mansion, which is open to the public, still operate a sugar plantation and offer a twenty-minute film with rare footage on plantation life and sugar processing in the early part of this century.

Cherry Tree Hill, a knoll at 850 ft/260 m, commands a magnificent view of the Atlantic and the Scotland District. About 1 mi/1.6 km south of Cherry Tree Hill stands the seventeenth-century Morgan Lewis Mill, the only windmill of the 580 that once operated in Barbados that still has its wheelhouse and arms intact. Here and farther south at Walker's Savannah and Chalky Mount, one can see large clusters of columnar cactus, an endemic species that grows over 6 ft/1.8 m tall. The vegetation illustrates how microclimates can exist within small Caribbean islands such as Barbados due to the wide variations in rainfall and winds.

Turner's Hall Woods

South of Morgan Lewis, beyond Greenland, a secondary road leads west to Turner's Hall Plantation and Turner's Hall Woods, 46 acres/18.6 hectares of natural deciduous or evergreen seasonal and semideciduous forest, considered the best example of the original vegetation that probably covered Barbados at the time of its discovery by Europeans. Thirty-two species of trees have been identified here. The woods consist mainly of bully or bullet, white cedar, West Indian locust, and fustic, a species belonging to the island's original flora, as well as dense stands of macaw palms. There are green monkeys here too.

The forest, popular for hiking and birding, is about 0.5 mi/0.8 km in length and up to 1,200 ft/366 m in width on a steep slope. It can be approached from the northeast end at the village of St. Simon via a road south of Belleplaine. Here a track that was once a road leads into the woods where one sees Spanish oak, wild clammy cherry, and mahogany, introduced in Barbados in the seventeenth century. After about 900 ft/274 m, the forest gets thicker and at the point where the track crosses a bridge and begins a sharp climb toward the Turner's Hall–Bridgetown Road, a barely noticeable track on the south leads through the best-preserved part of the woods where the trees are tallest and the canopy thickest.

Four layers of vegetation can be distinguished. Overhead are the trees forming a dense canopy 35 to 65 ft/11 to 20 m high and another layer of individual trees up to 120 ft/37 m tall protruding above the canopy. Lower shrubs and saplings comprise the third layer, and the herbs at ground level are the fourth. In addition to the common trees of the main canopy, there are a few deciduous ones such as hog plum and birch gum. The trees over 100 ft/30 m are locusts with girths up to 8 ft/2.4 m and silk-cotton with massive buttresses to support trunks that grow 8 to 12 ft/2.4 to 3.6 m in girth. There are sandbox trees, their trunks covered with sharp spikes, and fiddlewood, whose enormous leaves turn pink before falling. The cabbage palms reach 120 ft/37 m in height. Although the woods receive considerably less rain than a rain forest—it averages 60 to 70 in/152 to 177 cm—they have thirteen species of lianas, three epiphytes, and three ferns. Monkey tail is an aroid with leaves 18 in/46 cm long and 4 in/10 cm wide, found only in Barbados, Tobago, and Brazil.

Among the birds that populate the forest are the Lesser Antillean bullfinch, Carib grackle, gray kingbird, black-whiskered vireo, Caribbean elaenia, Zenaida dove, and scaly-naped pigeon, which only recently began colonizing Turner's Hall Woods.

On the south side of the woods lies the only uninhabited valley in Barbados, bounded by Moese Bottom on the west, White Hill on the south, and Haggatts to the east. People lived here until thirty years ago, but landslides and transport difficulties forced them to leave. The land is used for growing coconuts and mangoes and for grazing animals. Upon climbing east to the top of the ridge, one sees the change in vegetation: forest on the northwest side of the hill and scrub on the southeast side.

Surfers come to Bathsheba's boulder-strewn beach for strong Atlantic waves; hikers are drawn to the rugged beauty of the rockbound coves and hillsides.

A 5-mi/8-km hike from Turner's Hall Woods east, down through St. Simon and Haggatts Factory to Belleplaine and Windy Hill, takes at least two hours. A more difficult hike from Moese Bottom to Haggatts Factory following a riverbed takes about three hours and requires scrambling over rocks and bush. A hike from Turner's Hall Plantation north and west leads to Rock Hall village and Spring Head. It is a 4-mi/6.4-km round trip and takes two hours or more.

CHALKY MOUNT AND HACKLETON'S CLIFF

The East Coast Road from Belleplaine south along the Atlantic coast to Bathsheba follows the line of a railway that ran from Belleplaine to Bridgetown from 1882 to 1938. Until the road was built, large sections of the coast were inaccessible to vehicular traffic. The road passes under the peaks of Chalky Mount and The Potteries, a hilltop village where a few artisans carry on the tradition of working on wheels and use local ocher-colored clay to fashion pottery similar in design to those of Arawak and African traditions.

Chalky Mount is a curious three-pointed geological formation that, when viewed from a distance, resembles a man in repose with his hands crossed over his stomach. It is known locally as Napoleon. The red-flowered sorrel, which grows up to 3 ft/1 m tall here, is in full bloom in December and is known locally as the Christmas flower. A refreshing drink made from it is known to have been used in Egypt since ancient times.

Bathsheba, framed by the 1,000-ft-/305-m-high Chalky Mount on the northwest and Hackleton's Cliff on the southwest, is a fishing village and holiday resort. The landscape, often described as Cornwall-in-miniature, is strewn with masses of rock over which the Atlantic waves break. Flying fishes, common in Barbados waters, can be seen here.

ANDROMEDA GARDENS

A cliffside overlooking Bathsheba is the site of Andromeda Gardens, a mature tropical spread with a stream meandering through it. The gardens are renowned for their orchids. The plant life of Barbados is well represented and includes a large specimen of the bearded fig tree. The gardens, recently acquired by the National Trust, have a particular interest to botanists and horticulturists since the late owner's hobby was to transplant species here from different climatic conditions around the world to test their ability to grow in the Caribbean's tropical environment. The gardens are easily accessible by road; or one can make a 0.25-mi/0.4-km climb up the hill at Hillcrest, on the south side of Bathsheba.

THE RUGGED EAST COAST

The lighthouse at Ragged Point marks the easternmost reach of the island. From here north along the Atlantic coast to Bathsheba and Pico Tenerife, a distance of about 16 mi/26 km, is the island's most popular hiking area. It is possible to hike the length of the coast, but most people do it in short segments to enjoy interesting inland detours along the way.

Ragged Point to Consett Bay. 4 mi/6.4 km; two hours one way. From Ragged Point, a rough, stony trail about 150 ft/45 m inland follows the coast to the picturesque fishing village of Consett Bay, passing Culpepper Island and Skeete's Bay en route. About 0.25 mi/0.4 km offshore, the wreck of the *Countess of Rippon,* a metal-hulled steamer that went down in 1860, lies in 20 ft/6 m of water. It is not visible from land, but can be seen by snorkelers. From Bayfield the track continues to College Savannah west of Consett Point where one sees a double row of casuarina trees planted 300 ft/90 m apart; at the north end of the trees is the bed of the old railway. A sourgrass pasture follows the cliffs to Consett Bay.

Consett Bay to Martin's Bay. 3 mi/4.8 km; two hours. The hillside along the beach has evidence of bitumin which was mined commercially and exported from here at the turn of the century. About halfway, Bath is a popular picnic and swimming spot protected by a large barrier reef that is exposed at low tide. The government-operated picnic area has showers and toilet facilities. At the north end of Bath beach, a track continues to Congor Bay and around Studies Point, along the old railway bed to Martin's Bay, a small fishing village. The area has an abundance of seagrape, manchineel, and white wood trees. The trail parallels the East Coast Road with Hackleton's Cliff in the background.

Codrington College/St. John's Church/Martin's Bay Loop. 6 mi/9.6 km round trip; four hours. Codrington College, founded in the seventeenth century, is the oldest British school in the West Indies and one of the earliest institutions of higher education in the Western Hemisphere. Now a theological school, its entrance is marked by an avenue of majestic royal palms, often pictured in scenes of Barbados. The steep hike goes from Codrington College to St. John's Church via Consett Bay and Martin's Bay and returns via Quintyne, a natural freshwater spring marked by seven 80-ft-/24-m-high royal palms, just north of Bath. From the clifftop at St. John's Parish Church there are extensive views along the wooded face of Hackleton's Cliff and north to Bathsheba and beyond where strong Atlantic waves break against the coast. Built in 1836 to replace an earlier church destroyed by a hurricane, the graveyard of St. John's Church has tombstones from 1678.

Martin's Bay to Bathsheba. 3 mi/4.8 km; nintey minutes. Instead of climbing to St. John's Church, hikers can continue north at Martin's Bay to Bathsheba by following the railway track. The land is barren and rocky, and the sea is rough. A few freshwater springs drain across the land.

Bathsheba to The Choyce and Pico Tenerife. 4 mi/6.4 km; four hours. If hikers stay on the coast, rather than detouring to Hackleton's Cliff, they can follow the road that edges the coast north of Bathsheba to Windy Ridge and The Choyce, passing a beautiful stretch along Walker's and Long Pond beaches, which are popular for beachcombing. After The Choyce a trail leads to Pico Tenerife, a sharply pointed hill 300 ft/90 m above the sea that affords magnificent views of the rugged Atlantic coast. The steep track goes along a rocky, shrub-covered, windblown section of coast.

ANIMAL FLOWER CAVE

At Animal Flower Bay, directly east of North Point, the northernmost point of the island, there are sea caves with stalactites and stalagmites, accessible only by foot, and underwater caverns that can be reached only by scuba divers. Animal Flower Cave, the most popular of the sea caves, is a natural cavern in the cliffs. Although most of the rock formations of the coast have been shaped by the waves, the interior of Animal Flower Cave suggests that it is a karst cave formed inside the limestone and later opened to the sea. The cave derives its name from the sea anemones, known locally as animal flowers, that grow in pools on the rocks and in the cave. There are spectacular stands of cactus here too.

GRAEME HALL SWAMP

On the south coast, amid heavy development, the Graeme Hall Swamp is a 78-acre/31-hectare area that is Barbados's favored birding location. A track skirts the north side of the swamp. At daybreak one may see thousands of cattle egrets flying out of white mangrove trees, where they roost and nest. Other residents are green-backed heron, common gallinule (known here as red seal coot), Caribbean coot, and yellow, or golden, warbler. Among the migratory birds are osprey, belted kingfisher (known here as rainbird), greater and lesser yellowlegs, willet, double-crested cormorant, as well as finches, grassquits, and a variety of sandpipers, and terns.

At the fishing village of Oistins, a secondary road leads to South Point, the southernmost tip of Barbados where there is a lighthouse. The southeastern end of the island has a much indented coastline of beautiful bays and impressive rock formations and reefs lying just off the coast. The coast south of the international airport, particularly, has interesting rock formations—Pennyhole Rock, Salt Cave Point, Green Point, New Fall Cliff—and seasonal swamps. The area attracts swifts, terns, brown pelicans, gulls, brown boobies, and magnificent frigatebirds. Barbados receives many migrants, particularly shorebirds, some from as far away as the Arctic tundra en route to their wintering areas in South America.

Uncaged green, or vervet, monkeys, originally from West Africa, roam a mahogany forest in the Barbados Wildlife Reserve.

OUTDOOR ACTIVITIES

HIKING: As elsewhere in the tropics, the best and coolest hours for hiking are 6 to 10 A.M. or 4 to 6 P.M. The Barbados National Trust organizes free morning hikes starting at 6 A.M. for residents; visitors are welcome. The hikes, which attract as many as 300 people, are divided into three groups—fast, medium, and slow—and highlight nature as well as history and culture. Each hike is approximately 5 mi/8 km and lasts three hours. A different region is covered each week; schedules are available in advance from the National Trust and are published in local newspapers and visitors' guides. The Trust will also help arrange transportation. Hikers should wear a hat with a wide brim.

HORSEBACK RIDING: Four stables have riding and cross-country trekking. Information on stables is available from the Barbados Board of Tourism. Polo is played from September to March at the Polo Club (809-425-2260) on Saturdays and Wednesdays.

SWIMMING: The best beaches, with long strands of sand and calm waters, are along the Caribbean coast but they are tightly occupied by resorts; the same is true of the south coast as far as South Point. Much of the north, southeast, and east coasts is rockbound with coves and small beaches or long stretches washed by strong Atlantic waves. There is a series of quiet white sand beaches at Horseshoe Bay, Cluff's Bay, and Archer's Bay on the northwest coast, accessible only by secondary roads and tracks; Crane Bay on the southeast is one of the prettiest beaches on the island but often rough with Atlantic waves.

SNORKELING AND DIVING: Barbados is surrounded by coral reefs—an inner reef suitable for snorkeling and learning to dive and an outer barrier reef. It is one of the few locations in the eastern Caribbean that has a recompression chamber. The best areas for snorkeling are along the west coast, where the reefs lie in 20 to 30 ft/6 to 9 m of water within swimming distance of shore.

The barrier reefs are located from 0.25 to 0.75 mi/0.4 to 1.2 km offshore and require a boat to reach. The formations of those paralleling the west coast are somewhat unusual. They begin on a plateau at about 50 ft/15 m, drop to a valley of 80 to 100 ft/24 to 30 m, rise again to a height of 60 to 80 ft/18 to 24 m, and drop to another valley of 90 to 130 ft/27 to 40 m where the fish are larger and the water clearer. Divers will see moray eels, turtles, and squid as well as brightly colored parrotfishes and blue chubs, among others.

Barbados is popular with novices, but has limited interest for experienced divers, except those who are interested in shipwrecks and photographers who enjoy exceptionally clear water for taking pictures of invertebrate life.

For those who neither snorkel nor dive, a recreational submarine takes passengers to depths of 100 ft/30 m along the barrier reef. Excursions leave every two hours from 9 A.M. to 9 P.M. from the Careenage; the trip takes about 90 minutes with 45 minutes spent on the reef.

SURFING: Barbados offers surfing on the Atlantic coast around Bathsheba. Several surfing championships have been held here. The island has a factory that produces custom-made sailboards and surfboards and another that makes sails. Both companies do repairs.

WINDSURFING: The World Windsurfing Championships have been held here and are expected to return often. A combination of assets has made Barbados one of the prime windsurfing locations in the world with conditions particularly well suited to competition. First, there is a long reef of 4 to 5 mi/6 to 8 km along the south coast where for nine months of the year the tradewinds blow from the east, enabling windsurfers to reach for long distances.

Second, the reef not only protects the calm, inner waters near the shore, which are good for beginners, but outside the reef, the strong waves of the Atlantic break against the coral and over the reef, providing a real challenge in advanced windsurfing and great excitement for the sport of wave jumping. Slalom competition, in which competitors round buoys, and international wave-jumping competitions were held here in 1988. Barbados has become a training ground for competitors. Not only are conditions ideal for training but the island is less crowded than many other locations where windsurfing is popular. Moreover, the water is clean and warm year-round.

OTHER WATER SPORTS: There are facilities for sailing, parasailing, and deep-sea fishing; visitors make arrangements through local agencies and hotels. The Barbados Yacht Club (809-427-1125) is located east of Bridgetown on the south coast.

EXPLORING THE ISLAND

Barbados can be explored by car, bus, bike, or on foot. It has an extensive network of numbered roads—800 mi/1,280 km paved—and it is laced throughout with small roads bordered by fields of tall sugarcane that all look alike. So, while places are easily accessible, they are not always easy to find. A good map is essential to avoid getting lost. At the same time, in this island with the highest literacy rate in the Caribbean, where English is the native language, one need not go far before finding someone willing and able to help. The island is divided into eleven parishes or districts, each with a parish church.

All major highways—numbered 1 to 7—begin in Bridgetown in the southwest corner and stretch across the island from west to east like the ribs of a fan, often branching at midpoint to connect with other highways and creating a spiderweb across the island. For example, Highway 1 hugs the west coast on its way north to Speightstown where it bends east; Highway 2 is slightly inland from the west coast and points north/northeast until it meets Highway 1 at Farley Hill. The two roads combined with a few detours take one to Barbados's main attractions on a driving tour. Highway 7 skirts the south coast most of the way. The four highways in between—3, 4, 5, 6—cross the island northeast and east, ending at the east coast, the most popular area for hiking. Efficient as the system may sound, Bajans, as the people of Barbados are called, do not refer to roads by numbers, but rather give directions by location, destination, or the parish in which a place is located.

Cars, Mini Mokes, and vans are available for rent at prices comparable to those in the U.S. Driving in this former British Colony is on the LEFT. Visitors can use their U.S. driver's license to get a Barbados license, which is required and can be obtained quickly. Taxis are expensive unless one has several people with whom to share the cost, but there is a good, inexpensive public bus system that covers all parts of the island.

INFORMATION: In North America: Barbados Tourism Authority, 800 Second Ave., New York, NY 10017; 800-221-9831, 212-986-6516. In the U.K.: 263 Tottenham Court Rd., London W1P 9AA; 71-636-9448. In Barbados: PO Box 242, Bridgetown, Barbados, WI; 809-42-72623. Barbados National Trust, Ronald Tree House, No. 2, Tenth Ave., Belleville, St. Michael; 809-42-62421. The Trust is a private organization concerned with the preservation of the country's natural as well as cultural and historic heritage.

A Naturalist's Year in Barbados by Maurice Bateman Hutt, n.d.; *Exploring Historic Barbados* by Maurice Bateman Hutt (1981); *The Flora of Barbados* by Gooding, Lovelace, and Proctor. *The Ins and Outs of Barbados* by Keith and Sally Miller is an annual guide. Good topographical maps are available from bookstores and the Department of Lands and Surveys.

TRINIDAD AND TOBAGO

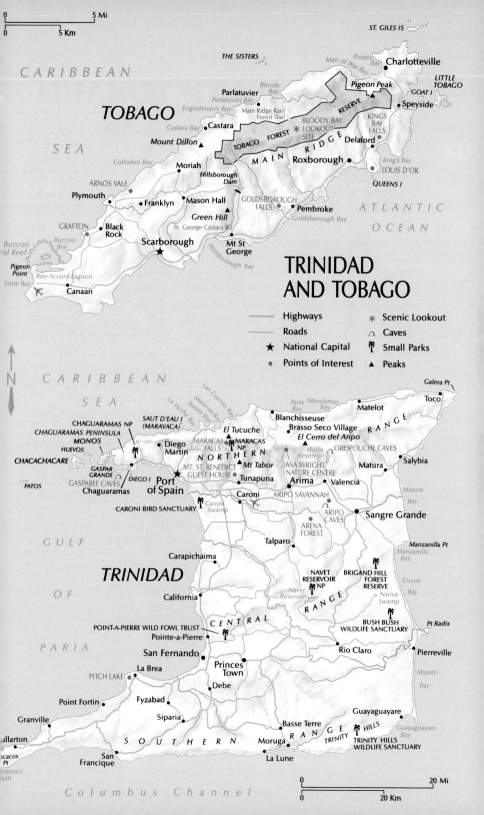

TRINIDAD AND TOBAGO

Legend:
- Highways
- Roads
- ★ National Capital
- ● Points of Interest
- ✳ Scenic Lookout
- ⌒ Caves
- 🌴 Small Parks
- ▲ Peaks

5 Mi
5 Km

TOBAGO

ST. GILES IS
THE SISTERS
Pirates Bay
Man of War Bay
Charlotteville
LITTLE TOBAGO
Parlatuvier
Bloody Bay
Pigeon Peak ▲
GOAT I
Parlatuvier Bay
Speyside
Englishman's Bay
Main Ridge Rain Forest Trail
RESERVE
KINGS BAY FALLS
Castara Bay
Castara
TOBAGO FOREST
BLOODY BAY LOOKOUT SITE
✳
Delaford
KINGS BAY
Mount Dillon ▲
MAIN RIDGE
Roxborough ●
King's Bay
LOUIS D'OR
Moriah ●
Hillsborough Dam
QUEENS I
ARNOS VALE
St. George-Castara Rd.
GOLDSBOROUGH FALLS
ATLANTIC OCEAN
Plymouth ●
Franklin ●
Mason Hall ●
Green Hill ▲
Pembroke
Goldsborough Bay
GRAFTON
Black Rock ●
Mt St George
Scarborough ★
Buccoo Reef
Buccoo Bay
Hillsborough Bay
Pigeon Point
Bon Accord Lagoon
Store Bay
Canaan ●

CARIBBEAN SEA

TRINIDAD

CARIBBEAN SEA
Galera Pt
Las Cuevas Bay
Maracas Bay
Toco
Baata Bay
La Vache Bay
Paria Bay
Mandamas Bay
Matelot
CHAGUARAMAS NP
SAUT D'EAU I (MARAVACA)
Blanchisseuse
RANGE
CHAGUARAMAS PENINSULA
El Tucuche ▲
Brasso Seco Village
MONOS
Diego Martin ●
MARACAS FALLS
El Cerro del Aripo ▲
HUEVOS
MARACAS NP
Hollis Reservoir
OROPOUCHE CAVES
CHACACHACARE
NORTHERN
ASA WRIGHT NATURE CENTRE
Matura
Salybia
GASPAR GRANDE
Mt Tabor ▲
MT. ST. BENEDICT GUEST HOUSE
Arima ●
GASPAREE CAVES
DIEGO I
Tunapuna
Valencia
Matura Bay
Chaguaramas
Port of Spain ★
Caroni ●
ARIPO SAVANNAH
PATOS
Caroni Swamp
ARIPO CAVES ⌒
CARONI BIRD SANCTUARY
ARENA FOREST
Sangre Grande ●

GULF
Carapichaima ●
Manzanilla Pt
Manzanilla Bay
OF
TRINIDAD
NAVET RESERVOIR
BRIGAND HILL FOREST RESERVE
California ●
CENTRAL
NP
Cocos Bay
PARIA
Navet Reservoir
Nariva Swamp
RANGE
POINT-A-PIERRE WILD FOWL TRUST
BUSH BUSH WILDLIFE SANCTUARY
Pt Radix
Pointe-a-Pierre ●
San Fernando ●
Rio Claro ●
Pierreville ●
La Brea ●
Princes Town ●
PITCH LAKE
Debe ●
Mayaro Bay
Point Fortin ●
Fyzabad ●
Granville ●
Siparia ●
Guayaguayare ●
ullarton
Basse Terre
Guayaguayare Bay
cacos Pt
Moruga ●
RANGE
TRINITY HILLS
San Francique ●
La Lune
TRINITY HILLS WILDLIFE SANCTUARY
SOUTHERN
Serpent's uth

Columbus Channel

20 Mi
20 Km

N

TRINIDAD AND TOBAGO

THE DUAL-ISLAND NATION of Trinidad and Tobago is something of an odd couple, differing in their origins, histories, and natural environments. Together they possess some of the most spectacular scenery, wildlife, and natural attractions in the Caribbean.

Trinidad, which is situated only 7 mi/11 km off the coast of Venezuela near the delta of the Orinoco River, was originally part of the South American mainland. Some scientists theorize that the separation occurred after the last ice age when the sea level rose; others maintain that it occurred more recently—less than 6,000 years ago—as the result of erosion caused by flooding of the Orinoco. Even today, the volume of water pouring into Trinidad's Gulf of Paria from the Orinoco is so great at times that the salt content of the Gulf is diluted to freshwater levels. The waters carry with them continental plants and animals that make their landfall in the southern reaches of Trinidad. As a result of its origins and proximity to the continent, Trinidad has the widest variety of flora and fauna of any island in the West Indies; most species are South American, not seen elsewhere in the Caribbean. Its birdlife is the most spectacular—425 species converge here.

Beautiful and serene Tobago lies 22 mi/35 km northeast of Trinidad on the continental shelf, east of the geological plate that divides North and South America. Partly because Tobago lies so near a geological plate, scientists have not yet agreed on the island's origin. Some suggest that the island broke loose from Trinidad itself. Others theorize that it broke loose from South America and "slid" across from Venezuela. (This would explain the presence of some plants and animals in both South America and Tobago but not in Trinidad, which now lies between them.) Still others note that there is igneous rock on the island and propose that Tobago, like the volcanic Lesser Antilles, rose from the sea and has acquired its flora and fauna from across the water.

On his third voyage, Columbus sighted the big island and named it La Trinidad after the three peaks of the southeast mountain range, which to him symbolized the Holy Trinity and today are known as the Trinity Hills. But rivaling European nations did not consider the island important, and the Spaniards were able to hold it for three centuries until 1797, when they were ousted by the British. In contrast, Tobago became a pawn in the struggle for power that raged in the West Indies among Spain, England, France, and other European powers. The island changed hands sixteen times, until finally in 1889 it asked to become a part of Trinidad. The two became an independent country in 1962.

TRINIDAD

Three parallel mountain ranges separated by wide plains run east–west across Trinidad. The deeply creviced mountains that cover the northern third of the island, known as the Northern Range, are an extension of the Andes of Venezuela. On their south side the mountains fall onto the wide Caroni Plain where nine rivers with dozens of streams wash down into two principal waterways: the Caroni River, which flows west into marshlands along the Gulf of Paria, and the Oropuche, which runs east to Matura Bay on the Atlantic. South of the plains the gentle limestone hills of the Central Range rise on a northeast–southwest angle at the island's midsection. Edging the south coast is the Southern Range, an unconnected series of mountains that peak at 1,010 ft/308 m in the forested Trinity Hills on the southeastern corner.

PORT OF SPAIN

Port of Spain, in Trinidad, is the capital and largest town of Trinidad and Tobago. The birthplace of the calypso and steel bands, it is the ultimate Caribbean kaleidoscope, reflecting many races and ethnic groups in its cuisine, music, dance, and religions. The busy port is at the head of a commercial and industrial corridor along the west coast that passes the international airport on its way south to the oil installations at San Fernando, the island's second largest town. Port of Spain may look all business and bustle, but it can serve as an introduction to the other face of Trinidad.

On the north side of town is Queen's Park Savannah, framed on its western perimeter by the Magnificent Seven—imposing buildings that were built at the turn of the century. On its north and northeast sides, the park is bordered by the Emperor Valley Zoo, Botanic Gardens, and presidential residence. In the northwest corner, below the level of the Savannah, is an area called The Hollows, where enormous trees shade open lawns in a setting of flower beds, lily ponds, and natural rocks. It is a peaceful place to picnic.

The Botanic Gardens, northeast of Queen's Park Savannah, were laid out in 1820. They have pretty walkways along manicured lawns with hedges of hibiscus and bougainvillea and seasonally changed flower beds. Among the large trees are tamarind, samaan, Brazil nut, and an avenue of palms. Flowering trees include the brilliantly red-leaved chaconia, the national flower, which grows in wooded areas especially along the north coast, and the yellow poui, an indigenous tree found throughout the country. Others are the flamboyant, or royal poinciana; jacaranda with lavender blue blossoms; pink poui, which is blossom-laden in February; and queen's-flower, whose pink flowers are seen from June to September. The pride of the gardens is its orchid collection, which includes some of Trinidad's 700 species.

West of the Botanic Gardens is the Emperor Valley Zoo. Begun in 1952 with a small number of local animals and birds, it now includes animals from around the world, although the emphasis remains on tropical fauna. Along the paths one can see a variety of monkeys including the two indigenous species: the weeping capuchin found in the Southern Range and in Bush Bush, a region of the Nariva Swamp; and the red howler, found in the Northern Range. Other forest mammals are deer, tree porcupine, peccary, crab-eating raccoon, agouti, and paca, a large rodent hunted in South America for its meat. The zoo also has a large number of reptiles including iguanas, four species of boas, and the spectacled caiman, called an alligator locally. Trinidad's forty-seven snake species include four venomous ones: bushmaster, fer-de-lance, and two colorful coral snakes.

Among the birds there is a handsome pair of channel-billed toucans, a species found particularly in the Arima and Aripo valleys of the Northern Range; a magnificent group of rare blue-and-yellow macaws; and scarlet macaws. The grounds of the zoo, Botanic Gardens, and Queen's Park Savannah are home to a variety of birds. Among them are several tanagers, particularly the palm tanager; the great kiskadee, one of Trinidad's most common birds; and the copper-rumped hummingbird and black-throated mango, two of the island's fourteen species of hummingbirds.

CHAGUARAMAS NATIONAL PARK

This park, located west of Port of Spain, covers the Chaguaramas Peninsula, the westernmost tip of the island with Mt. Catherine (1,768 ft/539 m) its highest peak, plus the offshore islands of Chacachacare, Huevos, Monos, Gaspar Grande, and the Diego Islands. One of the most arid areas of Trinidad, covered mostly with dry scrub, Chaguaramas is home to the red howler monkey. A track of about 6 mi/9.6 km from Carenage Bay, unsuitable for vehicles, leads to the summit of Mt. Catherine. It passes through woodlands with rock outcroppings and overlooks the Tucker Valley on the east, the main north–south corridor of the peninsula leading to popular beaches on the north.

Gaspar Grande, about a mile offshore, is a 1-mi-/1.6-km-long island that is a popular beach resort with daily boat service from Chaguaramas. The Gasparee Caves have impressive stalactites and stalagmites which can be viewed along recently renovated lighted walkways. There are picnic facilities in the adjacent area. At the west end of the Chaguaramas Peninsula across Scotland Bay, Monos, with many deep coves of white sand, is a favorite weekend getaway for affluent Trinidadians who have built elegant homes here. Huevos, where strong waves crash against the eastern shores, has a calm west coast, popular for snorkeling, fishing, and diving.

Clockwise from top left: copper-rumped hummingbird; violaceous trogon; oilbird; blue-gray tanager.

MARACAS BAY NATIONAL PARK AND FALLS

A high, winding road north of Port of Spain climbs up Saddle Road to the North Coast Road that comprises the Maracas North Coast Scenic Landscape, a scenic route through tropical-forest-clad mountains overlooking La Vache and Balata bays. It descends into the proposed Maracas Bay National Park, which fronts the Caribbean coast from Maracas Bay to Las Cuevas Bay where long stretches of palm-shaded golden sand are framed by the verdant north face of the Northern Range. Maracas Bay is one of the most popular swimming beaches in Trinidad, with Tourist Board bathing facilities. Lesser-known Tyrico Bay, 1 mi/1.6 km farther east, has dramatic wave action popular with surfers. Las Cuevas, 5 mi/8 km west of Maracas Bay, also has Tourist Board resort facilities. Experienced surfers like the strong wave action at the northwestern end of Las Cuevas, known as "the bowl." The road continues as far as Blanchisseuse.

Steep, difficult, and seldom-used trails from Las Cuevas Bay lead to the Caura and Maracas valleys on the south side of the Northern Range, but El Tucuche and Maracas Fall, two prime hiking destinations of the Maracas area, are more accessible from the south side of the range.

Maracas Fall—300 ft/90 m high and spectacular—is on the Naranja River in the mountains above the Maracas Valley; it is accessible from St. Joseph, a suburb about 6 mi/9.6 km east of Port of Spain. The road north follows the Maracas River to the village of the same name where a signposted secondary road on the right leads about a mile to walking trails. One trail of less than a mile is an easy walk through secondary forest to the base of the falls where there is a picnic and recreation area. A second trail, to be undertaken only by experienced hikers with a guide, is much more difficult and requires rock-hopping across the river and climbing up a steep, narrow, and often slippery path. It arrives at a point above the big falls and near a deep upstream pool where one can swim, though the water is quite cold.

EL TUCUCHE

An access point for the climb up El Tucuche, the island's second highest peak, is also along the Maracas Valley road. However, the 7-mi/11-km trek is complicated by many turns as it wends its way through old plantations, along abandoned roads, riverbeds, and overgrown paths, and over two mountain passes to the forest reserve from where a good trail winds up the steep-sided mountain to the summit. Hikers should have a local guide or the very explicit directions available in *The Nature Trails of Trinidad* by Richard ffrench and Peter Bacon to show the way. The last two hours pass through cool, dense tropical forests above 1,600 ft/488 m, where the canopy is at 90 ft/27 m or more and an understory is crowded with tree ferns, mountain palms, and epiphytes. The forest floor, covered with ferns and mosses, is brightened here and there with wild begonias. The forest reserve is also a wildlife sanctuary of 2,314 acres/936 hectares for animals such as deer, pacas, agoutis, and armadillos. Hikers might spot a rare scaly-naped or white-naped pigeon and orange-billed nightingale-thrush. More common are the beautiful green honeycreeper, violaceous euphonia with its bright yellow-orange chest and belly, and bay-headed tanager with a reddish-brown head and golden green body.

At the summit hikers enjoy spectacular views of the island. The hike takes four to five hours from Ortinola for experienced hikers in good condition accompanied by someone who knows the route. For information, one might contact the Trinidad and Tobago Field Naturalists' Club whose members make the trek each year during the dry season and have helped maintain the trail in the past.

CARONI SWAMP NATIONAL PARK
AND BIRD SANCTUARY

Caroni is the name of the river, the plains, and the mangroves stretching along the west coast south of Port of Spain. It also denotes a regional water management program that has been in formation for the past twenty years.

But to many, Caroni is most important as the home of the scarlet ibis, Trinidad's national bird, which daily at sunset stages one of nature's most spectacular shows.

The Caroni Bird Sanctuary is a 450-acre/180-hectare reserve within a mangrove swamp covering 40 sq mi/104 sq km. Just before sunset flocks of glowing, fire-engine-red birds begin to appear overhead. At first there are only a few, with their smoky-pink juveniles close by. Then the birds begin arriving by the dozens and, finally, by the hundreds, loudly flapping their 3-ft/0.9-m span of wings as they swoop down to alight at the top of mangrove trees spread in island clusters across the sanctuary. Soon, the brilliant scarlet adults and their young are joined by great numbers of snowy egrets and herons, which perch on the lower branches of the same trees to roost for the night. By the time dusk has fallen the birds have come in such numbers that they transform the little green islands into a sea of Christmas trees aglow with red and white decorations.

The ibis gets its brilliant red plumage from the carotene extracted from the crabs, shrimp, and snails on which it feeds. It takes about three years for the bird to achieve its intense red color. Although the scarlet ibis has been protected in Trinidad since 1962, its numbers in the Caroni Swamp have dropped in the past decade from 10,000 to an estimated 3,000 as a result of continued poaching and the alteration of the wetlands due to encroachment, pollution, and upstream water management programs.

In addition to the scarlet ibis, the Caroni Swamp area has one of the richest concentrations of wildlife in the Caribbean, with more than 150 species of birds, eighty kinds of fish, and a variety of reptiles. Guided boat trips to the sanctuary follow a winding course through canals, lagoons, and mangrove swamps to where the birds return in the evening. Along the way, one can see the four types of mangrove trees—red, white, black, and buttonwood—whose roots are the habitat of oysters, crabs, barnacles, and sponges. One of the most curious is the small four-eyed fish, which one is likely to spot as it beats its fins rapidly through the water searching for prey. Because the eyes of the fish are divided into segments, at water level it can see both under water as well as overhead. The species is about 12 in/ 30 cm in length. Among the largest fish are groupers and tarpon.

The park's hardest-to-see mammal is the nocturnal silky anteater, which is very difficult to maintain in captivity. Growing to a length of about 21 in/ 53 cm, it uses its forearms with two large claws for climbing and tearing food, and curls itself into a ball of silvery gray fur around a tree branch to sleep during the day. Its local name, "poor me one," is actually the cry of the common potoo, a nocturnal bird of the swamp. The swamp also has crab-eating raccoons and reptiles including the spectacled caiman and iguanas.

The most conspicuous birds are herons and egrets. The fork-tailed fly-catcher and blue-and-white swallow roost in the mangroves. There are yellow-headed caracaras, fulvous and black-bellied whistling-ducks, and yellow-breasted crakes. One of the most memorable night sights is the common potoo, which sits upright on the top of a dead tree with its beak held high, giving it a most imperious look.

Local travel companies offer tours to the park daily from Port of Spain, or one can join a boat trip at the dock near the signposted entrance to the park, west of the Uriah Butler (Princess Margaret) Highway. However, those interested in learning about the mangroves should visit with a natu-ralist guide, otherwise they will get a standard tour—little more than a boat ride to the scarlet ibis sanctuary to watch the birds at sunset.

From the boat dock there are walking trails along the marshes. One can also gain access from the south side, at the Cacandee Sluice at the junction of the Madame Espagnol and Guayamare rivers and the north–south canal. One can drive as close as 0.5 mi/0.8 km from the sluice gate from where a footpath runs along the Madame Espagnol River to the shore. Or, one can arrange with a fisherman to go to the sanctuary by boat; inquire locally.

MT. TABOR AND MT. ST. BENEDICT

Across the southern face of the Northern Range an accordion fold of ridges and river valleys stretches from the Maracas Valley on the west to the Rio Seco on the east and offers an almost endless range of choices for hikers and birders. Conceivably, one could hike from valley to valley across the moun-tain range, end to end. A more practical way, however, is to base oneself for short excursions in one of the country's two mountain lodges catering to birders and nature lovers: Mt. St. Benedict Guesthouse on the side of Mt. Tabor above Tunapuna, and Asa Wright Nature Centre in the mountains overlooking the Arima Valley. They offer comfortable accommodations within close range of mountain trails.

From Mt. St. Benedict Guesthouse at 800 ft/244 m, trails lead past the Abbey of St. Benedict to the peak of Mt. Tabor, 1,800 ft/550 m, where lookouts provide superb views of Port of Spain on the west, the Caroni Plains on the south, and El Tucuche on the north. Any morning soon after daybreak and late afternoon before sunset the trees around the guesthouse and those on the grounds of the abbey are alive with so many birds one can easily see thirty or more different species on a two-hour hike. The roads and trails are very steep but easy to climb. The guesthouse hosts nature photography seminars from time to time.

The green north face of the Northern Range overlooks Maracas Bay and its popular golden-sand swimming beach.

A huge mahogany tree directly in front of the guesthouse is usually full of green-rumped parrotlets and pairs of orange-winged parrots on the high branches. Hummingbirds, blue-gray, palm, and turquoise tanagers, violaceous trogons, and honeycreepers make an endless dance around the mango, guava, cashew, and other trees and flowering shrubs on the property. The lower montane forest by the abbey has common pauraque, ruddy quail-dove, rufous-browed peppershrike, and yellow oriole; overhead hawks and swifts soar and circle.

Asa Wright Nature Centre

Nestled deep in a rain forest at 1,200 ft/367 m on the lofty Northern Range is the Asa Wright Nature Centre, a private institution unique in the Caribbean. Established in 1967 on the Spring Hill Estate, a former cocoa-coffee-citrus plantation reclaimed by the forest, the Nature Centre is a hotel, bird sanctuary, protected wildlife reserve, and study area attracting amateur and professional naturalists alike. The former plantation house, located 7.5 mi/12 km north of the town of Arima and 0.5 mi/0.8 km west of a signposted entrance on the Arima–Blanchisseuse road, provides comfortable accommodations in the wild. The William Beebe Tropical Research Station, which has accommodations for scientists, student groups, and researchers, is located 3 mi/4.8 km south of the center, on the east side of the Arima–Blanchisseuse road.

A day on the hotel veranda, all but hidden in dense tropical vegetation, is like sitting in the middle of an aviary, except that the birds come and go freely from the surrounding rain forest. Within an hour one can see and photograph three dozen species including squirrel cuckoos, toucans, trogons, hummingbirds, and honeycreepers, among nature's most colorful creatures. Others that might be seen are the black-tailed tityra, scaly-naped pigeon, bat falcon, lilac-tailed parrotlet, and several woodpeckers.

A highlight of the Nature Centre is the sight of oilbirds, which make their home in Dunston Cave, located on the property. This is the only known, easily accessible nesting colony of the species. The oilbird, known locally as diablotin, is found only in the northern regions of South America and is the only nocturnal fruit-eating bird. First discovered for science in 1799, the plump birds, known as *guacharo* to the Native Americans who hunted them for food and lamp oil, feed mainly on palm nuts from which their flesh draws oil. Young birds remain in their nests for up to 110 days. At seventy days the nestling may weigh up to 1.5 lb/0.7 kg—50 percent more than its parent. Oilbird colonies can also be found in the Aripo Caves and the Oropouche Caves of the Northern Range, but they are relatively inaccessible.

Along the road into the Asa Wright Nature Centre, the thickly forested slopes are populated by bare-eyed and white-necked thrushes, blue-headed and orange-winged parrots, great antshrikes, and black-faced antthrushes. A clearing in the trees reveals a tall immortelle tree, heavy with the distinctive hanging nests of the crested oropendola. Here the beautiful black birds with bright yellow tails may be seen darting in and out of their nests as they bring corn, citrus, and other food to their young. The oropendolas nest in large colonies and their nests, woven together by the females from strips of vegetation, dangle as much as 5 ft/1.5 m below the branches.

The Nature Centre has mapped out five trails, ranging from easy half-hour strolls to difficult, winding, three-hour hikes, designed to maximize viewing of particular species within the immediate vicinity. The main trail heads down in front of the Nature Centre through a citrus orchard to the rain forest, passing a lek, or display ground, of the white-bearded manakin; one might also spot a channel-billed toucan feeding or sunning itself after a rain shower in a wild nutmeg tree. The bellbird trail branches west to where one can hear, if not see, the bearded bellbird, one of the most unusual birds of the forest, and a display ground—a horizontal branch high in the trees—of the golden-headed manakin. The male bellbird, with a black and white body and brown head, has a beard of black stringy wattles hanging from his throat. He perches and feeds high on the branches of thick forests and is hard to see—but not to hear. He has two completely different calls. One is a loud clank like the pounding of metal; the other, from which the bird's name derives, is soft like the ringing of a bell.

Another trail from the Nature Centre makes a loop through cocoa, coffee, and banana groves, where hikers are likely to see a blue-crowned motmot or golden-olive woodpecker, and leads to another display ground of the white-bearded manakin. A more difficult trail, which crosses a stream, takes one to an area of morpho butterflies, whose iridescent royal blue makes them among the most beautiful creatures of the forest. The longest and most difficult trail—slippery when wet—is a three-hour hike on steep slopes through dense forests with canopies over 100 ft/30 m above the ground and thick with lianas, bromeliads, and other rain-forest vegetation.

The path to the Dunston Cave is an unmarked extension of the main trail. The oilbird home is actually not a cave but a chasm carved from bedrock by a stream that runs through the property. One can visit the site only by arrangement with the Nature Centre and must be accompanied by a guide. Day visitors are welcome and upon payment of a nominal fee may use the trails. Nature seminars and painting sessions are held in summer, photography workshops in fall. The Nature Centre is also a good base for exploring the northern slopes of the Northern Range and the Blanchisseuse region on day trips arranged by the Centre or on one's own.

ARIMA TO BLANCHISSEUSE

Whether one starts from the Asa Wright Nature Centre or another location, the entire road from Arima to Blanchisseuse on the north coast is a splendid route that climbs from sea level to about 2,000 ft/610 m in 10 mi/16 km, providing scenic wonders at every turn. And turns there are—as many as 387 by one count. The road passes through dense montane and secondary forests laced with gigantic bamboos, carpeted with ferns, and colored with the red blossoms of mountain rose. Branching from the main artery are trails along logging and mining tracks, old plantation roads, and footpaths which can be explored for an hour or a day. At about 1,500 ft/450 m the Lalaja Road, 6 mi/9.6 km from Arima, winds east around the ridge between the Arima and Guanapo valleys. It can be negotiated for about a mile or two by car or jeep, but after that one must hike.

North of the Asa Wright Nature Centre, trails along Las Lapas Trace and Andrews Trace at 1,800 ft/550 m overlooking the Lopinot Valley lead through the montane forest where in a few minutes one can spot yellow-legged thrush, speckled tanager, Antillean euphonia, and two dozen more species of birds that prefer high elevations. But the highlight is the display court of the white-bearded manakin. Here, three dozen or more males—round balls of white fluff with a small black cap and black wings giving them the appearance of minuscule seals—flit about in the lower branches of the bush and strut on their courts in the lek (a clearing in the forest) in hopes of attracting a mate. A lek might have as many as seventy courts, each male having staked out his territory where he has cleared the vegetation. Quiet and motionless viewers can remain within a few yards to watch and photograph the delightful, amazing display.

On the north side of the ridge, the Arima–Blanchisseuse road makes a wide swing into the valley through a pass and offers magnificent views across the heavily forested mountains bright with the orange blossoms of immortelle. Overhead, turkey vultures, hawks, and other birds of prey soar on the hot air rising from the valley. At certain bends, the vistas open down the valley to the Caribbean. These vantage points are also an opportunity to scout the treetops for toucans, trogons, and American swallow-tailed kites and to see hummingbirds, honeycreepers, and tanagers around the flowering bushes near at hand. At every turn the rain forest is crowded with huge ferns and elephant ears and draped with lianas.

Approximately halfway to Blanchisseuse a secondary road eastward leads to Brasso Seco Village from where there are 7 mi/11.2 km of track through mora forests to Paria Bay and Mandamas Bay by the sea. Hikers need a local guide to find their way; topographical maps are not sufficient as the route has many forks and turns.

The main road passes through the hamlet of Morne le Croix, where a large hedge of blue vervain by the roadside is well known for attracting ruby-topaz and tufted coquette hummingbirds. The road continues to Blanchisseuse Village on the Caribbean coast. About 3 mi/4.8 km west of the village at the Damien River, there are scenic rocky cliffs and empty white sand beaches for swimming. Las Cuevas, about 5 mi/8 km to the west as the crow flies, is connected by a good road. East of Blanchisseuse, a sheltered lagoon at the mouth of the Marianne River is often the place to spot a green kingfisher in the bamboo and gray kingbird or yellow oriole in the coconut palms.

Further east, Paria and Mandamas bays are turtle nesting grounds as well as swimming beaches. East from Blanchisseuse to Matelot where the mountains drop directly into the sea, the Paria Main Road, as it is known, is only a path not a road. The entire region of the northeast range is the wildest in Trinidad where even local naturalists do not go without guides from the area. Experienced bushwhackers who have proper equipment and make adequate preparation could hike and camp in this little-explored region. Hikers must be on the lookout for snakes. Birders note: the area is the home of the rare Trinidad piping-guan, known locally as pawi or paui, which usually is regarded as Trinidad's only endemic species, though some authorities say it is a form of one of the South American piping-guans.

The scarlet ibis, Trinidad's national bird, nests in spectacular numbers in the tops of mangrove trees in the Caroni Bird Sanctuary.

EL CERRO DEL ARIPO AND ARIPO CAVES

The highest peak in Trinidad, El Cerro del Aripo (3,083 ft/940 m), can be reached partway by a very steep, winding road that starts about 4 mi/6.4 km east of Arima. The road follows the Aripo River for about 10 mi/16 km via Aripo Village to the entrance of Dandrade Trace. Here, a park sign posts the distance to the summit as 9 mi/14.4 km. The trail is difficult to follow; one should arrange for a guide in Aripo Village. The up-and-down trail passes through jungle-thick upper montane forest, down limestone cliffs, and across streams. It is also the trail to Aripo Caves, Trinidad's largest cave system, where oilbirds can be seen from the entrance. Only fully equipped spelunkers should venture beyond the cave entrance. Some rare species of hummingbirds and the rare Trinidad piping-guan may be seen in the area. Ruiz Trace above Aripo Village passes a lek of the bearded bellbird.

MATURA BEACH AND THE LEATHERBACK TURTLE

Four of the world's seven species of marine turtles—the green, hawksbill, olive ridley, and leatherback—nest on Trinidad's beaches. The leatherback, the only one known to nest here in large numbers, is the largest, growing up to 7 ft/2 m in length and weighing more than 1,000 lb/454 kg. The peak nesting period is April to June, but the female may start arriving at Matura Beach in March and continue to nest into late August. The leatherback is known to travel great distances in the open sea and farther into cold water than other species, but it nests only on tropical shores. The government was pressured into passing laws in 1975 to protect the turtles and prohibit hunting during the nesting season from March to September.

ARIPO SAVANNAH AND FOREST

The rectangle between Arima and Matura on the north and Navet Reservoir and Manzanilla Point on the south is cultivated lowlands interspersed with forests and savannas and giving way to the country's largest freshwater swamp, Nariva, along the Atlantic coast. The entire area is a birder's paradise.

The Aripo Savannah directly south of Valencia is the last relatively undisturbed savanna in Trinidad and offers an outstanding example of a marsh formation comprising marsh forest, palm marsh, and savanna. Triangular in shape, it is located largely along the Long Stretch Forest Reserve between the Aripo and Quare rivers. Its eastern side encompasses scientific and wilderness zones of marsh forest interspersed with savanna bordered by palm. The western side has been reforested with native species, while the south has commercially harvested Caribbean pine forests.

The wildlife includes mongoose, agouti, paca, opossum or manicou, and deer. Among the birds are the rare or endangered scarlet-shouldered parrotlet, seen only in the Aripo Savannah; sulphury flycatcher; lesser elaenia, which nests only here; red-bellied macaw; and Moriche oriole.

On the southwest side of the Aripo Savannah, the Arena Forest is an evergreen seasonal forest rich in birdlife with many of the species common to the Northern Range, such as manakins, toucans, trogons, and tanagers. It is a good area for rufous-tailed jacamar and white-bellied antbird, as well as the crimson-crested woodpecker and grassquits. At its heart is the Arena Dam, an area populated with herons, egrets, and other water birds. One needs a Water and Sewage Authority permit (see page 453) to visit.

BRIGAND HILL

If one had to select the best places in eastern Trinidad to hike, see birds, and enjoy magnificent views, Brigand Hill should be at the top of the list. Once a cocoa plantation, the hill has been overtaken by rain forest where bamboo, ferns, and epiphytes mix with fruiting and flowering trees in a diverse concentration that attracts many birds. The hill, now a forest reserve, has a forestry station and lighthouse at the summit and several lookouts that put one at the level of the treetops, making it easy to spot birds that favor the heights and are normally difficult to see from ground level. The road to the summit is paved and easy to walk, but it is very steep and should be taken at a slow pace. At the top, particularly after a quick tropical shower, birders are likely to spot various tanagers, elaenias, and golden-olive woodpeckers, distinguished by a red crown and cheek. There will likely be a black vulture or two keeping watch atop the lighthouse.

From the summit, too, one has a sweeping view of the east coast from Manzanilla Point on the north to Point Radix on the south. This narrow strip of land with thousands of coconut palms divides the endless roll of Atlantic breakers from the great span of the Nariva plains and swamp, seen in the foreground. Occasionally in the distance on the southeast, flares from oil rigs at sea are visible. The turn-off for Brigand Hill is from the Plum Mitan Road, a side road of the Sangre Grande–Manzanilla Highway. Inquire locally for directions.

NARIVA SWAMP AND BUSH BUSH WILDLIFE SANCTUARY

South from the village of Lower Manzanilla, along a highway bordering Manzanilla and Cocos bays, is a 17-mi/27-km stretch of palm-shaded golden sand, one of the longest beaches in the Caribbean. Be warned, however: pretty as it may look, an undertow makes parts of this coast dangerous for swimmers. The Tourist Board has facilities for bathing and picnicking at Manzanilla Bay, but there are no hotel or other tourist developments.

West of the road is the Nariva Swamp, the largest expanse of freshwater marshes in Trinidad, fed by the waters of the Navet and lesser rivers and streams flowing east from the Central Range. At the eastern edge of the swamp the Nariva River is bordered with mangroves; if manatees remain in Trinidad's waters, they will be found here. Unfortunately, the ones seen most often are those caught in the nets of fishermen harvesting catfish.

The swamp has an abundance of birdlife but there are no organized boat trips like those at Caroni Swamp. However, it is easy to spot birds along the road and down tracks in marshy areas used for rice cultivation. Wattled jacanas paddle among water hyacinths, and the yellow-headed caracara, silvered antbird, and Moriche oriole are also present.

Within the swamp is the 3,840-acre/1,554-hectare Bush Bush Wildlife Sanctuary, established in 1968 and intended to protect the country's endangered macaws and parrots as well as monkeys. Unfortunately, squatters, grazing cows, and fires from the illegal slash-and-burn method of agriculture have destroyed much of the environment. Though dwindling, flocks of red-bellied macaws do arrive daily at sunset to roost at the tops of the Moriche palms, one of the dominant trees of the marshes.

The collared peccary is a piglike mammal that lives in the rain forest above the Arima Valley. It has musk glands on its back and can inflict severe wounds with its tusks.

The hawksbill turtle, whose shell is prized for jewelry and ornaments, is one of four turtle species that nest on Trinidad's beaches.

TRINITY HILLS WILDLIFE SANCTUARY AND THE MUD VOLCANOES

In the mountains of the Southern Range, whose three-peaked Trinity Hills gave Trinidad its name, an area of 16,020 acres/6,483 hectares directly west of Guayaguayare was made into a wildlife sanctuary in 1934. It has forests of native mora trees and wildlife including monkeys, pacas, armadillos, agoutis, deer, porcupines, and opossums. Among the birds are parrots, toucans, bellbirds, scaly-naped pigeons, violaceous euphonias, gray seed-eaters, and Trinidad euphonias. To reach the highest point of the range, at 1,010 ft/308 m, one must drive approximately 4 mi/6.4 km west of Guaya-guayare, passing en route a track to the mud volcano of Lagon Bouffe.

Mud volcanoes are formations in the earth's surface created by gases sweeping through the subsurface mud via faults in the earth's crust. Mud bubbles up through the surface, and as it dries, it builds up in cones sometimes as high as 20 ft/6 m. The mud bubbling up is cool, not hot like the bubbling mud typically seen in volcanic craters. At Princes Town, east of San Fernando, a mud volcano known as the Devil's Woodyard, regarded as a holy site by some Hindus of the area, apparently was thought to be the only such phenomenon in the country when it erupted around 1852. But in 1964 another mud volcano was discovered in Moruga. There are now approximately twenty mud volcanoes registered in southern Trinidad; they are associated with the strata typical of oil-bearing rocks.

From the main road of the Trinity Hills, a narrow, steep path of about 2 mi/3.2 km leads into the forest and along the ridge to the summit. From the summit one has views of the forest, Guayaguayare Bay, and the Columbus Channel, as the sea between the south coast of Trinidad and Venezuela is known. Permission to visit Trinity Hills must be obtained in advance from the TRINTOC (Trinidad and Tobago Oil Company) in Pointe-a-Pierre.

POINTE-A-PIERRE WILD FOWL TRUST

A most unlikely collaboration of conservationists and industry has resulted in one of the most beautiful and interesting spots in Trinidad. Less than an hour's drive south from Port of Spain at Pointe-a-Pierre, two lakes surrounded by 15 acres/6 hectares of coastal wilderness comprise the Pointe-a-Pierre Wild Fowl Trust, entirely within the compound of the TRINTOC's refineries and petrochemical complex. The refuge is a private, nonprofit effort established in 1966 to protect and repopulate Trinidad and Tobago's endangered species. It is also a haven for hundreds of migratory birds and waterfowl, with more than 86 species recorded. The Trust serves as a public environmental educational center, particularly for schoolchildren, as well as a research center. An ancillary activity has been the protection of other wildlife, particularly nesting turtles.

As an enhancement of the natural woodlands vegetation, the Trust has planted forty different kinds of fruit and forest trees, from orange and mango to the showy African tulip, in order to attract a wide variety of birds. There are nature walks around both lakes and a few benches at vantage points where one can sit in a beautiful park setting to watch waterfowl at close range. Those with patience are rewarded with the sight of purple gallinule, wattled jacana, and an occasional pied water-tyrant strolling the water lilies; green-backed and tricolored herons and olivaceous cormorants scan from the posts and rails, an anhinga suns on a log, and a host of ducks swim about. Usually dancing about in the trees are barred antshrikes, white-winged becards, yellow-hooded blackbirds, yellow orioles, red-breasted blackbirds, yellow-bellied elaenias, and a variety of flycatchers and tanagers including perhaps a migrating summer tanager, whose red plumage makes it stand out. Disguised in the grass are colonies of saffron finches, and flitting about the flowering bushes above them are copper-rumped hummingbirds.

Among the indigenous species in the breeding program are black-bellied, fulvous, and white-faced whistling-ducks, white-cheeked pintail, and Muscovy duck. The latter, once extirpated here, has been bred and reintroduced into the wild by the Trust. Other extirpated or highly endangered species in the program are blue-and-yellow macaw and yellow-headed and blue-headed parrots. Because the sanctuary is operated solely by volunteers, one must arrange a visit in advance. Contact Pointe-a-Pierre Wild Fowl Trust, c/o 42 Sandown Rd., Goodwood Park, Point Cumana, Trinidad, WI; tel. 809-637-5145. Visitors may bring a picnic lunch.

PITCH LAKE

The area south of San Fernando at Fyzabad has the country's largest oil field. On the southwest coast at La Brea is the Pitch Lake, the largest deposit of asphalt in the world. Often described as resembling a gigantic parking lot, the lake covers approximately 89 acres/36 hectares to a depth of 250 ft/75 m. Discovered in 1595 by Sir Walter Raleigh, who used the pitch to caulk his ships, the asphalt was formed millions of years ago when the "lake" was a huge mud volcano into which asphaltic oil flowed. Underground gases facilitated the mixing of the oil and mud, some elements evaporated, and the substance that remains is the asphalt. There are many other types of bitumen or natural asphalt deposits throughout the world, but the quantity of the substance here is unusually great and of good quality. Speculation is that at the present extraction rate of about 300 tons per day the lake will last another fifty years or so.

ICACOS POINT AND SOLDADO ROCK

The southwestern tip of Trinidad at Icacos Point is a nature conservation reserve made up of mangroves bordering the southern straits, known as the Serpent's Mouth, where Venezuela's Orinoco River empties. The offshore island of Soldado Rock, 6 mi/9.6 km west of the Point, is a 1.5-acre/0.6-hectare sanctuary for nesting brown noddies and sooty terns. Brown pelicans, magnificent frigatebirds, and laughing gulls are also seen.

TOBAGO

Tiny Tobago, 22 mi/35 km northeast of Trinidad, is like a garden paradise. The diversity and density of plants, trees, birds, and butterflies in so small a space is probably greater here than anywhere else in the Caribbean. The display on land is but a mere invitation to the spectacular show in the aquamarine waters surrounding the island. So natural and abundant is the wildlife that the birds and fish seem almost tame.

The Main Ridge, a verdant mountain spine, rises almost directly from the sea and covers two-thirds of the island along a northeast–southwest angle. It reaches its highest points in the north at Pigeon Peak, 1,700 ft/518 m, and

Man of War Hill, 1,800 ft/560 m, and at Centre Hill, 1,900 ft/580 m, at about the island's center. Tobago is still an island of farmers and fishermen. Save for mountainsides too steep to farm or abandoned plantations that have returned to the forest, the lower mountain slopes and the rolling hills and lowlands of the south end where most of the people live are intensively cultivated with coconuts, bananas, and other tropical fruits and vegetables.

Scarborough, 8 mi/13 km from the airport on the Atlantic or windward side, is the principal port and capital. From its historic Fort King George one can have a sweeping view of the island and the windward coast. In its small Botanic Gardens one can see a great variety of tropical flora.

Buccoo Reef Restricted Area

Located in the leeward waters on the west end of Tobago, the Buccoo Reef Restricted Area, proposed as a marine park, is a 2.7-sq-mi/7-sq-km sea and land reserve of shallow-water reefs, lagoons, mangroves and a narrow strip of land. Several features make Buccoo Reef distinctive. While it is the most southerly of the coral reefs of the Caribbean (save a small one at Toco off Trinidad), it is located in a region with non-Caribbean influences, particularly from August to October when it receives some of the outflow of the Orinoco River. Buccoo Reef is really five major reef flats arching out in the shape of a broad horseshoe from Pigeon Point on the west to Buccoo Bay on the east. This shape shelters the interior lagoon from the heavy northeast Atlantic swells that impact other areas around the island.

Buccoo Reef is the island's leading tourist attraction, a mixed blessing because too many people with a disregard for or lack of knowledge of the reef's delicate environment have caused extensive damage. Although the reef has been protected by legislation for nearly two decades, the government has never seriously enforced the law. It is now under pressure from environmentalists to do so, however. The most recent improvement has been the placement of channel markers in the lagoon to help safeguard the reef from destruction caused by boats and their anchors.

The lagoon has gardens of coral with staghorn, starlet, and brain corals and sea fans. The crest of the reef around the lagoon is unusually broad, ranging from 600 to 900 ft/180 to 270 km in width. The outer reef on the east and west slopes seaward to about 60 ft/18 m where there are elkhorn, flower, and large star corals. The great variety of fishes includes rock beauty, Caribbean red snapper, Nassau grouper, yellow goatfish, queen triggerfish, parrotfishes, trumpetfishes, angelfishes including the large, colorful queen angelfish, squirrelfishes, and barracudas, along with an occasional hawksbill turtle and eagle ray, among many other creatures.

From Little Tobago, a bird sanctuary also called Bird of Paradise Island, one can see the forests of Tobago's Main Ridge.

The south side of the restricted area has a lagoon, Bon Accord, with extensive patches of turtle grass edged by a thin band of red mangrove trees that host sea life as well as birds and butterflies. The mangroves, accessible from land by a trail on the south side, are a popular birding area for the rufous-vented chachalaca, the national bird of Tobago, which may be sighted here in company with the common moorhen, white-cheeked pintail, roseate spoonbill, and various herons, egrets, and plovers. Tobago has 181 species of birds, of which eighty-six are known to breed here; eleven of the breeding species do not occur in Trinidad.

Pigeon Point is a small spit of land with an idyllic palm-fringed white sand beach overlooking the Caribbean on the west and the Bon Accord mangroves on the east. Because of its proximity to Buccoo Reef, the airport (within walking distance), and many hotels, Pigeon Point is also one of the island's most popular swimming beaches. It has bathing facilities; there is an entrance fee.

GRAFTON, ARNOS VALE, AND FRANKLYN ESTATE

Tobago's entire Caribbean coast is made up of one beautiful beach after another—some with resorts, others untouched. Leatherback turtles nest on the beaches between Buccoo and Plymouth from April to June. Slightly inland, Grafton Estate, a former resort and bird sanctuary on an old coconut plantation that has returned to the bush, has easy walking trails.

Farther north, Arnos Vale, a rustic resort on a tiny cove that was once part of a sugar plantation, is one of the most romantic, enchanting spots in the Caribbean. The lodge is situated on a hillside in the former estate storehouse, so completely encased in tropical foliage that it resembles a tree house. From the terrace one can watch a blazing Caribbean sunset to a chorus of jacamars, motmots, doves, and mockingbirds. There are numerous paths and trails up the hillside leading to Sunset Point, another vantage point for watching fabulous sunsets. The cove has an exceptionally good shallow reef with large elkhorn coral, sea fans, and sponges and a shallow-water wall with star coral—all suited to snorkelers and novice divers. The reef attracts schools of grunts, blue tangs, parrotfishes, and angelfishes.

An abandoned road from Arnos Vale north to Golden Lane and Culloden Bay is now a hiking trail of about 2 mi/3.2 km. Culloden Bay has a magnificent stretch of reef, one of several of Tobago's reefs that have been proposed for protection as scientific research areas. West of Arnos Vale by the road that now links Scarborough and Golden Lane, another abandoned plantation, Franklyn Estate, has impressive ruins of a waterwheel and other machinery that have become a part of the forest. Around the ruins and under the spreading arms of huge samaan, calabash, and other trees shading old cocoa and coffee plants, it is easy to spot woodpeckers, motmots, and doves within a few minutes' search.

MT. DILLON

From Golden Lane a road twists and turns through the deep green mountains along cliffs overlooking coves and the Caribbean en route to Mt. Dillon, a windswept promontory rising 1,000 ft/300 m above the sea. Tobago's birds are so abundant that even on Mt. Dillon, where gale-force winds blow, a hollow limb of a barren tree has been found to hold a thimble-sized nest of the black-throated mango hummingbird with two chicks.

From the cliffside there is a spectacular view of the length of the island—Pigeon Point, Buccoo Reef, and the forested peaks of the Main Ridge. On the southwest horizon is Trinidad. In the foreground by the sea are a series of deep coves with lovely beaches shaded by palms, ferns, and giant bamboo. Behind them rise the green mountains, colored with the orange blossoms of immortelle, where trails lead to pretty waterfalls. Now and then one will see the hanging nests of the crested oropendola. Castara, a popular swimming beach by the little village of the same name, has bathing facilities; Englishman's Bay, Parlatuvier Bay, and Bloody Bay can be reached by short trails from the main road. About 1.5 mi/2.4 km offshore are the Sisters, tiny rock islands with nesting brown noddies and sooty terns.

Main Ridge Rain Forest Trail

At Parlatuvier Bay a new road cuts inland through the mountains of the Main Ridge along the main artery between the leeward and windward coasts. It traverses the Tobago Forest Reserve and gives access to the Main Ridge Rain Forest Trail, the most accessible and best-maintained trail in Tobago. The Main Ridge Recreation Site and Hiking Trail, known locally as Bloody Bay Lookout Site, has a small Forestry Department cabin where a map of the trail is posted. The site captures a panoramic view of the coast overlooking Bloody Bay and the Sisters offshore. From this vantage point above the trees, it is easy in the late afternoon to see parrots flying about in the treetops in pairs—with their lifelong mates.

The lookout marks the western entrance of a looped trail that winds down through virgin rain forest along a tributary of the Bloody Bay River. The first forty-five minutes of trail is steep, downhill, and often slippery, but after the trail crosses the stream, it levels out and returns on an easy walking path to the eastern entrance on the main highway, about 1 mi/ 1.6 km east of the Lookout Site. If one starts from the lookout, covering the steepest part in the downhill direction first, the two- to three-hour hike is less tiring. Those who are short on time or who prefer to avoid the steep slope can enter from the eastern section to hike into the rain forest for about an hour and return by the same route. This covers the most beautiful part of the trail, passing enormous ferns and elephant ears and gigantic bamboos under a canopy reaching 50 to 60 ft/15 to 18 m. Along the way, hikers will see numerous species of hummingbirds, including perhaps the rare white-tailed sabrewing feeding on the heliconia blossoms, and jacamars, with their brilliant iridescent plumage glistening in the sunlight that filters through the trees. Overhead the unmistakable quack of parrots can be heard. The western end of the trail passes a lek of the blue-backed manakin where one might see the males in their mating display.

Hillsborough Dam

The Windward Road between Scarborough and Speyside, a fishing village toward the north end of the island, hugs the coast as it winds its way through bayside hamlets and fishing villages and along the luxuriant countryside where the trees are heavy with mangos, papayas, or limes. A few miles north of Scarborough at Mount St. George, a road inland climbs to the Green Hill Waterfall, one of several with trails and picnic facilities.

The Mount St. George–Castara road zigzags farther up the mountain to the Hillsborough Dam, providing breathtaking views of the coast. Along the way there are frequent opportunities to spot a blue-crowned motmot perched on the limb of a tree. Its long racquet-tipped tail makes its silhouette easy to recognize. At the reservoir, which is fed by streams running off the Main Ridge, herons, anhingas, and Caribbean martins are common. There are woodpeckers and trogons in the woods beyond the lake. A WASA permit may be needed to enter the reservoir area; inquire at the WASA station at the dam. Beyond the dam, a trail on an abandoned road climbs to the top of Main Ridge. Although the road to the dam is labeled Mount St. George–Castara on maps, it does not go across to the leeward coast.

From the Windward Road at Goldsborough Bay one can take a secondary road inland along the Goldsborough, or Great, River, then follow a footpath leading to waterfalls that drop through tropical vegetation into inviting pools. The walk takes about thirty minutes.

SPEYSIDE AND LITTLE TOBAGO

Speyside is a seaside village set against the forest of the Main Ridge. The area has been proposed as a marine park that would include Goat Island, one of the most unusual dive sites in the Caribbean, and the 280-acre/113-hectare Little Tobago, a bird sanctuary also known as Bird of Paradise Island. On the north side of Speyside, Blue Water Inn caters to birders, naturalists, and divers. It is close to the best diving in Tobago and operates its own boat to Little Tobago and St. Giles Islands off the north coast.

In 1909, an Englishman introduced several dozen greater birds of paradise on Little Tobago in hopes of establishing a haven from hunters who were decimating the species to supply feathers to the European fashion market. The birds lived until 1963, when a hurricane devastated the island and cut their number to a mere seven. This remnant, too, is presumed lost, since no birds have been sighted since 1983.

Although the exotic birds gave the island its fame, they were not its only attraction. Depending upon the time of the year, one can expect to see a good sampling of the other fifty-two bird species that have been recorded here, including some of the thirty-three kinds that breed here. The ground-nesting brown booby is on Little Tobago year-round as is the magnificent frigatebird, although the latter nests on the nearby St. Giles Islands. From about March to August, large tight colonies of sooty terns make their nests on the ground near the sea or the edge of a cliff, while brown noddies occupy thick cactus clumps or niches on cliffs. Bridled terns come from April through August, but in smaller numbers than their relatives. Laughing gulls, which breed here from April to September, usually build their

Distinctive coloring and a long racquet-tipped tail makes the blue-crowned motmot easy to identify.

nests on the steep slopes at Alexander Bay. Red-billed tropicbirds, which nest in the eastern cliffs, can be seen performing their aerial displays from December to July. Audubon's shearwaters are here year-round.

Little Tobago is arid and hilly and covered with xerophytic vegetation on its windward side. There is a network of marked trails ranging in length from a few hundred feet to a half-mile; each section is named and there are sheltered viewing stations. Along *Sea View Trail*, a short walk east along the lower parts of the island, one can see sooty terns, noddies, and laughing gulls at close range and tropicbirds and brown boobies in the distance. *George Ride Trail*, a forty-five-minute hike along the northeast–southwest ridge, winds up a slope through interior woodlands to a viewing station facing south across Alexander Bay where one can watch soaring tropicbirds, boobies, terns, and gulls. En route one is likely to see the familiar blue-crowned motmot and crested oropendola.

Little Tobago is 1 mi/1.6 km offshore at Speyside; the boat trip across the channel takes about twenty minutes and can be arranged through one's hotel or with a fisherman at the beach. The boat will return at a specific time or, for an additional charge, will wait for its passengers. In either case, one must be accompanied by a local guide. The crossing by boat is often quite rough, with whitecaps and swells; be prepared for a wet landing. Here, as elsewhere, birds are best seen in the early morning or late afternoon. Be sure to take water because there is none on Little Tobago.

Goat Island, a ten-minute ride from Speyside, has spectacular "Flying Reefs," so named because of their powerful surf and surge. Similar reef and sea conditions are found off the south and west of Little Tobago. They are only for advanced divers who have experience in drift diving. What makes the dive particularly exciting is that there are two currents—an upper one flowing southward and another below 100 ft/30 m circling north, so that if divers drift with the upper flow and then drop to the lower one, they are brought back near the starting point, gliding over the reef as one might glide through the air, a type of dive known as "flying the reef." It is a challenge even for experienced divers.

The reefs are constantly nourished by the clean, fresh waters of the Atlantic and abundant nutrients brought by the strong currents. The most celebrated, and particularly recommended for underwater photographers, is Japanese Garden, off the southern tip of the island beginning in about 20 ft/6 m of water and sloping quickly to 110 ft/33 m. The shallow area has huge sea whips, sponges unusual for their variety of colors, and sea fans with tube sponges grouped around them. At 90 ft/27 m there are large trees of black coral and large tube sponges. The fish are as colorful as the reef and include large schools of black-striped sergeant majors and purple creole wrasse and large queen and French angelfishes in the shallower parts.

MAN OF WAR BAY AND CHARLOTTEVILLE

A winding 3-mi/4.8-km road, the only cross-island connection at the north end of Tobago, connects Speyside with Charlotteville, a little fishing village on the northernmost bay of the island. Man of War Bay, shaped like a wide horseshoe, is one of the best natural harbors in the Caribbean. It is set in an amphitheater of heavily forested mountains which climb to heights over 1,800 ft/540 m at Pigeon Peak and Man of War Hill. Isolated and remote on the north shore of the bay, Charlotteville has kept the island's folkways more than any location on Tobago. Around the bay are seldom-used roads and trails to the top of the ridge overlooking the sea where one can see parrots, rufous-tailed jacamars, rufous-vented chachalacas, white-lined tanagers, and ruby-topaz hummingbirds.

The highest peaks are difficult hikes that require guides; however, an easy walk from the Speyside–Charlotteville road northeast on Observatory Road leads to Flagstaff Hill, an old lighthouse site. It has been developed by the Tourist Board as a lookout site with splendid views of St. Giles Islands off the northern tip of Tobago and Man of War Bay.

South of Charlotteville within walking distance of town are the Man-O-War Bay Cottages, a birdwatchers' and naturalists' enclave on the beach hidden in tropical gardens of papaya, breadfruit, and other fruit and flowering trees. It is situated on a 1,000-acre/400-hectare cocoa plantation where visitors are free to wander at will. Near the cottages one can see tanagers, thrushes, herons, flycatchers, and bananaquits; by the sea, frigatebirds and boobies; and in the forest, motmots and jacamars.

Approximately 650 acres/263 hectares of forest land adjacent to the plantation have been donated by the owners to the Jacamar Wildlife Reserve, intended to be a combination nature retreat and study center similar to the Asa Wright Nature Centre in Trinidad. The reserve is bounded on three sides by the Caribbean Sea and Atlantic Ocean, and on the fourth by a small track. The area is dominated by coastal primary forest and partially rejuvenated secondary forest on former plantation land. Tall canopy trees have epiphytes and bromeliads, while the lower story contains a variety of trees, shrubs, and wildflowers, from familiar heliconias to little-known mosses and liverworts. The sea cliffs of weathered rock have xerophytic vegetation of cacti, low brush, and dwarfed, windsheared trees.

Man of War Bay reefs are within swimming distance of shore. Directly in front of the cottages are two coral reefs that extend about 100 ft/30 m into the bay where angelfishes, trumpetfishes, squid, and other colorful creatures are abundant. At Lovers Beach on the south side of Man-O-War Cottages and Pirates Bay north of Charlotteville, snorkelers can walk directly to the reef. Offshore, Booby Island has a fringe reef in 3 to 80 ft/

TRINIDAD AND TOBAGO
450

1 to 27 m of water. Leatherback turtles nest on the bay from time to time. Man of War Bay is another area proposed as a marine park.

St. Giles Islands off the northern tip is a group of tiny islands and rocks comprising 72 acres/29 hectares, protected since 1968. They attract large flocks of magnificent frigatebirds, boobies, tropicbirds, and terns which nest here in large numbers. The islands and birds are best viewed by boat as landing is difficult and is not encouraged. Permits to go ashore normally are given only to researchers.

OUTDOOR ACTIVITIES

HIKING: Trinidad and Tobago offer endless opportunities for hiking, particularly in mountainous regions. *The Nature Trails of Trinidad* by R. ffrench and P. Bacon is an indispensable tool; it gives detailed information and maps on thirty hikes. Trinidad and Tobago Field Naturalists' Club (809-624-3321) has monthly field trips which visitors may join. Their members are the country's most knowledgeable and current sources on hiking trails for both islands.

CAMPING: The Trinidad and Tobago Tourist Office has developed camping sites at scenic spots around the country. One should contact them far in advance of a visit and expect to make repeated inquiries before receiving a reply. For serious naturalists the area between Blanchisseuse and Matelot with camping at Mandamas is a wild, little-explored area of the Northern Range. It comprises the full range of Trinidad's terrain, vegetation, and wildlife, including its poisonous snakes. No one, including local scientists, goes there without an experienced guide. Inquire from the Curator, Emperor Valley Zoo, or the Trinidad and Tobago Field Naturalists' Club for names of guides.

CAVING: Although Trinidad is known to have several cave systems, speleology is a fairly new science here and caving is not a developed sport. The best-known caves are those with oilbirds, namely, Aripo Caves, which are accessible on a path cut by the Tourist Board but are considered dangerous. The sea caves on the northwest coast at La Vache Point also are said to have oilbirds. The Tamana Caves in the Central Range have great numbers of bats.

SWIMMING: Trinidad has many beaches on the Caribbean coast from Balata Bay to Las Cuevas and on offshore islands such as Monos, but nothing there can measure up to the idyllic—and empty—powdery beaches of Tobago. Almost any stretch of beach in Tobago could make the Caribbean's Top Ten list. Beaches on the Caribbean coast, particularly Parlatuvier and Bloody Bay, where bathers must hike in from the main road, offer exquisite beauty. Bathers should also be aware that spots along Trinidad's and Tobago's coasts, particularly on the Atlantic, have strong undertows; one should inquire locally about swimming.

SNORKELING AND DIVING: Tobago was one of the first locations in the Caribbean to be discovered by dive enthusiasts three decades ago, but the lack of promotion and the rugged nature of the diving in some places, particularly in the best locations, has left the island as something of a last frontier. Tobago is almost completely surrounded by fringe reef, much of it within swimming distance from shore and in water as shallow as 3 to 30 ft/1 to 9 m. It offers great diversity, including fascinating drift dives for advanced divers. The reefs are incredibly beautiful and outstanding for

Clockwise from top: preening male anhinga; white ibis; lesser yellowlegs; brown pelican; black-bellied whistling-duck.

the variety and color of their marine life. The clarity of the waters, with visibility up to 150 ft/45 m, makes it a paradise for underwater photographers, as well.

Beginners and novice divers are happy with any of the Caribbean reefs on Tobago's leeward coast. Grouper Ground, a site with gentle drift diving for experienced divers, is on the western tip, opposite Pigeon Point. Here basket sponges are as large as bathtubs. Divers planning to drift-dive and "fly the reefs" around Speyside must be in good physical condition and have good diving skills and water stamina.

Tobago has six dive operators, one each at Pigeon Point, Crown Reef, Turtle Beach, and Charlotteville, and two at Speyside. Glass-bottom boat trips to Buccoo Reef leave daily from Pigeon Point, Buccoo Point, and Store Bay.

FISHING: From Trinidad, the cliff-bound Bocas Islands on the northwest are the prime location for deep-sea fishing for kingfish, mackerel, wahoo, bonito, yellowtail tuna, barracuda, dolphin, snapper, and grouper. On Tobago the main locations are the northern shores and around St. Giles Islands. Inquire at your hotel for arrangements.

SAILING AND BOATING: Sailing is a popular, private sport but is almost non-existent on a commercial basis. The Yachting Association, located in Chaguaramas, holds almost weekly races. Members of other yacht clubs visiting the island should inquire through their associations. Angostura Race Week in

Tobago in May brings the sailing season to a close with many fun events. Power-boat racing is also a big sport; the major yearly event is the 90-mi/144-km Great Race between Trinidad and Tobago in early August.

SURFING: Although a young sport here, surfing has become very popular during the last decade. The Surfing Association of Trinidad and Tobago, 73 Ariapita Avenue, Port of Spain (809-627-3294), is eager to assist visitors. Surfing can be enjoyed year-round. The north coast of Trinidad is the most popular location. From Maracas to Blanchisseuse there are four surfing breaks: Maracas Bay with waves from 2 to 10 ft/0.6 to 3 m and favored for body surfing; Las Cuevas with waves from 3 to 10 ft/1 to 3 m; Damiens Bay in Blanchisseuse, the most consistent, with waves from 4 to 13 ft/1.2 to 4 m; and Rock Break, where the waves break off a rock and range from 4 to 15 ft/1.2 to 4.5 m. Toco Point, the northeastern tip of Trinidad jutting into the Atlantic, catches the most swell action, with swells in winter up to 18 ft/5.5 m. From Galera Point west to Matelot, where the road ends, there are five locations.

On Tobago, Rocky Point at Mount Irvine Bay is considered one of the finest point breaks in the Caribbean; it has been a mecca for surfers since the early 1960s.

WINDSURFING: The main area for windsurfing is Trinidad's Chaguaramas Bay.

EXPLORING THE ISLANDS

Trinidad has a fairly wide network of roads on which it is possible to reach most areas of the country within one to two hours from the capital. Major population centers are served by good, well signposted roads; they have very heavy traffic. Small towns have adequate secondary roads, while remote mountain and rural regions must be reached by

track or by foot. No maps are complete or completely accurate.

Trinidad has an inexpensive public bus system along the Eastern Main Road and between major towns. Those with plenty of time can get around this way, provided they are willing to walk or hike to their destination at the end of the line. Otherwise one must use taxis, which are expensive, or a rented car, whose rates are comparable to those in the U.S. Driving in this former British Colony is on the LEFT. For those who are good at planning and making their own arrangements, Trinidad does not present particularly difficult problems except expense, the frequent need to obtain permits to visit certain areas, and the limited hotel choices outside of the capital. Locally operated tours also tend to be overpriced. Visitors may want to use one of the two mountain lodges (Asa Wright Centre or Mt. St. Benedict Guesthouse) for most of their stay.

Because so many foreign visitors to Trinidad are bird watchers and naturalists, the country probably has more knowledgeable nature guides than any other location in the Caribbean. Although a guide is not essential except in remote areas, those who sightsee without a guide are likely to miss many of the best attractions. Consequently, on a first visit to Trinidad, many people—including those who normally shun group travel—might find their trip more rewarding if they joined a nature tour organized by specialists. Caligo Ventures of Armonk, New York, and Questers Worldwide Nature Tours and Wonder Bird Tours, both of New York City, design tours specifically for birders and naturalists, with experienced nature guides as leaders. Wonder Bird also arranges special programs for wildlife photographers and scientists.

Tobago has a network of corkscrew roads by the sea and through the mountains reaching most parts of the 27-mi/43-km-long island. But distances here are deceiving. The drive of 24 mi/38 km from the airport on the south along the windward coast to Speyside takes almost two hours. Some new roads are excellent, many old ones are terrible, and others have simply been abandoned for lack of maintenance.

Tobago has had a long-standing love-hate relationship with tourists—most of whom come from Trinidad rather than other parts of the world. A myriad of on-again, off-again development projects has left this otherwise Garden of Eden with a haphazard patchwork of overpriced tourist-class hotels and funky guesthouses where the setting is intended to make up for the shortcomings.

Trinidad and Tobago are connected by a high-frequency air shuttle operated by BWIA, the national carrier. The flight takes about twenty-five minutes. There is also interisland sea transportation by ferry which takes about five hours.

INFORMATION: In the U.S.: Trinidad and Tobago Tourist Board, 25 West 43rd St., Suite 1508, New York, NY 10036; 212-719-0540; 800-232-0082. There is no office in Canada. In the U.K.: 8A Hammersmith Broadway, London W67 AL; 81-741-4466. In Trinidad: Trinidad and Tobago Tourist Board, 134-138 Frederick St., Port of Spain, Trinidad, WI; 809-623-1932. A Natural History Festival is held annually in October; contact the Tourist Board headquarters for information.

Trinidad and Tobago Field Naturalists' Club meets on the second Thursday of each month at St. Mary's College, Frederick St., Port of Spain; publishes *Living World* (every two years); has monthly outings for members and will accommodate visitors with advance notice; tel: 624-3321. The Crusoe Reef Society, P.O. Box 890, Port of Spain, is concerned with protecting the marine environment.

A Guide to the Birds of Trinidad and Tobago by Richard ffrench (1980); *The Nature Trails of Trinidad* by Richard ffrench and Peter Bacon (1982); *A Birder's Guide to Trinidad and Tobago* by W. Murphy (College Park, MD: Peregrini Enterprises, 1987). *The Naturalist* is an independent magazine, with articles written mostly by members of the Trinidad and Tobago Field Naturalists' Club.

PERMITS: WASA, Water and Sewage Authority, Farm Road, Valsayn, St. Joseph, Trinidad, WI, for permission to visit certain forest and watershed areas.

ARUBA

CURACAO

BONAIRE

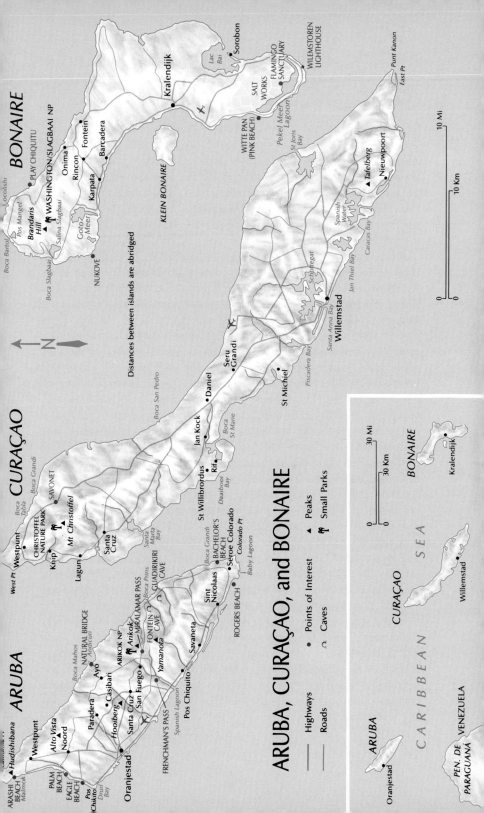

ARUBA, CURAÇAO, and BONAIRE

ARUBA

Hudishibana ▲
ARASHI BEACH
Malmok
Westpunt
PALM BEACH
Alto Vista ▲
EAGLE BEACH
Noord
Pos Chikito
Druif Bay
Oranjestad
Paradera
Casibari
Santa Cruz
Hooiberg ▲
San Fuego
FRENCHMAN'S PASS
Spanish Lagoon
Pos Chiquito
Boca Mahos
NATURAL BRIDGE
Andicuri
Ayo
ARIKOK NP
Arikok ▲
Yamanota ▲
FONTEIN CAVE
GUADIRIKIRI CAVE
MIRALAMAR PASS
Boca Prins
Savaneta
Sint Nicolaas
BACHELOR'S BEACH
Seroe Colorado
Colorado Pt
ROGERS BEACH
Baby Lagoon

CURAÇAO

Westpunt
West Pt
Boca Tabla
Boca Grandi
SAVONET
CHRISTOFFEL NATURE PARK
Mt Christoffel ▲
Knip
Lagun
Santa Cruz
Boca Grandi
Boca San Pedro
St Willibrordus
Rif
Boca St Marie
Boca
Daaibooi Bay
Santa Marta Bay
Jan Kock
Daniel
Seru Grandi
St Michiel
Piscadera Bay
Santa Anna Bay
Willemstad
Schottegat
Jan Thiel Bay
Caracas Bay
Spanish Water
St Joris Bay
Tafelberg ▲
Nieuwpoort
East Pt
Punt Kanon

BONAIRE

Lac
Bocalishi
PLAY CHIQUITU
Pos Mangel
Boca Bartol
Boca Slagbaai
Brandaris Hill ▲
WASHINGTON/SLAGBAAI NP
GotoMeer
Salina Slagbaai
NUKOVE
Fontein
Barcadera
Onima
Rincon
Karpata
Kralendijk
Lac Bai
Sorobon
FLAMINGO SANCTUARY
WILEMSTOREN LIGHTHOUSE
Punt Kanon
East Pt
SALT WORKS
Pekel Meer Lagoon
WITTE PAN (PINK BEACH)

KLEIN BONAIRE

Distances between islands are abridged

N

Legend
— Highways
— Roads
● Points of Interest
▲ Peaks
♙ Small Parks
∩ Caves

10 Mi
10 Km

CARIBBEAN SEA

ARUBA
Oranjestad

CURAÇAO
Willemstad

BONAIRE
Kralendijk

PEN. DE PARAGUANÁ
VENEZUELA

30 Mi
30 Km

ARUBA

ARUBA IS SOMETHING OF A MODERN MIRACLE. In thirty years it has been transformed from an island of little more than sand and brush into one of the most popular resorts in the Caribbean with sophisticated tourist facilities catering to visitors from three continents. Yet, while the south coast, the area of greatest tourist development, has changed, the island's northern half is largely untouched.

A dry, low-lying island 20 mi/32 km in length only 15 mi/24 km off the coast of Venezuela, Aruba has rocky, desert terrain similar to that of the American southwest. Less than 20 in/50 cm of rain falls annually, concentrated in a few showers and an occasional downpour between October and January. Except for undulations here and there, the land is flat, rising slightly toward the center and north in hills up to 623 ft/190 m. Aruba is ringed by coral reefs that grew around an ancient mountain core when the oceans were higher than they are today. The west and south coasts have miles of calm, palm-fringed white sand beaches considered to be among the most beautiful in the Caribbean. In contrast, where strong winds and salt-spraying waves batter the coast, the landscape is rugged and as desolate as the surface of the moon. Along the rockbound shores there are coves with white sand beaches, caves with prehistoric drawings, sand dunes, and black pebble beaches. Throughout the island, Aruba's trademark, the distinctive, windsculpted divi-divi tree can be seen.

Aruba was discovered in 1499 by Alonso de Ojeda and became a Dutch possession in 1636. Except for a short period of British control in the early nineteenth century, it has remained Dutch. The island was largely ignored until 1824 when gold was discovered. Its production lasted almost a century and was followed by oil prosperity until 1985, when Exxon closed its refinery. In 1986, Aruba left the Netherlands Antilles group to become a separate autonomous entity within the Kingdom of the Netherlands and tourism, now Aruba's mainstay, is growing by leaps and bounds.

Aruba was one of the few places in the West Indies where the European conquerors allowed the indigenous people to live in relative peace. About half of today's population are said to be direct descendants of the Arubaes, a tribe of the Cacquetios—the Arawaks from South America who also inhabited Bonaire and Curaçao when the Europeans arrived. The Arawak heritage, more strongly reflected here than in other Caribbean islands, sets the Arubans apart.

Oranjestad and Palm Beach

The capital, Oranjestad, is a neat, clean town of Dutch colonial and modern architecture easy to cover in an hour's stroll. Wilhelmina Park is a colorful tropical garden named for the former Dutch queen. The De Man Shell Collection (18 Morgenster Street) has a private display of shells with rare and unusual pieces. It is housed in the owner's home, but open to the public (297-8-24246). West of town at Druif Bay, where the coastline bends north, there is an almost continuous 7-mi/11-km stretch of powder-fine sand along Eagle Beach and Palm Beach. This is the most developed part of the island with the majority of its luxury hotels, casinos, restaurants, and water-sports facilities. Eagle Beach is the venue for the annual international windsurfing competition and has a jogging track at its western end.

Along Palm Beach, the seaside hotels are surrounded by flowering gardens, relieving an otherwise barren landscape. Bananaquits, when not stealing the sugar from the dining tables, peck at soft fruits on the trees or sip nectar from the flowers. Hovering around the flowers and flowering shrubs are green-throated caribs and black-faced grassquits. In gardens the tropical mockingbird and the beautifully colored orange troupial feed on juicy fruits, but in the countryside, or *kunucu* as it is called in Papiamento, the language of Aruba and the Netherlands Antilles, they eat the fruit of the organ-pipe cactus. (In Arawak, *kunucu* originally meant a plot of land for agriculture, but now the term is widely used to mean rural areas. In Aruba, the Spanish word *campo* is also used for "countryside.")

Along Aruba's shores, the most common seabirds are brown pelicans, which are often accompanied by laughing gulls. Royal terns perch on the buoys marking swimming areas and magnificent frigatebirds, which roost in patches of mangroves on the south coast and north end, appear overhead. From September to March, ruddy turnstones can be seen strolling the seaweed.

Bubali Pond

On the north side of Eagle Beach at Pos Chikito, Bubali Pond is a bird sanctuary; it is located south of De Olde Molen, a nineteenth-century Dutch windmill that is now a restaurant and a landmark. The pond was once used as a pan for making salt from sea water, but now a sewage-treatment plant releases its processed water here. The pond has fish and attracts a great variety of birds. Flocks arriving at sunset are a particularly memorable sight. Pelicans are here in large numbers, as are black olivaceous cormorants, which can be seen perched on the rocks with their wings spread to dry. Of the several species of herons, black-crowned night-herons are

Strong cross-island winds carved and weathered several rock formations on Aruba, among them the Casibari boulders, which one can climb to get panoramic views.

particularly numerous; active in the early morning, in the evening, and at night, they roost in trees, shrubs, or along the water's edge during the day. Here and in the mangrove thickets on the south shore, the green-backed, the smallest of the herons, can be seen along with great blue, little blue, and tricolored herons. Abundant, too, are great egrets with long, black legs and yellow bills, and snowy egrets with yellow feet and black legs. Black-necked stilts are breeding residents seen throughout the year. Groove-billed anis are seen here and throughout the island. Yellowlegs and spotted sandpipers are at the pond during the winter months as are blue-winged teal, wigeon, and lesser scaup. One might also see barn and bank swallows. Some of the pond's casual visitors from Venezuela include glossy and scarlet ibis and the large wood stork. Ospreys fly over the coast and are sometimes seen at the pond. The ABC islands—Aruba, Bonaire, and Curacao—are particularly interesting for birders because, in addition to their own bird species and stray ones from Venezuela, they are the first landfall for many northern migrants on their autumn trans-Gulf migration route.

CALIFORNIA POINT

On the northern end of Aruba, Hudishibana, a small hill marked by the California Lighthouse, is a pelican feeding ground. To the northeast, California Point is one of several locations on Aruba with a dramatic, exotic landscape of sand dunes. Off Cudarebo (also spelled Kudarebe), the northwest tip, lies the *Californian*, wrecked in 1891, in 15 to 30 ft/4.5 to 9 m of water. Beyond the wreck there is a gradual slope with sponges, gorgonians, and big brain corals that almost break the surface at low tide. The strong currents here carry large numbers of fish through the offshore waters. This shallow area between Aruba and Venezuela has led some to think that Aruba was once part of the South American continent. However, most scientists believe that Aruba broke off from a northern formation and slid down the continental shelf to where it now rests.

The main road from California Point returns southeast along a stretch of dry, desolate terrain characterized by towering rock formations and scattered hills with the highest being Alto Vista (236 ft/72 m), which is worth climbing for its nice views. Only the hardiest of salt-resistant species, such as crabgrass, survive here. Among the ground-hugging pioneers are *yerba di cusinchi*, a tiny brown cushion-like plant that grows between rocks; and *banana di rif*, which can be recognized by its thick, fleshy leaves that resemble minuscule bananas.

The region is home to the shy iguana, which has a particular fondness for hibiscus flowers. Common on the roadside is the *blausana*, or *cododo*, a lizard species whose adult males grow up to 12 in/30 cm in length and have copper-blue coloring that is especially bright on the tail. The "blueies," as they are known, look for food scraps in picnic areas, aggressively chasing away competitors with their foreleg-waving display. An endemic anole called *waltaca* in Aruba and *kako* in Curaçao grows up to 8 in/20 cm long. Seen on trees, they change colors like a chameleon from cream to gray and black.

HOOIBERG

Almost in the center of the island is the conical Hooiberg (541 ft/164 m), known as the Haystack, whose silhouette can be seen from almost any location. The curious volcanic formation is covered with dry woodlands of *kibrahacha*, or yellow poui, white manjack, and other flowering trees together with wild sage and a variety of cacti. A flight of several hundred steps leads to the top where, on a clear day, the view reaches to the Venezuelan coast. Among the bird species that populate the hill are the spectacular orange and black troupial, which sings from the treetops here and throughout the island, and the yellow oriole, similar to the troupial except for its yellow, instead of black, head. The oriole's bottle-shaped nests hang down as much as 2 ft/0.6 m from the end of branches, sometimes three or more per branch. Crested bobwhites and several kinds of doves scurry about in the underbrush.

On the south side of the Hooiberg, the Canashito area has caves with Arawak petroglyphs, one of several places where they can be seen. Hooiberg and Casibari on the north are littered with huge boulders that have been carved and weathered into bizarre shapes by the strong winds that blow across the island. Similar rock formations can be found elsewhere on the island. Ayó, northeast of Hooiberg, has been dubbed the Stonehenge of Aruba. Rare burrowing owls live here in holes they dig under the boulders. East of Ayó, a track leads through a pretty palm plantation to the coast at Andicuri Bay, a good picnic location.

THE NATURAL BRIDGE

On the northeast coast at Boca Mahos the land drops sharply into a turbulent sea. The force of the thundering waves has given rise to a popular misconception that the natural bridge here and similar formations along the coast were carved out of the coral cliffs by the sea. Actually, the openings were made from the land side. The entire north coast consists of coral rock formations with various levels, some now above sea level and some still below; the bridges were formed when weak spots in the coral were dissolved and washed away by rainwater running off the land.

SPANISH LAGOON

About midway along the south coast, Spanish Lagoon is a long finger of mangrove-edged water with a bird refuge at its northeastern end. The thickets have three mangrove species—red, white, and buttonwood. (Mangroves are found elsewhere on the south coast: at Pos Chiquito on a spit of land known as Isla di Oro; at the small town of Savaneta, the former capital of Aruba; and on the reef islands facing Savaneta.)

Among the great variety of birds attracted to Spanish Lagoon, egrets and herons are the most common. A small colony of pelicans is found in the mangroves on the reef; frigatebirds roost there at night. Along the entire coast one can see Sandwich terns, including both the northern form, whose bill is black with a yellow tip, and the southern form, often called the cayenne tern, with an all-yellow bill. The two interbreed in Aruba, indicating that they are not separate species as was once thought. Breeding colonies of Sandwich terns are found on the reef islands at San Nicolas Bay. Common terns breed there as well as on the northeast coast.

On the north side of Spanish Lagoon in front of Barcadera Harbor, a reef about 600 yds/550 m from shore starts at the surface and drops to about 80 ft/24 m depth. It is part of a 2-mi/3.2-km reef that runs along the south coast and has abundant gorgonians and elkhorn and staghorn corals that attract squirrelfishes, parrotfishes, French angelfish, groupers, grunts, barracuda, sharks, and other fish common to the Caribbean. Farther out at sea, a deeper reef has 100-ft/30-m walls. The area is also popular for sportfishing. Close to shore, is De Palm Island, a privately developed recreation and sports center specializing in snorkeling and diving. Daily bus and boat excursions to De Palm Island leave directly from Palm Beach hotels.

FRENCHMAN'S PASS

South of Spanish Lagoon, Mangel Halto, which means "tall mangroves" in Papiamento, has a pretty beach with a reef within swimming distance from shore. Inland from Pos Chiquito, a road around the north end of the lagoon goes through Frenchman's Pass, a cactus-lined drive with panoramic views of the countryside; French and Spanish buccaneers fought a battle here in the seventeenth century. Tracks from the main road go north and south to the lagoon and bird refuge and to the ruins of the Balashi gold mill, a relic of Aruba's gold rush, built in 1898. A plant noticeable in this area is the rubber vine, whose white latex can be made into rubber. It was introduced into the West Indies early in the century to be developed for commercial purposes; instead, it spread so quickly that it became a pest, wrapping itself around trees and strangling them.

Aloe vera, known locally as *haloe*, grows wild throughout Aruba. It was widely cultivated for medicinal use in the past, but its production declined greatly after lower-priced synthetics reduced the market. In the traditional method of processing aloe, the bitter juice was drained from the leaves and then boiled. Some of the big outdoor ovens used for that purpose are still in operation in the area and cultivation continues on a small scale. Aloe is used throughout the Caribbean for sunburn: one simply cuts the leaf and rubs the yellow juice on the skin.

PUNTA BASORA

The southeastern end of the island, marked by the Colorado Lighthouse, has beautiful white sand beaches overlooking some of Aruba's main dive locations where there are large gardens of elkhorn and staghorn coral, basket sponges, and sea fans. The Point lies south of Sint Nicolaas, which was the island's second largest settlement until 1985 when the oil refinery here was closed. On the south side of the Point are two secluded beaches, Salina and Manzalina, better known as Rodgers Beach and Baby Lagoon, where one can snorkel from shore. Both beaches lie at the foot of Seroe

Colorado, the former residential community for the oil company staff; the houses are available for rent to vacationers.

On the north side, Boca Tabla, popularly referred to as B.A. or Bachelor's Beach, has a reef starting about 50 ft/15 m from shore, sloping first to about 60 ft/18 m and then dropping to 160 ft/48 m. Diving here is for experienced divers; currents are strong and sharks and barracuda are frequent visitors. The area offers drift diving as well. Farther north, Boca Grandi is a popular picnic spot. All the waters around Punta Basora are prime sport-fishing grounds.

North of Sint Nicolaas is an arid, windswept region where the asymmetrical *watapana*, commonly known as the divi-divi tree, is the dominant feature. The tree's odd shape is caused by the *passaat*, the Papiamento name for the constant strong winds that blow predominantly from the east. Although all wind-sheared trees with this shape are commonly called divi-divi, several species grow in this manner. Among them are mesquite, known locally as *kwihi;* thorny acacia, known as *hubada;* West Indian cherry; and *watakeli.* In sheltered places on the island's leeward side the same species grow normally. The *watapana* has small, fragrant blossoms and thick, curled pods whose high tannin content made it a valuable commercial product to the European tanning industry from the mid-1700s up to the last century. The name *divi-divi*—which means "ear" in the Arawak language—refers to the *watapana* pod, which resembles a human ear.

Among the most widespread of Aruba's many cactus species is the prickly pear, whose disks or arms snap off and root easily. Their dispersion is aided greatly by wandering goats, to whom the thorny disks attach. Candle cactus, whose flowers bloom at night, appears here in several varieties, collectively called *kadushi.* One candle cactus species endemic to the Dutch Leeward Islands is *breba,* a huge tree-like plant often over a hundred years old. Another of the *kadushi,* organ-pipe cactus, called *datu* in Curaçao, is less branched than *breba* and is often used for making cactus fences. Barrel cactus, or Turk's-head, called *bushi,* is abundant at Seroe Colorado and the windward coast. The cutting down of trees or cacti on public lands in Aruba is prohibited by law.

GUADIRIKIRI AND FONTEIN CAVES

Many caves are found in the Seroe Colorado area and to its north. Near the coast, Huliba Cave is a small underground passage with stalagmites and stalactites. The large Guadirikiri Cave has two high-ceilinged caverns and

The wind-shaped sand dunes at Boca Prins, on Aruba's north shore, are nesting spots for loggerhead, green, and hawksbill turtles.

an opening at the top that lets in some light; it is home to a large number of bats. Aruba's bat species include insectivores, a fish-eating species, and pollen- and honey-eating bats, some of which feed at orchids. None carries the rabies virus. The Fontein Cave with fine Arawak petroglyphs is the most interesting one. Aruba's largest cave is in the heart of the Seroe Colorado area and is the subject of a $3 million project that is awaiting government approval; the project, aimed at opening the cave to the public, would take three years to complete.

BOCA PRINS

Boca Prins, a cove with sand dunes constantly being reshaped by the strong wind, has rugged, weathered cliffs and a bridge formation known as Boca Druif, or Dragon Mouth. Between Boca Prins and the pretty beach of Dos Playa—and along many beaches in Aruba—seagrape and *cocorobana*, a low shrub with thick silver-gray leaves, are abundant. Here, too, are manchineel trees. Their shade may look tempting, but one should exert caution because the sap from the leaves can cause blisters, and the trees' small green fruit is poisonous.

Aruban beaches are visited by four species of sea turtle from April through August. Green turtle, known locally as *turtuga blanco*; loggerhead or *cawama;* and hawksbill visit the sandy coves on the north and east coasts. Only the leatherback visits the beaches on the south and west.

ARIKOK NATIONAL PARK

The road between Boca Prins and Santa Cruz runs through the Miralamar Pass between Aruba's highest hills and affords views over the countryside with farms, rolling hills, and great diorite rock formations. The triangle of land north of the road between Boca Prins and San Fuego, and bounded on the east by the coastline as far as Boca Keto, comprises the Arikok National Park with Mt. Arikok (577 ft/176 m), the island's second highest hill, as its focal point. At the foot of the hill is a small garden with an old restored adobe house. The garden has most species of trees and bushes found on Aruba and attracts birds and butterflies, the native hare, and iguanas. It can be reached by car from the San Fuego–Boca Prins Road.

Around the hill are some rare species that were once abundant, such as lignum vitae, known locally as *wayaca*, whose extraordinarily hard wood and other properties made it a valuable commercial product. The tree is an evergreen and can be recognized by its light blue flowers and orange heart-shaped fruits. Even rarer is the brazilwood or dyewood, which has an exceptionally deep-grooved and twisted trunk. Petroglyphs can be seen on rocks at Arikok.

Yamanota

The area south of the San Fuego–Boca Prins Road—measuring about 2 mi/ 3.2 km north to south and 4 mi/6.4 km east to west—is known as Yamanota. The area, which includes the island's highest hill, Mt. Yamanota (617 ft/ 189 m), has been proposed as a national park by FANAPA (Aruba Foundation for Nature and Parks), the island's principal conservation group. The area is dry, particularly on the south and east, but even here the fields can turn from dusty gray to green after a winter rain. A paved road leads to the top of Mt. Yamanota, but most other hiking trails are dirt paths.

The Yamanota area is the home of the brown-throated parakeet, a bright green and yellow bird which is almost as large as a parrot. The birds make their nests in caves and in termite nests and feed on seeds and fruits, favoring particularly the fruit of the organ-pipe cactus. They fly in small groups and can be seen close to houses in dry seasons. Other birds of the area are bare-eyed pigeon and flycatchers, of which the most common is the brown-crested flycatcher, which makes its nest in tree cavities. The ruby-topaz hummingbird is seen in the hills around the blooms of trees and cacti and also in gardens, hovering about the flowering bushes. Often the road-sides are brightened with the pink flowers of coralita, or coral vine, and the trumpet clusters of purple scopet, similar to morning glories. Here or in gardens one might see the rufous-collared sparrow, which is found else-where in the Caribbean only in the border region of southern Haiti and the Dominican Republic.

The sparsely inhabited Yamanota area is home to Aruba's two snakes—both endemic subspecies: the harmless santanero and the venomous tropi-cal rattlesnake, called *colebra* or *cascabel* in Papiamento. The area also has goats, lizards, and feral donkeys. Development and loss of habitat has decreased Aruba's wildlife, but efforts by FANAPA and other conservation-ists are being made to reverse the trend.

Outdoor Activities

Hiking: Aruba does not have marked hiking trails, but many tracks lead off the main roads; distances are not great between the roads and points of inter-est. Excursions for hikers and those in-terested in animals, birds, and plants are led by naturalists and take from three to six hours: inquire at the Aruba Tourism Authority or at Corvalu Tours (297-8-21149), whose owner, Julio Maduro, is Aruba's best known naturalist.

Horseback Riding: Daily except Sunday, Rancho El Paso (297-8-23310) offers trail riding through the country-side on *paso fino* horses imported from South America. The mounts are noted for their smooth gait.

Swimming: Unquestionably the most beautiful waters for swimming are those that bathe the soft sands of Palm Beach, but there are many other white sand beaches with calm waters along the leeward coast and some protected areas on the windward coast. Baby Lagoon at Seroe Colorado is only 4 to 5 ft/1.2 to 1.5 m deep, and the calm waters are especially suited for children and inexperienced swimmers. The dramatic waves of the north coast are great for viewing and as a picnic setting, but not for swimming. One should inquire locally before swimming anywhere along the windward coast.

SNORKELING AND DIVING: Aruba is surrounded by coral reefs and has some interesting shipwrecks. Generally, the reefs on the leeward side are in calm waters and offer both shallow-water coral gardens within swimming distance of shore and deepwater reefs and walls that drop 100 ft/30 m and more. Snorkeling and diving can be arranged through hotels or directly with dive operators, most of whom are located on the leeward coast in the vicinity of Eagle and Palm beaches.

The area between Druif Beach and Arashi, suitable for snorkeling or shallow diving, has the gentlest current. At Arashi Beach, a reef of elkhorn coral lies on a sandy bottom in 20 to 40 ft/6 to 12 m of water within swimming distance from shore. Baby Lagoon on the southeast corner has the best visibility. The windward coast has many bocas, or small bays, but for the most part, they are only for experienced divers accompanied by local experts; the water is usually rough and the currents strong.

Two wrecks can be viewed by snorkelers as well as divers. An oil tanker from World War II, the *Pedernales*, lies in 20 to 40 ft/6 to 12 m of water near the Holiday Inn. At Malmok, the wreck of the *Antilla*, a German cargo ship scuttled by the Germans at the start of World War II, rests in 60 ft/18 m of water. The wreck, broken in two parts, is surrounded by small basket sponges, gorgonians, and other formations.

BOATING: Catamarans and other boats for picnic cruises and glass-bottom ones for viewing the coral are available through hotels and water-sports operators. Yachting is not a sport of general interest here, but there is a nautical club at the mouth of Spanish Lagoon.

DEEP-SEA FISHING: Sport-fishing is big in Aruba. Half- and full-day, fully equipped charters are available through one's hotel or directly from boat operators. Less than a mile or two from shore, the sea is rich with kingfish, tuna, bonito, wahoo, blue and white marlin, and many more.

WINDSURFING: The same strong winds that shape the divi-divi tree and keep the island cool have made Aruba one of the leading windsurfing locations in the Caribbean. For 300 days of the year there are guaranteed winds of 15 knots, and they often blow up to 20 knots. In June, when the annual international windsurfing competitions are under way at Eagle Beach, the winds get up to 25 knots and more. The prime windsurfing location, Fisherman's Huts, is north of the Holiday Inn on Palm Beach. For those who are not ready for competition or have not yet taken up the sport, hotels along the quiet waters farther south on Palm Beach have equipment and instructors. Bachelor's Beach on the southeast coast is a favorite spot for those with advanced skills; Rodgers Beach has light surf.

EXPLORING THE ISLAND

Aruba has a good network of roads, most radiating from Oranjestad, the capital. No road completely encircles the island. By using a series of connecting roads one can make a loop from Palm Beach around the northwest end and return inland via Noord. Several circuits can be followed through the center of the island, heading north-northeast from Oranjestad to the Natural Bridge via Paradera; or via the

Hooiberg, Casibari, and Ayó through the countryside to the windward coast at Andicuri.

Toward the south and southeast, the main highway from Oranjestad to the airport continues on the south coast to Spanish Lagoon, Savaneta, and Sint Nicolaas. A detour around the old oil installations leads to Punta Basora. Alternatively, one can loop through Sint Nicolaas to Fontein and Boca Prins on the northeast coast, returning via the Miralamar Pass between the island's two highest hills to Santa Cruz, a crossroad almost in the center of the island. From Santa Cruz, roads branch north to Boca Mahos and the Natural Bridge; northwest along the Hooiberg to Casibari and thence to Palm Beach; and south to Frenchman's Pass. The Aruba Tourism Authority at the airport or near the dock has copies of *Aruba Holiday*, a free tourist guide with a map of the main roads, and other literature.

Rental cars are readily available and are the best mode of transportation around the island. Buses run fairly regularly from downtown on Smith Boulevard near the Tourism Authority to the resorts along Eagle and Palm beaches, stopping to pick up and discharge passengers near the main hotels en route.

Note that laws prohibiting the export of material of biological importance, dead or alive, from the land or waters have been passed to protect all the Netherlands Antilles and Aruba.

INFORMATION: In the U.S.: Aruba Tourism Authority, 1000 Harbor Blvd., Weehawken, NJ 07087; 201-330-0800. In Canada: 86 Bloor St. West, Suite 204, Toronto M5S 1M5; 416-975-1950. In Europe: Amalia Straat 16, 2514 JC, The Hague, Holland; 070-35-66-220. In Aruba: 172 L. G. Smith Blvd., Eagle, Aruba; 297-8-21019. *Discover Aruba's Wildlife*, published in 1982 by STINAPA-Aruba (now known as FANAPA), is a guide to flora and fauna and available at bookstores and some hotel gift shops.

The Natural Bridge at Boca Mahos near Andicuri, like other natural bridges along the northeast coast, was formed when rainwater runoff from land dissolved weak spots in the coastal coral rock formations.

CURAÇAO

CURAÇAO IS A MINI HOLLAND in the tropics complete with waterways and colorful houses. It is a cosmopolitan capital and bustling port juxtaposed against a rugged landscape of windswept shores, chalky mountains, and arid terrain where the cactus grows as tall as trees and there are only a few roads. It has two of the best nature parks—on land and undersea—in the Caribbean. And like its neighbors, Aruba and Bonaire, it is a landfall for migrating birds on their trans-Gulf flight.

Curaçao is the capital and largest island of the Netherlands Antilles (its sister islands are nearby Bonaire, and Saba, St. Eustatius, and St. Maarten in the eastern Caribbean). Given its low, undulating terrain with rocky hills here and there, Curaçao's countryside resembles the Arizona desert with reddish clay soil that supports a scrub vegetation on a rainfall of barely 22 in/55 cm a year. The land is greener toward the northern end, mostly national parkland, where the hills peak at over 1,200 ft/300 m. The slim, 38-mi-/61-km-long island lies well south of the Caribbean hurricane path on a northwest–southeast axis between Aruba on the west and Bonaire on the east. Klein Curaçao, an uninhabited island, lies to the southeast.

Quiet seas wash Curaçao's western leeward coast; wild surf crashes against the windward north. Along the perimeter of its rocky shores there are small coves with narrow, sand-and-pebble beaches and several large bays or lagoons with very narrow entrances and wide basins. These waterways, with their many fingers and inner islands, are one of Curaçao's distinctive features. Some lagoons are used for commerce, others for sport. Completely surrounding the island are reefs where a fabulous underwater world of coral and fish is only now being discovered by divers.

The island's first known inhabitants were the Curaçaos, a clan of the Caquetios, one of the Arawak tribes that came to the Caribbean from South America. Alonso de Ojeda reached the island in 1499, the first European to do so, and the Spaniards made their first settlement in 1527. A century later, however, they abandoned Curaçao to Holland, which made it a possession of the Dutch West India Company. The French and British, who coveted Curaçao's natural harbors and strategic location, tried several times to dislodge the Dutch but without success. A young Peter Stuyvesant became governor in 1642, only three years before he was named the director-general of the Dutch colony of New Amsterdam, which today we call New York.

Under the Dutch, the island was divided into plantations, some of which prospered on salt mining rather than agriculture. Slavery was abolished in 1863, and Curaçao remained a sleepy little island until 1914 when oil was discovered in Venezuela and the Royal Dutch Shell Company, attracted by Curaçao's excellent harbor, built one of the world's largest oil refineries there. This oil prosperity lasted through most of this century and brought workers from many nations who added to Curaçao's polyglot culture.

WILLEMSTAD

Throughout the Caribbean, the islands are brushed with their European heritage but in no place is the picture painted more vividly than in Willemstad, Curaçao's capital, an architectural gem. The town is built around Santa Anna Bay, which is entered through a channel, 4,200 ft/1,280 m long and only 270 ft/82 m wide, that opens on to the Schottegat, an inner bay covering 150 acres. The picturesque harbor is lined with brightly painted Dutch colonial houses with red gabled roofs.

The west side of the harbor, Otrabanda, is connected to the east side by a pontoon bridge that serves as a pedestrian walkway; it is opened several times daily to allow ships to pass. About a mile from the bridge, the Curaçao Museum (van Leeuwenhoek Street), housed in a building dating from 1853, has exhibits on the island's history from pre-Columbian times to the present. Along the shore, the Rif Recreation Center is a jogging, walking, and recreation boulevard; a fitness center is being added.

Northwest of Willemstad, the road crosses the peaceful countryside, or kunucu, where sheep and goats graze in patchwork fields fenced with neatly crisscrossed candle cactus and dotted with small adobe houses. *Kunucu*, an Arawak word, originally was used to mean a piece of land given by a landowner to a slave to grow subsistence crops, but now means any rural area. The dry, rocky terrain—freshest in November and December when it rains—is covered with mesquite and tall cacti wrapped with tiny orchids or draped with brightly colored bougainvillea. The divi-divi tree is ever present: its branches, shaped by the wind, grow in one direction at a right angle from the trunk.

Throughout the kunucu, one also sees many of Curaçao's sixty remaining *landhuizen*, or plantation houses, some dating from the seventeenth century and once surrounded by fortified walls. From Landhuis Seru Grandi on the Grote Berg (big hill), there is a fine view of the Hato plain, stretching north along desolate coastal scenery to Boca San Pedro. At Daniel, the road forks west to Sint Willibrordus, a small village, and the seventeenth-century Landhuis Jan Kock, where salt from nearby ponds was once produced for the herring industry in Holland. The manor house has a museum that includes heavy furniture made from the mahogany that once grew on the plantation. From the village, unpaved roads and tracks suitable for hiking lead over the Rif, a pretty area surrounding Salina St.

On the southern leeward coast, quiet Caribbean waters bathe Daaibooi Beach, one of the few public beaches on Curaçao.

Marie, a salt pond by the sea. Other roads—some paved, some dirt—lead to small, secluded beaches along a stretch of Valentijns Bay. Some are on undeveloped private property and visitors may need permission to proceed, but Daaibooi Beach, reached by a paved road, is public land.

CHRISTOFFEL NATURE PARK

The hilly north end of Curaçao is dominated by the rocky peak of Mt. Christoffel (1,238 ft/375 m) and tabletop Mt. Hyronimus (759 ft/230 m). The Christoffel Nature Park, commencing north of Sint Hyronimus, spreads over 3,500 acres/1,860 hectares, or about half of the terrain in the northern fifth of the island. The park (open daily from 8 A.M. to 3 P.M.) is composed of three contingent plantations—Savonet, Zorgvlied, and Zevenbergen—acquired by the government and placed in the care of STINAPA, the Netherlands Antilles National Parks Foundation. The park protects more than 500 varieties of plants, an estimated 150 bird species, as well as iguanas, feral donkeys, and the Curaçao deer, a subspecies of the American white-tailed deer (Curaçao is said to be the only Caribbean island that has had deer since pre-Columbian times). The region has unusual rock formations, ancient shells, endemic snails, and caves with bats and Arawak petroglyphs.

The vegetation is dominated by mesquite, century plants, divi-divi, and groves of gigantic cactus. Orchids are found in abundance. There are rare palm species and remnants of dyewood and indigo, both once grown for their commercial value. Nature guides and an excellent guidebook are available at the park entrance, located on the main highway that passes through the east side of the park.

Approximately 20 mi/32 km of road, divided into four signposted, color-coded routes, wander through the park. Three are driving routes, named after the plantations through which they pass; the fourth is a footpath to the top of Mt. Christoffel.

Savonet Route (blue; 5.6 mi/9 km; signs 1–10) offers an introduction to the common trees and plants of Curaçao. It leaves from the visitors' center and winds east, and then north, to caves sheltering bats and petroglyphs. A new Museum of Natural and Cultural History occupies the old Savonet plantation house. A footpath just beyond the first sign passes under the shade of tall mahogany and poisonous manchineel trees to the estate's former *hofi*, or orchard. At the second sign, there are three common trees—mesquite, divi-divi, and thorny acacia—that observers often confuse but whose differences become apparent upon closer scrutiny. Mesquite, widely used for charcoal, has light yellow flowers. Thorny acacia can be recognized by its very long thorns and yellow flowers. The divi-divi

Curacao's dry desert terrain supports its national tree, the divi-divi, which typically grows with branches blown laterally by the wind.

tree has curved pods, which were once in great demand by European tanneries because of their high tannin content.

The road descends to a dry bed, known locally as *rooi*, which has water only after a heavy rain. One is cautioned about bringamosa, an endemic shrub with small white, heart-shaped leaves: the hairs on its leaves and branches secrete a substance that makes the skin itch and swell. Fortunately, an antidote, jatropha or *flaira*, grows in the same area. Its small red flower yields a fruit whose juice stops the burning sensation of bringamosa when rubbed on the skin.

At sign 6, a footpath goes to the top of a jagged limestone hill where one has a view of the north coast overlooking Boca Grandi on the east and Mt. Christoffel on the west. From Boca Grandi, the route returns along the coast past ancient Arawak petroglyphs (sign 9) and the entrance to two caves (sign 10).

Zorgvlied Route (green; 7.5 mi/12 km; signs 11–17) is a ninety-minute circuit through the central and north area of the park. It returns along the eastern flank of Mt. Christoffel, crossing the footpath that goes to the summit. From the visitors' center the route heads north to the ruins of Zorgvlied estate house.

At sign 14, from the hilltop known as Rancho Grande, there is a wide panorama across the northwest. The island's complex geology is in evidence: the underlying rock is the 100-million-year-old Curaçao Lava Formation; over the base is sedimentary rock from the 70-million-year-old Knip Formation; and overlying this are more recent limestone terraces. The route returns along a ridge—the most scenic part of the circuit—to the base of Mt. Christoffel, where the footpath to the summit begins (it takes about an hour). Overhead one can often spot white-tailed hawks, a small number of which breed on the island.

Zevenbergen Route (yellow; 6.8 mi/11 km; signs 18–23) is a winding road that circles the southwest area of the park over undulating hills and gives access to viewpoints with splendid panoramas of the west coast. One can also get to the trail up Mt. Christoffel from here. Two species of orchids are found only here: the purple *Schomburgkia humboldtii*, which blooms in July and August; and the white orchid *Brassavola nodosa*, which flowers mainly in December and January but can be seen at other times if there has been rain.

Christoffel Trail (red) is the footpath; it offers grand panoramic views and is the most rewarding route for birders. It starts from the visitors' center and goes up a dry riverbed to the foot of the mountain, where the ascent begins. Alternatively, one can drive to the base of the mountain, cutting an hour off the three-hour hike.

Birds that populate the *rooi* are the rufous-collared sparrow, common ground-dove, Zenaida dove, and white-tipped dove. The elusive scaly-naped pigeon, known locally as the St. Christoffel pigeon, is more likely to be heard than seen. Equally shy is the bare-eyed pigeon, recognized by the white patch on its wing. On the slope, hummingbirds, parakeets, tropical mockingbirds, and troupials may be seen. The long, bottle-shaped nests of the yellow oriole are seen hanging from the branches of thorny scrub. A black head distinguishes the yellow and black troupial from the oriole, which has a yellow head. Troupials can also be a beautiful bright orange.

Near the top of the mountain, the track becomes very steep, and it can be slippery after a rain; hikers must use hands and feet to proceed to the top. The track passes a cluster of large balsam apple trees, also known as the autograph tree. It originates as an epiphyte on the trunk of a tree, but once it roots, it overtakes the supporting tree. The panorama from the summit extends to Bonaire in the east and Venezuela in the south.

WESTPUNT

On the north side of the park, the highway passes by a side road to Boca Tabla, a grotto where the surf pounds the windward shores. The highway loops around the north end to Westpunt, an old fishing town on the rocky cliffs above the quiet, fantastically colored turquoise sea of the leeward coast. Below is a small beach with coarse sand and rock. From Westpunt the road returns south through the undulating hills of the west coast via Knip, Jeremi, Lagun, and Santa Cruz, where rocky coves covered with cactus and acacia woods protect little beaches, some reached by dirt roads or tracks. South of Santa Cruz is pretty Santa Marta Bay, a serpentine lagoon with beaches and rocky shores surrounded by green hillsides.

JAN THIEL LAGOON AND SPANISH WATER

The south coast from Willemstad and Jan Thiel Lagoon to Spanish Water is the island's main resort area with hotels and water-sports centers. Jan Thiel Lagoon is a residential area with a private beach open to visitors; there is a small admission charge. Farther east, Spaanse, or Spanish Water, is a beautiful lagoon with a long, narrow opening to the sea. A sheltered natural harbor with many hilly green fingers and coves, islands, and beaches, it is the center of the island's boating and fishing; the Curaçao Yacht Club is located here. On the east side of the entrance is Santa Barbara, a popular public beach with changing facilities. On the west side of the entrance to Spanish Water, a sliver of land separates the lagoon from Caracas Bay, a broad, deep-water anchorage marked by the round tower of Ft. Beekenburg, an unexpected medieval-style structure.

Curaçao Underwater Park

The 1,500-acre/607-hectare Curaçao Underwater Park protects some of Curaçao's finest reefs, stretching for 12.5 mi/20 km from the Princess Beach Hotel, just west of Jan Thiel Lagoon, to the eastern tip of the island. Visibility here is up to 150 ft/46 m. Buoy no. 3 is the start of an underwater trail with numbered signs that is reached by boat from the Princess Beach Hotel or Seaquarium. An excellent guide written by Tom van't Hof, the marine biologist who directed the park's development, has an explanatory profile of the reef. Permanent mooring buoys for boats are positioned.

Princess Beach Hotel (1) has reef so diverse and colorful, one almost need go no further. Its structure is typical of Curaçao's reef. It starts with a shallow terrace, suitable for snorkelers, where elkhorn and staghorn corals and gorgonians are abundant. It drops to 30 to 40 ft/9 to 12 m from where the reef slopes at a 45-degree angle. The types of corals differ according to depth: brain, sheet, and star corals on the lower slope; mountain star, leaf, flower, and yellow pencil corals on the upper slope. Fishes include chromis, wrasses, foureye butterflyfish, and sergeant majors, among others.

Bapor Kibra (2) has two vertical outcroppings at 110 to 120 ft/33 to 36 m covered with colorful sponges and black coral. Fish include French angelfish, rock beauty, yellowtail snapper, as well as porgies, barracudas, and groupers.

Boca di Sorsaka (3), a snorkeling trail in front of the Jan Thiel Lagoon, is rich in sponges and small black corals. *Jan Thiel* (4), immediately west of Jan Thiel Bay, is best at the dropoff (50 to 60 ft/15 to 18 m depth) with great varieties of corals, sponges, and gorgorians. *Lost Anchor* (7) is close to the cliff at Caracas Bay. The mooring is connected to a heavy old chain, probably from a ship's anchor, that starts at 10 ft/3 m and has been measured to 283 ft/86 m; its origin remains unknown, however. Caracas Bay is unusual geologically because it originated in a landslide that, geologists estimate, sent 375 million tons of rock to the bottom of the sea. At *Towboat* (8) an old boat sits upright in only 20 ft/6 m of water. *Punt'i Piku* (10) has outstanding large pillar corals and sheets of mountain star coral. Mooring buoys 11 to 16 are in water that is often choppy; the sites are only for experienced divers.

Curaçao Seaquarium

At Bapor Kibra, east of the Underwater Park entrance, is the Curaçao Seaquarium, a private facility where more than 400 species of fish, corals, and sponges native to Curaçao waters are on view. (Its hours are 10 A.M. to 10 P.M. and there is an admission fee.) A glass-bottom boat departs frequently from here on thirty-minute excursions over the reef.

TAFELBERG

Dominating the landscape on the east side of Spanish Water is a sheer, chalky mountain, Tafelberg, or Table Mountain (637 ft/194 m). For thousands of years seabirds gathered here, depositing their guano. Rainwater carrying dissolved guano combined with the underlying limestone to produce a formation with a high content of phosphoric acid, and as much as 100,000 tons of phosphate were once mined here annually. Barn owl nests have been observed in the cliffs of Tafelberg, and ospreys are often seen flying along the coast.

OUTDOOR ACTIVITIES

HIKING: The best hiking in Curaçao is found in Christoffel Nature Park, which has four signposted routes. Some coves with swimming beaches on the leeward coast must be reached on foot or via dirt roads suitable for hiking. The dirt roads and tracks of the north coast lead hikers to wild desolate scenery where strong waves crash against rocky shores.

HORSEBACK RIDING: Rancho Alegre at Landhuis Groot St. Michiel (599-9-681616) and Ashari Ranch at Kaya Groot Piscadera A-23 (699-9-686250) offer riding across kunucu. Arrangements can be made through hotels or directly.

SWIMMING: Recently, several beaches on the leeward coast within a mile or so east and west of Willemstad have been developed or improved by the addition of white sand and the building of breakwaters. Visitors pay a fee and have access to changing facilities and water sports. On the southeast coast, St. Barbara at the entrance to Spanish Water is the beach most popular with Curaçaoans. Outside the metropolitan area, the leeward coast offers coves with small beaches where swimmers are likely to be by themselves, except perhaps on weekends. Some beaches are on private property and permission or payment of a fee is needed for admittance; some have changing facilities. Generally, the windward coast is too turbulent for safe swimming.

SNORKELING AND DIVING: Long overshadowed by Bonaire, Curaçao is only now beginning to get attention as a dive location. The island is completely surrounded by fringing reef, much of which is virgin territory. In addition to its Underwater Park, Curaçao has more than three dozen coves and beaches, most with reefs within swimming distance from shore. One of the most convenient is Piscadera Bay near Willemstad and Blauw Bay to the west of it. Farther along the west coast, Lagun Beach has snorkeling and diving from shore on a dropoff that begins in 30 ft/9 m. At Kalki Beach, a sheltered cove just south of Westpunt, the underwater terrain resembles the undulating landscape seen from Mt. Christoffel.

Curaçao has a good number of full-service dive shops, almost all located at hotels. Most can also make arrangements for fishing and other water sports. In 1988, Curaçao's first hotel for divers opened.

DEEP-SEA FISHING: Sports fishing is very popular in Curaçao, with anglers going for marlin, tuna, dolphin, wahoo, sailfish, kingfish, and others. Boats are available for charter, either half- or full-day, and can be arranged through one's hotel or the marinas at Spanish Water. Only hook-and-line fishing is permitted in the Curaçao Underwater Park.

SAILING: Small craft such as Sunfish are available at hotels. Yachting is popular with Curaçaoans, who hold regattas frequently, but sailing is not commercially developed for tourists. The Yacht Club at Spanish Water is very active.

WINDSURFING: The constant northeast trade winds that cool the island and shape the divi-divi tree have also made windsurfing one of Curaçao's most popular sports. Annually in June, the island hosts the Curaçao Open International Pro-Am Windsurf Championship, which attracts the top masters from around the world. The most popular area for windsurfing is on the southeast coast between Princess and Jan Thiel beaches; it is also the venue for the annual competitions. The protected lagoon Spanish Water is recommended for novices.

EXPLORING THE ISLAND

Curaçao has a network of good roads crossing the island between Willemstad—Curaçao's capital and port—on the south and the airport on the north. From the Willemstad suburb of Julianadorp, a major artery leads west across the center of the island, forking to the west coast via Santa Marta Bay to Westpunt, or continuing north through the Christoffel Nature Park to Westpunt. East and south of Willemstad, there are many good roads as far as Spanish Water. The eastern end of the island has only a few dirt roads and tracks. Surprisingly, a great deal of Curaçao's coast is accessible only by dirt roads and tracks and some parts can be reached only by walking. Most secondary roads were newly signposted in 1987.

Willemstad is built around Santa Anna Bay, with a narrow, picturesque harbor where Fort Amsterdam, the oldest part of town, and the Punda, the shopping street, are easily covered on foot. The west side of the harbor, known as Otrabanda, is connected by a pedestrian bridge. A vehicle bridge spans the north side of the bay and connects the town with the roads that circumnavigate it.

Car rentals are readily available and are a must for touring the island. Driving is on the RIGHT. A valid foreign driver's license may be used. All road signs are in kilometers. Most dirt roads are well packed and can be traversed by car, except after a heavy rain when they are too muddy. Inquire locally about road conditions. Road maps are readily available.

There is regular bus service in the Willemstad metropolitan area and to the populated areas of the island. From Willemstad, the central departure points are the Waaigat (next to the post office) in Punda, and the Riffort in Otrabanda. Taxis can be found here too, or they can be requested by telephone (599-9-616577). There are taxi stands at the airport and at hotels. Fares, for up to four passengers, should be agreed upon with the driver in advance. There is a surcharge after 11 P.M. To get to Otrabanda, it is prudent to walk across the pontoon bridge and take a taxi from the west side of the harbor; otherwise, the taxi must circle a long distance around the bay.

INFORMATION: In North America: Curaçao Tourist Board, 400 Madison Ave., Suite 311, New York, NY 10017; 212-751-8266. In Europe: Curaçao Tourist Bureau Europe, Vasteland 82-84, 3011 BP Rotterdam; 010-4142639. In Curaçao: Curaçao Tourism Development Bureau, Pietermaal 19, P.O. Box 3266, Curaçao, NA; 599-9-616000.

Books: *Excursion-Guide to Christoffel Park Curaçao*, STINAPA No. 30, Curaçao: STINAPA, 1984. *Guide to the Curaçao Underwater Park*, by Tom van't Hof and Heleen Cornet, STINAPA No. 12, Curaçao: STINAPA, 1983. *Curaçao Underwater, A Diving and Snorkeling Guide*, by G. S. Lewbel, 1985. *Birds of the Netherlands Antilles*, by K. H. Voous, 1983.

BONAIRE

BEST KNOWN AS A MECCA for scuba divers because of its fabulous underwater life, the semiarid, coral island of Bonaire is blessed with a bounty of natural beauty on land as well—and the foresight to protect both. The island boasts three nature sanctuaries—one for birds and wildlife, another for flamingos, and a third for marine life. All this is on an island only 24 mi/38 km long and 5 mi/8 km wide.

Covered mostly with desert vegetation, Bonaire's landscape has almost as much variety as its seascape; it ranges from barren, rocky hills and salt ponds to green parklands with freshwater lakes and palm-framed ocean beaches. Along the shore strong waves crashing against volcanic rock and coral have created ridges, unusual lava formations, grottoes, and caves. Some of the latter have Arawak petroglyphs.

The second largest island of the Netherlands Antilles, Bonaire is located 30 mi/48 km east of its sister island of Curaçao. Low humidity and constant tradewinds help ensure a pleasant year-round climate with the average temperature about 82°F/28°C. Asymmetrical divi-divi trees, common in the Netherlands Antilles, are blown into their characteristic shape by the strong winds that also help keep the island cool. The rainfall is barely 10 in/25 cm per year and falls normally between October and May.

The boomerang-shaped island has three distinct areas: a hilly, greener north end; a somewhat flatter middle with a landscape similar in appearance to the American southwest; and a flat south end with salt pans, sand dunes, and mangrove swamps. Three-quarters of a mile off Bonaire's west coast is Klein (meaning "little") Bonaire, a flat, uninhabited island of about 3 sq mi/7.8 sq km.

Inhabited by the Arawaks at the time of its discovery in 1499 by Amerigo Vespucci, the Italian navigator for whom the Americas were named, the tranquil island was named *bo-nah* by Vespucci after the Arawak word meaning "low land." When the Spaniards' attempt to colonize the island failed, they took the entire Arawak population to Hispaniola as slaves. Later, when the Dutch took control, they imported African slaves to work the salt pans. Today, the petroglyphs of the Arawaks and the slave quarters of the Africans are the only vestiges of the island's brutal history.

Page 478 and 479: Greater flamingos, sometimes 10,000 of them at a time, inhabit the Flamingo Sanctuary in southeast Bonaire, and can also be seen at other island feeding grounds.

WASHINGTON-SLAGBAAI NATIONAL PARK

The northwestern end of Bonaire, the hilliest and greenest area, is covered by the 13,500-acre/5,463-hectare Washington-Slagbaai National Park, a wildlife sanctuary and showcase for the island's flora and fauna; the park includes Brandaris Hill, the island's highest point at 784 ft/228 km. Most of the land in the park is situated on what was once the Washington plantation producing divi-divi trees, aloe, charcoal, and goats. The owner of the plantation, before his death in 1967, sold the land to the government on the condition that it would never be developed for commercial use. This move gave birth to the Netherlands Antilles National Parks Foundation, which in 1974 became the custodian of the newly designated national park, the first of its kind in the Netherlands Antilles. Four years later the area was expanded with the addition of the Slagbaai plantation on its southern flank and was given its present name.

The park boasts a variety of features: dry lowland vegetation with salt licks, freshwater lakes, secluded beaches, rocky coasts and caverns, and bird sanctuaries where as many as 120 species of birds—some unique to Bonaire—have been sighted. Some sources put the number as high as 150 species, which is not surprising since Bonaire is in the path of bird migration between North and South America.

Among the most abundant species in the park are bananaquit, black-faced grassquit, gray kingbird, tropical kingbird, yellow oriole, and several species of flycatchers and warblers. Bonaire is also home to five species of doves and a large number of parakeets and parrots, including the protected lora, or yellow-shouldered parrot, also called the Bonaire parrot. Some of the best places to view birds are Salina Mathijs, a salt flat which is home to greater flamingos from October to January, located immediately past the park entrance. Here one can also see sandpipers and black-necked stilts. Nearby Playa Chiquitu has a white sand beach for picnics, but it is dangerous for swimming because of the strong surf. Here, the sand dunes are a particular feature of the landscape, their contours adorned with white-flowered seaside lavender.

Pos Mangel, another pond at the northern tip of the island near Boca Bartol, is a watering place for a great variety of birds in the late afternoon, especially the snowy egret, yellow-crowned night-heron, olivaceous cormorant, brown pelican, and brown booby. Near the lighthouse on the northeast coast, Boca Cocolishi (which means "shell" in Papiamento, the language of the Netherlands Antilles) is a bay of black sand with a deep, rough seaward side and a calm, shallow basin separated by a coral ridge. The basin and the black sand of the beach were formed by small pieces of coral, mollusks, and mollusk shells. One can see hermit crabs in the sand and in the shallow water of the secluded beach.

Salina Slagbaai, on the west side of the park near Boca Slagbaai, is a large bay popular for picnics and swimming. From about January to July it is also a feeding ground for greater flamingos. Bronswinkel Well at the foot of Brandaris Hill is a favorite watering hole for pigeons and parakeets. Among the less common birds one may see are the black-whiskered vireo, the pearly-eyed thrasher, and the yellow-and-black-colored yellow oriole, whose bottle-shaped nests can sometimes be seen hanging from the outer branches of trees. Mosquitoes can be bothersome in the area.

Goto Meer, a saltwater lagoon on the park's southwestern corner, also attracts large numbers of flamingos. About 2 mi/3.2 km west of the Goto Meer, at Nukove, there are beaches for swimming, hidden caves, and some of the island's most popular picnicking and snorkeling locations.

The park has unusual rock formations and a surprising variety of vegetation. The most conspicuous are prickly pear and two species of candle cactus. There is an abundance of acacia, mesquite (a favorite perch of the Bonaire parrot), the ever-present divi-divi, and a variety of aloe.

Although Bonaire has few mammals, feral goats and donkeys roam the park. There are seven species of lizards, including an iguana and an anole, a yellow tree lizard native to Bonaire. The iguanas are most easily seen in Slagbaai, the southwestern area of the park.

The park can be toured easily by car or on foot on one of two well-marked routes: a 15-mi/24-km track marked with green arrows, and a 22-mi/35-km one marked with yellow arrows. The roads are somewhat rough in spots, as can be expected in wilderness settings. Tracks and walking trails from the main roads also give access to the shore and beaches. The park is open daily and has an entrance fee; a guidebook is available at the visitors' center at the entrance, which is located on the northeastern side of the park.

FLAMINGO SANCTUARY

In contrast to the hilly north end, the southern part of the island is flat, dry, and covered with white hills of salt that shimmer in the bright sun. Here, between salt pans more than 150 years old and the Pekel Meer Lagoon, is a 135-acre/55-hectare flamingo sanctuary and breeding ground, one of the largest in the Western Hemisphere, attracting as many as 10,000 greater flamingos. Due to the flamingo's extreme sensitivity to noise, direct access to the sanctuary is prohibited; one can drive only along the perimeter. Viewers usually leave their vehicles by the road and walk quietly along the edge of the lagoon where they can get close enough to see the birds through binoculars and photograph them through a telephoto lens.

On the coast south of the salt-loading pier is Witte Pan, or Pink Beach, one of the longest stretches of beach on Bonaire. The beach parallels the south side of the Pekel Meer Lagoon. Along the beach one sees tiny huts, once the sleeping quarters of slaves who worked the salt pans.

On the southern tip of the island stands the Willemstoren Lighthouse, built in 1831. Here, the road turns north to Lac Baai, or Lake Bay, which has a pretty beach and mangroves. On the north side of the bay at Sorobon there is a small naturists' hotel with its own clothes-optional beach, which nonguests may use upon payment of an entrance fee.

THE NORTH COAST

The countryside is called *kunucu*—the word is Arawak in origin—and in no place is the kunucu more wild than on Bonaire's north coast, where the moonscape terrain is strewn with lava formations and the vegetation, sparse as it is, struggles to survive. A surfaced road runs along the north side via Fontein where one can view Arawak petroglyphs on rock faces near the road. Other coastal areas have caves but they are accessible only by hiking on dirt roads or tracks: one, on the way to Onima, has petroglyphs.

BONAIRE MARINE PARK

In the 1970s, the increasing fame of Bonaire as a tourist destination led to an awareness of the need for a long-term program to protect the island's extraordinary coral reefs. With the help of the International Union for Conservation of Nature and Natural Resources and the World Wildlife Fund, STINAPA (Netherlands Antilles National Parks Foundation) received a grant in 1979 for the creation of the Bonaire Marine Park.

The park incorporates the entire coastline of Bonaire and neighboring Klein Bonaire, and the sea between. All marine life is completely protected. Fishing and the collecting of fish, shells, or corals—dead or alive—are prohibited, as is spearfishing. Boats of less than 12 ft/3.6 m may use a stone anchor, but all others must use permanent moorings and cannot anchor except for emergencies. All park activities are controlled by government legislation and a marine-environment management program. The Karpata Ecological Center, which is the administrative headquarters for STINAPA and the Bonaire Marine Park, has an ecological research facility and an information center where brochures and information are available.

Most diving and other recreational activity in the park takes place on the island's leeward side and the reefs surrounding Klein Bonaire. These reefs have a narrow, sloping terrace extending seaward to a drop-off at 33 ft/10 m. Thereafter the bottom may slope further or fall off in a vertical wall extending to a depth of 100 to 200 ft/30 to 60 m.

Bonaire's reefs contain some of the most beautiful coral formations in the Caribbean. They are famous for their variety of corals—the park's guide-book describes eighty-four species—and include an abundance of sponges, particularly purple tube sponges, elkhorn and sheet coral, and four kinds of brain coral. The corals are widely distributed but certain species flourish at specific depths or zones. The Shore Zone, at 3 ft/1 m, features knobby brain coral; the Elkhorn Zone, from 3 to 13 ft/1 to 4 m, has a predominance of elkhorn and fire coral; the Staghorn Zone, 13 to 23 ft/4 to 7 m, is populated with staghorn, yellow pencil, mountainous star, and brain corals. Gorgonians, mountainous star, flower, leaf, giant brain, and smooth starlet corals are found in the Drop-off Zone, 23 to 40 ft/7 to 12 m, and in the Upper Reef Slope, 40 to 83 ft/12 to 25 m.

In rich, healthy reefs, fish life is abundant. More than 272 species have been identified, and although it is impossible to predict which fish can be seen in a given place, some do have preferred habitats. In the shallow Shore and Elkhorn zones, wrasses, yellowtail snapper, and parrotfishes are abundant. In the Staghorn Zone one can see reef shrimp, butterflyfishes, damselfishes, trumpetfishes, rock beauty, and various angelfishes. In the deeper Reef Slope there are numerous crinoids, groupers, black margates, and spotted and green moray eels. Even nondivers can see a great deal on glass-bottom boat tours because visibility in Bonaire's waters is excellent and major coral formations are close to shore.

KLEIN BONAIRE

Less than a mile west of Kralendijk is the tiny uninhabited islet of Klein Bonaire. Its 1,500 acres/607 hectares are flat and rocky and covered with desert vegetation similar to that of Bonaire. It has several white sand beaches that are picnic destinations for day-trippers. But it is not the land that attracts visitors; rather, they come to see the spectacular reefs. Sixteen sites around the perimeter have been charted. They range from shallow-water gardens thick with elkhorn coral to coral slopes that drop to 150 ft/46 m, supporting great varieties of sponges, gorgonians, large star corals, and brain corals. One site, known as Forest, has dense forests of black coral at 40 ft/12 m and a purple tube sponge almost 7 ft/2 m long growing horizontally from the slope at 60 ft/18 m. Among the fish one is likely to see are white mullet, yellowtail snapper, tiger grouper, parrotfishes, trumpetfishes, and spotted moray eel. No Name Beach, popular for picnics, is a good snorkeling location.

OUTDOOR ACTIVITIES

CAVING: Bonaire is honeycombed with caves, particularly along the coast where more than forty caves have been found in only the past decade. At Barcadera, on the west coast, steps lead down to the Cueva Barcadera, where the water basin at the entrance was used, it is said, to lure wild goats into captivity. The opening to the cave is small; only experienced spelunkers should venture in; they need lights and must crawl on hands and knees to explore it.

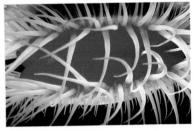

Left to right: hermit crab; flame scallop.

SWIMMING: Most of Bonaire's beaches are small coves rather than long stretches of sand. They have clear water and reefs to protect them, and some have caves and small grottoes. The best swimming is on the leeward or western side where the waters are calm. In general, neither swimming nor diving on the windward side is recommended due to the strong currents and rough seas.

SNORKELING AND DIVING: Bonaire is recognized as one of the best scuba-diving areas in the world, with more than eighty dive spots. In many places, divers can wade from the shore to the reefs, enabling them to enjoy unlimited viewing and diving from the beach any time of the day or night. The proximity of the reefs to the shore is also ideal for snorkelers, particularly the 0.25-mi/0.4-km stretch of marked underwater trails in shallow water along the shoreline.

The best reefs are found along the quiet west coast, within the protected lee of the island and sheltered by Klein Bonaire. Among the beaches for walk-in snorkeling and scuba are Angel City near the Salt Works at the south end of the island; A Thousand Steps, north of the Bonaire Beach Hotel; and Nukove, on the southwestern side of the Washington/Slagbaai National Park. The rocky coral shore at Boca Bartol has elkhorn coral and sea fans and many species of colorful reef fish.

Bonaire is one of the Caribbean's best-equipped dive centers; most hotels cater to divers and have excellent dive operations on their premises. They offer learn-to-dive vacations as well as advanced training and underwater photography. Films on Bonaire's underwater world are shown at various hotels on alternating evenings. And divers can hire an underwater video camera operator to film their diving experiences. Deluxe live-aboard boats that carry their own dive equipment are also available.

Habitat, the region's first hotel specifically for divers, is owned by dive pioneer Don Stewart, an American better known on the island as Captain Don. He was fighting almost singlehandedly for laws to protect the Caribbean's marine life long before environmental protection became a fashionable cause, and has been honored by the Bonaire government by having a dive site named for him.

FISHING: Half- and full-day charters with all provisions are available through hotels. Bonaire's offshore fishing grounds beyond the Marine Park are abundant with mackerel, tuna, wahoo, barracuda, and swordfish, and many other fish.

BOATING: Boats of all types can be seen in the harbor at Kralendijk. Some offer day trips with lunch and snorkeling around Klein Bonaire. The Bonaire Sailing Regatta in mid-October draws fishermen and pleasure sailors from all over the Caribbean to compete in various categories according to the size, design, and purpose of their craft. The regatta includes yachts, sailfish, dinghies, windsurfers, Hobie Cats, fishing sloops, among others, and contestants ranging from twelve-year-old apprentices to sixty-five-year-old master sailors.

Exploring the Island

Bonaire has a very limited number of surfaced roads; the others are dirt roads and tracks. A car, or in some places a four-wheel-drive vehicle, is necessary for exploring the island and can be arranged at the airport upon arrival or through one's hotel. Driving is on the RIGHT.

There is no public bus system, but there are taxis. An island tour can be arranged through one's hotel or the tourist bureau. The office distributes a free booklet, *Bonaire Holiday*, which has road maps.

From Kralendijk, a surfaced road of 9 mi/14.4 km runs west along the coast, where most of the island's resorts are located, to the national park boundary. Here it forks, giving way to tracks and footpaths along the west shore to Nukove, a prime snorkeling area; alternatively, it turns north to Rincon, the oldest settlement on the island. From Rincon a dirt road leads northwest to the national park entrance. The west coast road also branches twice to Rincon—6 mi/10 km north of the capital (beyond the water distillation plant), and farther on at Karpata. Rincon can also be approached from the east on a road that runs from the capital to the north side of the island via Fontein.

On the south side of Kralendijk, a surfaced road makes a loop around the southern tip of the island via the Pekel Meer Lagoon and returns north along the east coast to Kralendijk and up north to Rincon; it also has a branch that leads to the west coast beaches south of the capital.

INFORMATION: In the U.S.: Bonaire Gov't. Tourist Office, 444 Madison Ave., Suite 2403, New York, NY 10022; 212-832-0779; 800-826-6247. In Canada: % RMR Group, Taurus House, 512 Duplex Ave., Toronto M4R 2E3; 416-485-8724. In Bonaire: Kaya Simon Bolivar 12, Kralendijk; 599-7-8322 or 8649.

Books: STINAPA (Netherlands Antilles National Parks Foundation), P.O. Box 706, Netherlands Antilles, WI, has published *Excursion-Guide to the Washington-Slagbaai National Park Bonaire*, No. 29, 1984; *Field Guide to the National Park Washington-Slagbaai Bonaire*, No. 23, 1982; and *Guide to the Bonaire Marine Park* by Tom van 't Hof (No. 11).

The strong winds that keep the semi-arid island of Bonaire cool also force the branches of the divi-divi tree to grow leeward, almost at a right angle to the trunk.

INDEX

The type in this book was set in Century Expanded
on the Mergenthaler Linotron 202
at Graphic Arts Composition, Inc., Philadelphia, Pennsylvania, USA.

The book was printed and bound
by Toppan Printing Company, Tokyo, Japan.